ARCO

Everything you need to score high on

AP
ENGLISH
LITERATURE
AND
COMPOSITION

Fourth Edition

MACMILLAN • USA

Fourth Edition

Copyright © 1997, 1993, 1990 by Laurie Rozakis, Ph.D.

Macmillan Reference USA
A Simon & Schuster Macmillan Company
1633 Broadway
New York, NY 10019-6785

An Arco Book

ARCO and colophon is a registered trademark of Simon & Schuster, Inc.
MACMILLAN and colophon is a registered trademark of Macmillan, Inc.

Manufactured in the United States of America

10 9 8 7 6 5 4 3 2

Library of Congress Number: 97-070069

ISBN: 0-02-861715-0

Contents

PART 5. ANALYZING DRAMA

PART 6. THREE SAMPLE EXAMINATIONS IN ENGLISH COMPOSITION AND LITERATURE

List of Works

Preface to the Third Edition

The third edition retains the most popular features of the first two editions: the separate writing section, full texts of pivotal literary works, plot summaries of other novels, essays, poems, and plays, a guide to holistic scoring, and sentence variety.

But there's been a great deal added that makes this book even more useful. The completely revised "Introduction" now includes a guide to taking the English Advanced Placement Examination, "Preparing to Take the Examination." This section lists important dates and information about special accommodations, such as a braille examination. The "Introduction" also has material on the new AP Awards and a handy list of addresses and telephone numbers for The Advanced Placement Program and the College Board. "The Short Answer Portion: Should You Guess?" answers the most frequently asked questions about how to take this part of the examination.

In addition, the section on sentences has been even further expanded. This new material focuses on different sentence types and the most common sentence errors. The grammar section has been revised, too.

All the reading lists—short stories, novels, poetry, essays, and drama—have been revised to include greater depth and scope and reflect the College Board's growing awareness of ethnic variety. As a result, there are a great many more works by women, minorities, and modern writers included.

Finally, we've even streamlined the format to make the book easier to use. You'll find a lot of material is now in chart format, set off in boxes.

Thanks for your continued support!

Acknowledgments

"Among School Children" and "Sailing to Byzantium" reprinted with permission of Macmillan Publishing Company from *The Poems* by W. B. Yeats, edited by Richard J. Finneran. Copyright 1928 by Macmillan Publishing Company, renewed 1956 by Georgia Yeats.

"Design" and "Fire and Ice" from *The Poetry of Robert Frost* edited by Edward Connery Lathem. Copyright 1923, 1930, 1939, © 1969 by Holt, Rinehart and Winston. Copyright 1936, 1951, © 1958 by Robert Frost. Copyright © 1967 by Lesley Frost Ballantine. Reprinted by permission of Holt, Rinehart and Winston, Publishers.

Note on Reading Lists: Suggested reading lists are provided for short stories, novels, satire, essays, poetry, and drama. The works included on these lists offer a wide range of literature of recognized literary merit. Any of these works would be suitable for discussion and analysis on the Advanced Placement exam. All of them will help to increase your appreciation for and understanding of our literary heritage.

Introduction

WHAT IS THE ADVANCED PLACEMENT PROGRAM?

Advanced Placement is a program of college-level courses and examinations that allow high school students to earn advanced placement and/or college credit. Currently, AP courses and exams are given in sixteen major areas: art, biology, chemistry, computer science, economics, English, French, German, government and politics, history, Latin, mathematics, music, physics, psychology, and Spanish.

For information about the AP Program and its policies, you can write or call:

Advanced Placement Program
The College Board
45 Columbus Avenue, New York 10023-6992
(212) 713-8066

Educational Testing Service
AP Services, P.O. Box 6671
Princeton, New Jersey 08541-6671
(609) 771-7300

HISTORY OF THE ADVANCED PLACEMENT PROGRAM

The Advanced Placement program administered by the College Entrance Examination Board has grown remarkably over the past two decades. From an original 104 high schools sending Advanced Placement candidates to 130 colleges, the program has expanded to include some 3,500 secondary schools and more than 2,000 colleges and universities. About 360,000 students participate in the AP program each year. More than 100,000 examinations a year are taken in English alone.

WHY TAKE AN AP COURSE?

Aside from the obvious pleasure inherent in studying more challenging material, earning advanced placement in college lets you skip work you've already done in high school and, perhaps, even participate in an internship or study abroad. You may be able to graduate from college earlier, enter graduate school sooner, or begin a career more quickly. Because of AP credit, you may also be able to take additional courses, and explore areas of interest that would not otherwise fit into a busy school program. Advanced Placement courses also represent a very significant savings in college tuition. Tuition for a full year's course can be as much as $2,500. The institutions that grant credit for a score of 3 or more are listed in *Sophomore Standing Through the Advanced Placement Program,* available through the College Board. It is recommended that you contact the director of admissions at the colleges you are considering to ask about specific AP policies. Request this information in writing.

THE ADVANCED PLACEMENT COURSES IN ENGLISH

The Advanced Placement program now offers two courses and examinations in English: English Language and Composition, and English Literature and Composition. The two different Advanced Placement courses are designed to represent the two types of freshman English generally offered in colleges and universities. Each examination represents a full-year college introductory English course. Either course can substitute for a year's worth of English credit. Consequently, students may take either examination, but not both.

The English Literature and Composition course:
- for students trained in literary analysis
- more than 90,000 examinations are given yearly

English Language and Composition
- for students who have attained the reading and writing skills generally expected at the end of the freshman year of college but who may not have studied literary analysis
- more than 30,000 examinations are given yearly

Each examination is three hours long. One hour is devoted to multiple-choice questions; two hours to essays. Each examination is graded according to the same scale:

5	extremely well qualified
4	well qualified
3	qualified
2	possibly qualified
1	no recommendation

"5" papers demonstrate	originality and imagination. They are clearly focused discussions made up of coherent arguments of exceptional clarity. These papers leave the reader convinced of the soundness of the discussion, impressed with the quality of the writing style, and stimulated by the intelligence and insight of the writer.
"4" papers demonstrate	a solid, logical, and persuasive discussion, but they lack the originality or insight of the "5" papers. Further, the development lacks the grace and style of the "5" papers, and may seem a bit predictable and plodding.
"3" papers demonstrate	a thorough but not totally convincing discussion of the topic, marked by the sense that the writer has not completely thought out the issue. In addition, there are some writing errors that may distract the reader from the argument.
"2" papers demonstrate	an attempt made to organize the essay, but the structure is flawed and the supporting detail is weak. There may be serious problems with the mechanics of correct written English.

"1" papers demonstrate a lack of understanding; either they do not address the topic directly or fail to answer the question. They draw obscure, irrelevant, or bizarre conclusions and are seriously deficient in the conventions of standard written English.

The English Literature and Composition examination tests both your writing ability and knowledge of literature. Ordinarily, the examination consists of one hour of multiple choice questions followed by two hours of essay questions. The essay section counts for 55% of the total grade; the multiple-choice section counts for 45%. Examinations can be divided in a number of ways. Some typical examinations may look like this:

A. 55 minutes devoted to multiple-choice questions on a poem
    20 minutes devoted to an essay about a prose passage
    25 minutes devoted to an essay about a poem
    45 minutes devoted to a general essay
    45 minutes devoted to a general essay

B. 25 minutes devoted to multiple-choice questions on a poem
    25 minutes devoted to an essay about the poem questioned above
    45 minutes devoted to a general essay
    45 minutes devoted to an essay on a prose passage
    40 minutes devoted to a general essay

C. 45 mintues devoted to a multiple-choice questions on two poems
    30 minutes devoted to an essay comparing the two peoms
    60 minutes devoted to a general essay
    45 minutes deovted to a general essay

The multiple-choice section tests your ability to read poetry and/or prose sections carefully to discern meaning and identify specific literary techniques. You will be expected to be familiar with such terms as connotation, denotations, metaphor, simile, irony, syntax, tone, etc. The essay section stresses your skill in organizing your thoughts coherently, developing ideas fully, responding to general questions with specific evidence, and writing clearly and vividly. The Advanced Placement Grading Committee will look especially for your ability to mold language, to utilize and recognize imagery and symbolism, point of view, audience, mood, and tone. But a knowledge of literary convention alone by no means guarantees success in either examination. You must have a knowledge of the various models of writing—narrative, descriptive, expositive, and persuasvie—and an ability to use them properly. A close study of sample essays in this text will assist you in developing a clear and well-organized essay style.

The English Language and Composition examination, like the English Literature and Composition exam, is made up of multiple-choice and essay questions. In this test, however, the multiple-choice questions test your ability to rework sentences and analyze the language of prose passages. The essays require you to demonstrate your skill in using various rhetorical styles. Usually, the test consists of one hour of multiple-choice questions followed by two hours of essay writing. The essay section counts for 55% of the total grade; the multiple-choice section, 45%.

PREPARING TO TAKE THE EXAMINATION

January: Talk about taking the examination with your English teacher, guidance counselor, and the AP Coordinator at your school. Make sure that these people understand that you wish to take the examination.

If you need special accommodations, such as a braille exam, speak with your school's AP Coordinator or write to the College Board.

Fees: As of 1992, candidates must pay a $65 fee to take the examination. The College Board will reduce fees by $12-15 for qualified students who can demonstrate financial need. Do *not* send money to the College Board. Your school's AP Coordinator will have this information.

May: Examinations are given. In 1993, for example, the AP examination days were May 5-7, 10-14, and 17-18.

June: If you do not want all your AP grades reported to your colleges, you must notify the College Board by June 15.

July: The scores are sent to you and your designated colleges and universities. In cases of a scoring conflict, the College Board allows up to one year for the multiple-choice section to be rescored and retotaled by hand. The essay sections cannot be reread.

In 1992, the AP program introduced three awards to honor those students who have earned outstanding AP achievement. The *Scholar Award* honors students who earn grades of 3 or higher on three or more AP examinations.

The *Scholar with Honor* and *Scholar with Distinction* awards are available for those students who go beyond these criteria.

THE SHORT ANSWER PORTION: SHOULD YOU GUESS?

You will need to answer about half of the multiple-choice questions correctly to earn a multiple-choice score that equals a total grade of 3. What about guessing? Your score on the multiple-choice questions is based on the number of questions you answer right minus a percentage for incorrect answers. For questions with four choices, for instance, one-quarter of a point is subtracted for each incorrect answer. Therefore, just running down the page and filling in answers will not help you earn a better grade. But, do make *educated guesses*—eliminate one or more answers and then guess from the remaining choices.

Part 1

Diagnostic Test and Analysis

General Directions for the Diagnostic Test

This test was constructed to be representative of what you will encounter on the Advanced Placement exam. Take the test in a quiet room without distractions, following all directions carefully and observing all time limits. Try to get as close as possible to actual test conditions, and take the test in one sitting. The more carefully you match test conditions, the more accurate your results will be, and the better able you will be to evaluate your strengths and weaknesses.

CONTENT OF THE TEST

There will most likely be a poem with questions that require you to be aware of the following things:

Figures of speech	These can include such terms as metaphor, simile, analogy, personification, hyperbole, etc. You will have to know what each figure of speech is and be able to recognize examples found in the body of the verse.
Poetic types	These can include the sonnet, ode, narrative verse, ballad, dramatic monologue, hudibrastic verse, doggerel, etc. You will have to know one type from the other and be able to tell what type a particular selection represents and why.
Poetic style	This includes the choice of language and figures of speech, the arrangement of words, such as inversion, and the reason for the poet's specific choice. You may be asked to explain how the techniques used fit in with the theme and reinforce it.
Poetic movements	There are a variety of poetic trends and movements, such as the Symbolists, the Metaphysical poets, or the Realists. You will have to know the characteristics of each group and be able to tell with which school the poem you are looking at is most closely allied. Of course, there are a great many poets who are not linked to any formal "school" of poetry.
Meter, rhyme, rhythm	You will have to be able to distinguish such basic poetic metric patterns as iambic pentameter, and be able to establish the rhyme scheme of a poem. You will also have to know how to "scan" a poem to discover its rhythm.
Author	While there is no way you will be able to give a full biography of any author, you will be required in some instances to establish something about the author from his/her verse. Thus, you may be asked what the author's attitude is toward something based on a poem, or when he/she may have lived, or what his/her attitude toward a certain subject matter may be.

Tone and mood	You will be able to tell the prevailing mood or tone of a work from its word choice and arrangement. The mood could be elevated and lofty, or depressing and bitter.
Meaning	Probably the single most important aspect of poetic interpretation is discovering the meaning—the theme—of the poem. What is it that the author is saying? Why did the author write this poem? What is the author telling us? What lines or phrases help you to arrive at this conclusion? You will be expected to do a close textual analysis, isolating specific words and phrases to prove your points.

For prose passages, you will most likely have to be aware of:

Tone	Again, the prevailing mood of the piece, established through word choice and arrangement.
Theme	What is the author's meaning? Why did the author write this passage? What, if anything, did he/she hope to accomplish?
Speaker	Do not confuse the *speaker* of the work with the *author;* they are rarely the same. Often the author adopts a *mask* to present a specific theme.
Technique	Word choice, sentence variety and length, punctuation, figurative language, etc. all combine to form the *style* of a piece.

You may be asked to do any and all of the following: Compare two poems; compare two prose passages; respond to a prose passage or a poem; explain the author's theme in a prose or poetic passage; or answer a series of questions on poetry or prose and then write an essay.

THE LITERARY ESSAY

In addition, the test includes a literary essay, in which you are given a selection of works of "recognized literary merit" with which to answer a question. Occasionally, a list will *not* be provided. In these instances, you are expected to select a literary work that is acknowledged to be of value. In most cases, this eliminates "best sellers" and relies instead on the books that are seen as "classics." If in doubt, err on the side of safety: select a work that you have studied in class and know is well regarded by educated people.

You will have to give *clear, specific examples* drawn from the text of the book(s) you use. In addition, you will be expected to show evidence of a firm grasp of grammar, usage, vocabulary, and writing techniques. See Unit 2, Essay Writing Guide, for specific details and examples.

Diagnostic AP Examination

SECTION 1

Part A: Time—20 minutes

Directions: Read the following poem and answer the questions that follow it.

UPON A SPIDER CATCHING A FLY

Thou sorrow, venom elf.
  Is this thy play,
To spin a web out of thyself
  To catch a fly?
5   For why?

I saw a pettish wasp
  Fall foul therein:
Whom yet thy whorl pins[1] did not clasp
  Lest he should fling
10   His sting.

But as afraid, remote
  Didst stand hereat,
And with thy little fingers stroke
  And gently tap
15   His back.

Thus gently him didst treat
  Lest he should pet,[2]
And in a froppish,[3] waspish heat
  Should greatly fret[4]
20   Thy net.

Whereas the silly fly,
  Caught by its leg,
Thou by the throat took'st hastily,
  And 'hind the head
25   Bite dead.

This goes to pot, that not
  Nature doth call.[5]
Strive not above what strength hath got,
  Lest in the brawl
30   Thou fall.

This fray seems thus to us:
  Hell's Spider gets
His entrails spun to whip cords thus,
  And wove to nets,
35   And sets.

To tangle Adam's race
  In's[6] stratagems
To their destructions, spoil'd, made base
  By venom things,
40   Damn'd sins.

But mighty, Gracious Lord,
  Communicate
Thy Grace to break the cord; afford
  Us glory's gate
45   And state.

We'll nightingale sing like,
  When perched on high
In glory's cage, Thy glory, bright:
  Yea, thankfully,
50   For joy.

—*Edward Taylor*

1. *whorl pins* are used to hold thread on a spindle.
2. *pet* means irritable.
3. *froppish* means cranky, irritable.
4. *fret* means break, rupture.
5. *that not/Nature doth call* means those who do not rely on a person's inborn ability to distinguish good from evil.
6. *In's* means in his.

5

1. What is the analogy in the sixth stanza?
   (A) The spider bit the fly's head off. In a similar manner, "Hell's Spider" (line 32) is poised to bite off the venom elf's head.
   (B) The venom elf (line 1) calls man to brawl, but "Hell's Spider" comes between them.
   (C) Man will go to ruin if he does not follow natural reason. The spider "bags" his victim, just as Satan catches his victim, man.
   (D) Man must allow himself to be called by Nature. If he fails to respond to this natural summons, Satan will "bag" him.
   (E) Man "flies" as the insect does; nonetheless, Satan is ready to "bag" him.

2. Who is "Hell's Spider" in line 32?
   (A) Satan
   (B) Man
   (C) The black widow spider
   (D) The venom elf
   (E) A representative of Adam's race

3. What are the "venom things" in line 39?
   (A) Base metals that poison man
   (B) "Damn'd sins" that sting man to death and destruction
   (C) Strands of the web that entangle man
   (D) The entrails of "Hell's Spider"
   (E) The spider's poison

4. What is the "cord" in line 43?
   (A) The cord that guards Heaven's gate. The poet wants to break it and be allowed to enter Heaven.
   (B) The cord that connects the child to his mother
   (C) The whip cord the spider uses to trap the fly
   (D) The cord that the devil uses to trap man
   (E) The cord that the venom elf uses to entrap man

5. What is the figure of speech in the seventh stanza?
   (A) A metaphor
   (B) A simile
   (C) An analogy
   (D) Personification
   (E) Hyperbole

6. What does that figure of speech in the seventh stanza mean?
   (A) The activity of the spider is similar to man's fall from grace.
   (B) The activity of the fly is similar to man's fall from grace.
   (C) The activity of the nightingale is similar to man's fall from grace.
   (D) Entrails are compared to the venom elf and the spider's whip cords.
   (E) God's grace is personified in the spider.

7. What is the figure of speech in the last stanza?
   (A) Metonymy
   (B) Synocdoche
   (C) Metaphor
   (D) Simile
   (E) Mixed metaphor

8. In the final stanza, the nightingale symbolizes
   (A) the spider
   (B) the fly
   (C) man
   (D) God
   (E) the sweet bird of youth

9. How is the entire poem an analogy?
   (A) Fly : spider :: man: devil
   (B) Spider : fly :: man : devil
   (C) Venom elf : spider :: devil : man
   (D) Venom elf : nightingale :: spider : fly
   (E) God : man :: spider : venom elf

10. This poem would be described as metaphysical because
    (A) it is witty, subtle, highly intellectual
    (B) it uses many elaborate and surprising figures of speech
    (C) it compares two very dissimilar things
    (D) it uses an extended conceit
    (E) all of the above

11. The poem is an example of a(n)
    (A) sonnet
    (B) ode
    (C) hudibrastic verse
    (D) doggerel
    (E) none of the above

12. The author is most likely
    (A) an atheist
    (B) an agnostic

(C) religious
(D) irreligious
(E) a biologist

13. The rhyme scheme here is best described as
    (A) *abbaa*
    (B) *ababb*
    (C) *aabaa*
    (D) *aabca*
    (E) *ababa*

14. The tone of this poem is
    (A) intense and agitated
    (B) thoughtful and morose
    (C) witty and light
    (D) resigned and pessimistic
    (E) irreligious

15. Which of the following statements is *not* true about the poem?
    (A) The poem compares two very dissimilar things.
    (B) The poet is a very learned man.
    (C) The poet believes Satan is ready to catch his victims at any moment.
    (D) Man is silly, vulnerable, and easily destroyed by Satan's traps.
    (E) The poet is little concerned with religion; he is actually dealing with the material world of insects.

16. The poet switches topics to make his comparison in line
    (A) 31
    (B) 15
    (C) 36
    (D) 20
    (E) 46

Part B: Time—25 minutes

Directions: Read the two poems that follow and discuss each of the following:
1. How the two authors view old age and how their views differ from one another
2. What effect this difference in view has on the *tone* of each poem
3. Differences in *style* between the two poems

Cite specific lines from each poem to make your point clearly.

THE LAST LEAF

I saw him once before,
As he passed by the door,
  And again
The pavement stones resound,
5 As he totters o'er the ground
  With his cane.

They say that in his prime,
Ere the pruning-knife of Time
  Cut him down,
10 Not a better man was found
By the Crier on his round
  Through the town.

But now he walks the streets,
And he looks at all he meets
15 Sad and wan,
And he shakes his feeble head,
That it seems as if he said,
  "They are gone."

The mossy marbles rest
20 On the lips that he has pressed
  In their bloom,
And the names he loved to hear
Have been carved for many a year
  On the tomb.

25 My grandmamma has said—
Poor old lady, she is dead
  Long ago—
That he had a Roman nose,
And his cheek was like a rose
30 In the snow.

But now his nose is thin,
And it rests upon his chin
  Like a staff,
And a crook is in his back,
35 And a melancholy crack
  In his laugh.

I know it is a sin
For me to sit and grin
  At him here;
40 But the old three-cornered hat,
And the breeches, and all that,
  Are so queer!

And if I should live to be
The last leaf upon the tree
45   In the spring,
Let them smile, as I do now,
At the old forsaken bough
  Where I cling.

                —*Oliver Wendell Holmes*

TERMINUS

It is time to be old,
To take in sail:—
The god of bounds,
Who sets to seas a shore,
5 Came to me in his fatal rounds,
And said: 'No more!
No farther shoot
Thy broad ambitious branches, and thy root.
Fancy departs: no more invent;
10 Contract thy firmament
To compass of a tent.
There's not enough for this and that,
Make thy option which of two;
Economize the failing river,
15 Not the less revere the Giver,
Leave the many and hold the few.
Timely wise accept the terms,
Soften the fall with wary foot;
A little while
20 Still plan and smile,
And,—fault of novel germs,—

Mature the unfallen fruit.
Curse, if thou wilt, thy sires,
Bad husbands of their fires,
25 Who, when they gave thee breath,
Failed to bequeath
The needful sinew stark as once,
The Baresark marrow to thy bones,
But left a legacy of ebbing veins,
30 Inconstant heat and nerveless reins,—
Amid the Muses, left thee deaf and dumb,
Amid the gladiators, halt and numb.'

  As the bird trims her to the gale,
I trim myself to the storm of time,
35 I man the rudder, reef the sail,
Obey the voice at eve obeyed at prime:
'Lowly faithful, banish fear,
Right onward drive unharmed;
The port, well worth the cruise, is near,
40 And every wave is charmed.'

                —*Ralph Waldo Emerson*

SECTION 2

Part A: Time—45 minutes

Directions: Read the two selections that follow. Then write an essay comparing and contrasting the *tone* of the first selection with that of the second. Use specific examples from each selection to make your points clearly. The first excerpt is from *The American Crisis* by Thomas Paine; the second, *Speech in the Convention, at the Conclusion of its Deliberations, September 17, 1787,* by Benjamin Franklin.

SELECTION 1

These are the times that try men's souls: The summer soldier and the sunshine patriot will in this crisis, shrink from the service of his country; but he that stands it NOW, deserves the love and thanks of man and woman. Tyranny, like hell, is not easily conquered; yet we have this consolation with us, that the harder the conflict, the more glorious the triumph. What we obtain too cheap, we esteem too lightly:—'Tis dearness only that gives everything its value. Heaven knows how to put a proper price upon its goods; and it would be strange indeed, if so celestial an article as FREEDOM should not be highly rated. Britain, with an army to enforce her tyranny, has declared that she has a right (*not only to*) TAX but "to BIND *us in* ALL CASES WHATSOEVER," and if being *bound in that manner,* is not slavery, then is there not such a thing as slavery upon earth. Even the expression is impious, for so unlimited a power can belong only to GOD....

I have as little superstition in me as any man living, but my secret opinion has ever been, and still is, that God Almighty will not give up a people to military destruction, or leave them unsupportedly to perish, who have so earnestly and so repeatedly sought to avoid the calamities of war, by every decent method which wisdom could invent. Neither have I so much of the infidel in me, as to suppose that he has relinquished the government of the world, and given us up to the care of devils; and as I do not, I cannot see on what grounds the king of Britain can look up to Heaven for help against us: a common murderer, a highwayman, or a house-breaker, has as good a pretence as he ....

I once felt all that kind of anger, which a man ought to feel against the mean principles that are held by the tories: A noted one, who kept a tavern at Amboy, was standing at his door, with as pretty a child in his hand, about eight or nine years old, as I ever saw, and after speaking his mind as freely as he thought was prudent, finished with this unfatherly expression, *"Well! give me peace in my day."* Not a man lives on the continent but fully believes that a separation must some time or other finally take place, and a generous parent should have said, *"If there must be trouble, let it be in my day, that my child may have peace,"* and this single reflection, well applied, is sufficient to awaken every man to duty. Not a place upon earth might be so happy as America. Her situation is remote from all the wrangling world, and she has nothing to do but to trade with them. A man

can distinguish himself between temper and principle, and I am as confident, as I am that GOD governs the world, that America will never be happy till she gets clear of foreign dominion. Wars, without ceasing, will break out till that period arrives, and the continent must in the end be conqueror; for though the flame of liberty may sometimes cease to shine, the coal can never expire....

The heart that feels not now is dead; the blood of his children will curse his cowardice, who shrinks back at a time when a little might have saved the whole, and made *them* happy. I love the man that can smile in trouble, that can gather strength from distress, and grow brave by reflection. 'Tis the business of little minds to shrink; but he whose heart is firm, and whose conscience approves his conduct, will pursue his principles unto death. My own line of reasoning is to myself as straight and clear as a ray of light. Not all the treasures of the world, so far as I believe, could have induced me to support an offensive war, for I think it murder; but if a thief breaks into my house, burns and destroys my property, and kills or threatens to kill me, or those that are in it, and to *"bind me in all cases whatsoever"* to his absolute will, am I to suffer it? What signifies it to me, whether he who does it is a king or a common man; my countryman or not my countryman; whether it be done by an individual villain, or an army of them? If we reason to the root of things we shall find no difference; neither can any just cause be assigned why we should punish in the one case and pardon in the other.

SELECTION 2

Mr. President,

I confess, that I do not entirely approve of this Constitution at present; but, Sir, I am not sure I shall never approve it; for, having lived long, I have experienced many instances of being obliged, by better information or fuller consideration, to change opinions even on important subjects, which I once thought right, but found to be otherwise. It is therefore that, the older I grow, the more apt am I to doubt my own judgment of others. Most men, indeed, as well as most sects in religion, think themselves in possession of all truth, and that wherever others differ from them it is so far error. Steele,[1] a Protestant, in a dedication, tells the Pope, that the only difference between our two churches in their opinions of the certainty of their doctrine, is, the Romish Church is *infallible,* and the Church of England is *never in the wrong.* But, though many private persons think almost as highly of their own infallibility as of that of their sect, few express it so naturally as a certain French lady, who, in a little

dispute with her sister, said, "But I meet with nobody but myself that is always in the right." *"Je ne trouve que moi qui aie toujours raison."*

In these sentiments, Sir, I agree to this Constitution, with all its faults—if they are such, because I think a general government necessary for us, and there is no *form* of government but what may be a blessing to the people, if well administered; and I believe, further, that this is likely to be well administered for a course of years, and can only end in despotism, as other forms have done before it, when the people shall become so corrupted as to need despotic government, being incapable of any other. I doubt, too, whether any other convention we can obtain, may be able to make a better constitution; for, when you assemble a number of men, to have the advantage of their joint wisdom, you inevitably assemble with those men all their prejudices, their passions, their errors of opinion, their local interests, and their selfish views. From such an assembly can a *perfect* production be expected? It therefore

---

1. *Steele* most likely refers to Richard Steele, the English essayist.

astonishes me, Sir, to find this system approaching so near to perfection as it does; and I think it will astonish our enemies, who are waiting with confidence to hear that our counsels are confounded like those of the builders of Babel, and that our States are on the point of separation, only to meet hereafter for the purpose of cutting one another's throats. Thus I consent, Sir, to this Constitution, because I expect no better, and because I am not sure that it is not the best. The opinions I have had of its *errors* I sacrifice to the public good. I have never whispered a syllable of them abroad. Within these walls they were born, and here they will die. If every one of us, in returning to our constituents, were to report the objections he has had to it, and endeavor to gain partisans in support of them, we might prevent its being generally received, and thereby lose all the salutary effects and great advantages resulting naturally in our favor among foreign nations, as well as among ourselves, from any real or apparent unanimity. Much of the strength and efficiency of any government, in procuring and securing happiness to the people, depends on *opinion,* on the general opinion of the goodness of that government, as well as of the wisdom and integrity of its governors. I hope, therefore, for our own sakes, as a part of the people, and for the sake of our posterity, that we shall act heartily and unanimously in recommending this Constitution, wherever our influence may extend, and turn our future thoughts and endeavors to the means of having it *well administered*.

On the whole, Sir, I cannot help expressing a wish, that every member of the convention who may still have objections to it, would with me on this occasion doubt a little of his own infallibility, and, to make *manifest* our *unanimity,* put his name to this instrument.

Part B: Time—30 minutes

Questions 1–22 refer to the following poem.

THANATOPSIS

To him who in the love of Nature holds
Communion with her visible forms, she speaks
A various language; for his gayer hours
She has a voice of gladness, and a smile
5 And eloquence of beauty, and she glides
Into his darker musings with a mild
And healing sympathy that steals away
Their sharpness ere he is aware. When thoughts
Of the last bitter hour come like a blight
10 Over thy spirit, and sad images
Of the stern agony, and shroud, and pall,
And breathless darkness, and the narrow house
Make thee to shudder and grow sick at heart—
Go forth, under the open sky, and list
15 To Nature's teachings, while from all around—
Earth and her waters, and the depths of air—
Comes a still voice—
           Yet a few days, and thee
The all-beholding sun shall see no more
In all his course; nor yet in the cold ground,
20 Where thy pale form was laid with many tears,
Nor in the embrace of ocean shall exist
Thy image. Earth, that nourished thee, shall claim
Thy growth, to be resolved to earth again,
And, lost each human trace, surrendering up
25 Thine individual being, shalt thou go
To mix forever with the elements,
To be a brother to the insensible rock
And to the sluggish clod which the rude swain
Turns with his share and treads upon. The oak
30 Shall send his roots abroad and pierce thy mold.

Yet not to thine eternal resting place
Shalt thou retire alone; nor couldst thou wish
Couch more magnificent. Thou shalt lie down
With patriarchs of the infant world—with kings,
35 The powerful of the earth—the wise, the good.
Fair forms, and hoary seers of ages past,
All in one mighty sepulcher. The hills
Rock-ribbed and ancient as the sun; the vales
Stretching in pensive quietness between;
40 The venerable woods; rivers that move
In majesty; and the complaining brooks
That make the meadows green; and, poured
    round all
Old Ocean's gray and melancholy waste—
Are but the solemn decorations all
45 Of the great tomb of man. The golden sun,
The planets, all the infinite host of heaven,
Are shining on the sad abodes of death
Through the still lapse of ages. All that tread
The globe are but a handful to the tribes
50 That slumber in its bosom. Take the wings
Of morning, pierce the Barcan wilderness,
Or lose thyself in the continuous woods
Where rolls the Oregon, and hears no sound
Save his own dashings—yet the dead are there;
55 And millions in those solitudes, since first
The flight of years began, have laid them down
In their last sleep—the dead reign there alone.
So shalt thou rest, and what if thou withdraw
In silence from the living, and no friend
60 Take note of thy departure? All that breathe

Will share thy destiny. The gay will laugh
When thou art gone, the solemn brood of care
Plod on, and each one as before will chase
His favorite phantom; yet all these shall leave
Their mirth and their employments, and shall
65   come
And make their bed with thee. As the long train
Of ages glides away, the sons of men,
The youth in life's green spring, and he who goes
In the full strength of years, matron and maid,
70   The speechless babe, and the gray-headed man—
Shall one by one be gathered to thy side,

By those who in their turn shall follow them.
So live, that when thy summons comes to join
The innumerable caravan which moves
75   To that mysterious realm, where each shall take
His chamber in the silent halls of death,
Thou go not, like the quarry slave at night,
Scourged to his dungeon, but, sustained and
    soothed
By an unfaltering trust, approach thy grave
80   Like one who wraps the drapery of his couch
About him, and lies down to pleasant dreams.

—William Cullen Bryant

1. In lines 1–17, what does the poet say man should do when torn by thoughts of death?
   (A) Seek diversion.
   (B) Think instead of "darker musings" and the "eloquence of beauty."
   (C) Listen to Nature.
   (D) Ignore Nature's promptings, for they offer false hopes.
   (E) Continue his daily routine and push such thoughts firmly aside.

2. What will Nature be able to offer man, according to the poet?
   (A) The sluggish clod
   (B) The insensible rock
   (C) Healing sympathy
   (D) The magnificent oak
   (E) The company of fascinating people

3. In lines 17–57, what comfort does the poet believe Nature offers man when he is facing death?
   (A) The beauty of the open sky and still waters
   (B) A "magnificent couch" decorated with glories
   (C) The warm embrace of the ocean
   (D) Old friends and fond memories
   (E) None at all; it is cold and unyielding.

4. Who has shared Nature's "magnificent couch"?
   (A) The patriarchs of the infant world
   (B) Good people
   (C) Wise men
   (D) Kings
   (E) All of the above

5. In lines 57–72, why is dying without being mourned not important?
   (A) Since you are already dead, you have little use for what the living say.
   (B) It is actually very important, for it determines your fate.
   (C) Mourning customs are hypocritical at best, for few of us are really concerned about anyone else's mortality.
   (D) Mourning is unnecessary, for all who are unaware of the person's passing will be joining him soon enough.
   (E) It offers little comfort to the survivors.

6. In lines 73–81, what *is* important to the poet and the poem's meaning?
   (A) That man will live in continuing trust with Nature
   (B) That man set his affairs in order before his death
   (C) That man make his peace with his neighbors
   (D) That man summon his friends and relatives to his side before his passing
   (E) That man fight death to the last, not surrendering his will to Nature's

7. Why must man base his faith in Nature?
   (A) There is nothing else to comfort him.
   (B) So that when he faces death, he can be secure in the knowledge that Nature will sustain him and make him a part of the natural order.
   (C) Nature will reward him with riches beyond his wildest dreams.
   (D) There is no Supreme Being for Man to seek.
   (E) There is no reason.

8. What does the "mighty sepulcher" in line 37 most nearly mean?
   (A) The tomb
   (B) Clay
   (C) Nature
   (D) Earth
   (E) The individual grave

9. To what does the above term refer?
   (A) The final resting place of the wicked
   (B) The mighty grave of all
   (C) The mighty grave of the worthy
   (D) The afterlife
   (E) The process by which man is forgotten

10. What is the "destiny" spoken of in lines 60–61?
    (A) Rebirth
    (B) Death
    (C) Joining with the Supreme Being
    (D) Mourning
    (E) Accepting Nature

11. What poetic technique does the author use in the final two lines?
    (A) Simile
    (B) Personification
    (C) Alliteration
    (D) Apostrophe
    (E) Inversion

12. What is death compared to in these final two lines?
    (A) Mourning
    (B) Nature
    (C) Rebirth
    (D) Sleep
    (E) The ocean

13. When the author published this poem in a new edition, he added lines 1–17, up to "Yet a few days, . . .". What purpose did this serve?
    (A) It explained the *theme* more fully.
    (B) It established the *tone* more firmly.
    (C) It framed the poem by clearly defining the subject matter.
    (D) It made the poem conform to an established literary form.
    (E) It introduced Nature and offered a bit of hope.

14. At the same time as the above additions were made, he also added the final 16 lines, beginning with "As the long train." Why did he do this?
    (A) They allow him more room for additional figures of speech.
    (B) They offer hope and consolation.
    (C) They establish the poem as a ballad.
    (D) They ask man to fear death as a worthy opponent.
    (E) They complete the rhyme pattern.

15. The view expressed in this poem most clearly shows the influence of
    (A) the Realistic school
    (B) the Naturalist school
    (C) the Imagist movement
    (D) the Symbolist movement
    (E) the Romantic movement

16. The poem presents a movement from
    (A) life to death
    (B) death to rebirth
    (C) doubt to hope to doubt
    (D) ecstasy to joy to sorrow
    (E) faith to rebirth

17. The poem is a(n)
    (A) villanelle
    (B) dramatic monologue
    (C) sonnet
    (D) ballad
    (E) none of the above

18. All of the following are true about the language of the poem EXCEPT:
    (A) The poet uses poetic contraction such as "list" for "listen."
    (B) Sentences and phrases are inverted for poetic effect.
    (C) The words are selected to call for two different levels of interpretation.
    (D) The words are not unusual or difficult to define.
    (E) The poet makes frequent references to Nature.

19. The language of the poem can best be described as
    (A) labored
    (B) economical
    (C) extravagant
    (D) awkward
    (E) ill suited to the subject matter

20. The speaker of the poem is
    (A) nature
    (B) the dead
    (C) the "powerful of the earth"
    (D) the poet
    (E) different in different stanzas

21. The following line is an example of what poetic technique? "Yet a few days, and the all-beholding sun shall see no more in all his course."
    (A) Oxymoron
    (B) Conceit
    (C) Inversion
    (D) Personification
    (E) Synecdoche

22. The *tone* here is intended to be
    (A) comforting
    (B) frightening
    (C) neutral
    (D) passive
    (E) excited

SECTION 3

Time—60 minutes

Directions: Select a major character from any work of recognized literary merit and show how that character is human in that he or she possesses both good and bad traits. It is this balance between the two extremes that makes us "human," and this is true in literature as well as life. Be sure to include specific examples from the work under discussion to make your point. If you wish, you may select from the following list:

Madame Bovary	*The Scarlet Letter*
Ethan Frome	*The Adventures of Huckleberry Finn*
Vanity Fair	*Moby Dick*
The Red Badge of Courage	*Lord Jim*
Hamlet	*Catch-22*
The Portrait of a Lady	*The Turn of the Screw*

ANSWERS AND EXPLANATIONS FOR DIAGNOSTIC TEST

Section 1, Part A

1. (C) The poem is using the analogy of a spider and a fly to show how Hell's spider—Satan—traps Adam's race—man. (A) is partly correct, for the spider did indeed bite the fly's head off, as the lines "Whereas the silly fly,/Caught by its leg,/Thou by the throat took'st hastily,/And 'hind the head/Bite dead" (stanza 5) tell us. The rest of the question is not correct, though, for the "venom elf" mentioned in the first line does not refer to the *fly*, as the answer choice implies, but rather to the spider. (B) is not correct, for again, the "venom elf" refers to the spider, not the fly. (D) is not correct for the poem does not say that man must allow himself to be called by Nature. Rather, the sixth stanza explains that man must listen to his inborn ability to tell right from wrong. This choice is far too general and thus fails to answer the question. (E) is wrong, for the poem does not say that man flies. An ability to fly would have nothing to do with Satan's power to ensnare man.

2. (A) As mentioned in the first answer above, "Hell's Spider" is Satan, the devil. We can tell this is so by the eighth stanza, specifically in the phrase "Adam's race," in line 36, referring to mankind. Only the devil would be able to entrap man. Thus (B), Man, cannot be correct. (C) is equally wrong, for nowhere in the poem is a black widow spider mentioned. (D) The "venom elf" mentioned in the first line refers to a spider spinning a net to catch a fly, not to the devil himself, and (E) the representative of "Adam's race" is the one being trapped, not the one doing the trapping.

3. (B) In keeping with the analogy between the spider (Satan) and the fly (man) set up above, it follows that the "venom things" that trap man would be his sins. (A) cannot be correct, for base metals have nothing to do with spiders and flies and the battle between Satan and man. (C) is partly correct, for man is indeed tangled in a web, but the comparison is more fully expressed in answer (B). (D) and (E) may appear to be correct, but a closer examination reveals that nowhere is poison considered.

4. (D) The cord is the devil's way to trap man. (A) makes no sense, for the poet would not beg God's grace to break the cord. God's grace is awarded to man to ease sins. (B) There is no mother-child discussion here, and so this choice is incorrect. (C) looks like a correct answer at first glance, but by this point in the poem, we are beyond the spider-fly analogy, and so an answer with the devil and man is more suitable. The same is true for answer choice (E).

5. (C) The figure of speech here is an analogy, as a comparison is constructed between the spider of the beginning of the poem and the devil. Each sets traps to ensnare its prey. (A) is wrong, for a metaphor is a comparison between two objects in a *brief* and *succinct* manner. Unless it is an "extended metaphor," it would rarely stretch more than a line, and certainly not through a whole poem. (B) A simile is a kind of metaphor that uses either "like" or "as" to make the comparison, as in "He eats like a horse." (D) Personification gives human attributes to objects, and (E) hyperbole is exaggeration for literary effect.

6. (A) The spider traps the fly as the devil traps man: Each constructs clever snares for its unsuspecting prey. (B) appears to be a correct answer, but the analogy between the fly and man is not close enough to select this as a better answer than (A). A fly cannot reason and escape from a trap; a fly cannot stop himself from sinning. (C) is wrong, for nowhere in stanza 7 is a nightingale mentioned. (D) is wrong, for entrails are not *compared* to the spider. (E) We cannot see God's grace in the spider, for the spider is identified with the devil.

7. (D) As mentioned in answer 5, a simile is a brief comparison using "like" or "as." The line in the last stanza, "We'll nightingale sing *like* . . . ," as man in heaven is likened to a bird singing with joy, is the correct choice here. (A) means using the name of one object for that of another of which it is a part or related, such as "scepter" for "sovereignty." (B) is a figure of speech in which part is used for the whole, as when modern poet and dramatist T.S. Eliot says a "pair of ragged claws" in referring to crab in his poem "The Love Song of J. Alfred Prufrock." (E) is a metaphor that has portions that do not fit together, as in "sailing to the crosswalk of life," for a crosswalk would not be found on the ocean.

8. (C) Man, washed free of his sins, will sing gloriously in heaven, says the poet. Lines 43–44, "Thy Grace to break the cord; afford/Us glory's gate" is a clue to this, especially the word "Us."

9. (A) The fly is caught by the spider in the same way as man is caught by the devil, the poet claims. None of the other answers correctly expresses this relationship.

10. (E) To answer this question correctly, you would have to know what the metaphysical poets, a group who wrote during the seventeenth century in England, believed in and practiced. All of the choices listed in the question are characteristic of this movement. You will be expected to have a knowledge of the main poetic and literary movements, and be able to distinguish between them. Study the material in the Poetry Unit and the Novel Unit concerning this aspect of the exam.

11. (E) Again, a knowledge of basic poetic *forms* is required to correctly answer this. A sonnet, for example, is a poem that has 14 lines, either an English (Shakespearean) or an Italian (Petrarchian) rhyme scheme, and iambic pentameter rhythm. An ode, (B), is a lyric poem that expresses a great deal of emotion, usually concern-

ing exalted figures. Originally, it was sung rather than recited. (C) Hudibrastic verse is mock-heroic verse in tetrameter couplets, and doggerel, (D), is poorly-written and -regarded verse. All of these are discussed in the Poetry Unit.

12. **(C)** The final two couplets tell us that the author is most likely a very religious person, as the poem concludes with the wish that God will wash away the devil's traps and afford us all His grace. In this light, choices (A), (B), and (D) would not fit. Choice (E), a biologist, has little to do with the poem, as it does not focus on what we would consider "natural" or "nature" phenomena.

13. **(B)** We figure rhyme scheme by assigning a letter to each word that rhymes. For example, Cat (A)/ Bat (A)/ Mat (A)/ would all be assigned the same letter as they all rhyme. The next word that does not rhyme, such as "like," would be assigned the letter "B".

This continues for the length of the poem. (B) is the correct choice, as

elf	A	wasp	A
play	B	therein	B
thyself	A	clasp	A
fly	B	fling	B
why	B	sting	B

is how we would assign the letters for the rhyme scheme.

14. **(C)** "Witty and light" best expresses the *tone* of the poem. The tone of a work of literature is the particular manner or style, the mood of a piece of writing. It is determined through the author's choice of words and their placement. Here, the very comparison between Satan and the spider and a fly and man establishes the general tone, for were the author to be (A), intense and agitated, or (D), resigned and pessimistic, we would have had a different choice of analogy. The ending also, with its vision of redemption, would not fit in with selections (A) and (D). The very subject of the work—God's grace and man's acceptance or rejection of the devil's snares—contradicts choice (E).

15. **(E)** As established in previous answers, the poet is very much concerned with religion. Thus, the only answer that is *not* true would be (E). The questions that have the word *not* or *only,* or any other qualifier, must be read very carefully; they are often answered incorrectly because they are read too quickly and the *not* is ignored.

16. **(A)** The switch is made in line 31, where the poet says "This fray seems thus to us . . ." and ties the spider to the devil and the fly to man to make his point.

Section 1, Part B

"Terminus" is a calm, dignified, realistic statement of an old man accepting his age and fast-approaching death. The first line—"It is time to be old"—can be cited to support this. Lines 39–40—"The port, well worth the cruise, is near,/And every wave is charmed."—also illustrate this. It is a poem of serious and deep contemplation, whereas, in contrast, "The Last Leaf" is light and playful in tone. The majority of the figures of speech in "The Last Leaf" are comic, with the exception of those used in the final verse. Images such as "the pruning-knife of Time" (line 8) has "Cut him down" (line 9) and "his nose . . . rests upon his chin/Like a staff" (lines 31–33) are examples of the comic tone of "The Last Leaf" which show how it differs from "Terminus." But the figure in the final stanza is sad and lonely, for the last leaf upon the tree in the spring is even sadder than the last leaf in autumn. This leaf has been able to survive the winter, and surrounded by the new leaves bursting forth, must now wither away and die. Also, in the final stanza, the poet, who has maintained his distance from his subject, now identifies with him, looking forward to the time when *he* will be "the last leaf upon the tree/In the spring."

Section 2, Part A

The first speech has an emotional tone, trying to incite the audience into a frenzy of fighting. It can be called inflammatory or incendiary, as phrases such as "I cannot see on what grounds the king of Britain can look up to Heaven for help against us; a common murderer, a highwayman, or a house-breaker, has as good a pretence as he . . ." illustrate. He is calling the king names, trying (with great success, as it turned out) to incite the people to revolution. The second speech, in contrast, is far more deliberate and reasoned in tone with far fewer quotable, incisive phrases. The first speech strives for a soapbox approach, to reach the common man, the general audience, while the second has a more rational tone for a more elevated and educated audience.

Section 2, Part B

1. **(C)** The poet feels that man should listen to Nature when thoughts of death obsess him. Lines 2–3 tell us that "she speaks/A various language" and line 7 explains Nature's "healing sympathy." Lines 8–15 specifically instruct man to shake off his thoughts of the "last bitter hour" by going forth to Nature, under the open sky, and "list" (listen) to what the Earth and waters and air can tell.

2. **(C)** This is a direct quote from the poem (line 7), as mentioned in question 1.

3. **(B)** The phrase "Couch more magnificent" is found in line 33. The author is saying that nothing could be more majestic than to share eternity with the most powerful the earth has known—kings, the wise, the good.

4. **(E)** Lines 34–37 list all those who are buried in the earth.

5. **(D)** The line "All that breathe/Will share thy destiny" (lines 60–61) explains that mourning is not necessary, for in time all will pass on to Nature's bed.

6. **(A)** The poet is very concerned that man live in trust with Nature. The lines "Thou go not, like the quarry slave at night,/Scourged to his dungeon, but, sustained and soothed/By an unfaltering trust, approach thy grave . . . and lies down to pleasant dreams" (lines 77–81) tell us this.

7. **(B)** The entire poem is concerned with man's acceptance of the natural order, that man will live and die according to Nature's rules and thus all will work in a great cosmic harmony.

None of the other choices fit with the poem's meaning.

8. **(D)** A "sepulcher" is a tomb, and "mighty" means grand. Here, the earth is the grandest tomb of all, for it is the largest and holds all the great, wise, and mighty from all time.

9. **(B)** See the answer for question 8 for an explanation.

10. **(B)** The "destiny" is death, what all people, no matter how great or small, hold in common. None of the other choices are always true, for we have no assurance that all will have to mourn, (D), or accept Nature, (E).

11. **(A)** A simile is a comparison using "like" or "as," and here we have "*Like* one who wraps the drapery of his couch/About him. . . ," comparing sleep with a warm and comfortable blanket to the grave's shroud. Both, the poet claims, should be approached calmly and with trust. (B), personification, is giving human qualities to inanimate objects, and (C), alliteration, is the repetition of the initial letter, as in "Peter Piper picked a peck of pickled peppers." (D), apostrophe, is addressing someone who is not present, as if the author here were to say, "Dear Nature . . ." Inversion, (E), occurs when portions of the sentence are switched around for literary effect.

12. **(D)** Death is compared to sleep, as the reader is instructed to approach death as if it were but sleep on a warm couch.

13. **(E)** The new lines offer more hope, speaking as they do of "gayer hours" (line 3), "voice of

gladness" (line 4), and "healing sympathy" (line 7). The poet had come under fire for what many saw as a bleak picture of death, although he intended it to offer great comfort.

14. **(B)** Again, these lines offer a bit of hope and unify the beginning and the end of the poem. Rarely will an author add anything simply to allow room for more figures of speech, (A); the poetic devices add to the meaning, not substitute for it. The poem is not a ballad, (C), and nowhere is death to be feared or battled. See the final lines.

15. **(E)** The major influence on "Thanatopsis" by William Cullen Bryant is a movement called Romanticism, which flourished during the nineteenth century. Some of the ideas of the movement reflected in this poem include a belief in the changeable, variable state of the physical world (often called "mutability") and the feeling that all is prey to decline and decay. The Romantics also felt that even though everything changes and declines, God remains absolute and reveals Himself through His greatest, though changeable, creation—Nature. Bryant also used many of the writing techniques of the Romantic school. There is a great reliance on artificially inflated diction and syntax. The Romantics felt that old-fashioned, out-of-date word order and choice could be used to establish a serious and philosophical tone. Thus we find words like "thou," "thy," and "shalt," as well as contractions such as "list" for "listen." Even in the nineteenth century, which seems so long ago, no one was speaking in this manner. Inversion, discussed previously, was also a Romantic technique. Also referred to as anastrophe, it is the movement of a word or phrase from its normal and expected position in the sentence for poetic effect or emphasis. It can also be used to maintain poetic rhythm and rhyme. As shown above, Bryant made extensive use of this technique.

16. **(A)** The poet speaks of life in the beginning, and concludes with a discussion of the way in which a person should approach death—calmly, and with trust in Nature.

17. **(E)** (A) A villanelle is a short poem of fixed form, five tercets followed by a final quatrain, having rhyme and refrains. This is not the case with "Thanatopsis." (B) A dramatic monologue is a poem that has one person telling a dramatic story, such as Robert Browning's "My Last Duchess." There is no story, no narrative, here. (C) A sonnet is a poem of 14 lines having a very specific rhyme and rhythm, which is not the case here either, and (D), a ballad, is a simple narrative poem, usually having a romantic theme and able to be set to music and sung. "Thanatopsis" is none of these.

18. **(C)** There is only one level of interpretation here, the poet's belief that Nature will welcome man and comfort him and that man's death will unite him firmly with the universe and the natural order of life. Be careful with questions that have the word EXCEPT in them, for they can be tricky to read.

19. **(A)** The inversions and poetic contractions, such as "list" for "listen," make the poem difficult to read. In no way would the language be economical (B), for there are a great many words here, and a case could be made that this would have been a better, more effective poem, if the author had used fewer. The language is not *best* described by either (C) or (D), although a case could be made for both, as well as (E). Remember to select the answer that *best* completes the question, even though there will be choices that appear to be correct. There is always one that is most accurate.

20. **(D)** The speaker makes no pretensions to be Nature or the "powerful of the earth," choices (A) and (C). The voice remains the same throughout the poem, and thus choice (E) is not correct.

21. **(C)** This is an inversion, as the words are switched out of their expected order. The sentence would most usually read, "Yet a few days, and the all-beholding sun shall not see any more in all his course." (A) An oxymoron is a seeming contradiction, such as "cruel kindness." (B) A conceit is an elaborate metaphor or extended comparison, and (D), personification, is giving human qualities to inanimate objects. (E) A synecdoche is the use of a part for a whole or a whole for a part, such as "five sails" for five ships.

22. **(A)** The poet intends to comfort man about death. We can see this especially in the final lines.

Section 3

The essay asks that you show both the good and bad traits a character possesses to conclude that the character is "human" like all of us. Briefly, a chart could be used to show these character traits. In *The Adventures of Huckleberry Finn*, for example, we see that Huck, the main character, is "human" because he has the following balance of good and bad traits:

Good

Risks eternal damnation ("All right, then, I'll go to hell") to rescue Jim after he is sold to the slave traders for "forty dirty dollars."

Works hard at school and tries to learn; initially does try to stop Tom from the worst of the plans to "rescue" Jim at the end of the book.

Bad

Plays three progressively dangerous and humiliating tricks on Jim—the nickel/hat trick, the snake trick where Jim gets bitten, and worst of all, the "trash" incident.

Goes along with Tom on the escape plans at the end of the book, which are very dangerous. Tom is shot and wounded. Abandons his studies with ease when his father kidnaps him from cabin.

The same can be done for Shakespeare's *Hamlet:*

Good

Wrestles with his conscience before he will kill Claudius—he must have proof.

Well loved by the common people, shown especially in Act V with the gravediggers—he had the "common touch"

Honest, decent, kind, possessor of a keen conscience (scenes with Horatio).

Bad

When he does have proof—Claudius's confession in his private room—does not act and compounds the tragedy.

Treats Ophelia very shabbily when he feels she has thrown him over; treats his mother as poorly when he comes close to killing her in the "closet" scene. Ghost stops him.

Indecisive and too much given to brooding—see Act I with his mother's comments.

HOW TO USE THE DIAGNOSTIC TEST

1. Take a look back at each section and see where you did well and where you did poorly. Did you find the poem very hard to analyze or the essay difficult to organize? Did the prose passages and essay stump you? On a sheet of paper, note which sections were hard for you and which questions you could not answer.

2. You will have a list that will look something like this:
   Simile?
   Metaphor?
   How to organize essay?
   What's *tone*?

3. Now, go through this book and write down the page numbers of the sections that explain what you need to know.
   Simile?   p. ——
   Metaphor?   p. ——
   How to Organize essay? p. ——

4. Do not spend much time on those sections you understood. Rather, to make the best use of this book and the time allowed, focus on the sections that you found most difficult. Make sure all your questions are answered.

5. When you have finished all your study, take the three simulated exams at the end of this book. After each exam, make note of the questions you missed and the concepts that gave you trouble. Go back to the study sections for additional help in your own personal troublespots before attempting the next exam.

Part 2

Essay Writing Guide

Step by Step to High-Scoring AP Essays

1. Before you do anything else, make sure that you understand exactly what is required of you. Ask yourself the following questions:

   • What must I prove?

   • How much time do I have to complete the essay?

   • What form—novel, short story, poem, drama—am I required to use?

   • How many works or characters or aspects must I consider? One? Two?

   • Is the work or are the works that I have selected of "recognized literary value"? It is usually best to select works that you have covered in class or that have come from the AP reading list. Avoid works that have been made into recent popular movies and stick with something that you are sure will be acceptable. This is not the time to experiment with outside reading.

   • Who are they asking me to select? A main character? A supporting player? The narrator? Is the person that I have selected the proper one?

   • Do I know the work well enough to be sure of the details? Do I have the chronology straight: Do I recall the actual order of events? Do I know the characters? Can I spell their names? Can I recall their various relationships? This is crucial, for the success of your thesis will directly depend on the strength of your *detail*, and major errors in this area can seriously weaken your essay. Make sure you know the work. Before you finalize your choice, make a list of all the important and relevant details from the works you are considering.

2. After you have thought out all of the above, rephrase the thesis statement in your own words to make sure that you understand what you will have to do. Try several different variations and double-check selection of characters, etc. Again, be sure you have the correct and necessary information from the works.

3. Construct an outline, either jotted or topic (see Organizing Your Thoughts, page 25). Make sure that you have included all the correct details in the correct order. Check that you have included all you need to make your point. Do not be afraid to include dialogue and specific quotes, if you can recall them. You will find that if you know a book or play well, many important interchanges will come to mind. These might include such crucial details as Hamlet's "To be or not to be" speech; Huck Finn's famous denial of public conscience, "All right, then, I'll go to hell," or his last lines, as he "lights out for the territory ahead of the rest;" Macbeth's "Lay on Macduff" speech, just to name a few. These are the *specific details* that can make the difference between a *good* paper and a *great* one. It is a good idea to prepare several books and poems, noting details and lines that impressed you. **This does not mean that you will insert lines wherever you can to impress the reader; they must, of course, directly prove your point or they are valueless. But if you have carefully outlined several different works, the specific details will come to mind.**

4. Write the introduction. This is a very important part of your paper, as we will discuss later in detail. It establishes your thesis and captures your reader's attention. If the thesis is incorrect, the paper will not prove the point; if the introduction is dull and lifeless, the reader's attention will drift, and he may miss some of your points. Make sure you rephrase the question, include title and author, and establish what you will prove.

5. Write the first draft. Of course, it is always best to write more than one draft of a paper, but you may not have the time to do so. Thus, it is important that you follow the outline to make sure that you have included all your salient points. Do not count on having the time to complete two drafts, but keep in mind that if you are so fortunate, your paper will be the better for it. Never leave extra time at the end; use every minute that you are allowed.

6. Make sure that you *proofread* very carefully. This can be one of the most important steps in any paper, for no matter how valid your points, how clear your examples, if you have made a great many careless writing errors, you will lose credit. While your essay will be evaluated holistically (on the total impression it makes), errors can distract your reader and reduce the effectiveness of your arguments. Try to leave your paper for a few moments, perhaps look over the short answers or another essay, and then go back to it refreshed. *Always* make sure that you have time to proofread, and be as careful as you can to read what is there, not what you *think* is there.

SCORING

The short answer questions on both the English Literature and Composition exam and the English Language exam are machine scored, as per Educational Testing Service standard practice. The essays, however, are read individually by specially trained high school and college teachers who gather for five days during the late spring. Your essays are evaluated on the basis of a single, overall impression. This method of grading is called "holistic scoring," as it concentrates on a single, overall effect rather than focusing on individual errors. Holistic scoring assumes that error count alone cannot accurately reflect competency levels. In other words, the whole piece of writing is greater than the sum of its parts. On the positive side, *minor* writing errors that do not seriously affect the content of your paper will be overlooked, for the reader will be concentrating on the total effect of your paper. On the negative side, although ETS has a high level of reliability, your paper will likely only be read once. This places more emphasis on effective introductions, conclusions, and clear, specific details.

Generating Your Thoughts

It is always difficult to begin writing—especially so on a pressured exam, where you have precious little time to map out your ideas. There are few things as disheartening as staring at a blank sheet of paper, wondering where to start. You don't have the luxury of sitting and thinking for awhile, musing on the various aspects your topic presents. You are not allowed to bounce your ideas off others; you have no recourse to primary or secondary texts. There will most likely be no opportunity for a second draft or extensive revision. Your first draft will have to stand as your final effort.

How do you begin? Is it best to just take a few deep breaths and plunge right in? Or are you perhaps better off planning for a few moments, even though it seems like everyone around you is already writing? Almost all writers agree that planning results in a better finished product, especially when there is little or no time for revision. Planning helps your ideas flow with greater logic and order. It also guarantees that all important details will be included in their proper places.

Therefore, even though it might appear that everyone else has already begun writing, *always* try to set aside some time to plan what you are going to say and how you are going to say it. Naturally, the time you spend planning depends on how much time you have to write your essay. Use the chart that follows to determine how much time you should allocate to planning your essay:

If you have 20 minutes for your essay	plan for 3–5 minutes
If you have 25 minutes for your essay	plan for 5 minutes
If you have 30 minutes for your essay	plan for 5 minutes
If you have 40 minutes for your essay	plan for 5–7 minutes
If you have 45 minutes for your essay	plan for 7 minutes
If you have 60 minutes for your essay	plan for 7–10 minutes

Now that you know approximately how much time to set aside for planning your essay, let's look at ways to best use that time.

Writers all have their own ways of generating ideas, but what works well for one person may be ineffective for another. Below are three different ways to get your thoughts flowing. Try all three with the simulated AP essay questions in this text. Experiment to discover which method works best for you. Then, use that method or a combination of methods on the actual test.

One possible way to begin is to *brainstorm*. First, re-read the question. Then, put your pen on the paper—and don't lift it up again until you have finished brainstorming! Now, allowing yourself about 2 minutes, write down all the ideas that you can concerning the question. These can be single words or phrases. You can abbreviate or use dashes (—) or slashes (/) to save time. The most important thing about successful brainstorming is to continue writing, as quickly as you can. Don't worry if a few of your ideas seem irrelevant to the topic, or if you write the same idea twice, or if you misspell some words. If you can't think of anything to write but still have time left, continue writing, even if you write your name or the date. You should be able to generate a list of about 15 different ideas within the 2 minute time frame. For example, let's brainstorm with this simulated AP essay question:

"... show how the main character is unwilling or unable to accept members of his or her community or family and is thus isolated and alone. Also explain how the author prepares the reader for this rejection of human companionship. Consider at least two elements of fiction such as theme, setting, characterization, or any other aspect of the writer's craft in your discussion."

Brainstorming sample

—Hamlet	—father dead
—mother remarried/uncle/2 months	—R & G spies
—Ophelia cut off	—ghost
—distrusts Claudius	—distrusts mother
—contemplates suicide	—"to be or not to be"
—Claudius/murder plot/England	—has only Horatio
—play within a play	—black cloak
—madness	—battlements at night

Now you have a list of ideas you can use to begin writing. While not every idea will fit, you should have enough to begin arranging your ideas into a coherent whole, a topic discussed at length in the next section, "Organizing Your Thoughts." But first, let's look at a second way to generate ideas, freewriting.

Some writers find it easier to think in sentences rather than words or phrases. When they begin brainstorming, they find themselves writing down very long phrases that grow into sentences, even brief paragraphs. If this description fits your writing style, you might find it easier to generate ideas through *freewriting*. With brainstorming, you write down *words or phrases*; with freewriting, you write down *sentences*.

Allowing about 3 to 4 minutes, or about twice as long as you set aside for brainstorming, write down all the ideas you have concerning the test question in complete sentences, tying your ideas together in a loose, off-the-top-of-your-head paragraph. By no means will this be a finished composition; rather, it is a very brief paragraph designed to get you thinking. By nature it will be somewhat rambling, poorly-organized, and perhaps even confusing in places—but it will serve to get your ideas flowing and establish a starting place for your composition. Let's freewrite the same simulated AP question:

> ". . . show how the main character is unwilling or unable to accept members of his or her community or family and is thus isolated and alone. Also explain how the author prepares the reader for this rejection of human companionship. Consider at least two elements of fiction such as theme, setting, characterization, or any other aspect of the writer's craft in your discussion."

Freewriting sample

Even though he tries to establish meaningful contact with people in his family (Gertrude/Claudius) and community (Laertes, Ophelia, Rosencrantz and Guildenstern), he fails and is alone. Shakespeare prepares the reader for this by using characterization and theme. He comes back to his home Denmark because he thinks that he is going to attend his father's funeral. Imagine his surprise when he discovers that he is also witnessing his mother's marriage (funeral baked meats/irony). He is isolated because he is unable to talk to his mother after she has remarried (Act I, and later scene in her room), and he really does not trust his uncle. Later we find out how perceptive this is. His girlfriend cuts him off; his friends R & G are disloyal.

There is a lot missing from this brief paragraph (including the main character's name!), yet it serves well as a springboard for a focused, well-developed essay. Notice how this freewriting establishes the primary points to be discussed, lists the main characters, and begins introducing some specific detail. Although there is little here that directly addresses the second half of the question: "Consider at least two elements of fiction such as theme, setting, characterization, or any other aspect of the writer's craft in your discussion," we do have enough generated to begin arranging a formal response.

The third method of generating your thoughts involves *asking questions*. There are two different ways to do this. One frequently used method is called *QAD* (Questions, Answers, Details); the second method involves asking yourself the traditional journalistic questions. Let's take a look at QAD first.

As with brainstorming and freewriting, the QAD method of generating ideas is designed to take only a few moments. Consult the chart on page 25 to best pace your time on each individual AP essay question. QAD is especially useful on a factual literature essay. Here is a sample pertaining to tragedy and *Macbeth*:

Question	Answer	Details
What is tragedy?	representations of serious actions which turn out disastrously for the main character(s)	1. involves a character for whom we have sympathy 2. serious occurrence 3. circumstances beyond one's control 4. results in hero's death

This should take a few moments to briefly outline. Next, zero in on the question, and fill in the chart with details pertaining to it. The following is an example from *Macbeth*.

QUESTION	ANSWER	DETAILS					
		WHAT HAPPENS?	WHERE?	WHEN?	WHY?	HOW?	WHO?
What is a situation involving a serious or calamitous occurrence?	Macbeth goes to the cave of the witches.	He sees three visions.	Appearing from the cauldron.	After seeing Banquo's ghost at the feast.	Because of his uncertainty and fear regarding his position as King.	He reacts by deciding to continue his killing.	Macduff's family.

Another way of asking questions to generate ideas focuses on the 5 W's and H: Who? What? When? Where? Why? and How?

Again, working within the time frame outlined on the chart for generating ideas, select whichever variations on these questions apply to your topic. Here are some suggestions:

Who
—was involved?
—does this concern?
—does this affect?

What
—happened?
—was the cause?
—were the results?
—does this mean to the plot or theme as a whole?

When
—did it happen? (try to narrow your response down to a specific time or page
   number)
—will the results be apparent?

Where
—did it happen?

Why
—did it happen?

How
—did it happen?

You will most likely find this method of generating ideas even more useful if you narrow down your questions to best suit your specific topic—the more specific the question, the more focused your response. Consider again the simulated AP question with which we have been working:

> "... show how the main character is unwilling or unable to accept members of his or her community or family and is thus isolated and alone. Also explain how the author prepares the reader for this rejection of human companionship. Consider at least two elements of fiction such as theme, setting, characterization, or any other aspect of the writer's craft in your discussion."

Here are some questions to consider:

- What work will I use?
- Is it a work of recognized literary value?
- Who is the main character?
- What in the book tells me that this character is unwilling or unable to accept people?
- How does the author use theme to anticipate the character's rejection of people?
- How does the author use symbolism to anticipate the character's rejection of people?

To summarize, there are many different ways to generate ideas; we have discussed but three of the most common. Select the method—or combination of methods—that best suits your individual style of composition. Also consider the nature of the specific AP question you are being asked—different methods work better with different questions—and the amount of time you have. Regardless of the method(s) you ultimately adopt, successful prewriting techniques can greatly improve the quality of organization and detail in your composition. These techniques can make it easier for you to begin writing, and help to ensure that you will make the best use of your time.

Exercises: Generate ideas for each of the following simulated AP questions by using *brainstorming, freewriting,* and *asking questions.* You can try all three methods on each question, but make sure to try each method at least once.

1. Read the two poems that follow. Then compare the mood of the first with the mood of the second, showing how the mood of each poem serves to define and reinforce the theme. Use specific lines from both poems to support your discussion. Time—45 minutes.

WHEN I WAS ONE-AND-TWENTY

When I was one-and-twenty
   I heard a wise man say,
"Give crowns and pounds and guineas
   But not your heart away;
Give pearls away and rubies
   But keep your fancy free."
But I was one-and-twenty,
   No use to talk to me.

When I was one-and-twenty
   I heard him say again,
"The heart out of the bosom
   Was never given in vain;
'Tis paid with sighs a plenty
   And sold for endless rue."
And I am two-and-twenty,
   And oh, 'tis true, 'tis true.

          —*A.E. Housman*

WITH RUE MY HEART IS LADEN

With rue my heart is laden
   For golden friends I had,
For many a rose-lipt maiden
   And many a lightfoot lad.

By brooks too broad for leaping.
   The lightfoot boys are laid;
The rose-lipt girls are sleeping
   In fields where roses fade.

          —*A.E. Housman*

2. Explain how any three poetic devices Gerard Manley Hopkins uses in "Pied Beauty" contribute to the poem's theme. You may select from the following list: alliteration, sound devices, meter, rhythm, rhyme, figurative language, vocabulary, word use, color use. Time—45 minutes.

PIED BEAUTY[1]

Glory be to God for dappled things—
   For skies of couple-colour as a brindled cow;
      For rose-moles all in stipple upon trout that swim;
Fresh-firecoal chestnut-falls; finches' wings;
   Landscape plotted and pieced—fold, fallow, and plough;
      And all trades, their gear and tackle and trim.

All things counter, original, spare, strange;
   Whatever is fickle, freckled (who knows how?)
      With swift, slow; sweet, sour; adazzle, dim;
He fathers-forth whose beauty is past change:
        Praise him.

          —*Gerard Manley Hopkins*

3. Select a major character from any work of recognized literary merit and show how that character is unable to adjust successfully to his or her environment. Be sure to include specific examples from the work to make your point. Time—60 minutes.

---

[1]*Pied* means of two or more colors, variegated.

Organizing Your Thoughts

One of the best ways to organize material you have generated through brainstorming, freewriting, asking questions, or a combination of these methods is to use an *outline*. Outlines are especially effective in literary essays where you must be sure to include all the necessary details in the correct order. There are four main kinds of outlines: jotted, topic, sentence, and paragraph. Each one is useful in certain circumstances, depending on the subject, the time allotted, and how secure you feel with the material.

THE JOTTED OUTLINE

The jotted outline is the simplest way to quickly organize the material you have generated through brainstorming or freewriting. When using the asking questions method, an outline is not usually required as the basis of the composition is already established. Like most writers, you are apt to find the jotted outline especially useful if you are pressed for time, which is certainly the case on the AP exam.

With the jotted outline, you arrange the brief phrases you have gathered into a logical whole. At the same time, you must delete any words or phrases from your original list that are irrelevant to the topic as well as add any new material you require to fully flesh out your thesis. Use parallel phrasing to keep your thinking straight. Here's a jotted outline for a typical AP essay on literature:

Question
"A sharp insight can change a person's life for better or worse. Select a character from a recognized work of literary value and show how this is true."

Outline
Thesis: Huckleberry Finn has a sharp insight which changes his life for the better.

1. Huck—typical upbringing for child in 1830s—taught blacks inferior to whites
2. Meets Jim/Jackson's Island/strike up closer friendship/travel down Mississippi
3. Begins to see Jim as person/story of Jim's daughter's deafness/Jim's aim to buy wife and children
4. Huck/sharp insight/Cairo/lies to slave traders; gets $40/"All right, then, I'll go to hell"—letter to Miss Watson/rescue of Jim

Now you have a chronological list of items you will consider to make your point. You can refer to your outline to make sure you discuss all your points clearly.

THE TOPIC OUTLINE

If time permits, the topic outline will usually help you organize your thoughts more throughly than the jotted outline. The topic outline takes the jotted outline one step further. The jotted outline *lists* words or phrases that represent main ideas; the topic outline, in contrast, *arranges* these brief phrases in a highly formalized structure. Again, keep these phrases parallel to further encourage logical thinking. Your thoughts will thus be ordered in an *inductive* manner, as your major points are set upward in tiers of ascending importance, and *deductive*, as your major headings are divided into smaller and smaller subheads. You mark headings and subheadings by alternating numbers and letters as you proceed downward from Roman numeral I through captial A to Arabic 1 and little a, until you reach, if you need them, parenthesized (1) and (a). You indent equal headings equally, so that they fall into the same column, Roman under Roman, capital under capital, and so on, in this manner:

I. _____
   A. _____
      1. _____
      2. _____
   B. _____
      1. _____
         a. _____
           (1)_____
              (a)_____
              (b)_____
           (2)_____
         b. _____
      2. _____
II. _____
   A. _____
   B. _____
   C. _____
   D. _____
      1. _____
      2. _____
      3. _____
         a. _____
         b. _____

Headings always come in pairs; you cannot have a I without a II, an A without a B, a 1 without a 2, etc. This is because an unpaired heading suggests a detail is too small for separate treatment, and should really be part of a larger heading directly above. Let's take another look at the question on "sharp insight":

I. Topic paragraph
   A. Topic sentence—title, author, thesis statement
   B. Material that will be covered in PP2—first events leading up to sharp insight
   C. Material that will be covered in PP3—conclusion on sharp insight
   D. transition into PP2

II. Beginning of proof
   A. Topic sentence—restatement of thesis
   B. Huck's upbringing/attitude toward slaves
   C. Huck meets Jim on Jackson's Island/begin down Mississippi
   D. Scene with Jim's tale of daughter's deafness/Huck begins to realize Jim a person with feelings
   E. Scene right before Cairo—Jim reminds Huck how good Huck has been to him

    F. Huck has beginning of insight with slave traders at Cairo—lies for Jim to slave traders/accepts $40

    G. Thesis statement—Huck begins to accept Jim as a person, has insight that Jim is "white inside"

III. Climax of insight
    A. Topic sentence—brief recounting of events leading up to selling of Jim
    B. King sells Jim for "40 dirty dollars." Huck decides to write letter to Miss Watson/letter itself
    C. Huck rips up letter/says, "All right, then, I'll go to hell!" Decides to risk eternal damnation (refer to II B) to save his friend. Sudden realization
    D. Huck and Tom rescue Jim
    E. Concluding sentence

IV. Conclusion
    A. Topic sentence—Huck experiences sudden insight/realizes that Jim a human being, despite all he has been taught about blacks
    B. Summarize PP2
    C. Climax of sudden realization—Huck risks eternal damnation to save Jim
    D. Conclusion—scene at Cairo: Huck begins to accept Jim

This is the type of outline that you will use most frequently on the AP examination, for it is well worth the time to clearly organize your thoughts before you begin to write. In this manner, you can make sure that you have included clear details (Cairo, quotes, etc. as shown) and made your point.

THE SENTENCE OUTLINE

The sentence outline requires more time than either of the previous two methods, but it can be very helpful if you tend to think in longer phrases or you find it useful to plan even more tightly before you begin to write. Because it forces you to think out your plan so carefully beforehand, it can greatly speed up your writing time. Few outlines will be as complete as the one that follows, but you can see how easy writing an essay will be with an outline this full.

> Thesis: Holden Caulfield, the main character in J. D. Salinger's *The Catcher in the Rye,* is removed from the mainstream of society for a variety of reasons and is more independent than the person who must rely upon others. One critic has linked him to other characters in American literature who live alone, and dubbed this kind of character "the American Adam." Compare Holden's isolation with the isolation of any other character in American literature.*

I. Holden is isolated from society, even though he attempts to make contact with others.
    A. Holden first visits his old history teacher from Pencey Prep, Mr. Spencer.
        1. Although Holden admires Spencer, they fail to make contact as Spencer reads Holden's failing examination paper to him.

*See R.W.B. Lewis, *The American Adam: Innocence, Tragedy and Tradition in the Nineteenth Century.* Chicago: The University of Chicago Press, 1955.

        2. Things get even worse as the teacher forces Holden to listen to the pathetic note Holden had added to his paper.

        3. Even though Holden sees that Spencer is trying to help him end his isolation, the older man fails to establish a link, symbolized by the magazine he throws failing to reach the bed.

  B. Holden next has a conversation with his roommate, Ward Stradlater, and again we see his isolation.

        1. Stradlater, whom Holden considers a "phony," has Holden writing his essays for him.

        2. Stradlater ignores what Holden has to say about Jane Gallagher, Holden's friend, more intent on her physical appearance than her basic humanity.

        3. Although Stradlater invites Holden to join them on the date, he is unable to bring himself to establish a bond.

II. Huckleberry Finn, from *The Adventures of Huckleberry Finn* by Mark Twain, is also isolated from society.

  A. Huck has no family.

        1. His mother died when Huck was born.

        2. His father, a drunken bum, abuses Huck by locking him in a cabin alone for three days.

        3. Although his guardians, the Widow Douglas and Miss Watson, mean well, neither is able to become "family" to him.

  B. Huck's actions set him off from society.

        1. Huck runs away to Jackson's Island to escape his abusive Pap.

        2. Huck sails down the Mississippi River with a runaway slave, Jim, surviving by "borrowing" food.

        3. Huck risks what he considers eternal damnation to save Jim from a return to slavery.

        4. At the end of the book, Huck "lights out for the territory ahead of the rest," running away once again.

An outline this complete might not be possible in the time allowed on the exam, but some students find it a useful method for their particular writing styles. There is one final method of outlining, more useful for summaries of reading than for preparation of essays, and that is the paragraph outline.

THE PARAGRAPH OUTLINE

The paragraph outline strengthens your ability to organize your paragraphs by topic sentences, since in this type of outline you write a topic sentence for each and every one of your paragraphs. Since your paragraphs are many and your divisions few, it is most convenient to use a combination of Roman and Arabic numerals. A paragraph outline could look like this:

I. Holden seems unable to maintain even the most tenuous link with others.

    1. As he is having breakfast in a cheap cafeteria, Holden meets two nuns, and is filled with pity for them.

    2. He gives them ten dollars, even though he is running out of money himself, and tries to buy them breakfast, which they refuse.

    3. Holden and the nuns have a long conversation about literature and it appears that the meeting will go well after all.

4. But as they part, Holden blows smoke at the nuns, which disturbs him a great deal.
5. He feels as though he has behaved very badly and wonders if he should have given them more money. Even in this seemingly innocent meeting, Holden is unable to establish a link with others.

This type of outline is generally too detailed to be useful in a literature essay for a timed examination, but it will be handy for extended reading assignments, term papers, or any untimed and extensive essay.

To outline your reading, you first summarize the essay into one sentence. Then you go back through the essay, writing down a series of sentences that summarize the main ideas as they come along. You may use the author's own words, but it is generally easier to summarize with your own briefer statements. Then you arrange the statements into major and minor importance, and rearrange them in the proper order.

OUTLINING TECHNIQUES

The following points will make your outlines clearer and more helpful in structuring your essays:

1. **Title.** Set the title off from the text of the outline. Do not underline it or place it in quotes. Make it as specific as you can, even if your essay will not be as specific as your title. This will help focus your thoughts more clearly.

2. **Capitalization.** Capitalize only the first word of each heading (and other words that would normally be capitalized).

3. **Punctuation.** Put periods after headings that are complete sentences, but not after phrases.

4. **Headings.** Whenever possible, make headings grammatically parallel. Try not to mix headings—some nouns, some sentences, some fragments. This may not always be possible, of course, if you are rushed for time, but it will make the actual writing of the essay easier if the headings are parallel.

Outlining Exercise

Directions: Construct a topic outline on the following simulated AP question using the form provided below. Try to be as specific as possible and keep your headings and subheadings as parallel as possible.

"Failure in human relationships results when one shirks the normal responsibilities of one's position in life." Show how this is true with one character from a recognized work of literary value.

I. _____
    A. _____
    B. _____
    C. _____
    D. _____

II. _____
    A. _____
    B. _____
        1. _____
        2. _____
    C. _____
        1. _____
        2. _____
    D. _____

III. _____
    A. _____
    B. _____
        1. _____
        2. _____
    C. _____
        1. _____
        2. _____
    D. _____

IV. _____
    A. _____
    B. _____
    C. _____
    D. _____

Possible Answers: (Using *The Scarlet Letter* by Nathaniel Hawthorne)

I. Topic paragraph
   A. Topic sentence—rephrase question/Arthur Dimmesdale avoids his responsibilities.
   B. Material in PP2—Arthur's involvement with Hester Prynne
   C. Material in PP3—Arthur's involvement with Chillingworth and the town
   D. Lead-in PP2

II. Beginning of thesis
   A. Topic sentence—rephrase question and answer
   B. Arthur's affair with Hester/birth of Pearl/scene with Arthur beseeching Hester to reveal her lover/irony/denial of responsibility
      1. Detail on Arthur's role
      2. Detail on Arthur's normal responsibility
   C. Hester, disgraced, has to support Pearl alone/psychological and physical
      1. Economic—seamstress—because of Arthur's failure to support them
      2. Problems with Pearl—no father
   D. Summary of above

III. Conclusion of thesis
   A. Topic sentence—Arthur's responsibility extended beyond Hester to Chillingworth and the town.
   B. Responsibility to Hester's husband, Chillingworth
      1. Chillingworth "leech"
      2. Ripping aside of vestments
   C. Responsibility to town
      1. Secret guilt—bloody scourge in closet
      2. Town worships him, the more the guilt increases

IV. Conclusion
   A. Summary of thesis
   B. Summary of PP 2
   C. summary of PP 3
   D. General conclusion

The Elements of Writing Style

Your *writing style* conveys your personality, which is your individual voice. Many different elements combine to create your writing style, including diction, figurative language, tone, degree of formality, rhythm, grammatical structure, organization, and sentence variety. Let's take a close look at the last element, sentence variety.

Varying your sentences can alert your reader to a change in thought and to an especially important point. Sentence variety can also make the difference between a lackluster essay and one that sparkles. The following chart reviews nine of the most common ways to start your sentences:

INTRODUCTORY SENTENCE ELEMENTS

Introductory Element	Job—Acts as—Does the Work of	Ends or Begins With	"Clue"	Example
1 ADVERB	Modifies the verb which follows close by	Often ends with -ly	Will have a comma following it	*Quietly*, the cat stalked the bird.
2 PREPOSITIONAL PHRASE	Acts as a modifier Adjective or Adverb	Ends with a noun or pronoun	Begins with a preposition	*In December*, we prepare to take the AP test in English.
3 DEPENDENT CLAUSE	Has a subject and a verb	Begins with a subordinate conjunction; ends with a comma	Cannot stand alone	*Because he overslept*, he missed his bus.
4 MAIN CLAUSE	Has a subject and a verb	May be joined by a coordinate conjunction to another main clause	May stand alone as a sentence	*We can all leave for the dance*, if you are ready now.
5 VERBAL	Used as a noun, adjective, or adverb in a sentence	Begins with the word *to*; ends in -ing, -ed, -en, -t	Has a "hint" of action	*Shaking with fear*, the defendant stood before the jury.
6 INFINITIVE	A *verbal* used as a noun, adjective, or adverb	Begins with the word *to*	Can be changed into a gerund	*To shop in that store* is a true nightmare.
7 PARTICIPLE	A *verbal* used as an adjective—will modify a noun or pronoun	Ends in -ing, -ed, -en, -t	Followed by a comma	*Swollen by the melted snow*, the river rose over the farmland.
8 GERUND	A *verbal* used as a noun	Ends in -ing	Can put "the act of" in front of it	*Eating* in out-of-the-way restaurants can be an adventure.
9 ADJECTIVE	Modifies a noun or pronoun	Generally comes before the word it modifies	Demonstrative, indefinite, and possessive adjectives often begin sentences	*Those* students are rarely late for class.

SENTENCE VARIETY

There are four main kinds of sentences:

Simple: a single subject and verb group, although either may be plural

> *Examples:* Last July was unusually warm.
> Mary and John worked and studied together. (plural subject, plural verb)

Compound: two or more simple sentences joined in one of the three ways described below. A compound sentence unites two ideas, but it does not necessarily show the relationship between them. Compound sentences can be formed in the following ways:

1. semicolon (;)

   Example: The sun scorched the land; the lack of rain made it untillable.

2. comma + coordinating conjunction (and, but, or, for, so, yet, nor)

   Example: The sun scorched the land, and the lack of rain made it untillable.

3. semicolon + conjunctive adverb

   Example: The sun scorched the land; however, the farmers were able to irrigate successfully.

Conjunctive adverbs help you convey relationships within a sentence. They create logical connections in meaning, as the following chart shows:

Conjunctive Adverbs	
emphasis	certainly, indeed
addition	also, furthermore, moreover, besides
contrast	however, still, nevertheless, conversely, nontheless, instead, otherwise
comparison	likewise, similarly
result	therefore, thus, then, hence, consequently, accordingly
time	next, then, meanwhile, subsequently, finally

Complex: one independent clause and one or more subordinate (dependent) clauses

> *Example:* After Mary came home from work, Bill went to get a haircut.

Subordinating one part of a sentence gives one idea more importance than another. Usually, place the more important idea in the independent clause. As with conjunctive adverbs, select the subordinating conjunction that best conveys the relationship between ideas as indicated in the following chart:

Subordinating Conjunctions	
condition	if, even if, provided that, unless
effect	so, so that, that, in order that
cause	because, as
contrast	though, although, even though
location	where, wherever
choice	whether, rather than, than
time	after, before, once, since, until, when, whenever, while

Compound-Complex: at least two independent clauses and at least one dependent clause. The dependent clause can be part of the independent clause.

Example: When the heat comes, the lakes dry up, and farmers fear crop failure.

Sentence Errors

A **fragment** lacks either a subject or a complete verb, or does not express a complete thought.

Example: The cross-eyed lion with the shaggy orange mane. (lacks a verb)

A **run-on** sentence incorrectly runs together two complete ideas without using a conjunction or punctuation. A comma splice incorrectly joins two independent clauses with a comma.

Example: Elmer walked into the room, he found a mouse in his desk.

You can correct a run-in sentence in three ways:
①Divide it into two separate sentences. Elmer walked into the room. He found a mouse in his desk.
②Use a coordinating conjunction in place of the comma. Elmer walked into the room, and he found a mouse in his desk.
③Use a subordinating conjunction in place of the comma or in the beginning of the sentence. When Elmer walked into the room, he found a mouse in his desk.

How to Vary Sentences

1. Compound Sentence Elements

Sections of sentences may be compounded, eliminating wordiness. Elements that may be compounded include subjects, verbs, direct objects, predicate nouns and adjectives, other adjectives, and entire predicates. More than two compounded elements become a series.

Examples:

Compound predicate adjective: My sister is *obstinate, obsessed,* and *zealous.*
Compound verb: She *cheers, coaxes,* and *curses* the players.
Compound predicate: He *stares at the plays, yells in anger,* and *raises his fist.*

2. Appositives

An appositive (a noun) renames the noun it is placed immediately after. it eliminates wordiness and is especially useful when identifying characters for a literature essay.

Example:

Subject first: The President of the Board of Education, *a frequent visitor to the schools,* is well known to all the students.

Appositive first: *A frequent visitor to the schools,* the President of the Board of Education is well known to all the students.

3. Adverbs

An adverb may be placed at the beginning of a sentence. It adds variety to your writing by allowing the sentence to begin with something other than its subject.

Example:

Frequently, he praises the teacher and commends her teaching style.

4. Subordinate Clauses

There are three types of clauses, each with its own list of subordinate conjuntions.

An adverbial clause. The adverbial clause describes by telling how, where, why, when, or under what condition. It can be placed in many positions within the sentence, adding great variety to your writing. If such a clause is placed at the beginning of the sentence, it must be set off by a comma. Look for these words:

How	Where	When	Why	Under what condition
as if as though	where wherever	while when whenever as before after since until	because since as so that	if unless though although

Examples:

While he stares at the television, he speaks to his sister.
He speaks to his sister *while he stares at the television.*

An adjective clause. The adjective clause describes a noun by telling which, what kind of, or how many. It cannot be moved within the sentence and is most often placed after the noun it describes. If it is surrounded by commas, it can be removed from the sentence. If it is not, it is essential to the sentence and cannot be removed. Look for these words:

which	what kind of	how many
who whom whomever whoever that	what whatever	which whichever

Examples:

My grandfather, *who is a sports enthusiast,* watches ballgames every weekend. (Because it is surrounded by commas, the clause can be removed from the sentence.)

He gets a big bowl of popcorn *which he eats in front of the television.* (Because it is not surrounded by commas, this clause cannot be removed from the sentence.)

A noun clause. The noun clause, like a noun, may be used as a subject, direct object, indirect object, predicate noun, or object of a preposition. Look for these words:

what	who	how	that
whatever	whoever	however	whether
whomever	where	why	whom
wherever			

Examples:

As the subject of the sentence; *What he does every weekend* seems ridiculous to me. As the direct object: He really loves *what he does on the weekend.*

Elliptical clause. The elliptical clause is any of the three types discussed above with some of the unnecessary words omitted in order to eliminate wordiness. Be very careful not to remove necessary words and create a confusing sentence.

Example: While he stares at the plays, he yells at the television.

becomes ◊ While staring at plays, he yells at the television. (Note how "he" and "the" have been removed, and "stares" is replaced by "staring.")

5. Prepositional Phrases

A prepositional phrase contains a preposition + either a noun or a pronoun. It can function either as an adjective or an adverb. As an adjective, it cannot be moved and must be placed next to the noun it describes or after a linking verb. As an adverb, it may be placed in several different positions within the sentence.

Commonly Used Prepositions				
about	below	for	near	till
above	beneath	from	of	to
according to	beside	in	off	toward
across	besides	in addition to	on	towards
after	between	in place of	on account of	under
against	beyond	in front of	out	until
along	by	in spite of	out of	up
around	by way of	in regard to	outside	up to
at	despite	inside	over	upon
because of	down	instead of	since	with
before	during	into	through	within
behind	except	like	throughout	without

Examples:

Adjective: A computer nut *like my father* spends all Sunday at the terminal.

Adverb: *During the winter,* he works far into the night.

6. Gerund and Infinitive Phrases

Gerunds and infinitives are verbs used as nouns. An infinitive is the "base" (unconjugated) form of a verb; it is always in the form of *to + the verb*. Gerunds always end in "ing." Gerunds, which cannot serve as a sentence's main verb, are always used as nouns. Gerund or infinitive phrases begin with a gerund or infinitive. They function within a sentence in the same way as any of the five noun functions (as a subject, direct object, indirect object, predicate noun, or object of a preposition). Use such phrases sparingly, since they can create awkward and wordy sentences.

Examples:

Infinitive phrase as a subject: *To be a musician* is my friend's goal.

Infinitive phrase as a direct object: She wants *to practice the drums all day.*

Gerund phrase as a subject: *Having us all listen* is an essential part of her practice.

Gerund phrase as a predicate noun: Her goal is *watching us all writhe in agony.*

7. Present and Past Participal Phrases

Present and past participles are verbs used as adjectives. A present participle is the -ing form, and a past participle is the -ed form. Present and past participial phrases begin with present or past participles. They function as any other adjective or adjective phrase. Sophisticated and concise, a participial phrase must be placed carefully next to the noun it describes. If it is not, the meaning of the sentence can be confused.

Examples:

Present participial
phrases: *Staring at the screen,* he cheers the team.

Past participial
phrase: *Surrounded by bowls of food,* he munches in front of the TV.

Notice how switching the order of the two phrases in the last example would confuse the meaning of the sentence. "He munches in front of the TV surrounded by bowls of food" implies that the TV—not the man—is surrounded by food.

Remember that the most effective sentence is that which expresses your thought most clearly, concisely, and gracefully. This means that no one sentence style is better than another; complex sentences are not "better" than compound sentences, and so forth. Select the sentence style that best expresses what you have to say. The most effective writing styles are usually a mixture of different sentences, including simple, compound, and complex.

Practice Sentence Variety

Exercise 1: Rewrite the following paragraph to vary the sentences. You may combine sentences, reduce sentences to clauses, or rephrase as needed, but you must not change the meaning of the original paragraph.

> Uncle Sam was my Aunt Helen's husband. Uncle Sam did nothing for a living. He appeared to have no past. He came from Blackheart, Indiana. This one fact was known about him. Nobody seemed to know anything else about him. A picture of Blackheart emerged for me. The picture was reconstructed from Uncle Sam's conversation. The reconstructed picture showed that Blackheart consisted mainly of ball parks, pool rooms, and hardware stores. Aunt Helen came from Medford. Medford consisted of shopping malls, movie theatres, and food stores. What could have brought my Uncle Sam and Aunt Helen together? The other members of our family spoke freely of their relations. Some of these relations were real. Some of these relations were imaginary. Uncle Sam spoke of no one. Uncle Sam did not even speak of a parent.

Here is one possible revision. Remember that there are many possible and equally correct ways to revise any essay to vary sentences and create interest.

> Uncle Sam, my Aunt Helen's husband, did nothing for a living and appeared to have no past. We knew only that he came from Blackheart, Indiana, and from his conversations about his childhood home, I was able to reconstruct what it must have been like. A picture emerged of a small town consisting chiefly of ball parks, pool rooms, and hardware stores. Aunt Helen, in contrast, came from Medford, which was made up of shopping malls, movie theatres, and food stores. We all wondered what could have brought these two together. The family spoke of their past, discussing real and imaginary relations, but Uncle Sam spoke of no one, not even a parent.

Exercise 2: Shift the sentence elements in each of the following examples for greater sentence variety and better writing style. Then decide which version of each sentence is best suited to your subject, audience, and style.

1. A bowling team was formed this winter for the first time in the history of the school.
2. A mysterious figure stepped cautiously into the darkened room.
3. Sally, a voracious reader, keeps the librarian busy supplying her with books.
4. Candidates for a driver's license must take the written examination to prove their knowledge of traffic regulations.
5. The children, when their mothers are working, are cared for in nursery schools.
6. The audience, tired and hot, soon became impatient.
7. We were frightened by the explosion and dared not move from our places.
8. More than half the 90,000 acres under cultivation had not been ruined by the recent drought.
9. Accept the plan we have proposed if you have nothing better to offer.
10. There will never be a real compromise between such stubborn adversaries.
11. Sorters stand around the village store and chat with one another while waiting for the afternoon mail to be sorted.
12. A small boy, sobbing bitterly, ran toward me.

Possible Answers

Choose the sentence that is the most concise and graceful. Below are some suggested responses, although you may prefer the original sentences to the revised versions because they better reflect your personal writing style.

1. For the first time in the history of the school, a bowling team was formed this winter.
2. Cautiously, a mysterious figure stepped into the room.
3. A voracious reader, Sally keeps the librarian busy supplying her with books.
4. To prove their knowledge of traffic regulations, candidates for a driver's license must take the written examination.
5. When their mothers are working, the children are cared for in nursery schools.
6. Tired and hot, the audience soon became impatient.
7. Frightened by the explosion, we dared not move from our places.
8. The recent drought had not ruined more than half the 90,000 acres under cultivation.
9. If you have nothing better to offer, accept the plan we have proposed.
10. Between such stubborn adversaries there will never be any real compromise.
11. While waiting for the afternoon mail to be sorted, sorters stand around the village store and chat with one another.
12. Sobbing bitterly, a small boy ran toward me.

LOOSE AND PERIODIC SENTENCES

English sentences can be classified according to the form they take: simple, compound, complex. They can also be grouped according to style: loose and periodic.

In the loose sentence, the subject and predicate often come near the beginning of the sentence, and subordinate parts follow. The sentence is grammatically complete before its conclusion. For example:

> Then, having reached the dingy, grimy, and rickety depot station, we would get out, walk rapidly across the tracks of the station yard where we could see great flares and steamings from the engines, and hear the crash and bump of freight cars shifting, the tolling of bells, and the sounds of great trains on the rails.

Grammatically and logically, the sentence above could have ended after the word "out." It could also end after "yard" and "engines."

Another kind of sentence, much less frequently used, is the periodic. Here, the writer withholds his meaning until the very end and the reader is held in suspense. The sentence cannot end early either grammatically or logically. Here is an example:

> And to all those familiar sounds, filled with their exultant prophecies of flight, the voyage, morning, and the shining cities—to all the sharp and thrilling odors of trains—the smell of cinders, acrid smoke, and of musty, rusty freight cars, the clean pineboard of crated produce, and the smells of fresh stored food—oranges, coffee, tangerines, and bacon—there would be added now all the strange sights and smells of the coming circus.

It is impossible to end this sentence before the phrase at the end, for the full meaning is withheld until that point and the sentence would be a fragment without its final portion.

Practice Writing Loose and Periodic Sentences.

Exercise

1. If we wish to remain free, if we wish to maintain justice, if we hope to be esteemed throughout the world, we must be prepared to defend, whenever it is threatened, the liberty of each individual citizen.
2. With the trumpets blaring, the drums booming, and the children screaming their wild delight, the marchers passed in review.
3. We have done our best, although our dreams have now faded, our efforts have proved fruitless, and we have tasted the bitterness of defeat.

Possible Answers

1. This is a periodic sentence, as the meaning is at the end. A loose version would read as follows:

   We must be prepared to defend, whenever it is threatened, the liberty of each individual citizen, if we wish to remain free, if we wish to maintain justice, if we hope to be esteemed throughout the world.

2. This is also a periodic sentence, as the meaning is at the end. A loose version would read as follows:

   The marchers passed in review, with trumpets blaring, drums booming, and children screaming their wild delight.

3. This is a loose sentence, and a periodic version would be:

   Although our dreams have now faded, our efforts have proved fruitless, and we have tasted the bitterness of defeat, we have done our best.

SUPPLYING DETAILS

The most effective way to get your point across to your reader is through the use of detail: sharp, specific words selected to appeal to the senses and make the reader experience what you are describing. In a literary essay, the details are drawn from the work under discussion, and must be as specific as you can possibly make them. This means that quotes or paraphrases that directly make your point would be especially effective. In this way, your reader will understand your point while becoming convinced that you have read the book carefully.

The following passage from Thomas Wolfe's *Of Time and the River* illustrates effective use of detail. Read it and answer the questions that follow.

October is the richest of seasons. The fields are cut, the granaries are full, the bins are loaded to the brim with fatness and from the cider press the rich brown oozings of the York Imperials run. The bee bares to the belly of the yellow corn, the fly gets old and fat and blue, he buzzes loud, crawls slow, creeps heavily to death on a sill and ceiling, the sun goes down in blood and passion across the bronzed and mown fields of Old October.

Questions

1. What is the main impression here?
2. List the details that create the impression.
3. How is the paragraph organized?
4. Describe the sentences—variety, length, etc.
5. What letter or sound predominates?

Answers

1. The main impression is of fullness and richness as autumn closes.
2. There are a great many details to select: "rich brown oozings," "bronzed and mown fields," "bins loaded to the brim," etc.
3. The action of the poem moves from outside (the fields) to the inside (bins, cider press) back to the outside (sun goes down in blood). It can also be viewed as top to bottom: fields cut down, sun setting, standing for the closing of a season.
4. The sentences are very long and flowing, mainly compound and simple.
5. "M" and "O," suggesting richness and fullness, are the main letters.

Now do the same with this passage from Harper Lee's *To Kill a Mockingbird*:

> Maycomb was an old town, but it was a tired old town when I first knew it. In rainy weather the streets turned to red slop, grass grew on the sidewalks, the courthouse sagged in the square. Somehow, it was hotter then: a black dog suffered on a summer's day; bony mules hitched to Hoover carts licked flies in the sweltering shade of the live oaks on the square. Men's stiff collars wilted by nine in the morning. Ladies bathed before noon, after their three o'clock naps, and by nightfall were like soft teacakes with the frosting of sweat and sweet talcum.
>
> People moved slowly then. They ambled across the square, shuffled in and out of the stores around it, and took their time about everything. The day was twenty-four hours long but seemed longer.

Questions

1. What is the main impression here?
2. What details add to this impression?
3. What sound is used over and over?
4. Describe the sentences.

Answers

1. The main impression is heat and slowness.
2. The details include words such as "sagged," "wilted," and "ambled."
3. "S" is used to suggest heat and slowness.
4. The sentences are long, again suggesting exhaustion, and include all three types: simple, compound, and complex.

WORD CHOICE

Another important element of writing style is word choice. Saying exactly what you mean in a way that is fresh, clear, and correct can make your writing both interesting and effective. Following are some examples of poor word choice that can result in low scores on the AP exam:

Clichés

Clichés are phrases that have become stale and overused. They are to be avoided in your writing because they show a lack of imagination and an inability to convey exactly what you mean.

Clichés include such commonplace phrases as:

sweet as sugar	slow but sure	raining cats and dogs
tried and true	sick and tired	hard as nails

Wordiness

A tendency to ramble on or to bury your point in excess verbiage may cause readers to lose patience with your essay and to award you an unacceptably low score for your work. Get to your point quickly, with a lot of relevant detail but no unnecessary words.

Practice Eliminating Wordiness

Eliminate unnecessary words by striking out every unessential word in the sentences that follow:

Exercise

1. We watched the big, massive, black cloud rising up from the level prairie and covering over the sun.
2. Far away in the distance, as far as anything was visible to the eye, the small, diminutive shapes of the settlers' huts were outlined in silhouette against the dark sky.
3. Modern cars of today, unlike old cars of yesteryear, can be driven faster without danger than old ones.
4. When what the speaker was saying was not audible to our ears, I asked him to repeat again what he had said.
5. It was in this mountain vastness that the explorers found there the examples of the wildlife for which they had sought for.

Possible Answers

1. Eliminate: big, up, level, over
2. Eliminate: Far away, as far as anything was visible to the eye, small, in silhouette
3. Eliminate: of today, of yesteryear, than old ones
4. Eliminate: what, was saying, to our ears, again
5. Eliminate: It was, that, there the examples of, for which, had, for

Ambiguity

Ambiguity occurs when the reader is unsure of the meaning of your sentences. There are several different ways it can occur:

1. *Misplaced Modifiers.* When a phrase, clause, or word is placed too far from the word that it describes, the sentence fails to convey the exact meaning and may produce confusion or amusement.

Examples:

Misplaced phrase: Francis caught sight of the bus passing through the kitchen door.

Obviously the bus did not pass through the kitchen door. The phrase "through the kitchen door" modifies "caught sight of" and should be placed nearer to it, rather than next to "passing." The sentence should read: "Through the kitchen door, Francis caught sight of the bus passing."

Misplaced clause: They bought a cat for my brother that they call Spot.
The clause "that they call Spot" describes "cat," not "brother." The sentence should read: "They bought a cat that they call Spot for my brother."

Misplaced word: To get to the pool we nearly traveled three miles.
The word "nearly" describes "three." The sentence should read: "To get to the pool we traveled nearly three miles."

Practice Eliminating Misplaced Modifiers

Correct misplaced modifiers by revising the sentences that follow. Some of the sentences may be correct as given.

Exercise

1. We came upon a hospital rounding the corner.
2. The shrub was given to us by a relative that was supposed to flower in the spring.
3. The qualified doctor can only prescribe medicine.
4. Occurring in May, we were astonished by the event.
5. Reserve a room for the lady with a bath.

Possible Answers

1. Rounding the corner, we came upon a hospital.
2. The shrub that was supposed to flower in the spring was given to us by a relative.
3. Only a qualified doctor can prescribe medicine.
4. The event that occurred in May astonished us.
5. Reserve a room with a bath for the lady.

2. *Dangling Constructions.* When the noun or pronoun to which a phrase or clause refers is missing or in the wrong place, you have an unattached, or dangling, phrase or clause. (A *phrase* is two or more words having neither a subject nor a predicate. A *clause* is a group of words having both a subject and a predicate.) An example of a dangling construction that could result in ambiguity follows:

While driving along the highway, a fatal head-on collision was seen.

This is incorrect because it lacks a noun or pronoun—*who* saw the collision? The correct version would read: "While driving along the highway, *we* saw a fatal head-on collision."

Practice Eliminating Dangling Constructions

Correct dangling constructions by choosing the correct word or group of words for each of the sentences that follow on page 49.

Exercise

1. All the next week, (driving, while driving, as I drove) back and forth to school, the scene remained clear in my mind.
2. Though (we were troubled, troubled) by many worries, the results were better than we could have hoped.
3. The tomb of the Egyptian pharaoh commanded attention (as we came, coming) into the hall.
4. (Rushing, As she rushed) down the hall, her hat fell off.
5. (After failing, Since they had failed) the test, the teacher advised them to study more.

Answers

1. as I drove 2. we were troubled 3. as we came 4. As she rushed 5. Since they had failed

3. *Faulty Pronoun Reference.* When you are not sure what a pronoun is referring to, you have an ambiguous sentence. For example:

> Because my children had so many toys, I gave *them* to the local charity. (What was given away? The children or the toys?)

> Mr. Smith operated a wheat farm, and his daughter hopes to become *one.* (She hopes to become a farm?)

Frequently Misused Words or Word Pairs

There are a great many English words that are often confused. Here are just a few examples of words whose meaning every AP student should know.

Advise, Advice. *Advise* is a verb (people advise students); *advice* is a noun. (The teacher gave us good advice.)

Altogether, All Together. *Altogether* means "completely," while *all together* means "all at one time," as in "We repeat the motto all together at each meeting."

Disinterested, Uninterested. *Disinterested* means "fair, without prejudice," as in "disinterested judge." *Uninterested* means "not concerned," as in "uninterested in sports."

Effect, Affect. *Effect* is most often used as a noun meaning "result" as in "The effect of the war was felt for years afterward." *Affect* is most often used as a verb meaning "to influence," as in "Alcohol affects the brain."

Have, Of. *Have* is a verb; *of* is a preposition. Never write something like "He might *of* helped him."

He/She. Avoid using this awkward construction. Whenever possible, reconstruct the sentence in the third person (they) or use either "he" or "she" consistently.

Healthy, Healthful. *Healthy* means "possessing good health," as in "a healthy individual." *Healthful* means "to bring about good health," as in "healthful climate."

Its, It's. Its is the possessive form, meaning "belonging to it." *It's* is a contraction for *it is.*

Lead, Led. *Lead* is a noun, a metal (as in "The pipe was made of lead."). *Led* is the past tense of the verb "to lead."

Loose, Lose. *Loose* is an adjective that means "free, unattached," while *lose* is a verb meaning "to part with unintentionally."

Man. Today, neutral terms are preferred. Consider using *people, humans,* and *humanity* instead of terms such as "man" or "mankind."

Passed, Past. *Passed* is the past tense of "to pass," a verb that means "to go by." *Past* has three possible uses:

1) As an adjective meaning "having taken place at a prior time" as in "He was in charge at past meetings."
2) as a noun meaning "time gone by" as in "let the past go!"
3) as a preposition meaning "beyond" as in "We missed the turn and drove past the train station."

Stationary, Stationery. *Stationary* means "staying in one place," as in "The satellite appeared stationary." *Stationery* means "letter paper," as in "Hotels often provide stationery."

Than, Then. *Than* is a conjunction used in comparisons; *then* means "at that time."

That, Which, Whom. "That" refers to animals or people, "which" refers only to things, and "who/whom" refers only to people."

Their, They're, There.

Their means "belonging to them," and shows ownership.
They're is a contraction for "they are."
There means "in that place."

Unique. means "one of a kind." As such, it cannot be used with a modifier, as in "most unique." Instead, it is used alone, as in "That is a unique vase."

Who's, Whose. *Who's* is a contraction for "who is"; *whose* is a possessive, showing "belonging to whom."

Your, You're. *Your* means "belonging to you"; *you're* is a contraction for "you are."

1. passed   2. affect   3. past   4. advice   5. than, who's, than.

Practice Using Word Pairs

Choose the correct word by completing each of the sentences that follow.

Exercise

1. Did you see that bus as it (passed, past) the intersection?
2. How will the new tax (affect, effect) your home?
3. My American history teacher had a lot of time to make up for (past, passed) errors.
4. On his doctor's (advice, advise), he returned to work.
5. He is taller (then, than) his sister, (who's, whose) younger (than, then) he is.

Answers

1. passed   2. affect   3. past   4. advice   5. than, who's, than.

Verbs Often Confused

Just as there are pairs of words that get confused and result in loss of credit on your AP essays, so there are verbs that are frequently misused. Study the following groups of verbs and make sure you know how to use them correctly.

Accept, Except *Accept* is a verb meaning "to receive"; *except* is a conjunction or a preposition that means "other than" (everyone except me; excepted from a rule).

Affect, Effect *Affect* means "to influence"; *effect*, "to bring about."

Aggravate, Annoy *Aggravate* is a verb that means "to make worse." It is only used to refer to conditions, as in "Loud music aggravates a headache." *Annoy* is a verb meaning "to irritate," as in "Don't annoy me."

Borrow, Lend *Borrow* means "to take with the intention of returning"; *lend*, "to give with the intention of getting back."

Bring, Take *Bring* means, "to carry toward the speaker"; *take*, "to carry away from the speaker."

To Lie means to "recline"
present: The cat lies (is lying).
future: The cat will lie.
past: The cat lay.
perfect: The cat has lain, will have lain.

To Lay means to "put" or "put down."
present: The player lays (is laying) his dice down.
future: The player will lay his dice down.
past: The player laid his dice down.
perfect: The player has laid, had laid, will have laid his dice down.

Precede, Proceed. *Precede* means "to go before in rank and time"; *proceed*, "to move forward, advance."

Practice Using Verbs Often Confused

Choose the correct word by completing each of the sentences that follow.

Exercise

1. I had (lain, laid) awake all night, worried about the exam.
2. (Bring, Take) this paper to the nurse.
3. Where did you (lie, lay) the book I was reading?
4. If anyone wants that book, tell him it (lays, lies) on the table.
5. At first people were not allowed to leave the ship, women and children (accepted, excepted).

Answers

1. lain   2. take   3. lay   4. lies   5. excepted

Incorrect Expressions

The following chart summarizes the most commonly misused expressions.

Incorrect	Correct
1. Try *and* do better	Try *to* do better
2. The reason is *because*	The reason *is that*
3. *Being that*	*Since*
4. *This here* place	*This* place

Incorrect	Correct
5. Give me *them* books	Give me *those* books
6. *That there* dog	*That* dog
7. Different *than*	Different *from*
8. He (she, it) *don't*	He (she, it) *doesn't*
9. *Due to* sickness	*Because* of sickness
10. Five *foot* tall	Five *feet* tall
11. He (She) swims *good*	He (She) swims *well*
12. They *had ought* to	They *ought* to
13. My *mother, she says*	My *mother says*
14. *This here* rabbit	*This* rabbit
15. *In "Poe"* it tells about	*"Poe"* tells about
16. *Irregardless*	*Regardless*
17. Kind of *a*	*Kind of*
18. *Like* he told you	*As* he told you
19. *Me and my friend* went	*My friend and I* went
20. *Most* always	*Almost* always
21. *Off of*	*Off*
22. A *real* good dinner	A *really* good dinner

Agreement

The elements of a sentence must "match." This refers especially to subjects and verbs, or pronouns and antecedents (the word to which a pronoun refers). Here are a few rules to keep in mind:

1. A singular verb requires a singular subject. A plural verb requires a plural subject.
   EXAMPLE: Too many commas in a paragraph often (cause, causes) confusion.
   The correct answer is *cause,* for the plural subject requires a plural verb. Remember that a great many verbs in English that are singular end in *s.*

2. Subjects that are singular in meaning but plural in form (such as measles, news) require a singular verb.

3. Singular subjects connected by or, nor, either . . . or, neither . . . nor require a singular verb.
   EXAMPLE: Either the witness or the defendant (is, are) lying.
   The correct answer is *is,* for the subjects are connected by either . . . or.

4. A compound subject connected by *and* requires a plural verb.
   Exception to this rule: A compound subject that is considered as one unit is paired with a singular verb.
   EXAMPLE: The long and short of the matter (is, are) that we lost the race.
   The answer is *is* because "long and short" is considered as one unit.

5. If a subject is made up of two or more nouns or pronouns connected by *or* or *nor,* the verb agrees with the nearer noun or pronoun.
   EXAMPLE: Neither Mary nor my aunts (is, are) arriving for the winter.
   The answer is *are,* for *aunts* are plural.
   EXAMPLE: Either you or she (is, are) to blame.
   The answer is *is* to agree with the closer pronoun.

6. A pronoun agrees with its antecedent. The antecedent is the word to which the pronoun refers.

EXAMPLE: If anyone questions the safety of the journey, refer (him, them) to me. The answer is *him* to agree with the singular pronoun *anyone*.

Singular Pronouns		
anyone	everyone	someone
no one	one	each
either	neither	anybody
everybody	somebody	every (person, etc.)
many a (person, etc.)		

Practice Agreement

Choose the correct word by completing each of the following sentences.

Exercise

1. There, hiding in the tall reeds, (was, were) six bandits.
2. There (was, were) a dog and a mouse in the chair.
3. The books they read (shows, show) they are advanced students.
4. Each of the women (observes, observe) all the rules.
5. Everybody (was, were) asked to remain standing.

Answers

1. *were* to agree with the plural subjects *bandits*
2. *were* to agree with the compound subject connected by *and*
3. *show* to agree with the plural subject books
4. *observes* to agree with the singular pronoun *each*
5. *was* to agree with the singular pronoun *everybody*

Case

Pronouns can be confusing because they have different forms for different uses. The following chart reviews pronoun usage:

Pronouns as Subjects (Nominative Case)	Pronouns as Objects (Objective Case)	Possessive (Possessive Case)
I	me	my, mine
you	you	your, yours
he	him	his
she	her	her, hers
it	it	its
we	us	our, ours
they	them	their, theirs
who	whom	whose
whoever	whomever	whoever

Let's review the rules for correct pronoun usage:

1. A pronoun used as a subject is in the subject (nominative) case.
   EXAMPLES: (Who, Whom) do you believe is the most nervous?
   (*Who* is the subject of the verb *is*.)
   I believe no one is as nervous as (she, her).
   (*She* is the subject of the understood verb *is* (as *she is*).
   Exception: A pronoun used as the subject of an infinitve takes the objective case.
   EXAMPLE: My teacher expects John and (I, me) to pass.
   (*Me*, together with *John*, is the subject of the infinitive phrase *to pass*. The entire phrase *John and me to pass* is the object of *expects*.)
2. A pronoun used as a predicate nominative takes the subject (nominative) case. A noun or pronoun after any form of *to be* (is was, might have been, etc.) is called a predicate nominative.
   EXAMPLE: It was (we, us) students who studied the hardest. (Use *we* as the predicate nominative after the verb *was*.)
3. A pronoun used as the direct object of a verb, object of an infinitive, object of a preposition, or indirect object takes the objective case.
   EXAMPLES: (Who, Whom) will you send to study with us?
   (*Whom* is the direct obejct of the verb *will send*.) Between you and (I, me), there have never been any real problems.
   (*Me* is the object of the preposition *between*.)
4. A pronoun used in apposition with a noun is in the same case as that noun.
   EXAMPLES: Two students, Henry and (he, him), wrote exceptionally well.
   (The pronoun must be in the subject (nominative) case—*he*—because it is in apposition with the noun *students*, which is in the subject case.)
5. A pronoun that expresses ownership is in the possessive case. Remember that nouns that express ownership (mine, yours, his, hers, its, ours, theirs, etc.) never require an apostrophe. Don't confuse possessive pronouns with contractions.

Possessive Pronoun	Contraction
its	it's (it is)
your	you're (you are)
their	they're (they are)
whose	who's (who is)

NOTE: The word "its' " is not a correct form of either "its" or "it's." It has no meaning at all in English and, therefore, has no use.
EXAMPLE: He became an expert on the theater and (its, it's) greatest starts.
(*Its* is the correct spelling of the possessive case, which is needed here to express ownership. The word *it's* is a contraction, meaning "it is.")

Practice Case

Exercise

Write the correct choice in each sentence and state the reason for your answer.

1. He bought the cake for Debbie and (she, her).
2. Bill and (I, me) have been elected to the General Organization.
3. The heroes are (they, them).
4. (We, Us) girls want to study together.
5. Call for Elizabeth and (I, me) later today.
6. The principal is (she, her).
7. The leaders are Bob and (he, him).
8. My mother and (I, me) changed the tire.
9. He asked all of (us, we) boys for our opinion.
10. May I use (your's, yours)?

Answers

1. *her*, object of the preposition "for"
2. *I*, subject of the sentence
3. *they*, predicate nominative (note "are," a form of "to be")
4. *We*, subject of the sentence
5. *me*, object of the preposition "for"
6. *she*, predicate nominative ("is" as a form of "to be")
7. *he*, predicate nominative ("are" as a form of "to be")
8. *I*, subject of the sentence
9. *us*, object of the preposition
10. *yours*, correct possessive form

Parallel Structure

Parallel structure means that ideas of the same rank or significance are in the same grammatical form. A look at the following examples will illustrate this important element of writing style.

EXAMPLE: Mailing a letter a few days too early is better than (to run, running) the risk of its arriving late.
The verbal noun *running* is required to match or parallel the verbal noun *mailing*.

EXAMPLE: You should always eat foods that are nourishing and (tasty, taste good).
The predicate adjective *tasty* parallels the predicate adjective *nourishing*.

EXAMPLE: To do the job required is more difficult than (to plan, planning) heroic actions.
The infinitive *to plan* parallels the infinitive *to do*.

Practice Parallel Structure

Exercise

Complete each of the following sentences.

1. I expected her to be angry and (that she would scold, to scold) him.
2. The modern train has the advantages of strength and (being speedy, speed, moving quickly).
3. To complete a task at once is better than (to fret, fretting) about it.
4. He enjoys dancing, skating, and (to go swimming, going swimming, swimming).
5. He appeared tired and (a disappointed man, disappointed).

Answers

1. to scold
2. speed
3. to fret
4. swimming
5. disappointed

PUNCTUATION

Another essential ingredient of writing style is punctuation. The ability to use different forms of punctuations to express your ideas will give variety, coherence, and strength to your writing. Punctuation also provides a key to the logic of your argument; for example, when a reader sees a colon in your work, he/she knows that you intend to present a series of items or to explain more fully an idea that you have just stated. In the same way, readers know that sentences connected with a semicolon are closely related to each other.

It is assumed that every AP student knows how to use periods and question marks correctly. Here then are some of the less familiar rules of punctuation.

Use Commas . . .

1. To set off words of direct address (words that tell to whom a comment is addressed).
   EXAMPLE: Mr. Smith, that is the reason I was not in class.

2. To set off words in apposition (words that give additional information).
   EXAMPLE: A heavy sleeper, my mother is always the last to awake.

3. To set off a direct quotation.
   EXAMPLE: "Tomorrow I begin my new job," he said.

4. To set off a parenthetic (interrupting) expression.
   EXAMPLE: These prices, Lord help us, are the highest in town.

5. After interrupting words at the beginning of a sentence.
   EXAMPLE: Oh, I am glad to hear that.
   Interjections to be set off by a comma include: Yes, no, well, etc.

6. Before a conjunction (and, but, or, for) in a compound sentence, unless the compound sentence is very brief.
   EXAMPLE: Bill is not in the office today, but he will be here tomorrow.

7. After each item in a series, except, of course, the last.
   EXAMPLE: For dinner we had porkchops, applesauce, peas, and carrots.

8. To set of contrasting expressions.
   EXAMPLE: The boys, not the men, did most of the chores around the farm.

9. After an introductory prepositional phrase.
   EXAMPLE: Along the route from the bus terminal to the hotel, the major was treated to a brass band.

10. After an introductory subordinate clause.
    EXAMPLE: When I received an A in English, my parents were very surprised.

11. After an introductory participial phrase.
    EXAMPLE: Frightened by our approach, the badger fled.

12. To set off nonessential participial phrases.
    EXAMPLE: The child, weakened by loss of fluids, fell asleep.

13. After the opening of an informal letter.
    EXAMPLE: Dear Sue,

14. After the close of any letter.
    EXAMPLE: Sincerely,

NOTE: With closing quotation marks, the comma is always inside.

Use A Semicolon. . .

1. To divide items in a series when the items contain commas.
   EXAMPLE: The following directors were named: Charles Lawrence, president; Robert Aristedes, vice-president; Jennifer Fink, secretary.

2. Between main clauses that contain commas.
   EXAMPLE: Charles Smith, the hero, dotes on Mary Capone; and he eventually gives up his throne to save Harry Capone, Mary's husband.

3. Between main clauses when the conjunction (and, but, or for) has been left out.
   EXAMPLE: We have made several attempts to reach you by telephone; not a single call has been returned.

4. Between main clauses connected by however, moreover, nevertheless, for example, consequently etc.
   EXAMPLE: It was really a lovely car; consequently, she felt no urge to return it.

NOTE: With closing quotation marks, the semicolon is outside.

Use A Colon. . .

1. After the word "following" and any other word that indicates a list or series.
   EXAMPLE: We had the following for lunch: fruit, cheese, broiled chicken, mashed potatoes, green beans, salad, and dessert.

2. Before a quotation of greater than five lines.

3. Before part of a sentence that explains or gives an example of what has just been stated.
   EXAMPLE: We have a firm rule: We will not be undersold.

4. After the opening of a business letter.
   EXAMPLE: Dear Mr. Fuller:

NOTE: With closing quotation marks the colon is outside.

Use A Dash. . .

1. To show a sudden change in thought.
   EXAMPLE: We have a republican student council—of course, we are not allowed to set all the rules—that allows us a voice in governing the school.
   Avoid excessive use of the dash in a formal paper, as it makes for a breathless and casual tone.

2. Before a summary of what has just been stated.
   EXAMPLE: Staying on the football team, maintaining high grades, keeping my part-time job—everything depends on the use of the family car.

Use Parentheses. . .

1. To enclose additional information.
   EXAMPLE: The decline in profits in the past three years has been marked (see chart on page 49).

2. To enclose numbers or letters.
   EXAMPLE: A book owned by a public library is usually catalogued by (1) a title card, (2) an author card, (3) a subject card.

Use Brackets. . .

1. To enclose information that interrupts a direct quotation.
   EXAMPLE: She said, "I tutored Sam with his math [in fact, she saved him from failing] when he had Mr. Smith as a teacher."

Use Quotation Marks. . .

1. To set off titles of short works (essays, short stories, etc.).
2. To set off definitions.
3. To set off direct quotations.

Use Apostrophes. . .

1. To indicate ownership.
   To form the possessive of singular nouns and indefinite pronouns, add *'s*. Use only an apostrophe, without an *s*, when the noun already ends in *s*.
   EXAMPLES: "The Mon*k's* Tale" is one of Chauce*r's Canterbury Tales.*
   When he would arrive at Mar*y's* home was anyon*e's* guess.
   For goodnes*s'* sake, the bos*s'* son got fired!

   To form the possessive of a plural noun (those ending in *s* or *es*) add only the apostrophe.
   EXAMPLES: Two week*s'* sick leave and three month*s'* medical allowance are available to those who were laid off.
   The Lopeze*s'* children are always ready to add their two cent*s'* worth.

   Use an apostrophe with only the last noun in a compound word or to show joint possession.
   EXAMPLES: My brother-in-la*w's* book was left in Debbie and Barr*y's* apartment.
   The editor-in-chie*f's* responsibility ended on Tuesday.

2. Use an apostrophe to show that letters have been omitted in contractions or to show that numbers have been left out of dates.
   EXAMPLES: I should*n't* have, but it could*n't* have been avoided.
   The *'85* champions were better than the *'86* winners.

3. Use an apostrophe and add an *s* to form the plural of numbers, letters, or words used as words.
   EXAMPLES: When you write, make sure your *1's* and *7's* can be easily read.
   Too many *very's* can decrease the effectiveness of your speech.

Practice Punctuation

Exercise 1: Insert all necessary punctuation in each of the following sentences.

1. All the people who have not presented proper identification will be excluded from the train.
2. Yes I have been there
3. How often do you consider Mr Smith said how exciting it is to visit foreign lands
4. Huntington High is the only school that beat us last year but we fully expect to beat them in a rematch
5. At the start of the walk through the city everyone was in a good mood
6. For these reasons my fellow citizens I need your vote
7. The first moon walk was July 20 1972
8. Paul Parker the head of the debating team is in my science class
9. The results I am not at all pleased to say took us by surprise
10. Don't you agree that parents not small children should be held responsible

Exercise 2: Change each word and phrase in parentheses to its possessive form.

1. The (college library) holdings are extensive.
2. My (sister-in-law) car is new and shiny.
3. (Lerner and Loewe) play *My Fair Lady* was based on (George Bernard Shaw) play *Pygmalion*.
4. (Harold Robbins) and (Stephen King) novels are best sellers.

Answers—Exercise 1

1. No punctuation need be added.
2. Yes, I have been there.
3. "How often do you consider," Mr. Smith said, "how exciting it is to visit foreign lands?"
4. Huntington High is the only school that beat us last year, but we fully expect to beat them in a rematch.
5. At the start of the walk through the city, everyone was in a good mood.
6. For these reasons, my fellow citizens, I need your vote.
7. The first moon walk was July 20, 1972.
8. Paul Parker, the head of the debating team, is in my science class.
9. The results, I am not at all pleased to say, took us by surprise.
10. Don't you agree that parents, not small children, should be held responsible?

Answers—Exercise 2

1. college library's
2. sister-in-law's
3. Lerner and Loewe's, George Bernard Shaw's
4. Harold Robbins', Stephen King's

CAPITALIZATION

In the same way that careless mistakes with punctuation can lose you points—as well as confuse the points you are trying to make—so errors in capitalization can mar an otherwise fine essay. Review the rules that follow to make sure that your essays are as correct as possible.

1. Capitalize the opening word of a sentence and of a direct quotation. Do not capitalize the second half of a divided quotation, unless it begins a new sentence.
   EXAMPLE: "*If* you go three blocks south," the man explained, "*you* will see the library."

2. Capitalize the first word of a line of poetry, unless the poet did not do so.

3. Capitalize the salutation of a letter, as well as the noun or title in the salutation.
   EXAMPLE: Dear Pat, Dear Uncle Sam,

4. Capitalize only the opening word of the complimentary close of a letter.
   EXAMPLE: Very truly yours,

5. Capitalize the first word of each item in an outline.
   EXAMPLE: I. Driver training
   　　　　　　A. In the classroom
   　　　　　　B. Behind the wheel

6. Capitalize proper nouns and proper adjectives.
   EXAMPLES: Shakespeare, Shakespearean play
   Do not capitalize the second part of hyphenated numbers.
   EXAMPLE: Forty-second Street
   Do not capitalize north, south, east, west when used to indicate direction.
   Do not capitalize seasons.

7. Capitalize names of historical events, eras, documents, organizations, institutions, names of languages, nationalities, races, religions, references to the Supreme Being.

8. Capitalize titles before a person's name.
   EXAMPLE: Captain Smith
   Do not capitalize titles used alone, except for very high government officials.

9. Capitalize titles of parents and relatives not preceded by a possessive word (your, mine, etc.).
   EXAMPLE: I saw Father with Uncle Harry.
   Exception: If a name follows a title, capitalize the title, even when preceded by a possessive word.
   EXAMPLE: My Uncle George plays racketball.

10. Capitalize titles of books, plays, etc. but do not capitalize articles (a, an, the), conjunctions, or short prepositions in titles.
    EXAMPLE: *The Old Man and the Sea*

11. Capitalize titles of newspapers and magazines, but do not capitalize the word *the* before the title unless it begins the sentence.
    EXAMPLE: the *New York Times*.

12. Capitalize titles of courses.
    EXAMPLE: Psychology 101, Mathematics 212
    Do not capitalize school subjects, except languages.
    EXAMPLE: I am taking psychology, mathematics, history, and English.

13. Capitalize brand names, but not the product.

14. Capitalize the words *I* and *O*, but not *oh*, unless it begins the sentence.

15. Capitalize personifications.
    EXAMPLE: O Liberty! O Liberty!

Practice Capitalization

Exercise

Correct the capitalization in each of the following sentences.

1. go one mile South then turn East and you will come to the Empire state building.
2. He said that spring came late this year, but we were all looking forward to Summer, for we were to visit the pacific ocean and yellowstone national park.
3. "If you go to New england," the man said, "Be sure to visit the Doctor and my uncle George."

Answers

1. Go one mile south then turn east and you will come to the Empire State Building. (Capitalize the first word of a sentence; do not capitalize "south" and "east" when used to give directions; capitalize proper names such as the "Empire State Building.")
2. He said that spring came late this year, but we were all looking forward to summer, for we were to visit the Pacific Ocean and Yellowstone National Park. (Do not capitalize the seasons; capitalize proper names.)
3. "If you go to New England," the man said, "be sure to visit the doctor and my Uncle Sam." (Capitalize the names of geographic locations; do not capitalize the continuation of a quote; do not capitalize common nouns such as "doctor"; capitalize a title if it follows a name, even if it is preceded by a possessive word.)

Revising and Editing Your Essay

Revising involves revamping thesis statements and supporting details to more closely answer the question. It also includes adding additional examples and reworking existing material. *Editing* entails eliminating redundancy and correcting grammar, usage, spelling, and punctuation.

Ideally, you would have ample time to completely redraft your essay. But, this is rarely possible on the AP test. Most often, your first draft stands as your final draft, with perhaps some minor attention paid to surface errors. Even if you do have time to revise and edit, you might be unwilling to mark up your carefully written paper. You might decide to let a few errors slide by rather than turn in a sloppy-looking final copy.

It's *always* best to correct any errors and do whatever editing and revising you can. Consider writing on every other line and printing, especially if your handwriting is difficult to read. Make your correction marks clear and simple—avoid big X's. Cross out words with a single line and write the correction neatly. If you need to move blocks of copy, make sure your reader understands what you intend. Use the following proofreader's symbols to clarify your corrections:

delete (remove)

new paragraph

no new paragraph

insert a letter, word, sentence

insert a space

transpose a letter, word, sentence

close up

rewrite as a capital letter *cap*

rewrite as a lower case letter *lc*

Pace yourself carefully to ensure you will have time to correct the most damaging errors in composition and style. The following chart can help you plan your time most effectively:

Allocate Your Time	
If you have 20 minutes for your essay	revise for 3–5 minutes
If you have 25 minutes for your essay	revise for 5 minutes
If you have 30 minutes for your essay	revise for 5 minutes
If you have 40 minutes for your essay	revise for 5–7 minutes
If you have 45 minutes for your essay	revise for 7 minutes
If you have 60 minutes for your essay	revise for 7–10 minutes

Writing an Essay on Prose

The AP essay question takes many different forms. Following are descriptions of the kinds of essay questions you are likely to encounter on your exam.

SAMPLE QUESTIONS

1. Two works will be presented, perhaps two essays, two speeches, or two poems. You will be asked to read both selections and write an essay in which you explain what qualities in the first work make it superior to the second work. You will be expected to be conversant with the conventions of that genre. Thus, if the works are prose, you will be expected to discuss descriptive language, tone, and theme. If the selections are poems, you will discuss figurative language, tone, mood, irony, and various poetic devices. In either case, you will be expected to isolate *specific examples* from each work to construct your comparison/contrast essay.

2. Again, two selections of the same genre will be presented. You will be expected to isolate the *themes* of each and compare them. This may take the form of a question that reads: "Write an essay based on the works above in which you discuss how the author's conception (or description or portrait or portrayal, etc.) of the theme differs from one work to the other." You will be expected to select specific details from the works to support your conclusion. The themes may be the same or they may be radically different, or there may be subtle shades of difference in how each author's *tone* or mood colors the definition of the subject under discussion.

3. You will be asked to select a character from a work of recognized literary value and discuss one aspect of this character or the character in relation to the theme of the work under discussion. There may be a list of authors or works below the question, but you are usually free to select from any work of comparable excellence. Because you must choose a work that you are sure is valued by the literary community, you should stick to works that you have treated in class. You may be asked why the character is good and worthy of your admiration, or why the character is a villain and deserves the treatment he is accorded. In all cases, you will be expected to place the character in the novel and discuss his actions in relation to other characters in the work in order to prove your point. Thus, if you were trying to show that the King from Mark Twain's *The Adventures of Huckleberry Finn* was a villain, you would discuss how he sold Jim for "forty dirty dollars" into slavery, just when it appeared that Jim would be able to rejoin his family. You could also discuss his various "scams"—The Royal Nonesuch, the temperance revivals, the swindle of the Wilkes sisters.

4. You will be asked to read a prose selection and discuss how the author's *style* reveals the *theme* of the work. You will be expected to consider various elements of style such as tone, diction, figurative language, sentence length and variety, detail, and so forth. This means that you will have to take the passage "apart" and look at each section very carefully, then put it back together and reconsider the meaning.

5. There is occasionally an essay that is not based on literature. In this case, you may be asked to respond to a brief passage and show how you agree or disagree. You

may be presented with a definition of a certain item, place, or feeling and be asked to write your own version of a definition. If they give you a passage on "love," for instance, you will be expected to write your own definition of love, drawing from your own experience *specific examples* to support your claims. You may, of course, use literary examples if they fit and serve to back up your thesis.

6. The final portion of a play, a novel, an essay, or a narrative poem may be considered either very important or simply as a gathering up of the loose ends of the plot. You will be asked to evaluate the final portion of a work, discussing its importance to the rest of the work. Obviously, you will have to demonstrate a clear knowledge of the rest of the work and prove how the ending relates to the body as a whole. This will again call for specific examples, names, dates, and places to back up your thesis.

STUDENT RESPONSES WITH EVALUATIONS

Analyze the following examples of student essays and explain why each one does or does not fulfill the AP requirements. Use the questions below as guidelines for your evaluations.

1. Does the essay answer the question?
2. Are the examples specific and well-selected?
3. Is the writing clear? Does it reflect all the elements of writing style: grammar and usage, spelling and punctuation, parallel structure and placement of modifiers, word choice and sentence variety?
4. What specifically can be done to improve this essay? For example, rewrite sentences that are dull or incorrect, rearrange portions of the essay, and add specific examples where needed.

Questions for Essays A–E:

"Failure in human relationships results when one avoids the normal responsibilities of one's position in life." Show how this is true for any one character from any work of recognized literary value that you have read. Time—30 minutes.

Essay A

FAILURE IN HUMAN RELATIONSHIPS

People fail in their relationships when they avoid the responsibilities of their particular position in life. In *The Glass Menagerie,* Tom Wingfield, a young man frustrated by life and its difficulties, gives us a perfect example of this unfortunate situation.

Tom's expected responsibility is to support his mother and sister because his father deserted the family. In the thirties, when this story takes place, women had little chance of finding work outside the home. Amanda, the mother, had tried to obtain work selling magazine subscriptions over the telephone, and the little that she was able to make went to send her handicapped daughter to secretarial school. Tom had a job in a warehouse and did the best he could to sustain the family. The problem began when Amanda began to criticize everything Tom did, including his eating habits, his smoking, and his movie-going. Her constant carping created a great deal of friction between them, as he began to resent her and their relationship deteriorated. Amanda told Tom that he was responsible for the family until his sister Laura was married, but Tom wanted no part in finding his sister a suitable husband. He avoided fulfilling his responsibilities by deserting the family and joining the Merchant Marines.

While it is obvious that Amanda's nature did not help her relationship with her son, if Tom would have attempted to resolve their difficulties, perhaps things could have turned out differently. However, as a result of not providing for the family and fulfilling his expected responsibilities, Tom's relationship with his mother failed.

Analysis of Essay A

Introduction. The use of a title is good, for it helps the writer as well as the reader to focus on the topic. Note that the title is correct as written, since it is not underlined or set in quotes. Note also that the title is not ornate or overly clever; something that zeroes in on the topic is all that is necessary. Do not waste time fashioning a clever title. You are better off devoting that time to the essay itself.

The first sentence is well-written, a clear restatement of the thesis. While it could be made more interesting through the use of a quote or a brief anecdote from the work, it nonetheless gets to the point and alerts the reader to the topic.

The second sentence can be improved: The author's name is missing, and the description of Tom is too general. Be specific in describing the topic of your AP essay. In this instance, the writer should have mentioned Tom's desire for freedom versus the necessity of supporting his mother and sister.

The topic paragraph needs *at least* one more sentence to flesh it out. As a rule of thumb, the topic paragraph (or any paragraph, for that matter) needs at least three sentences to be complete. These include a topic sentence, a body sentence, and a clincher sentence, for a paragraph is an essay in miniature. Naturally, a body paragraph needs more than three sentences in order to provide specific examples of the points you wish to make. One possible solution for this topic paragraph is to move up the first sentence of paragraph 2 ("Tom's expected responsibility. . .") and write a new topic sentence for paragraph 2.

Body. If the first sentence is going to remain in the paragraph, it has to be more closely related to the sentence that follows. As it stands the style is choppy and weak.

The third sentence of paragraph 2 has a lot of good specific detail, but it could be improved by adding the name of the daughter, Laura, to parallel the inclusion of the name of the mother, Amanda.

Sentence 4 ("Tom had a job in a warehouse. . .") can be improved. Where did he work? How much did he make? Did he really do his best to support the family? A great deal more detail can be added here.

Sentence 5 ("The problem began. . .") is not totally correct. Actually, the problem began much earlier, when Tom's desire to be a poet was thwarted by the family's need. There is no doubt that Amanda's constant carping created a rift between them, but Tom already bitterly resented the lot he had been appointed in life. To suggest otherwise is to miss the nuances in the play.

The remainder of paragraph 2 is too vague and partially incorrect. It is not true that "Tom wanted no part in finding his sister a suitable husband," for Tom did indeed bring home his friend, Jim (ironically a young man Laura had long admired), as a possible suitor. Again, the writer overlooks the play's nuances.

Conclusion. The first sentence of paragraph 3 must be rewritten, for its meaning is not proven in the essay. The writer offers no proof that either of the characters could have healed the breach. The last sentence is fine.

This paper would receive a grade in the range of C+ to B−, a 3 on the Advanced Placement grading scale. The basic outline is good, but the essay lacks specific details and includes some inaccurate statements.

Essay B

In *The Glass Menagerie,* by Tennessee Williams, Tom Wingfield fails in human relationships by avoiding his normal responsibilities. After his father left the family to pursue his own pleasures, Tom, the son, was left to support the family, his mother, Amanda, and his sister, Laura, who lived together in a run-down tenement house. But he found himself unable to take his mother's constant criticism, and desperate to salve what remained of his future, Tom deserted the family to seek his own life.

When Tom's father, a telephone man in love with long distances, deserted the family, Tom had to abrogate his dream of becoming a poet and secure a job that offered immediate financial remuneration. He accepted sixty-five dollars a month as a worker in the Continental Shoemaker's Warehouse, a job he loathed. His nights were his only times of "freedom," when he could escape to the movies and enter a world of wonderful dreams. There was also a stage show, and the magician Malvolio would escape from a nailed-shut coffin. Obviously, this is a symbol for Tom's condition, nailed into a coffin by the circumstances of his life. But after awhile Tom realized that he could not escape forever into the dream world of the movies. As he told his friend Jim, "It's our turn now to go to the South Sea Island. . .I'm tired of movies and I am about to move!" When Jim asks him where he is going to move, he replies, "I'm starting to boil inside. Whenever I pick up a shoe, I shudder a little thinking how short life is and what I am doing." Rather than paying the light bill that month, Tom joined the Merchant Seamen Union, clearly announcing his intention to follow in his father's path and desert the family.

Tom fails in human relationships—especially his relationship with his mother, Amanda—when he fails to fulfill his normal responsibility of supporting the family. He feels that the family is stifling his ambition to be a poet, and that he has done enough to support them. He leaves to find his own destiny.

Analysis of Essay B

Introduction. This introduction is more fully expanded than the one that we first looked at, as each character is mentioned and relationships are briefly explained. Pay close attention to the thesis as it is stated: Tom found himself unable to withstand his mother's constant criticism, and so he left the family. Also change "salve" to either "save" or "salvage."

Body. The first sentence begins quite well, with the line "a telephone man in love with long distances" a most specific detail drawn directly from the play. The rest of the sentence, though, can be greatly improved by the removal of the "abrogate" and "remuneration." Both are used simply to impress the reader, and simpler words would be more effective in their places. Always choose the words best suited to the tone and style of your essay. Readers are impressed by the way you *use* the words you select.

The rest of the paragraph provides a wealth of specific detail, from the size of Tom's salary, to the name of the factory, to the description of the stage show. This shows that the writer knows the play well and can draw on very specific details to prove the point.

Conclusion. Here is where we become aware of the problem with this paper. Recall that in the introduction the writer carefully made the point that Tom found himself unable to withstand his mother's constant criticism and so he left to seek his own way. In the conclusion the writer states that the family is stifling Tom's ambition to be a poet. The problem is that the writer fails to prove either of these points in the essay. We get specific descriptions of how Tom feels nailed down and shut in, but we do not get any proof of the thesis stated in the introduction.

Thus, though this essay is far richer in detail than Essay A, it is actually a weaker paper, for the thesis is not proven. Essay B would receive a grade lower than a C, or a 2.5 on the AP scale.

Essay C

When one avoids the normal responsibilities of one's position in life, failure in human relationships will surely develop. This is true of Macbeth in William Shakespeare's play, *Macbeth*. In the beginning of the play, Macbeth is a loyal warrior to his king, Duncan, but as the play progresses he shuns his responsibilities and thus fails in human relationships.

As King Duncan's kinsman, Macbeth is one of the most trusted generals. His reputation was also achieved by his many loyal and brave acts during battle. Macbeth, already in possession of the title Thane of Glamis, is given the leadership of the armies in the war against the traitorous Thane of Cawdor. He upholds his reputation by fighting bravely for the king, and is rewarded by the good King with the title of the defeated Thane of Cawdor. This shows how Duncan is a fair and decent King, rewarding his men justly and generously for their bravery, and how Macbeth fights with distinction in the beginning of the play, fulfilling his normal responsibilities as a loyal thane. But all this changes right after the battle, when Macbeth encounters three witches.

Macbeth and his friend Banquo come upon three weird sisters as they journey home from battle. The witches tell Macbeth that he shall have a glorious future as Thane of Cawdor (he does not yet know he is to receive the title) and eventually King. Intrigued, Macbeth continues on his journey home to learn that he has indeed been given the title of the disloyal thane. This sparks his ambition and he first begins thinking about killing the King to hasten any chance he may have to become King himself. He tells his wife what has happened and she adds to his ambition, planning the ways to kill Duncan. They accomplish the heinous deed that night, stabbing the good and generous King and planting the daggers on his guards. It is at this point that he has deviated from his normal responsibilities as a loyal servant to his King, for killing one's king is one of the very worst deeds anyone could ever execute. From this point on, the play describes the destruction of all of Macbeth's relationships.

Anyone he viewed as a threat to his shaky power base was killed. He murders Banquo, for the witches had prophesized that Banquo's heirs would become king. He had intended to kill both Banquo and his son, Fleance, but Fleance escaped the murderers during the fray. He also murders Macduff's family in act IV, scene 2, for the loyal Macduff, another of Duncan's original soldiers, organized the rebellion against the now power-crazed Macbeth. The scene where Macbeth's soldiers murder Macduff's family—all the little "chickens"—shows us again how far Macbeth has moved away from his responsibility, how fully he has failed in human relationships.

Macbeth's denial of his normal responsibilities as a loyal soldier to the good King Duncan result in the destruction of all human relationships. By the end of the play he has become a murderous tyrant, devoid of all humanness.

Analysis of Essay C

Introduction. The introduction divides the answer into two parts: Macbeth's loyalty to the good King Duncan in the beginning of the play, and his later denial of his proper role as kinsman and thane. Check to make sure paragraph 2 discusses the first point; paragraph 3, the second.

The writing is adequate, but can be made more interesting by varying sentences or trying to catch the reader's attention with a quote or a brief anecdote.

Body. As mentioned above, the first part of the body should, if it is going to follow the outline suggested by the introduction, discuss Macbeth's fulfillment of his normal responsibilities in the beginning of the play. This it does, and very well, with a lot of specific details. The author discusses Macbeth's behavior during battle, and how the good King rewards him. This is crucial, for it must be shown that Macbeth is slaying a *good* king and thus committing a heinous deed. The setting aside of normal responsibilities would make no sense if Macbeth were killing an evil person—witness Macduff's actions in the end of the play. The final part of this paragraph is especially good, as the writer specifically says "This shows how. . ." These are key words and phrases that will help you keep your writing in focus, as you are forced by phrases such as "This proves. . .," "This illustrates," "This is an example of. . .," to keep on the topic.

Paragraph 3 is supposed to show that Macbeth fails in the execution of his normal responsibilities as a loyal thane and subject of the good king. Despite some syntax errors ("Macbeth and his friend Banquo come upon three weird sisters as they journey home from battle." Who is doing the traveling? The sentence is unclear as it stands.), the writer does a very good job of showing that in killing the king, Macbeth has violated the duties of any subject, much less a sworn supporter. The sentence "It is at this point that he has deviated from his normal responsibilities as a loyal servant to his king. . ." is especially good, for it ties up the rest of the paragraph and makes the point. The final sentence explains that the rest of the essay will show how all of Macbeth's relationships are destroyed.

The author does indeed prove the rest of his point, as he shows how Macbeth's relationships with Banquo, Fleance, and Macduff were destroyed when Macbeth set aside his normal and expected human responsibilities. The reference to "chickens"—recalling Macduff's impassioned speech upon hearing of the murder of his family—is good, for it is a moving and effective specific detail. The final sentence restates the topic and makes the point clear.

Conclusion. This is inadequate, recalling our discussion of a minimum of three sentences per paragraph. By recalling some of the specific details covered in the essay thus far, the author could easily expand upon the somewhat skimpy concluding paragraph.

This is a good essay, well organized and supported with specific detail. It would be in the A range, a 5 on the AP scale.

Essay D

Achilles, a character in Homer's *Iliad,* avoids his responsibilities and thus fails in human relationships. Achilles' duty was to lead the Achaeans into battle against the Trojans, but he let his personal feelings interfere with his duty as a soldier.

Achilles withdraws from the battlefield in anger, furious with Commander-in-Chief of the Achaean army, the greedy Agamemnon, who has threatened to take his mistress, Briseis, away from him. Achilles is maddened by Agamemnon's insolence, and despite his reverence for honor, retires from the battlefield. To placate Achilles' wounded pride, Agamemnon offers an apology, but Achilles will not accept it. Achilles' wounded pride and deep frustration with Agamemnon lead him to avoid his responsibility to the Achaean Army and lead to his failure in human relationships. He has an obligation to his fellow Achaeans, who greatly respect him and would honor him if he would return to battle. But he refuses to honor his responsibilities as a leader of men, and remains apart from his fellows.

One consequence of his withdrawal is the death of his dearest friend, Patroclus. Watching the enemy advance, standing on the sidelines, Achilles asks Patroclus to fight in his place, but Patroclus was not a warrior—he is Achilles' squire. Although he is inexperienced as a warrior, he feels it is his duty to honor Achilles' request. He goes to war in Achilles' armor and in the heat of battle is slain by Hector, a Trojan hero. This shows a failure on Achilles' part, for he had set aside his duty and forced another to take his place.

After Patroclus is killed, there is even greater fighting and vast destruction. There is an especially fierce battle around Patroclus' corpse, for the Trojans have taken it and the Achaeans are determined to recover it themselves. The Achaeans want Achilles to join in the Trojan War to recover Patroclus' corpse, which they hope will in some way alleviate Achilles' guilt for causing the death of his best friend. Hector instructs his Trojan allies to enter the conflict over the body, and the Trojans force back the Achaeans. Hippothus, a respected Achaean warrior, is slain. The ground runs red with blood.

Death and destruction follow Achilles' refusal to honor his responsibility to serve in battle. When he does finally join the battle, much destruction has already ensued, and his closest friend has been killed.

Analysis of Essay D

This response is a 5, an A, because it clearly proves the thesis that Achilles avoids responsibility and thus fails in human relationships. There is a good deal of clear, specific detail, and the style is mature and graceful. Note the variety of sentences, from the simple "Death and destruction follow Achilles' refusal to honor his responsibility to serve in battle" (5th paragraph) to two compound sentences in the first paragraph. Note how artfully the complex sentences have been crafted, with a variety of punctuation and stylistic devices. The writer has been especially successful in compressing a great deal of information into each sentence while retaining clarity and stylistic variation. We see this in the beginning of the second paragraph, where Agamemnon is both identified and characterized as the writer makes her point. The sentences exhibit an elegant agility as well. The dash in the second sentence of the third paragraph, for example, effectively shows a dramatic change in thought. The images are vivid, such as the startlingly effective, "The ground runs red with blood" in the fourth paragraph. It is also impressive to see how thoroughly the writer has studied and understood the work, keeping the characters and their relationships clear.

Essay E

When one abandons his normal responsibilities, failure in human relationships develops. Such is the case with Jason in Euripides' tragedy, *Medea*. Jason abandons his role as husband and father in order to marry a princess and raise his social status. In so doing, his relationship with his wife, Medea, is destroyed. In the ensuing carnage, he also loses his family and all that he held dear.

Jason's relationship with Medea, indeed his entire life, is destroyed when he neglects his normal responsibilities. Jason leaves his wife to marry the daughter of the King of Corinth, an action that will enable him to become King. He tells his wife that this will also benefit her, for it will enable their children to become royal. Although he attempts to rationalize his act, Medea believes that it is nothing other than abandonment, and her revenge leads to Jason's new wife's death. His abandonment of his normal responsibilities is at the root of this failure in human relationships.

As Jason neglects his responsibilities as a husband, he also sets aside his duties as a father. One of the main reasons he leaves Medea is to father more children, showing us that he seems to feel that families are replaceable. He soon learns otherwise, when Medea murders their children to spite him. Jason has lost his princess, his new family, his children by Medea. Because he leaves his children and neglects his paternal duties to them, Jason destroys his paternal relationships.

Jason's neglect of his responsibilities is all the more disturbing when one considers Medea's initial sacrifices. Herself once a princess in Colchis, Medea killed her own father to protect Jason in battle. She gives up her family and royal status to marry him. For Jason then to desert her, knowing all that she has done for him, makes his setting aside of human responsibilities all the more despicable.

Jason is a clear example of one who abandons his normal responsibilities and suffers for it. His relationship with his wife and children is destroyed. Because he places a higher social position above his family, he loses the most important relationship in his life. Euripedes' *Medea* shows Jason's mistake and the tragic price he must pay.

Analysis of Essay E

Again, this essay would receive a grade in the 5, or A range because it thoroughly proves the statement that rejecting one's responsibilities leads to failure in human relationships. Here, the writer shows through pertinent detail that Jason abandons his role as a husband and father to further his social ambition. In so doing, he destroys all that he once held dear, shattering relationships. As with Essay D, the writer's choice of words and images prove his point and provide sentence variety. Note how the level of syntax and diction combine to create a mature, effective style. Also notice how thoroughly the point is made, usually repeated at the end of each paragraph for emphasis and closure.

Question for Essay F and G

"A sharp insight can change a person's life for better or worse." Using any one recognized work of literary merit, show how this is true. Time—30 minutes.

Essay F

ONCE UPON A NIGHTMARE

In certain novels, there are characters who experience a sharp insight into the world around them which can alter their lives for better or worse. In Erich Maria Remarque's *All Quiet on the Western Front,* Paul Baumer is hurled into harsh surroundings and experiences just such an insight. Paul is a 19-year-old boy who enlists in the German Army during World War I and is immediately aware of the devastation war engenders. Paul's experiences lead him to realize many important things that will alter his life.

Paul's first insight occurred after a few months of feeling cold, hungry, and afraid. He began to wonder what he would do with his life should peace be declared that very day. He understands the fact that the education he has received in high school was trivial; it has left him unprepared for life. By being subjected to the nightmares associated with war, Paul suddenly realizes that he is too mature to re-enter school, and too old to become apprenticed in any skill. He characterizes himself, and others like him, as a lost generation. We can see from Paul's sudden realization that he is in a precarious position. He has missed all the fun and excitement associated with a normal high school life. He feels alienated and worried because the war has destroyed all his aspirations. Associated with this first sudden realization are several other moments of related awareness.

Paul experiences another insight when he returned home for 17 days. While on leave, he becomes aware of the fact that he no longer feels comfortable in his own home. He has an awkward feeling about himself; he is aware that it is he, not the home, that has changed drastically. The hastened maturity that he has undergone has caused him to drift away from his former way of life, and he has unwillingly become isolated from all that he was because of these changes.

There is another instance when he realizes a sudden change. He is temporarily stationed at a prison camp where he takes a long look at the other prisoners, Russians. He realizes that these men are really human beings just like his countrymen, his friends, and due to the decisions of their leaders, these people so like him have become enemies. Paul realizes that they could just as easily have become friends if the leaders had so decreed. This insight shows how confused Paul is, for he does not understand why he is fighting a war. He can see no difference between himself and the Russian prisoners, and is baffled that a simple word of command could set up barriers between people.

Paul Baumer has several sharp realizations during his experiences in World War I, all related to the changes he undergoes and the horrors that he witnesses. He was forced to mature too soon in order to cope with the blood, death, and constant bombardment. He feels lost, alienated from all that he once loved—friends, family, home. He has suddenly realized that he is a member of a confused, frightened, and wandering society, living out an unthinkable nightmare.

Analysis of Essay F

Introduction. The topic sentence is fine, a restatement of the thesis, but the rest of the paragraph can use improvement. The second sentence needs to be combined with the third, so that Paul is clearly identified. Also, the sentences could be better stated; this is an ideal place to work in sentence variety.

The most important problem with the opening, however, is the fact that the thesis is not answered. Was Paul's life changed for better or worse? What is it that he realizes? What is the *one* clear insight that he has that alters his life? Without this clear statement of purpose, the rest of the paper skirts around the issue, ending up showing a handful of insights, but not answering the question.

Body. The first sentence here again underscores the problem of the introduction: The question does not call for a "first insight"; rather, it asks that the author focus on *a* sharp insight. The next part of the body evinces the same problem, as does the final paragraph. Each of the several realizations is well proven, but unless they are all tied together into one, the thesis remains unproven.

Conclusion. The final sentence of the essay is what we have been looking for all along— as all the "little" things that Paul realizes come together into one sharp moment of awareness. The problem is that this is too slender a thread to tie an entire essay together; this must be stated at the end of each paragraph to fit the response to the question.

The paper would be in the low B range, a 3.5 on the AP scale.

Essay G

Sometimes a character in a story experiences a sharp insight which changes his life. This is true in *All Quiet on the Western Front,* by Erich Maria Remarque. In this novel, a young German soldier named Paul Baumer recounts the barbaric chaos he suffered through in the desperate days of the First World War.

Paul is not at all prepared for the hardships and extreme hatred of the enemy which is necessary for a soldier to possess in order to kill. After a few weeks on the battlefield, Paul realizes that his life as a child has come to an end, and he suddenly wishes that he could return to the simple life he had previously experienced. He expresses this as he says, "I am little more than a child; in my wardrobe still hangs short, boy's trousers—it is such a little time ago, why is it over?" Paul realizes suddenly that war has robbed him of his childhood.

After intentionally killing someone for the first time, the complete desolation of his situation comes forth as he whispers to the dead soldier, "I will fight against this war which has struck us both down; from you, taken life— and from me—? Life also. There is no hope of ever getting out of this." This sharp insight causes Paul to lose sight of his dreams of fame and glory, and he no longer wants to be involved in fighting and death. But he is compelled to continue—"We are insensible, dead men who through some trick, some dreadful magic, are still able to run and kill." Paul felt his life no longer had worth, and it is this last dreadful sharp insight which causes his death on a day "so quiet and still on the Western Front."

Paul Baumer experienced the sharp insight that war has robbed him of any hope for a normal life. He learns fear, despair, hoplessness, and finally death.

Analysis of Essay G

Introduction. This paper has the same fault as the one before; the thesis is not clearly answered. What is it that Paul realizes? How does this change his life?

Body. The first sentence is awkward, and despite the quote from the book, the point remains inconclusive. We are not convinced on the basis of the single quote that Paul has indeed been robbed of his childhood. More must be shown to clearly prove the thesis.

Again, it is a very good idea to use as many specific quotes and details as possible, but they have to be drawn to the thesis to be of any value. Here, we have the statement that "There is no hope of ever getting out of this," and are told that this is Paul's insight, yet a little further down we are told that he felt that his life no longer had worth. The question calls for a single insight, and these various ideas are not drawn together into a cohesive whole to make a single point. The final sentence is especially perplexing—how did the insight cause his death? What happened? Is it a real death or symbolic? All this must be shown through specific example, to make the point and receive maximum credit.

Conclusion. The conclusion, though far too short, provides a thesis that can be the basis of the paper—that war has robbed Paul of any hope for a normal life. If this were rephrased in the topic paragraph, the essay would far more easily prove the thesis.

The paper is in the low B, high C range, a 3 on the AP scale. Compare these two essays with Essays D and E on pages 70 and 71. Note especially how competently those writers proved the thesis.

Writing an Essay on Poetry

Following are some Advanced Placement questions on poetry. None are exact replicas of exam questions, but all are very much like what you will be asked. You will have the poem or poems in front of you as you answer the question. You will be expected to make close reference to the poems and quote specific lines and words to make your point clearly.

SAMPLE QUESTIONS

1. Often in poems the final lines resolve the situation presented in the rest of the work. This is especially true in Elizabethan (English) sonnets, where the final two lines, called the couplet, serve to sum up the situation and present the speaker's position. They have a different rhyme from the rest of the poem and are usually indented to set off their position more firmly. You will be asked to show how the final lines of a poem resolve the situation presented in the beginning. Thus, you will have to describe what happened in the beginning, what happens in the end, and how the two fit together. Time—15 minutes.

2. You will be required to strip a poem down to its basic elements and analyze how those elements work together to establish the theme, tone, or mood of the work. You will have to be aware of rhythm, rhyme, the speaker's attitude (not to confused with the poet's attitude; the speaker and the poet are not the same, as poets often assume masks to present their views), the elements of language, grammar, diction, etc. One of the most effective ways of discovering how all the elements interrelate is to rewrite the poem into a paragraph in your own words to help you make sure you understand what the speaker is saying. Then you can use this paragraph as a basis for your essay. You may also be asked to relate two poems to each other in this manner, and show how they are the same or different. Time—45–60 minutes.

3. Often poems, like prose works, present different views of people or events. You will be asked to break the poem down to its elements (to help you better understand it as well as demonstrate a knowledge of the parts of a poem) and then analyze how the different parts affect the theme or the tone. You can also be asked to show how the different parts relate to one another, how they fit together to produce a unified whole. You may also be asked to isolate one specific element, such as language or symbolism, and show how it operates within the whole. Time—45–60 minutes.

4. You may be asked to explain a poem's theme, its meaning, its "message." Why did the author write this poem? Was he/she trying to effect social change? Make a personal statement? Sway a specific group of people? Often, you will have to consider the elements of poetry in your analysis. These can include figurative language, metrical devices, etc. Time—30–45 minutes.

5. You may be required to analyze the tone or mood of a poem, or to compare the tones or moods of two different poems presented side by side. You will have to be aware of specific different tones, such as sarcastic, hopeful, depressed, etc. and how the elements of a poem contribute to the tone. See the sample responses to this question in the pages that follow. Time—45 minutes.

6. You may be required to "scan" a poem to determine its meter (the poetry section explains how to determine meter). Then, you may be asked how the meter and metrical devices relate to the theme and contribute to the total effect of the poem. Time—45 minutes.

7. You may be asked how any of the specific poetic elements, such as rhyme, figurative language, symbolism, etc. contribute to the author's desired end. Time—30 minutes.

8. You will be asked to trace and identify the poem's allusions, references to established works of literature, or well-known events or people outside the structure of the poem. Thus, you will have to be familiar with established works such as those of Shakespeare and Milton, works such as the Bible and ancient classical writings such as mythology. The best way to accomplish this is through wide reading of a variety of sources. You should also keep up with current events and be aware of well-known historical events and people. Time—45 minutes.

9. Read the poem below and then answer the questions that follow it. Time—30 minutes.

SONNET 10

Death, be not proud, though some have callèd thee
Mighty and dreadful, for thou art not so;
For those whom thou think'st thou dost overthrow
Die not, poor Death, nor yet canst thou kill me.
5 From rest and sleep, which but thy pictures be,
Much pleasure; then from thee much more must flow;
And soonest our best men with thee do go,
Rest of their bones and souls' delivery.
Thou'rt slave to fate, chance, kings, and desperate men,
10 And dost with poison, war, and sickness dwell;
And poppy or charms can make us sleep as well
And better than thy stroke. Why swell'st thou then?
One short sleep past, we wake eternally,
And Death shall be no more: Death, thou shalt die.
                                        —*John Donne*

1. Who is the speaker addressing? What is the speaker's attitude toward that which/who he is addressing? How does this affect the meaning of the poem?
2. What is the *form* of this poem? How is this specific form suited to the content of the poem? Specifically, how do the final two lines of the poem explain the theme and author's attitude?
3. According to the speaker, what different things affect the subject of the poem? What effect do these various things have on the poem's subject?
4. What do you think moved the poet to write this poem?

Suggested Responses

1. The speaker is addressing Death, which is personified as a living being. The speaker's attitude is defiant and bold, as he attack's Death's supposed invulnerability. The speaker's attitude reinforces the poem's meaning, that Death is not to be feared, for Death is but a brief passage to an eternal life.
2. The poem is a sonnet, as the title indicates. The final two lines indicate the sonnet's "turn," summing up the speaker's point, explained in #1.
3. The speaker charges that Death's supposed power is undercut (and finally destroyed) by the following realities: 1) We derive much pleasure from rest and sleep, which mirror Death; 2) Death is at the mercy of fate, chance, kings, desperate men; 3) Death lives with poison, war, and sickness; 4) Drugs ("poppy") and magic spells ("charms") induce sleep as well as Death; 5) Death is but a brief passage into eternal existence.
4. While answers will vary, mention that the author most likely lost a loved one or fears his own death.

10. Read the poem below and then answer the questions that follow it. Time—45 minutes.

DOVER BEACH

The sea is calm tonight.
The tide is full, the moon lies fair
Upon the straits;—on the French coast the light
Gleams and is gone; the cliffs of England stand,
5 Glimmering and vast, out in the tranquil bay.
Come to the window, sweet is the night-air!
Only, from the long line of spray
Where the sea meets the moon-blanched land,
Listen! you hear the grating roar
10 Of pebbles which the waves draw back, and fling,
At their return, up the high strand,
Begin, and cease, and then again begin,
With tremulous cadence slow, and bring
The eternal note of sadness in.

15 Sophocles long ago
Heard it on the Aegean, and it brought
Into his mind the turbid ebb and flow
Of human misery; we
Find also in the sound a thought,
20 Hearing it by this distant northern sea.

The Sea of Faith
Was once, too, at the full, and round earth's shore
Lay like the folds of a bright girdle furled.
But now I only hear
25 Its melancholy, long, withdrawing roar,
Retreating, to the breath
Of the night-wind, down the vast edges drear
And naked shingles of the world.

Ah, love, let us be true
30 To one another! for the world, which seems
To lie before us like a land of dreams,
So various, so beautiful, so new,
Hath really neither joy, nor love, nor light,
Nor certitude, nor peace, nor help for pain;
35 And we are here as on a darkling plain
Swept with confused alarms of struggle and flight,
Where ignorant armies clash by night.
—*Matthew Arnold*

1. Who is the speaker here? Who is he addressing?
2. What is the speaker's *mood*? Show what elements contribute to this mood.
3. Identify the elements of figurative language and show how they contribute to the tone and theme.
4. What is the *tone* of this poem? What details—specific words and events—contribute to the establishment of the tone?

5. What is the theme of this poem? What details contribute to this?
6. Which stanza sums up the meaning of the poem? How is this accomplished?
7. Write an essay in which you explain how the sights and sounds of the beach evoke a specific mood in the speaker. Identify the mood and show what elements contribute to its establishment.

Suggested Responses

1. The speaker is a man standing at a window. He is addressing the woman by his side.
2. The speaker is sad, melancholy. Note the sea's "eternal note of sadness" (line 14); "turbid ebb and flow/Of human misery" (17–18); and "It's melancholy, long. . ." (25).
3. Note especially the alliteration; internal as well as external rhyme; metaphors (ocean's sound compared to human misery, ocean's tides compared to ebb and flow of man's religious belief); similes ("Like the folds of a bright girdle furled"); and vivid imagery ("moon-blanched," "naked shingles of the world," "armies clash").
4. The tone is melancholy, almost bitter in the final stanza. See #2.
5. The theme is the need for human companionship to counter the world's bleakness and seeming hopelessness.
6. See the final stanza.
7. Answers will vary.

STUDENT RESPONSES WITH EVALUATIONS

Read the student essays on poetry that follow and explain why they do or do not fulfill the Advanced Placement requirements. Use the questions below as guidelines for your evaluations. Then read the critical analysis that follows each essay.

1. Does each essay answer the question? If there is more than one part to the question, are *all* parts answered?
2. Are there clear and specific examples drawn from the text itself to back up the points? Are the examples tied into the answer? In other words, does the writer use phrases like, "This shows that. . ." or "This proves that. . ." to make the point clearly?

3. Is the writing clear? Do the sentences flow smoothly? Are all portions of each paragraph and each essay logically connected? If there is a point made in the introduction, for example, is that point carried through the body to the conclusion?

4. Does the essay exhibit command of writing skill? Is it clear that the work has been proofread for careless errors? Does the work demonstrate knowledge of grammar and usage, spelling and punctuation, parallel structure, and placement of modifiers?

5. What about *style?* Is there variety in sentence structure? Are the words carefully selected for their specific nature and suitability to the essay?

Question for Essays A–C

Read the two poems that follow. Then, compare the *tone* of the first with the *tone* of the second. Show how they are the same and different. Use specific lines from each work to support your points. Time—45 minutes.

A MAN ADRIFT ON A SLIM SPAR

A man adrift on a slim spar
A horizon smaller than the rim of a bottle
Tented waves rearing lashy dark points
The near whine of froth in circles.
5   God is cold.

The incessant raise and swing of the sea
And growl after growl of crest
The sinkings, green, seething, endless
The upheaval half-completed.
10   God is cold.

The seas are in the hollow of The Hand;
Oceans may be turned to a spray
Raining down through the stars
Because of a gesture of pity toward a babe.
15 Oceans may become gray ashes,

Die with a long moan and a roar
Amid the tumult of the fishes
And the cries of the ships.
Because The Hand beckons the mice.

20 A horizon smaller than a doomed assassin's cap,
Inky, surging tumults
A reeling, drunken sky and no sky
A pale hand sliding from a polished spar.
        God is cold.

25 The puff of a coat imprisoning air:
A face kissing the water-death
A weary slow sway of a lost hand
And the sea, the moving sea, the sea.
        God is cold.
      —*Stephen Crane*

ON HIS BLINDNESS

When I consider how my light is spent,
Ere half my days, in this dark world and wide,
And that one talent which is death to hide
Lodged with me useless, though my soul more bent
5 To serve therewith my Maker, and present
My true account, lest he returning chide,
"Doth God exact day labor, light denied?"
I fondly ask: but Patience, to prevent
That murmur, soon replies: "God doth not need
10 Either man's work or his own gifts; who best
Bear his mild yoke, they serve him best. His state
Is kingly: thousands at his bidding speed
And post o'er land and ocean without rest.
They also serve who only stand and wait."
      —*John Milton*

Essay A

In "A Man Adrift on a Slim Spar," the author states "God is cold." The author feels that God does not care one way or the other if the man at sea lives or dies. The dying man is in a natural setting—the ocean. In this setting, the man is helpless and it is God, who created the ocean, who has the ability to rescue or take the life of the lost man. In line 26, "A face kissing the water-death," we realize that the man at sea will die. The author again states that "God is cold."

In John Milton's "On His Blindness," we read of a blind man who despite his handicap, asks God how he should serve Him. Patience replies in line 9, "God doth not need either man's work or his own gift's; who best bears his mild yoke, they serve him best." Here, the man seems to be deeply religious and devoted to serving God. God, appreciating the man's devotion despite his handicap, simply states those who bear what has been put upon them are serving God.

In the first poem, the speaker is angry with God. He resents that God allows a man to suffer at sea. In the second poem, however, the speaker is devoted to serving God and does not get angry at God because of the handicap of blindness, inflicted upon him by God. The second speaker has served God while the first has failed.

Evaluation of Essay A

The main problem with the student's treatment of "A Man Adrift on a Slim Spar" is that he does not address himself directly to the question of *tone;* rather, he provides a summary of the plot. While such summaries are necessary in many instances to establish the tone and answer the question, they cannot substitute for an answer that addresses itself to the question. The line "God is cold," repeated twice, does not explain the tone.

The problem persists into the second paragraph where the writer treats Milton's sonnet. Again, the question of tone is not resolved. While the writer correctly summarizes the plot, he does not answer the question.

As in paragraphs 1 and 2, the conclusion contrasts the plots of the two poems, but fails to explain the differences in tone.

This essay would receive a below-average grade, a D or a 1 on the AP scale, since it does not answer the question.

Essay B

"A Man Adrift on a Slim Spar" and "On His Blindness" have very different tones. The first poem depicts God as an unfeeling being who allows man to die needlessly. In this case, the man is drowning in the ocean. "The puff of a coat imprisoning air: A face kissing the water-death . . . God is cold." These lines show the poet's view that man is isolated and untouched by God. He is left alone on Earth in his fight for survival.

In contrast, "On His Blindness" views God as a power beyond question. Milton wonders why God has taken away his sight, robbing him of his ability to write. Patience's reply, "They also serve who stand and wait," signifies God's purpose that seemingly cruel and tragic things on earth have a meaning. Even though Milton has tragically lost his power to serve God, this writing ability, he is still serving God by keeping the faith.

In conclusion, "A Man Adrift on a Slim Spar" views God as unfeeling while Milton's "On His Blindness" sees God as caring. Both poems depict a tragic occurrence, a drowning and blindness. The difference between the two lies in the first poet's belief that God inflicts tragedy without a purpose while Milton views God's actions as purposeful. The difference in the two poems' tone lies in their view of God.

Evaluation of Essay B

This example, in sharp contrast to the one before it, addresses itself to the question of *tone* right from the start. The writer directly answers the question by telling us how the speaker feels about God. While there could be more examples more fully explained, the question is directly addressed.

There is a good transition—"in contrast"—between the first and second paragraphs. Here, however, the question of tone is not directly answered, even though it is alluded to in plot summary. Furthermore, the student should not assume that the speaker *is* the author. This may be true but it is still not an assumption we can safely make. This holds true for all literature.

The conclusion does serve to tie the essay together and answer the question, especially in the first line and the last one.

This is a better essay than Essay A, and would receive a grade in the B range, a 4 on the AP scale. Paragraph 2 needs to address itself more directly to the question, and more examples throughout the entire essay would be a significant improvement.

Essay C

The tone of the first poem, "A Man Adrift on a Slim Spar," differs markedly from the tone of the second, "On His Blindness." While each poet describes an omnipotent God, the first Supreme Being is cold and indifferent; the second, warm and compassionate.

On a literal level, the first poem describes a man vainly clinging to a slender scrap of wood in the middle of the fierce ocean. The poet carefully stacks the odds against the drowning man: the spar is "slim" (line 1), the "horizon smaller than the rim of a bottle" (line 2), the ocean endlessly "rearing lashy dark points" (line 3). God is all-powerful, the poet says, able to control the seas in the hollow of His hand, to make of them what He wishes. The ocean may be transformed into a gentle "spray/Raining down through the stars" because God feels compassion toward a child, or it may become a merciless storm that brings fishes and sailors alike to their brutal ruin—all at His whim. The man adrift in the ocean is doomed, his "pale hand sliding from a polished spar" as his face kisses "the water-death" and he sinks from sight. God is not actively against this man—or any man, for that matter—the poet says; rather, He is merely "cold," indifferent to the man's suffering and torment in the bitter cold ocean of life. The tone reflects this view of God, and so "A Man Adrift on a Slim Spar" is bitter and harsh. The second poem, however, is in a very different vein.

"On His Blindness" has a much more traditional view of God and His relationship to man, echoed in its more traditional form. A sonnet written with an abba/abba/cde/cde rhyme scheme, this poem depicts God as every bit as powerful as in the first example but a great deal more compassionate. The speaker begins by lamenting the loss of his vision, which renders his one talent, the ability to write, virtually useless. He is distraught because he desires above all else to serve God through his one talent, to be able to represent himself fully and glorify God through his prose and verse. God will not force him to perform tasks beyond his ability, he knows, such as compose verse in His honor without sight, but nevertheless he wishes to contribute to God's glorification. This is in marked contrast to the first poet's attitude, for he has no desire whatsoever to serve God in any capacity. God has allowed him but a slim spar and turned His back. The first speaker, then, never even discusses the notion of dedicating himself to God. In the Milton sonnet, on the other hand, God, in the form of Patience, reassures the speaker that those also serve who "stand and wait." God is King, the second poem states, and has thousands to actively carry out His bidding. The speaker need not worry that he has failed to properly honor his God.

The two situations are very different, as are the attitudes of the speakers. In the first, the speaker sees God as cold and indifferent and thus the tone emerges as bitter and harsh. In the second, the speaker sees God as compassionate and understanding, and thus the tone is gentle and reassuring.

Evaluation of Essay C

The introduction gets right to the point and answers the question clearly. While mentioning each poem by name so there will be no confusion, the writer specifically indicates what the *tone* is for each.

The plot summary provided in the second paragraph clearly contributes to answering the question, for it focuses on the theme. There is good sentence variety, especially in the varied use of punctuation. In the same way, the writer uses a great many carefully selected adjectives, such as "vainly," "slender" and "fierce," in the first sentence of the second paragraph alone. There are many clear examples drawn from the text, and each is used to make the point. From the line "God is not actively against this man. . ." to the end of the paragraph, the point is clearly stated and well supported by good specific examples.

The third paragraph on Milton's sonnet also addresses itself to the question. The two paragraphs are tied together with the last line of the second paragraph, lending unity to the whole. The first line of the third paragraph could perhaps be revised, for while the author justifies the inclusion of the rhyme scheme in the word "traditional," it is not germane to the discussion here. But the specific examples clearly state the tone, and the last portion of this paragraph makes a clear comparison between the two poems.

The conclusion sums up all that has been stated before and makes the point well.

This is a superior essay, well in the A range, a 5 on the AP scale. It makes the points carefully, with well-selected examples, and its style, with sentence variety and good word choice, contributes to the effectiveness of the answer.

Question for Essays D–H

Read the following poem and discuss the author's theme. 1) What is the *tone* of the first 12 lines of the poem? 2) What is the *tone* of the final two lines? 3) How are they different? 4) How is the form of the sonnet suited to this method of development? Time—30 minutes.

SONNET 130

My mistress' eyes are nothing like the sun;
Coral is far more red than her lips' red;
If snow be white, why then her breasts are dun;   3
If hairs be wires, black wires grow on her head.
I have seen roses damasked, red and white,
But no such roses see I in her cheeks;   6
And in some perfumes is there more delight
Than in the breath that from my mistress reeks.
I love to hear her speak; yet well I know   9
That music hath a far more pleasing sound:
I grant I never saw a goddess go;
My mistress, when she walks, treads on the ground. 12
 And yet, by heaven, I think my love as rare
 As any she belied with false compare.
       —William Shakespeare

Essay D

In Sonnet 130, by William Shakespeare, two different tones are expressed. The first, which makes up the first 12 lines of the sonnet, is sarcastic and witty. The second, which concludes the work, is more serious.

In the first 12 lines of the poem, the speaker describes his mistress in a sarcastic manner. He creates a visual representation through such phrases as "My mistress' eyes are nothing like the sun" and "coral is far more red than her lips red." But these descriptions in no way indicate that he does not love her, as the second part of the poem reveals.

In the final two lines we see the speaker's true feelings for his mistress. Although this woman does not have any of the traditional attributes mentioned in the Elizabethan love sonnet, she has something that he obviously values more—something in her manner and personality which he finds attractive.

The tone changes from sarcastic to serious as the poem progresses, although his feelings for his mistress remain the same throughout. Love is not always based on physical attraction; it goes deeper, within the heart, mind, and soul.

Evaluation of Essay D

The topic paragraph gets right to the point and clearly states the *tones* involved here. What is missing is a clear evaluation of the *theme* and a mention of how the sonnet form is suited to the poet's purpose. All these elements must appear in the topic paragraph in order to answer the question completely.

The second paragraph begins to establish the writer's meaning, but a great deal more can be done with examples to make that meaning clear. The writer should take us, step by step, through the poem to show clearly how the tone is sarcastic. There is a good transition in the final line of the second paragraph, leading logically into paragraph 3.

Paragraph 3, like paragraph 2, needs more specific examples to make the author's point. Again, examples must be taken from the poem and fully explained to show how the tone changes. This must be tied in with theme in this specific instance to make the author's point.

The concluding lines do establish the tone of the work, but the author failed to prove his conclusion clearly in the body of the essay.

This essay would be in the low B to high C range, a 3 on the AP scale. Although the writer obviously understood the poem, he did not provide enough specific examples to thoroughly prove his point.

Essay E

The tone of the first 12 lines of Shakespeare's Sonnet 130 are very different in meaning from the couplet at the end of the poem. While both parts of this work are concerned with love, the first part is much more sarcastic and even degrading, whereas the second part is much more flattering and compassionate.

In lines 1–12, the speaker insults his mistress by saying such things as "her eyes are nothing like the sun" and "If hairs be wires, black wires grow on her head." In all the traditional comparisons, she falls short.

The final two lines are much more loving. The poet states that although his mistress may have her faults—chief among them being her appearance—he loves her. There is much more to love than surface appearance and the poet wants to make this clear. This is stated in the final two lines.

Evaluation of Essay E

This introduction appears to be better than the one before it, for the author clearly states the *tone* of the poem. The *theme* can be inferred from the line "both parts of the work are concerned with love," but the question of the role of the sonnet in the tone and theme is not addressed.

The rest of the essay is not well written, however, as the examples provided (and there are far too few) are in no way tied into the author's point. This must be done to answer the question. The essay needs two or three times the number of examples given to fully answer the question.

This essay would be in the D range, a 1 on the AP scale, as it lacks clear examples and fails to make the point.

Essay F

The surprisingly sarcastic tone of Shakespeare's Sonnet 130 illustrates his strong feelings toward comparing love to beautiful images in life. Shakespeare uses lines 1–12 of the sonnet to create a picture of his mistress, and the reader learns that she does not measure up to the ideal of Elizabethan beauty. The woman is depicted as homely, pale, and awkward, with a shrill voice and bad breath. Even though her attributes cannot be expressed as the traditional comparisons to the sun or roses, she does possess qualities that make the speaker love her. This is evident in the last two lines, when the tone shifts from sarcastic and humorous to serious. The speaker states that he does indeed love her, and this love need not be compared to anything to make it stronger. His love for his mistress is true and can stand on its own. The sonnet form is suitable for this change in tone for the body illustrates the speaker's distaste for silly comparisons and the last two lines reinforce his point in a serious manner.

Evaluation of Essay F

The first line leads us right into the question, and while the writer does not tie in all five parts of the original assignment, she does answer this portion partially. There should be some specific lines drawn from the poem to back up her assertions that the woman is "homely, pale, and awkward." She also shows some knowledge of the traditions of Elizabethan love verse, referring to the sun and roses as traditional metaphors in the 16th century. There is a good transition to the question of the tone in the final two lines, but again it would be better were she to allude to the specific lines and quote those parts more germane to her argument. The final comment on the sonnet form can be enlarged to make the point clearer.

This essay is in the B– range, a 3.5 on the AP scale.

Essay G

The author's theme in Sonnet 130 is that beauty is not the most important priority in a relationship. Although the woman in the poem doesn't measure up to the traditional symbols of beauty such as the sun, coral, and a rose, she does possess other qualities which make him think that their love is very rare indeed. The tone of the first 12 lines of the poem is sarcastic and somewhat teasing, but in the final two lines the sarcasm is dropped, replaced by the author's feeling of genuine love for his mistress. Their love is truer than any "she belied with false compare." There is nothing phony about her—she is not a rose or a goddess, or any of the stereotypical love symbols—and he loves her all the more. The form of the sonnet is ideal for conveying this message, as the last two lines, with their specific rhyme, allow the speaker to clearly establish his theme.

Evaluation of Essay G

The writer's conclusion that beauty is not the most important aspect of a relationship is partly true here, but Shakespeare is also saying that the relationship he has with his mistress is such that it is diminished through false comparison, a point that should be made in the first few sentences. If the writer is going to say that Shakespeare feels that the woman has other qualities more valuable than beauty, he must be able to document those qualities, through specific examples drawn from the poem. The question is answered in the line that begins "The tone of the first twelve lines. . .," but this is not backed up with specific examples from the text. The same is true throughout the rest of the paragraph, especially in the final line, where the "specific rhyme" alluded to is not explained with examples.

The question is not fully answered and there are not enough examples to make the point clearly. The paper is in the C– range, a 2 on the AP scale.

Essay H

The tone of the first 12 lines of Shakespeare's Sonnet 130 contrast sharply to the tone of the final two, and this difference establishes the theme of the entire work. The first twelve lines of the poem parody the form and content of the typical love verse, as the woman fails to measure up to any of the traditional emblems of love and devotion. Thus, her eyes, the time-honored windows of the soul, lack the clear radiance of the sun, and her lips, the deep, rosy tint of coral. Her skin is mottled and dark; her hair, coarse wires. The tone is playful and mocking, as Shakespeare inverts all the accepted tools of the love sonneteer's trade to construct a series of false analogies. The tone of the final two lines, however, differs sharply. Frequently the final two lines of an Elizabethan sonnet, called the couplet, serve to sum up the meaning of the preceeding 12 lines and establish the author's tone. Such is the case here, for the couplet's tone and meaning differ markedly from the rest of the poem. These two lines are serious, not light and playful, as the author declares his love for the lady he has just pilloried at the stake of false comparison. He wrote this poem, he says here, to parody her tendency to compare their love to objects and in so doing, establish false analogies. Their love is a rare and serious thing, he states, not to be diminished through "false compare." The sonnet is well suited to this difference in tone, as the couplet in the end allows the author the opportunity to sum up the first 12 lines and establish the theme. Here, he abjures the parody of the first 12 lines to firmly and seriously declares his love.

Evaluation of Essay H

This example clearly answers the question fully, with style and grace. The first line ties in all the possible threads, tone, and theme, as well as alluding to the question of sonnet form by mentioning the last two lines. The next sentence follows logically, and the ones after that provide clear examples of the speaker's point. Next, the writer moves to the final two lines, and displays a knowledge of the conventions of the Elizabethan sonnet. The writer then shows, through specific example, how the final two lines differ in tone from the first twelve, and finally shows how the sonnet form is well suited to the theme of the poem.

This is a well-written essay, with clear examples and good word choice and sentence variety. It fully answers the question and would be in the A range, a 5 on the AP scale.

SUGGESTED READING LIST

The following books discuss the writing process, grammar and usage, and general rules of composition. These books are intended to supplement—not replace—actual writing practice.

Baker, Sheridan. *The Practical Stylist.* 3rd edition. New York: Thomas Y. Crowell, 1969.

Brooks, Cleanth and Robert Penn Warren. *Modern Rhetoric.* 3rd ed. New York: Harcourt Brace Jovanovich, 1970.

Cohen, Benjamin. *Writing about Literature.* Glenville, IL: Scott, Foresman, 1973.

Follet, Wilson. *Modern American Usage.* ed. Jacques Barzun. New York: Warner Publishing Company, 1987.

Hodges, John C. and Mary E. Whitman. *Harbrace College Handbook.* New York: Harcourt Brace Jovanovich, 1987.

Kane, Thomas and Leonard Peters. *Writing Prose.* 3rd edition. New York: Oxford, 1969.

Kirzner, Laurie and Stephen Mandell. *The Holt Handbook.* New York: Holt, Rinehart and Winston, 1987.

McCrimmon, James. *Writing with a Purpose.* Boston: Houghton Mifflin, 1973.

Lieberman, Leo and Jeffrey Spielberger. *Essential English Composition for College-Bound Students*. 2nd edition. New York: Arco, 1992.

McCrimmon, James. *Writing with a Purpose*. Boston: Houghton Mifflin, 1973.

Perrin, Robert. *The Beacon Handbook*. Boston: Houghton Mifflin Company, 1987.

Roberts, Edgar. *Writing Themes about Literature*. 3rd edition. New York: Prentice-Hall, 1973.

Sorenson, Sharon. *Webster's New World™ Student Writing Handbook*. 2nd edition, New York: Prentice Hall, 1992.

Strunk, E. and E.B. White. *The Elements of Style*. New York: Macmillan, 1972.

Warriner, John E. *Advanced Composition*. New York: Harcourt Brace Jovanovich, 1968.

Part 3

All About Prose

The Short Story

The actual definition of the short story has been subject to much discussion. It is impossible to distinguish a short story from a novel on any single basis other than length, and neither has a formally established length. As a general rule, the short story is narrative prose fiction shorter than a novel, usually not exceeding 15,000 words. It usually has fewer characters than a novel and a less involved plot—one main line of action rather than interwoven stories—but these rules are not hard and fast. Many works that cannot be classified are called "long stories" or "short novels" to illustrate the difficulty critics have had in pinning down this genre. One cannot say that a good short story has more unity than a novel, for frequently unity has no relation to the situation at all. A short story may deal with a briefer period of time, but again this may not always be the case. What happens most frequently is that a short story is, by nature of its length, less complex than a novel, and rather than tracing the development of a character, which is frequently the case with a novel, it focuses on a particular moment in that character's life and development. As Poe phrased it, the author of a short story strives to achieve a "single effect" in the pages allotted to him. While the short story has a rich and detailed history, it has frequently been eclipsed by its showier cousin, the novel.

BRIEF HISTORY OF THE SHORT STORY

The earliest known short stories date from the year 3000 B.C., Egyptian tales inscribed on papyrus and found entombed with other Egyptian effects.

The short story next appeared as an outgrowth of the oral tradition. The Anglo-Saxon epic *Beowulf,* ballads, and German folk tales, called *märchen* (the source of modern-day fairy tales) had their roots in the oral tradition, as did *The Iliad* and Hesiod's *Theogony,* a collection of Greek myths.

Other countries also contributed to the short story's rich legacy. From India came the *Jatakas,* the teachings of Buddha, around the year 500 B.C., and the *Panchatantra,* Hindu beast fables. In these fables, animals talked like human beings to make moral points. Aesop, the Greek slave who lived in the sixth century B.C., orginated similar fables that were written down in the first and second century A.D. By the Middle Ages, animal fables, like "The Owl and the Nightingale" (1225), were popular.

The Bible contributed also. The Old Testament abounds in examples of short stories: the tales of Ruth, David and Goliath, and Esther are all cases in point. In the New Testament, Christ's parables serve the same literary function.

The Middle Ages saw the appearance of many short narrative forms. The *conte dévot,* in the twelfth and thirteenth centuries, were short religious tales recounting saints' miracles and intended for pious instruction. The *Miracles of Mary* were especially popular, as they glorified the chivalrous devotion to ideal womanhood, as represented by the Virgin Mary. The *fabliaux,* originated in France in the thirteenth century, were short humorous verses that exposed human weaknesses in a bawdy and entertaining manner. Chaucer's *Canterbury Tales,* especially one like "The Miller's Tale," are examples of this genre (1387–1395). The *lai,* a secular short verse tale of romance, which dates from the thirteenth and fourteenth centuries, is also in this mode. The *exemplum,* an illustrated moral tale used in sermons, was intended to instruct, rather than entertain. Chaucer's "Pardoner's Tale" would be an exemplum.

By the early 1500's, prose began to replace verse. The invention of printing stimulated silent reading, displacing the oral tradition. Jest books, with puns and jokes, became popular. *Hundred Mery Tales,* which dates from 1526, is a noteworthy example.

The *novella,* a short prose tale, appeared as early as the fourteenth century in Italy. Boccaccio's *Decameron* and William Painter's later *Palace of Pleasure* (1566) show this trend. Parodies and burlesques also became popular.

In Spain, the picaro, a rogue who engaged in a series of adventures in which he managed to triumph over folly and vice, appeared in tales called *picaresques.* Cervantes' *Don Quixote* (1605) and Le Sage's *Gil Blas* (1715) are picaresques.

Prose sketches appeared in newspapers and magazines in England, depicting brief and realistic stories about middle-class life. These stories were overshadowed by the development of drama during the Renaissance, but achieved real success early in the eighteenth century in such British magazines as *Tatler* and the *Spectator.*

The Arabian Nights, romantic tales, sometimes overlaid with morality, date back to the eighth century, but they were first published in French in 1704. It is with the growth of the mass market and the rise of the commercial magazine in the nineteenth century that the modern short story really begins.

Washington Irving (1783–1859) is regarded by many critics as the father of the modern short story. He saw the purpose of fiction as entertainment, not instruction, and entertain he did by combining American and European history and folklore, social observation and humor.

Lavish gift books appeared in America during this time, richly illustrated and beautifully packaged, but full of banal tales of unrequitted love, ghosts, devils, and mad queens. For example, *The Atlantic Souvenir* (1826–1832) was a popular gift from young men to young women in the nineteenth century, much as candy or flowers are today. In the early part of the nineteenth century, with a few notable exceptions, the quality of popular fiction was low. Poe and Hawthorne stand out as exceptional writers during this time.

Poe Defines the "Well-Made Tale"

Edgar Allan Poe, who lived from 1809 to 1848, clearly established the boundaries and guidelines for the short story and greatly elevated the standards for shorter fiction. In his famous review of Nathaniel Hawthorne's *Twice-Told Tales* (1842), Poe laid down the "rules" for what has come to be called the "well-made tale."

In a skillfully constructed tale, according to Poe, "[the author] has not fashioned his thought to accommodate his incidents; but having conceived, with deliberate care, a certain unique or *single effect* to be wrought out, he then invents such incidents—he then combines such events as may best aid him in establishing this preconceived effect. If his very initial sentence tends not to the outbringing of this effect, then he has failed in his first step. In the whole composition there should be no word written, of which the tendency, direct or indirect, is not to the pre-established design."

Poe's rules were rigid in other regards, too. He felt that for unity of effect the ideal short story should be read without pause. For this reason, he limited the length of the story to one to two hours' reading time. The *effect* that Poe sought to create was terror, passion, or horror—or "a multitude of other such effects."

In his *Philosophy of Composition,* published in 1846, Poe established that the aim of the short story was to include not only *truth,* the satisfaction of the intellect, but *passion,* the excitement of the heart.

While some have ridiculed his theories as rigid, they have had great effect on the development of the short story.

Hawthorne Introduces the Concept of Romance

Nathaniel Hawthorne, who lived from 1804 to 1864, changed the course of the short story by constructing tales that spoke to the human heart and conveyed truths that held for all times.

Hawthorne saw romance as vital to the development of the short story. To this end, he saw the writer's imagination as the starting point and the artist's highest achievement as the faithful reproduction of his own imagination and conception of the world. In "Roger Malvin's Burial," for example, Hawthorne suggests that the imagination changes the outer world by "casting certain circumstances in the shade."

In the preface to his *House of the Seven Gables*, Hawthorne explained his concept of romance:

> When a writer calls his work a Romance, it need hardly be observed that he wishes to claim a certain latitude, both as to its fashion and material, which he would not have felt himself entitled to assume, had he professed to be writing a Novel. The latter form of composition is presumed to aim at *a very minute fidelity,* not merely to the possible, but to the probable and ordinary course of man's experience. The former—while, as a work of art, it must rigidly subject itself to laws, and while it sins unpardonably, so far as it may swerve aside from the truth of the human heart—has fairly a right to present the truth under circumstances, to a great extent, of the *writer's own choosing or creation.* If he think fit, also, he may manage his atmospherical medium as to bring out or mellow the lights and deepen and enrich the shadows of the picture. He will be wise, no doubt, to make very moderate use of the privileges here stated, and, especially, *to mingle the Marvellous rather as a slight, delicate, and evanescent flavor,* than as any portion of the actual substance of the dish offered to the Public (italics mine).

Hawthorne, then, saw the writer of romance as allowed to take a certain latitude with reality, to add details and situations that would not appear in the novel, due to the latter's strict observance of "reality." This is not to say that he was advocating what we would today call a "science-fiction" story; rather, he said that the writer was allowed to take certain liberties to enrich his story, but he must never stray so far from the truth as to make his reader doubt the veracity of the tale. While sometimes ignored or, in the case of Poe, maligned by their contemporaries, Hawthorne and Poe, working independently, helped shape the course of the modern prose tale.

HOW TO EVALUATE A SHORT STORY

1. First, establish the *plot,* the sequence of events in the story. Are they all external, or do some take place in characters' minds? The sequence of events may not be chronological (the order of time). The author may have established a flashback or retrospect, a recounting of an earlier episode than the one that has just been presented. Or the story can open *in medias res*—the middle of the action—and later show how the plot arrived at that point. You will find it helpful to construct a brief outline or a timeline of events to establish the chronology.

2. Next, focus on the *narrator*. Who is he/she? From what point of view is he/she relating the events? Is it one of the following three first-person views:

First-Person Observer   "I last met Smith in 1955."

First-Person Participant   "I had just gotten my first job and was looking for an apartment."

Innocent Eye   Told through a first-person narrator who is naive or unreliable, as when Faulkner has an idiot, Benjy Compson, narrate the first section of *The Sound and the Fury*. Although 33 years old, Benjy has the mind of a three-year-old, and thus the events are told from that point of view.

Or does he/she use a third-person narration?

Omniscient   Records the thoughts of all the characters

Selective Omniscient   Enters the minds of some characters to record their thoughts

Objective Omniscient   Simply records what is plainly visible

Editorial Ominscient   Records the characters' thoughts and also comments on them.

Can we trust the narrator or does he/she have an interest in the tale as a participant? Is he/she sane?

3. Then seek out the author's *theme* or main idea. Is the author's purpose simply to entertain or does he/she intend to comment on the human condition in some manner? What details and events contribute to the establishment of the theme?

4. If you have read other stories by the same author, determine how this one is similar, or different. Can you see a connection between this work and others by the same author?

5. Look for any *symbols*. Are there people or objects that stand for something greater than themselves? What do they represent and what was the author's purpose in creating them?

6. Examine the author's *point of view*. Is it evident from the story? Does the author have a specific attitude toward the events or characters he/she has created? Is the author involved or aloof? Does the author's attitude matter to this tale or is it irrelevant?

7. Determine whether you can discern a *time frame* for the story or whether the time is irrelevant to the tale. Does this story fit with others that were written in the same decade, say the 1920s or 1930s? Does it reflect the spirit of the times or does it transcend time to speak for all ages?

Use the techniques outlined to evaluate and analyze the three short stories that follow.

THE BLACK CAT
by Edgar Allan Poe

For the most wild yet most homely narrative which I am about to pen, I neither expect nor solicit belief. Mad indeed would I be to expect it, in a case where my very senses reject their own evidence. Yet, mad am I not— and very surely do I not dream. But tomorrow I die, and to-day I would unburden my soul. My immediate purpose is to place before the world, plainly, succinctly, and without comment, a series of mere household events. In their consequences, these events have terrified—have tortured—have destroyed me. Yet I will not attempt to expound them. To me, they have presented little but horror—to many they will seem less terrible than *baroques*. Hereafter, perhaps some intellect may be found which will reduce my phantasm to the commonplace—some intellect more calm, more logical, and far less excitable than my own, which will perceive, in the circumstances I detail with awe, nothing more than an ordinary succession of very natural causes and effects.

From my infancy I was noted for the docility and humanity of my disposition. My tenderness of heart was even so conspicuous as to make me the jest of my companions. I was especially fond of animals, and was indulged by my parents with a great variety of pets. With these I spent most of my time, and never was so happy as when feeding and caressing them. This peculiarity of character grew with my growth, and, in my manhood, I derived from it one of my principal sources of pleasure. To those who have cherished an affection for a faithful and sagacious dog, I need hardly to be at the trouble of explaining the nature or the intensity of the gratification thus derivable. There is something in the unselfish and self-sacrificing love of a brute, which goes directly to the heart of him who had had the frequent occasion to test the paltry friendship and gossamer fidelity of mere *Man*.

I married early, and was happy to find in my wife a disposition not uncongenial with my own. Observing my partiality for domestic pets, she lost no opportunity of procuring those of the most agreeable kind. We had birds, gold-fish, a fine dog, rabbits, a small monkey, and a *cat*.

This latter was a remarkably large and beautiful animal, entirely black, and sagacious to an astonishing degree. In speaking of his intelligence, my wife, who at heart was not a little tinctured with superstition, made frequent allusion to the ancient popular notion, which regarded all black cats as witches in disguise. Not that she was ever *serious* upon this point—and I mention the matter at all for no better reason than that it happens, just now, to be remembered.

Pluto—this was the cat's name—was my favorite pet and playmate. I alone fed him, and he attended me wherever I went about the house. It was even with difficulty that I could prevent him from following me through the streets.

Our friendship lasted, in this manner, for several years, during which my general temperament and character—through the instrumentality of the Fiend Intemperance—had (I blush to confess it) experienced a radical alteration for the worse. I grew, day by day, more moody, more irritable, more regardless of the feelings of others. I suffered myself to use intemperate language to my wife. At length, I even offered her personal violence. My pets, of course, were made to feel the change in my disposition. I not only neglected, but ill-used them. For Pluto, however, I still retained sufficient regard to restrain me from maltreating him, as I made no scruple of maltreating the rabbits, the monkey, or even the dog, when, by accident, or through affection, they came in my way. But my disease grew upon me—for what disease is like Alcohol!—and at length even Pluto, who was now becoming old, and

consequently somewhat peevish—even Pluto began to experience the effects of my ill temper.

One night, returning home, much intoxicated, from one of my haunts about town, I fancied that the cat avoided my presence. I seized him; when, in his fright at my violence, he inflicted a slight wound upon my hand with his teeth. The fury of a demon instantly possessed me. I knew myself no longer. My original soul seemed, at once, to take its flight from my body; and a more than fiendish malevolence, gin-nurtured, thrilled every fibre of my frame. I took from my waistcoat-pocket a penknife, opened it, grasped the poor beast by the throat, and deliberately cut one of its eyes from the socket! I blush, I burn, I shudder, while I pen the damnable atrocity.

When reason returned with the morning—when I had slept off the fumes of the night's debauch—I experienced a sentiment half of horror, half of remorse, for the crime of which I had been guilty; but it was, at best, a feeble and equivocal feeling, and the soul remained untouched. I again plunged into excess, and soon drowned in wine all memory of the deed.

In the meantime the cat slowly recovered. The socket of the lost eye presented, it is true, a frightful appearance, but he no longer appeared to suffer any pain. He went about the house as usual, but, as might be expected, fled in extreme terror at my approach. I had so much of my old heart left, as to be at first grieved by this evident dislike on the part of a creature which had once so loved me. But this feeling soon gave place to irritation. And then came, as if to my final and irrevocable overthrow the spirit of PERVERSENESS. Of this spirit philosophy takes no account. Yet I am not more sure that my soul lives, than I am that perverseness is one of the primitive impulses of the human heart—one of the indivisible primary faculties, or sentiments, which give direction to the character of Man. Who has not, a hundred times, found himself committing a vile or a stupid action, for no other reason than because he knows he should *not*? Have we not a perpetual inclination, in the teeth of our best judgment, to violate that which is *Law*, merely because we understand it to be such? This spirit of perverseness, I say, came to my final overthrow. It was this unfathomable longing of the soul *to vex itself*—to offer violence to its won nature—to do wrong for the wrong's sake only—that urged me to continue and finally to consummate the injury I had inflicted upon the unoffending brute. One morning, in cold blood, I slipped a noose about its neck with the tears streaming from my eyes, and with the bitterest remorse at my heart;—hung it *because* I knew that it had loved me, and *because* I felt it had given me no reason of offence;—hung it *because* I knew that in so doing I was committing a sin—a deadly sin that would so jeopardize my immortal soul as to place it—if such a thing were possible—even beyond the reach of the infinite mercy of the Most Merciful and Most Terrible God.

On the night of the day on which this most cruel deed was done, I was aroused from sleep by the cry of fire. The curtains of my bed were in flames. The whole house was blazing. It was with great difficulty that my wife, a servant, and myself, made our escape from the conflagration. The destruction was complete. My entire worldly wealth was swallowed up, and I resigned myself thenceforward to despair.

I am above the weakness of seeking to establish a sequence of cause and effect, between the disaster and the atrocity. But I am detailing a chain of facts—and wish not to leave even a possible link imperfect. On the day succeeding the fire, I visited the ruins. The walls, with one exception, had fallen in. This exception was found in a compartment wall, not very thick, which stood about the middle of the house, and against which had rested the head of my bed. The plastering had here, in great measure, resisted the action of the fire—a fact which I attributed to its having been recently spread. About this wall a dense crowd were collected, and many persons seemed to be examining a particular portion of it with very minute and eager attention. The words, "strange!" "singular!" and other similar expressions, excited my curiosity. I approached and saw, as if graven in *bas-relief* upon the white surface, the figure of a gigantic *cat*. The impression was given with an accuracy truly marvelous. There was a rope about the animal's neck.

When I first beheld this apparition—for I could scarcely regard it as less—my wonder and my terror were extreme. But at length reflection came to my aid. The cat, I remembered, had been hung in a garden adjacent to the house. Upon the alarm of fire, this garden had been immediately filled by the crowd—by some one of whom the animal must have been cut from the tree and thrown, through an open window, into my chamber. This had probably been done with the view of arousing me from sleep. The falling of other walls had compressed the victim of my cruelty into the substance of the freshly-spread plaster; the lime of which, with the flames, and *ammonia* from the carcass, had then accomplished the portraiture as I saw it.

Although I thus readily accounted to my reason, if not altogether to my conscience, for the startling fact just detailed, it did not the less fail to make a deep impression upon my fancy. For months I could not rid myself of the phantasm of the cat; and, during this period, there came back into my spirit a half-sentiment that seemed, but was not, remorse. I went so far as to regret the loss of the animal, and to look about me, among the vile haunts which I now habitually frequented, for another pet of the same species, and of somewhat similar appearance, with which to supply its place.

One night as I sat, half stupefied, in a den of more than infamy, my attention was suddenly drawn to some black object, reposing upon the head of one of the immense hogsheads of gin, or of rum, which constituted the chief furniture of the apartment. I had been looking steadily at the top of this hogshead for some minutes, and what now caused me surprise was the fact that I had not sooner perceived the object thereupon. I approached it, and touched it with my hand. It was a black cat—a very large one—fully as large as Pluto, and closely resembling him in every respect but one. Pluto had not a white hair upon any portion of his body; but his cat had a large, although indefinite splotch of white, covering nearly the whole region of the breast.

Upon my touching him, he immediately arose, purred loudly, rubbed against my hand, and appeared delighted with my notice. This, then, was the very creature of which I was in search. I at once offered to purchase it of the landlord; but this person made no claim to it—knew nothing of it—had never seen it before.

I continued my caresses, and when I prepared to go home, the animal evinced a disposition to accompany me. I permitted it to do so; occasionally stopping and patting it as I proceeded. When it reached the house it domesticated itself at once, and became immediately a great favorite of my wife.

For my own part, I soon found a dislike to it arising within me. This was just the reverse of what I had anticipated; but—I know not how or why it was—its evident fondness for myself rather disgusted and annoyed me. By slow degrees these feelings of disgust and annoyance rose into the bitterness of hatred. I avoided the creature; a certain sense of shame, and the remembrance of my former deed of cruelty, preventing me from physically abusing it. I did not, for some weeks, strike or otherwise violently ill use it; but gradually—very gradually—I came to look upon it with unutterable loathing, and to flee silently from its odious presence, as from the breath of a pestilence.

What added, no doubt, to my hatred of the beast, was the discovery, on the morning after I brought it home, that, like Pluto, it also had been deprived of one of its eyes. The circumstance, however, only endeared it to my wife, who, as I have already said, possessed, in a high degree, that humanity of feeling which had once been my distinguishing trait, and the source of many of my simplest and purest pleasures.

With my aversion to this cat, however, its partiality for myself seemed to increase. It followed my footsteps with a pertinacity which it would be difficult to make the reader comprehend. Whenever I sat, it would crouch beneath my chair, or spring upon my knees, covering me with its loathsome caresses. If I arose to walk it would get between my feet and thus nearly throw me down, or, fastening its long and sharp claws in my dress, clamber, in this manner, to my breast. At such times, although I longed to destroy it with a blow, I was yet withheld from so doing, partly by a memory of my former crime, but chiefly—let me confess it at once—by absolute *dread* of

This dread was not exactly a dread of physical evil—and yet I should be at a loss how otherwise to define it. I am almost ashamed to own—yes, even in this felon's cell, I am almost ashamed to own—that the terror and horror with which the animal inspired me, had been heightened by one of the merest chimeras it would be possible to conceive. My wife had called my attention, more than once, to the character of the mark of white hair, of which I have spoken, and which constituted the sole visible difference between the strange beast and the one I had destroyed. The reader will remember that his mark, although large, had been originally very indefinite; but, by slow degrees—degrees nearly imperceptible, and which for a long time my reason struggled to reject as fanciful—it had, at length, assumed a rigorous distinctness of outline. It was now the representation of an object that I shudder to name—and for this, above all, I loathed, and dreaded, and would have rid myself of the monster had I dared—it was now, I say, the image of a hideous—of a ghastly thing—of the GALLOWS!—oh, mournful and terrible engine of Horror and of Crime—of Agony and of Death!

And now was I indeed wretched beyond the wretchedness of mere Humanity. And *a brute beast*—whose fellow I had contemptuously destroyed—*a brute beast* to work out for *me*—for me, a man fashioned in the image of the High God—so much of insufferable woe! Alas! neither by day nor by night knew I the blessing of rest any more! During the former the creature left me no moment alone, and in the latter I started hourly from dreams of unutterable fear to find the hot breath of *the thing* upon my face, and its vast weight—an incarnate nightmare that I had no power to shake off—incumbent eternally upon my *heart*!

Beneath the pressure of torments such as these the feeble remnant of the good within me succumbed. Evil thoughts became my sole intimates—the darkest and most evil thoughts. The moodiness of my usual temper increased to hatred of all things and of all mankind; while from the sudden, frequent, and ungovernable outbursts of a fury to which I now blindly abandoned myself, my uncomplaining wife, alas, was the most usual and the most patient of sufferers.

One day she accompanied me, upon some household errand, into the cellar of the old building which our poverty compelled us to inhabit. The cat followed me down the steep stairs, and, nearly throwing me headlong, exasperated me to madness. Uplifting an axe, and forgetting in my wrath the childish dread which had hitherto stayed my hand, I aimed a blow at the animal, which, of course, would have proved instantly fatal had it descended as I wished. But this blow was arrested by the hand of my wife. Goaded by the interference into a rage more than demoniacal, I withdrew my arm from her grasp and buried the axe in her brain. She fell dead upon the spot without a groan.

This hideous murder accomplished, I set myself forthwith, and with entire deliberation, to the task of concealing the body. I knew that I could not remove it from the house, either by day or by night, without the risk of being observed by the neighbors. Many projects entered my mind. At one period I thought of cutting the corpse into minute fragments, and destroying them by fire. At another, I resolved to dig a grave for it in the floor of the cellar. Again, I deliberated about casting it in the well in the yard—about packing it in a box, as if merchandise, with the usual arrangements, and so getting a porter to take it from the house. Finally I hit upon what I considered a far better expedient than either of these. I determined to wall it up in the cellar, as the monks of the Middle Ages are recorded to have walled up their victims.

For a purpose such as this the cellar was well adapted. Its walls were loosely constructed, and had lately been plastered throughout with a rough plaster, which the dampness of the atmosphere had prevented from hardening. Moreover, in one of the walls was a projection, caused by a false chimney, or fireplace, that had been filled up and made to resemble the rest of the cellar. I made no doubt that I could readily displace the bricks at this point, insert the corpse, and wall the whole up as before, so that no eye could detect any thing suspicious.

And in this calculation I was not deceived. By means of a crowbar I easily dislodged the bricks, and, having carefully deposited the body against the inner wall, I propped it in that position, while with little trouble I relaid the whole structure as it originally stood. Having procured mortar, sand, and hair, with every possible precaution, I prepared a plaster which could not be distinguished from the old, and with this I very carefully went over the new brick-work. When I had finished, I felt satisfied that all was right. The wall did not present the slightest appearance of having been disturbed. The rubbish on the floor was picked up with the minutest care. I looked around triumphantly, and said to myself: "Here at least, then, my labor has not been in vain."

My next step was to look for the beast which had been the cause of so much wretchedness; for I had, at length, firmly resolved to put it to death. Had I been able to meet with it at the moment, there could have been no doubt of its fate; but it appeared that the crafty animal had been alarmed at the violence of my previous anger, and forbore to present itself in my present mood. It is impossible to describe or to imagine the deep, the blissful sense of relief which the absence of the detested creature occasioned in my bosom. It did not make its appearance during the night; and thus for one night, at least, since its introduction into the house, I soundly and tranquilly slept; aye, *slept* even with the burden of murder upon my soul.

The second and the third day passed, and still my tormentor came not. Once again I breathed as a freeman. The monster, in terror, had fled the premises for ever! I should behold it no more! My happiness was supreme! The guilt of my dark deed disturbed me but little. Some few inquiries had been made, but these had been readily answered. Even a search had been instituted—but of course nothing was to be discovered. I looked upon my future felicity as secured.

Upon the fourth day of the assassination, a party of the police came, very unexpectedly, into the house, and proceeded again to make rigorous investigation of the premises. Secure, however, in the inscrutability of my place of concealment, I felt no embarrassment whatever. The officers bade me accompany them in their search. They left no nook or corner unexplored. At length, for the third or fourth time, they descended to the cellar. I quivered not in a muscle. My heart beat calmly as that of one who slumbers in innocence. I walked the cellar from end to end. I folded my arms upon my bosom, and roamed easily to and fro. The police were thoroughly satisfied and prepared to depart. The glee at my heart was too strong to be restrained. I burned to say if but one word, by way of triumph, and to render doubly sure their assurance of my guiltlessness.

"Gentlemen," I said at last, as the party ascended the steps, "I delight to have allayed your suspicions. I wish you all health and a little more courtesy. By the bye, gentlemen, this—this is a very well-constructed house," (in the rabid desire to say something easily, I scarcely knew what I uttered at all),—"I may say an *excellently* well-constructed house. These walls—are you going, gentlemen?—these walls are solidly put together"; and here, through the mere frenzy of bravado, I rapped heavily with a cane which I held in my hand, upon that very portion of the brickwork behind which stood the corpse of the wife of my bosom.

But may God shield and deliver me from the fangs of the Arch-Fiend! No sooner had the reverberation of my blows sunk into silence, than I was answered by a voice from within the tomb!—by a cry, at first muffled and broken, like the sobbing of a child, and then quickly swelling into one long, loud, and continuous scream, utterly anomalous and inhuman—a howl—a wailing shriek, half of horror and half of triumph, such as might have arisen only out of hell, conjointly from the throats of the damned in their agony and of the demons that exult in the damnation.

Of my own thoughts it is folly to speak. Swooning, I staggered to the opposite wall. For one instant the party on the stairs remained motionless, through extremity of terror and awe. In the next a dozen stout arms were toiling at the wall. It fell bodily. The corpse, already greatly decayed and clotted with gore, stood erect before the eyes of the spectators. Upon its head, with red extended mouth and solitary eye of fire, sat the hideous beast whose craft had seduced me into murder, and whose informing voice had consigned me to the hangman. I had walled the monster up within the tomb.

Questions on "The Black Cat"

1. What is the sequence of events in this story? Are they external or internal?
2. Who is the narrator? What is the point of view used by the author?
3. Can we trust the narrator? Is he sane?
4. What is the author's purpose in writing this story?
5. If you have read any other stories by Poe, in what ways is this one similar or different?
6. What is the author's point of view here?
7. What is the "single effect" the author wishes to create in this tale? Isolate words from the first paragraph that contribute to that effect. Why did Poe use so many words in the first paragraph to build to an effect?
8. Where is the narrator in the first paragraph? Why? What will happen to him tomorrow?
9. Explain perverseness and discuss why the narrator feels these impulses.
10. Isolate and explain the purpose of the symbols used here.
11. What is the tone and mood of this tale?

Sample Essay Questions

1. How does "The Black Cat" illustrate Poe's theory of the "well-made tale"? Time—30 minutes.

2. Many twentieth-century short story writers, while acknowledging the importance of Poe's theories, have derided the "well-made tale" as artificial and contrived. Support or attack this point of view, using "The Black Cat" as proof. Time—45 minutes.

Answers to Questions on "The Black Cat"

1. The main character, driven mad by drink, has undergone a complete change of character. Previously docile and even-tempered, drink has transformed him into a madman who tortures animals and finally kills his wife. He is sentenced to die on the morrow. The events are internal, and we follow his thoughts in a flashback.
2. The narrator is not to be confused with the author—Poe did not kill anyone or torture small animals; even his highly-publicized drinking has been recently thought to be undiagnosed diabetes. The point of view is first-person participant.
3. The narrator is insane when under the influence of drink, but sane when he recounts the events here.
4. Using the conventional nineteenth-century notions of the effects of drink—it was widely believed that excessive drinking would drive men mad—Poe is entertaining us for a few hours. This is not a temperance tract.
5. Poe wrote three main "types" of stories: horror, detective, and "arabesques and grotesques," which were tales of weird and fantastic events. This story follows the pattern of his horror tales.
6. He is not entering into the morality of the character's action, for this is a tale to entice you through horror and entertain you for a few hours.
7. The effect is horror and terror, and words such as "wild," "terrified," "torture," and "horror" contribute to it. Poe felt that it was vital to establish the effect in the very first paragraph, and all words he used had to contribute to the effect.
8. The narrator is in jail for the murder of his wife, and he will be killed tomorrow.
9. Perverseness is the desire or the compulsion to do that which you know is wrong and destructive. The narrator acts this way because of drink.
10. Gallows, the bas-relief of the cat, the murder of the wife, all contribute to the horror.
11. The tone/mood is one of horror and terror.

Suggestions for Essay Answers

1. The "well-made tale" has a clear beginning, middle, and end. Discuss the divisions within this tale, showing how each is clearly defined. Then, consider the "single effect" he so highly prized—"terror, passion, or horror." This story is rich in terror and horror, and a good focal point would be the scene where the narrator sinks the ax into his wife's skull and then buries her in the wall. The mutilation of the cat, carving out its eyeball, would also establish this point. Finally, you could discuss how the topic paragraph immediately establishes the "single effect" and isolate the words and phrases that do so.
2. Your answer here will depend on your point of view concerning the "well-made tale."

If you like it . . .	If you dislike it . . .
Single effect of horror entertaining Story can easily be read within one sitting Unified, with beginning, middle, end; you know what's happening to each of the characters and can follow the plot	Single effect of horror is dull, need additional themes. You prefer longer less compressed tales. Predictable, with beginning, middle, and end; you prefer "slice of life" tales *you* have have to piece together to fully understand.

Let's examine a tale from Nathaniel Hawthorne in the same manner. Use specific details drawn from the tale to support your point of view.

THE BIRTHMARK
by Nathaniel Hawthorne

In the latter part of the last century there lived a man of science, an eminent proficient in every branch of natural philosophy, who not long before our story opens had made experience of a spiritual affinity more attractive than any chemical one. He had left his laboratory to the care of an assistant, cleared his fine countenance from the furnace smoke, washed the stain of acids from his fingers, and persuaded a beautiful woman to become his wife. In those days when the comparatively recent discovery of electricity and other kindred mysteries of Nature seemed to open paths into the region of miracle, it was not unusual for the love of science to rival the love of woman in its depth and absorbing energy. The higher intellect, the imagination, the spirit, and even the heart might all find their congenial aliment in pursuits which, as some of their ardent votaries believed, would ascend from one step of powerful intelligence to another, until the philosopher should lay his hand on the secret of creative force and perhaps make new worlds for himself. We know not whether Aylmer possessed this degree of faith in man's ultimate control over Nature. He had devoted himself, however, too unreservedly to scientific studies ever to be weaned from them by any second passion. His love for his young wife might prove the stronger of the two; but it could only be by interwining itself with his love of science, and uniting the strength of the latter to his own.

Such a union accordingly took place, and was attended with truly remarkable consequences and a deeply impressive moral. One day, very soon after their marriage, Aylmer sat gazing at his wife with a trouble in his countenance that grew stronger until he spoke.

"Georgiana," said he, "has it never occurred to you that the mark upon your cheek might be removed?"

"No, indeed," said she, smiling; but perceiving the seriousness of his manner, she blushed deeply. "To tell you the truth it has been so often called a charm that I was simple enough to imagine it might be so."

"Ah, upon another face perhaps it might," replied her husband; "but never on yours. No, dearest Georgiana, you came so nearly perfect from the hand of Nature that this slightest possible defect, which we hesitate whether to term a defect or a beauty, shocks me, as being the visible mark of earthly imperfection."

"Shocks you, my husband!" cried Georgiana, deeply hurt; at first reddening with momentary anger, but then bursting into tears. "Then why did you take me from my mother's side? You cannot love what shocks you!"

To explain this conversation it must be mentioned that in the center of Georgiana's left cheek there was a singular mark, deeply interwoven, as it were, with the texture and substance of her face. In the usual state of her complexion—a healthy though delicate bloom—the mark wore a tint of deeper crimson, which imperfectly defined its shape amid the surrounding rosiness. When she blushed it gradually became more indistinct, and finally vanished amid the triumphant rush of blood that bathed the whole cheek with its brilliant glow. But if any shifting motion caused her to turn pale there was the mark again, a crimson stain upon the snow, in what Aylmer sometimes deemed an almost fearful distinctness. Its shape bore not a little similarity to the human hand, though of the smallest pygmy size. Georgiana's lovers were wont to say that some fairy at her birth hour had laid her tiny hand upon the infant's cheek, and left this impress there in token of the magic endowments that were to give her such sway over all hearts. Many a desperate swain would have risked life for the privilege of pressing his lips to the mysterious hand. It must not be concealed, however, that the impression wrought by this fairy sign manual varied exceedingly, according to the difference of temperament in the beholders. Some fastidious persons—but they were exclusively of her own sex—affirmed that the bloody hand, as they chose to call it, quite destroyed the effect of Georgiana's beauty, and rendered her countenance even hideous. But it would be as reasonable to say that one of those small blue stains which sometimes occur in the purest statuary marble would convert the Eve of Powers to a monster. Masculine observers, if the birthmark did not heighten their admiration, contented themselves with wishing it away, that the world might possess one living specimen of ideal loveliness without the semblance of a flaw. After his marriage,—for he thought little or nothing of the matter before,—Aylmer discovered that this was the case with himself.

Had she been less beautiful,—if Envy's self could have found aught else to sneer at,—he might have felt his affection heightened by the prettiness of this mimic hand, now vaguely portrayed, now lost, now stealing forth again and glimmering to and fro with every pulse of emotion that throbbed within her heart; but seeing her otherwise so perfect, he found this one defect grow more and more intolerable with every moment of their united lives. It was the fatal flaw of humanity which Nature, in one shape or another, stamps ineffaceably on all her productions, either to imply that they are temporary and finite, or that their perfection must be wrought by toil and pain. The crimson hand expressed the ineludible grip in which mortality clutches the highest and purest of earthly mould, degrading them into kindred with the lowest, and even with the very brutes, like whom their visible frames return to dust. In this manner, selecting it as the symbol of his wife's liability to sin, sorrow, decay, and death, Aylmer's sombre imagination was not long in rendering the birthmark a frightful object, causing him more trouble and horror than ever Georgiana's beauty, whether of soul or sense, had given him delight.

At all the seasons which should have been their happiest, he invariably and without intending it, nay, in spite of a purpose to the contrary, reverted to this one disastrous topic. Trifling as it at first appeared, it so connected itself with innumerable trains of thought and models of feeling that it became the central point of all. With the morning twilight Aylmer opened his eyes upon his wife's face and recognized the symbol of imperfection; and when they sat together at the evening hearth his eyes wandered stealthily to her cheek, and beheld, flickering with the blaze of the wood fire, the spectral hand that wrote mortality where he would fain have worshipped. Georgiana soon learned to shudder at his gaze. It needed but a glance with the peculiar expression that his face often wore to change the roses of her cheek into a deathlike paleness, amid which the crimson hand was brought strongly out, like a bas-relief of ruby on the whitest marble.

Late one night when the lights were growing dim, so as hardly to betray the stain on the poor wife's cheek, she herself, for the first time, voluntarily took up the subject.

"Do you remember, my dear Aylmer," said she, with a feeble attempt at a smile, "have you any recollection of a dream last night about this odious hand?"

"None! none whatever!" replied Aylmer, starting; but then he added, in a dry, cold tone, affected for the sake of concealing the real depth of his emotion, "I might well dream of it; for before I fell asleep it had taken a pretty firm hold of my fancy."

"And did you dream of it?" continued Georgiana, hastily; for she dreaded lest a gush of tears should interrupt what she had to say. "A terrible dream! I should wonder that you can forget it. Is it possible to forget this one expression?—'It is in her heart now; we must have it out!' Reflect, my husband; for by all means I would have you recall that dream."

The mind is in a sad state when Sleep, the all-involving, cannot confine her spectres within the dim region of her sway, but suffers them to break forth, affrighting this actual life with secrets that perchance belong to a deeper one. Aylmer now remembered his dream. He had fancied himself with his servant Aminadab, attempting an operation for the removal of the birthmark; but the deeper went the knife, the deeper sank the hand, until at length its tiny grasp appeared to have caught hold of Georgiana's heart; whence, however,

her husband was inexorably resolved to cut or wrench it away.

When the dream had shaped itself perfectly in his memory, Aylmer sat in his wife's presence with a guilty feeling. Truth often finds its way to the mind close muffled in robes of sleep, and then speaks with uncompromising directness of matters in regard to which we practise an unconscious self-deception during our waking moments. Until now he had not been aware of the tyrannizing influence acquired by one idea over his mind, and of the lengths which he might find in his heart to go for the sake of giving himself peace.

"Aylmer," resumed Georgiana, solemnly, "I know not what may be the cost to both of us to rid me of this fatal birthmark. Perhaps its removal may cause cureless deformity; or it may be the stain goes as deep as life itself. Again: do we know that there is a possibility, on any terms, of unclasping the firm gripe of this little hand which was laid upon me before I came into the world?"

"Dearest Georgiana, I have spent much thought upon the subject," hastily interrupted Aylmer. "I am convinced of the perfect practicability of its removal."

"If there be the remotest possibility of it," continued Georgiana, "let the attempt be made at whatever risk. Danger is nothing to me; for life, while this hateful mark makes me the object of your horror and disgust—life is a burden which I would fling down with joy. Either remove this dreadful hand, or take my wretched life! You have deep science. All the world bears witness of it. You have achieved great wonders. Cannot you remove this little, little mark, which I cover with the tips of two small fingers? Is this beyond your power, for the sake of your own peace, and to save your poor wife from madness?"

"Noblest, dearest, tenderest wife," cried Aylmer, rapturously, "doubt not my power. I have already given this matter the deepest thought—thought which might almost have enlightened me to create a being less perfect than yourself. Georgiana, you have led me deeper than ever into the heart of science. I feel myself fully competent to render this dear cheek as faultless as its fellow; and then, most beloved, what will be my triumph when I shall have corrected what Nature left imperfect in her fairest work! Even Pygmalion, when his sculptured woman assumed life, felt no greater ecstasy than mine will be."

"It is resolved then," said Georgiana, faintly smiling. "And, Aylmer, spare me not, though you should find the birthmark take refuge in my heart at last."

Her husband tenderly kissed her cheek—her right cheek—not that which bore the impress of the crimson hand.

The next day Alymer apprised his wife of a plan that he had formed whereby he might have opportunity for the intense thought and constant watchfulness which the proposed operation would require; while Georgiana, likewise, would enjoy the perfect repose essential to its success. They were to seclude themselves in the extensive apartments occupied by Aylmer as a laboratory, and where, during his toilsome youth, he had made discoveries in the elemental powers of Nature that had roused the admiration of all the learned societies in Europe. Seated calmly in this laboratory, the pale philosopher had investigated the secrets of the highest cloud region and of the profoundest mines; he had satisfied himself of the causes that kindled and kept alive the fires of the volcano; and had explained the mystery of fountains, and how it is that they gush forth, some so bright and pure, and others with such rich medicinal virtues, from the dark bosom of the earth. Here, too, at an earlier period, he had studied the wonders of the human frame, and attempted to fathom the very process by which Nature assimilates all her precious influences from earth and air, and from the spiritual world, to create and foster man, her masterpiece. The latter pursuit, however, Aylmer had long laid aside to unwilling recognition of the truth—that our great creative Mother, while she amuses us with apparently working in the broadest sunshine, is yet severely careful to keep her own secrets, and, in spite of her pretended openness, shows us nothing but results. She permits us, indeed, to mar, but seldom to mend, and, like a jealous patentee, on no account to make. Now, however, Aylmer resumed these half-forgotten investigations; not, of course, with such hopes or wishes as first suggested them; but because they involved much physiological truth and lay in the path of his proposed scheme for the treatment of Georgiana.

As he led her over the threshold of the laboratory, Georgiana was cold and tremulous. Aylmer looked cheerfully into her face, with intent to reassure her, but was so startled with the intense glow of the birthmark upon the whiteness of her cheek that he could not restrain a strong convulsive shudder. His wife fainted.

"Aminadab! Aminadab!" shouted Aylmer, stamping violently on the floor.

Forthwith there issued from an inner apartment a man of low stature, but bulky frame, with shaggy hair hanging about his visage, which was grimed with the vapors of the furnace. This personage had been Aylmer's underworker during his whole scientific career, and was admirably fitted for that office by his great mechanical readiness, and the skill with which, while incapable of comprehending a single principle, he executed all the details of his master's experiments. With his vast strength, his shaggy hair, his smoky aspect, and the indescribable earthiness that incrusted him, he seemed to represent man's physical nature; while Aylmer's slender figure, and pale, intellectual face, were no less apt a type of the spiritual element.

"Throw open the door of the boudoir, Aminadab," said Aylmer, "burn a pastil."

"Yes, master," answered Aminadab, looking intently at the lifeless form of Georgiana; and then he muttered to himself, "If she were my wife, I'd never part with that birthmark."

When Georgiana recovered consciousness she found herself breathing an atmosphere of penetrating fragrance, the gentle potency of which had recalled her from her deathlike faintness. The scene around her looked like enchantment. Aylmer had converted those smoky, dingy, sombre rooms, where he had spent his brightest years in recondite pursuits, into a series of beautiful apartments not unfit to be the secluded abode of a lovely woman. The walls were hung with gorgeous curtains, which imparted the combination of grandeur and grace that no other species of adornment can achieve; and as they fell from the ceiling to the floor, their rich and ponderous folds, concealing all angles and straight lines, appeared to shut in the scene from infinite space. For aught Georgiana knew, it might be a pavilion among the clouds. And Aylmer, excluding the sunshine, which would have interfered with his chemical processes, had supplied its place with perfumed lamps, emitting flames of various hue, but all uniting in a soft, impurpled radiance. He now knelt by his wife's side, watching her earnestly, but without alarm; for he was confident in his science, and felt that he could draw a magic circle round her within which no evil might intrude.

"Where am I? Ah, I remember," said Georgiana, faintly; and she placed her hand over her cheek to hide the terrible mark from her husband's eyes.

"Fear not, dearest!" exclaimed he. "Do not shrink from me! Believe me, Georgiana, I even rejoice in this single imperfection, since it will be such a rapture to remove it."

"Oh, spare me!" sadly replied his wife. "Pray do not look at it again. I never can forget that convulsive shudder."

In order to soothe Georgiana, and, as it were to release her mind from the burden of actual things, Aylmer now put in practice some of the light and playful secrets which science had taught him among its profounder lore. Airy figures, absolutely bodiless ideas, and forms of unsubstantial beauty came and danced before her, imprinting their momentary footsteps on beams of light. Though she had some indistinct idea of the method of these optical phenomena, still the illusion was almost perfect enough to warrant the belief that her husband possessed sway over the spiritual world. Then again, when she felt a wish to look forth from her seclusion, immediately, as if her thoughts were answered, the procession of external existence flitted across a screen. The scenery and the figures of actual life were perfectly represented, but with that bewitching, yet indescribable difference which always makes a picture, an image, or a shadow so much more attractive than the original. When wearied of this, Aylmer bade her cast her eyes upon a vessel containing a quantity of earth. She did so, with little interest at first; but was soon startled to perceive the germ of a plant shooting upward from the soil. Then came the slender stalk; the leaves gradually unfolded themselves; and amid them was a perfect and lovely flower.

"It is magical!" cried Georgiana. "I dare not touch it."

"Nay, pluck it," answered Aylmer,—"pluck it, and inhale its brief perfume while you may. The flower will wither in a few moments and leave nothing save its brown seed vessels; but thence may be perpetuated a race as ephemeral as itself."

But Georgiana had no sooner touched the flower than the whole plant suffered a blight, its leaves turning coal-black as if by the agency of fire.

To make up for this abortive experiment, he proposed to take her portrait by a scientific process of his own invention. It was to be effected by rays of light striking upon a polished plate of metal. Georgiana assented; but, on looking at the result, was affrighted to find the features of the portrait blurred and indefinable; while the minute figure of a hand appeared where the cheek should have been. Aylmer snatched the metallic plate and threw it into a jar of corrosive acid.

Soon, however, he forgot these mortifying failures. In the intervals of study and chemical experiment he came to her flushed and exhausted, but seemed invigorated by her presence, and spoke in glowing language of the resources of his art. He gave a history of the long dynasty of the alchemists, who spent so many ages in quest of the universal solvent by which the golden principle might be elicted from all things vile and base. Aylmer appeared to believe that, by the plainest scientific logic, it was altogether within the limits of possibility to discover this long-sought medium; "but," he added, "a philospher who should go deep enough to acquire the power would attain too lofty a wisdom to stoop to the exercise of it." Not less singular were his opinions in regard to the elixir vitæ. He more than intimated that it was at his option to concoct a liquid that should prolong life for years, perhaps interminably; but that it would produce a discord in Nature which all the world, and chiefly the quaffer of the immortal nostrum, would find cause to curse.

"Aylmer, are you in earnest?" asked Georgiana, looking at him with amazement and fear. "It is terrible to possess such power, or even to dream of possessing it."

"Oh, do not tremble, my love," said her husband. "I would not wrong either you or myself by working such inharmonious effects upon our lives; but I would have you consider how trifling, in comparison, is the skill requisite to remove this little hand."

At the mention of the birthmark, Georgiana, as usual, shrank as if a redhot iron had touched her cheek.

Again Aylmer applied himself to his labors. She could hear his voice in the distant furnace room giving directions to Aminadab, whose harsh, uncouth, mis-shapen tones were audible in response, more likely the grunt or growl of a brute than human speech. After long hours of absence, Aylmer reappeared and proposed that she should now examine his cabinet of chemical products and natural treasures of the earth. Among the former he showed her a small vial, in which, he remarked, was contained a gentle yet most powerful fragrance, capable of impregnating all the breezes that blow across a kingdom. They were of inestimable value, the contents of that little vial; and, as he said so, he threw some of the perfume into the air and filled the room with piercing and invigorating delight.

"And what is this?" asked Georgiana, pointing to a small crystal globe containing a gold-colored liquid. "It is so beautiful to the eye that I could imagine it the elixir of life."

"In one sense it is," replied Aylmer; "or, rather, the elixir of immortality. It is the most precious poison that ever was concocted in this world. By its aid I could apportion the lifetime of any mortal at whom you might point your finger. The strength of the dose would determine whether he were to linger out years, or drop dead in the midst of a breath. No king on his guarded throne could keep his life if I, in my private station, should deem that the welfare of millions justified me in depriving him of it."

"Why do you keep such a terrific drug?" inquired Georgiana in horror.

"Do not mistrust me, dearest," said her husband, smiling; "its virtuous potency is yet greater than its harmful one. But see! here is a powerful cosmetic. With a few drops of this in a vase of water, freckles may be washed away as easily as the hands are cleansed. A stronger infusion would take the blood out of the cheek, and leave the rosiest beauty a pale ghost."

"Is it with this lotion that you intend to bathe my cheek?" asked Georgiana, anxiously.

"Oh, no," hastily replied her husband; "this is merely superficial. Your case demands a remedy that shall go deeper."

In his interviews with Georgiana, Aylmer generally made minute inquiries as to her sensations and whether the confinement of the rooms and the temperature of the atmosphere agreed with her. These questions had such a particular drift that Georgiana began to conjecture that she was already subjected to certain physical influences, either breathed in with the fragrant air or taken with her food. She fancied likewise, but it might be altogether fancy, that there was a stirring up of her system—a strange, indefinite sensation creeping through her veins, and tingling, half painfully, half pleasurably, at her heart. Still, whenever she dared to look into the mirror, there she beheld herself pale as a white rose and with the crimson birthmark stamped upon her cheek. Not even Alymer now hated it so much as she.

To dispel the tedium of the hours which her husband found it necessary to devote to the process of combination and analysis, Georgiana turned over the volumes of his scientific library. In many dark old tomes she met with chapters full of romance and poetry. They were the works of the philosophers of the middle ages, such as Albertus Magnus, Cornelius Agrippa, Paracelsus, and the famous friar who created the prophetic Brazen Head. All these antique naturalists stood in advance of their centuries, yet were imbued with some of their credulity, and therefore were believed, and perhaps imagined themselves to have acquired from the investigation of Nature a power above Nature, and from physics a sway over the spiritual world. Hardly less curious and imaginative were the early volumes of the Transactions of the Royal Society, in which the members, knowing little of the limits of natural possibility, were continually recording wonders or proposing methods whereby wonders might be wrought.

But to Georgiana the most engrossing volume was a large folio from her husband's own hand, in which he had recorded every experiment of his scientific career, its original aim, the methods adopted for its development, and its final success or failure, with the circumstances to which either event was attributable. The book, in truth, was both the history and emblem of his ardent, ambitious, imaginative, yet practical and laborious life. He handled physical details as if there were nothing beyond them; yet spiritualized them all, and redeemed himself from materialism by his strong and eager aspiration towards the infinite. In his grasp the veriest clod of earth assumed a soul. Georgiana, as she read, reverenced Aylmer and loved him more profoundly than ever, but with a less entire dependence on his judgment than heretofore. Much as he had accomplished, she could not but observe that his most splendid successes were almost invariably failures, if compared with the ideal at which he aimed. His brightest diamonds were the merest pebbles, and felt to be so by himself, in comparison with the inestimable gems which lay hidden beyond his reach. The volume, rich with achievements that had won renown for its author, was yet as melancholy a record as ever mortal hand had penned. It was the sad confession and continual exemplification of the shortcomings of the composite man, the spirit burdened with clay and working in matter, and of the despair that assails the higher nature at finding itself so miserably thwarted by the earthly part. Perhaps every man of genius in whatever sphere might recognize the image of his own experience in Aylmer's journal.

So deeply did these reflections affect Georgiana that she laid her face upon the open volume and burst into tears. In this situation she was found by her husband.

"It is dangerous to read in a sorcerer's books," said he, with a smile, though his countenance was uneasy and displeased. "Georgiana, there are pages in that volume which I can scarcely glance over and keep my senses. Take heed lest it prove as detrimental to you."

"It has made me worship you more than ever," said she.

"Ah, wait for this one sucess," rejoined he, "then worship me if you will. I shall deem myself hardly unworthy of it. But come, I have sought you for the luxury of your voice. Sing to me, dearest."

So she poured out the liquid music of her voice to quench the thirst of his spirit. He then took his leave with a boyish exuberance of gayety, assuring her that her seclusion would endure but a little longer, and that the result was already certain. Scarcely had he departed when Georgiana felt irresistibly impelled to follow him. She had forgotten to inform Aylmer of a symptom which for two or three hours past had begun to excite her attention. It was a sensation in the fatal birthmark, not painful, but which induced a restlessness throughout her system. Hastening after her husband, she intruded for the first time into the laboratory.

The first thing that struck her eye was the furnace, that hot and feverish worker, with the intense glow of its fire, which by the quanities of soot clustered above it seemed to have been burning for ages. There was a distilling apparatus in full operation. Around the room were retorts, tubes, cylinders, crucibles, and other apparatus of chemical research. An electrical machine stood ready for immediate use. The atmosphere felt oppressively close, and was tainted with gaseous odors which had been tormented forth by the processes of science. The severe and homely simplicitiy of the apartment, with its naked walls and brick pavement, looked strange, accustomed as Georgiana had become to the fantastic elegance of her boudoir. But what chiefly, indeed almost solely, drew her attention, was the aspect of Aylmer himself.

He was pale as death, anxious and absorbed, and hung over the furnace as it depended upon his utmost watchfulness whether the liquid which it was distilling should be the draught of immortal happiness or misery. How different from the sanguine and joyous mien that he had assumed for Georgiana's encouragement!

"Carefully now, Aminadab; carefully, thou human machine; carefully, thou man of clay!" muttered Aylmer, more to himself than his assistant. "Now, if there be a thought too much or too little, it is all over."

"Ho! ho!" mumbled Aminadab. "Look, master! look!"

Aylmer raised his eyes hastily, and at first reddened, then grew paler than ever, on beholding Georgiana. He rushed towards her arm with a gripe that left the print of his fingers and seized her fingers upon it.

"Why do you come hither? Have you no trust in your

husband?" cried he, impetuously. "Would you throw the blight of that fatal birthmark over my labors? It is not well done. Go, prying woman, go!"

"Nay, Aylmer," said Georgiana with the firmness of which she possessed no stinted endowment, "it is not you that have a right to complain. You mistrust your wife; you have concealed the anxiety with which you watch the development of this experiment. Think not so unworthily of me, my husband. Tell me all the risk we run, and fear not that I shall shrink; for my share in it is far less than your own."

"No, no, Georgiana!" said Alymer, impatiently; "it must not be."

"I submit," replied she calmly. "And, Alymer, I shall quaff whatever draught you bring me; but it will be on the same principle that would induce me to take a dose of poison if offered by your hand."

"My noble wife," said Aylmer, deeply moved, "I knew not the height and depth of your nature until now. Nothing shall be concealed. Know, then, that this crimson hand, superficial as it seems, has clutched its grasp into your being with a strength of which I had no previous conception. I have already administered agents powerful enough to do aught except to change your entire physical system. Only one thing remains to be tried. If that fail us we are ruined."

"Why did you hesitate to tell me this?" asked she.

"Because, Georgiana," said Aylmer, in a low voice, "there is danger."

"Danger? There is but one danger—that this horrible stigma shall be left upon my cheek!" cried Georgiana. "Remove it, remove it, whatever be the cost, or we shall both go mad!"

"Heaven knows your words are too true," said Aylmer, sadly. "And now, dearest, return to your boudoir. In a little while all will be tested."

He conducted her back and took leave of her with a solemn tenderness which spoke far more than his words how much was now at stake. After his departure Georgiana became rapt in musings. She considered the character of Aylmer, and did it completer justice than at any previous moment. Her heart exulted, while it trembled, at his honorable love—so pure and lofty that it would accept nothing less than perfection nor miserably make itself contented with an earthlier nature than he had dreamed of. She felt how much more precious was such a sentiment than that meaner kind which would have borne with the imperfection for her sake, and have been guilty of treason to holy love by degrading its perfect idea to the level of the actual; and with her whole spirit she prayed that, for a single moment, she might satisfy his highest and deepest conception. Longer than one moment she well knew it could not be; for his spirit was ever on the march, ever ascending, and each instant required something that was beyond the scope of the instant before.

The sound of her husband's footsteps aroused her. He bore a crystal goblet containing a liquor colorless as water, but bright enough to be the draught of immortality. Aylmer was pale; but it seemed rather the consequence of a highly-wrought state of mind and tension of spirit than of fear or doubt.

"The concoction of the draught has been perfect," said he, in answer to Georgiana's look. "Unless all my science have deceived me, it cannot fail."

"Save on your account, my dearest Aylmer," observed his wife, "I might wish to put off this birthmark of mortality by relinquishing mortality itself in preference to any other mode. Life is but a sad possession to those who have attained precisely the degree of moral advancement at which I stand. Were I weaker and blinder it might be happiness. Were I stronger, it might be endured hopefully. But, being what I find myself, methinks I am of all mortals the most fit to die."

"You are fit for heaven without tasting death!" replied her husband. "But why do we speak of dying? The draught cannot fail. Behold its effect upon this plant."

On the window seat there stood a geranium diseased with yellow blotches, which had overspread all its leaves. Aylmer poured a small quantity of the liquid upon the soil in which it grew. In a little time, when the roots of the plant had taken up the moisture, the unsightly blotches began to be extinguished in a living verdure.

"There needed no proof," said Georgiana, quietly. "Give me the goblet. I joyfully stake all upon your word."

"Drink, then, thou lofty creature!" exclaimed Aylmer, with fervid admiration. "There is no taint of imperfection on thy spirit. Thy sensible frame, too, shall soon be all perfect."

She quaffed the liquid and returned the goblet to his hand.

"It is grateful," said she with a placid smile. "Methinks it is like water from a heavenly fountain; for it contains I know not what of unobtrusive fragrance and deliciousness. It allays a feverish thirst that had parched me for many days. Now, dearest, let me sleep. My earthly senses are closing over my spirit like the leaves around the heart of a rose at sunset."

She spoke the last words with a gentle reluctance, as if it required almost more energy than she could command to pronounce the faint and lingering syllables. Scarcely had they loitered through her lips ere she was lost in slumber. Aylmer sat by her side, watching her aspect with the emotions proper to a man the whole value of whose existence was involved in the process now to be tested. Mingled with this mood, however, was the philosophic investigation characteristic of the man of science. Not the minutest symptom escaped him. A heightened flush of the cheek, a slight irregularity of breath, a quiver of the eyelid, a hardly perceptible tremor through the frame,—such were the details which, as the moments passed, he wrote down in his folio volume. Intense thought had set its stamp upon every previous page of that volume, but the thoughts of years were all concentrated upon the last.

While thus employed, he failed not to gaze often at the fatal hand, and not without a shudder. Yet once, by a strange and unaccountable impulse, he pressed it with his lips. His spirit recoiled, however, in the very act; and Georgiana, out of the midst of her deep sleep, moved uneasily and murmured as if in remonstrance. Again Aylmer resumed his watch. Nor was it without avail. The crimson hand, which at first had been strongly visible upon the marble paleness of Georgiana's cheek, now grew more faintly outlined. She remained not less pale than ever; but the birthmark, with every breath that came and went, lost somewhat of its former distinctness. Its presence had been awful; its departure was more awful still. Watch the stain of the rainbow fading out of the sky, and you will know how that mysterious symbol passed away.

"By Heaven! it is well-nigh gone!" said Aylmer to himself, in almost irrepressible ecstasy. "I can scarcely trace it now. Success! success! And now it is like the faintest rose color. The lightest flush of the blood across her cheek would overcome it. But she is so pale!"

He drew aside the window curtain and suffered the light of the natural day to fall into the room and rest upon her cheek. At the same time he heard a gross, hoarse chuckle, which he had long known as his servant Aminadab's expression of delight.

"Ah, clod! ah, earthly mass!" cried Aylmer, laughing in a sort of frenzy, "you have served me well! Matter and spirit—earth and heaven—have both done their part in this! Laugh, thing of the senses! You have earned the right to laugh!"

These exclamations broke Georgiana's sleep. She slowly unclosed her eyes and gazed into the mirror which her husband had arranged for that purpose. A faint smile flitted over her lips when she recognized how barely perceptible was now that crimson hand which had once blazed forth with such disastrous brilliancy as to scare away all their happiness. But then her eyes sought Aylmer's face with a trouble and anxiety that he could by no means account for.

"My poor Aylmer!" murmured she.

"Poor? Nay, richest, happiest, most favored!" exclaimed he. "My peerless bride, it is successful! You are perfect!"

"My poor Aylmer," she repeated, with a more than human tenderness, "you have aimed loftily; you have done nobly. Do not repent that with so high and pure a feeling, you have rejected the best the earth could offer. Aylmer, dearest Aylmer, I am dying!"

Alas! it was too true! The fatal hand had grappled with the mystery of life, and was the bond by which an angelic spirit kept itself in union with a mortal frame. As the last crimson tint of the birthmark—that sole token of human imperfection—faded from her cheek, the parting breath of the now perfect woman passed into the atmosphere, and her soul, lingering a moment near her husband, took its heavenward flight. Then a hoarse, chuckling laugh was heard again! Thus ever does the gross fatality of earth exult in its invariable triumph over the immortal essence which, in this dim sphere of half development, demands the completeness of a higher state. Yet, had Aylmer reached a profounder wisdom, he need not thus have flung away the happiness which would have woven his mortal life of the selfsame texture with the celestial. The momentary circumstance was too strong for him; he failed to look beyond the shadowy scope of time, and, living once for all in eternity, to find the perfect future in the present.

Questions on "The Birthmark"

1. Describe the tone of the story. What words and situations contribute to its creation?
2. All the characters can be described as "types." Indicate what these "types" might be and show how this stereotyping helps or hinders the story.
3. In the beginning of the story, Aylmer is depicted as a man with an all-consuming love for science. How, then, does his love for his wife fit into his life?
4. What is the theme here? What is Hawthorne saying to the reader?
5. At the time this tale was written, in the middle 1800's, Hawthorne was very close to many people who characterized themselves as Transcendentalists. Although his wife was an ardent Transcendentalist, Hawthorne never fully adopted the philosophy. The Transcendentalists held that there was some knowledge of reality that man could grasp through his intuition rather than his reason, that man and espe-

cially nature were inherently good, and that if left to his own devices, man would work things out in the best possible way for himself and his neighbors and friends. They felt that since man was good, no government was necessary (Thoreau's famous "that government is best which governs not at all"), and thus man needed no rules to control him. Hawthorne, in contrast, was drawn to the Puritan past of his ancestors, and felt that the past had a very real effect on man in the present. Show how Hawthorne was affected by Transcendentalism and then by his Puritan past. Use this story to make your case.

6. This tale can be considered an allegory, a narrative in which characters, action, and sometimes setting represent abstract concepts or moral qualities. Show how this statement is true.

7. Why do Aylmer's attempts to perfect his wife fail?

8. In what ways is this tale an example of the "well-made tale"? Consider plot, characters, unity of effect, setting, etc.

Answers to Questions on "The Birthmark"

1. The tone is heavy and somber, and there is a creepy Gothic atmosphere to the tale. The ill-omened dream, the Quasimodo-like appearance of Aminadab, Aylmer's unsuccessful experiments, and Georgiana's intrusion into the furnace room all foreshadow evil and failure. Hawthorne's old-fashioned language, such as "I shall quaff whatever draught you bring me" lends an air of strangeness to the setting. Hawthorne deliberately chose this ornate, almost archaic style to reinforce the story's eerie mood.

2. Aylmer is the mad scientist, his wife the beautiful and agreeable young lady, Aminadab the half-human lab assistant. The use of "types" helps the reader quickly recognize the character's role in the tale and allows the reader to focus on the theme rather than lengthy character identification.

3. See the last sentence of the first paragraph. Georgiana, a symbol of spirituality, ironically leads her husband deeper than ever into the mystery of science. In the end, she becomes the victim of his scientific attempts.

4. Hawthorne is telling the reader that we cannot attempt to control creation, that man is unable to attain perfection. In this he is allied to his Puritan heritage (one of his ancestors was the famous hanging judge in the Salem witchcraft trials of 1692) and its belief in God's firm control. Georgiana's tiny flaw was the hand of God, the mark that He stamps on all his creations to link them to Him. If she were to become perfect, she would be an angel, not a mortal.

5. Aylmer does not transcend or go beyond reality; rather, he looks at reality too closely. "He failed to look beyond the shadowy scope of time . . . to find the perfect future in the present." The Transcendentalists, such as Emerson and Thoreau, left no room for the darker, less cheerful view of man we find in Hawthorne's work.

6. Aylmer might stand for the higher intellect, the imagination that attempts to attain human perfection. Georgiana would stand for spiritual beauty, the earth's home for the spirit of the angels. Aminadab would be the purely physical side of man.

7. Only the Creator has the right to attempt to establish perfection, and anything that is perfect is, by definition, unsuitable for this world.

8. There is a clear beginning, middle, and end, and a "single-effect." In this case the effect is of terror and horror at what one person, acting out of love, can do to another.

Let's examine a modern tale.

THE BLANKET
by Floyd Dell

Petey hadn't really believed that Dad would be doing it—sending Granddad away. "Away" was what they were calling it. Not until now could he believe it of Dad.

But here was the blanket that Dad had that day bought for him, and in the morning he'd be going away. And this was the last evening they'd be having together. Dad was off seeing that girl he was to marry. He'd not be back till late, and they could sit up and talk.

It was a fine September night, with a silver moon riding high over the gully. When they'd washed up the supper dishes they went out on the shanty porch, the old man and the bit of a boy, taking their chairs. "I'll get me fiddle," said the old man, "and play ye some of the old tunes." But instead of the fiddle he brought out the blanket. It was a big, double blanket, red, with black cross stripes.

"Now, isn't that a fine blanket!" said the old man, smoothing it over his knees. "And isn't your father a kind man to be giving the old fellow a blanket like that to go away with? It cost something, it did—look at the wool of it! And warm it will be these cold winter nights to come. There'll be few blankets there the equal of this one!"

It was like Granddad to be saying that. He was trying to make it easier. He'd pretended all along it was he that was wanting to go away to the great brick building—the government place, where he'd be with so many other old fellows having the best of everything.... But Petey hadn't believed Dad would really do it, until this night when he brought home the blanket.

"Oh, yes it's a fine blanket," said Petey, and got up and went into the shanty. He wasn't the kind to cry, and, besides, he was too old for that, being eleven. He'd just come in to fetch Granddad's fiddle.

The blanket slid to the floor as the old man took the fiddle and stood up. It was the last night they'd be having together. There wasn't any need to say, "Play all the old tunes." Granddad tuned up for a minute, and then said, "This one you'll like to remember."

The silver moon was high overhead, and there was a gentle breeze playing down the gully. He'd never be hearing Granddad play like this again. It was as well Dad was moving into that new house, away from here. He'd not want, Petey wouldn't, to sit here on the old porch of fine evenings, with Granddad gone.

The tune changed. "Here's something gayer." Petey sat and stared out over the gully. Dad would marry that girl. Yes, that girl who'd kissed him and slobbered over him, saying she'd try to be a good mother to him, and all.... His chair creaked as he involuntarily gave his body a painful twist.

The tune stopped suddenly, and Granddad said: "It's a poor tune, except to be dancing to." And then: "It's a fine girl your father's going to marry. He'll be feeling young again, with a pretty wife like that. And what would an old fellow like me be doing around their house, getting in the way, an old nuisance, what with my talk of aches and pains! And then there'll be babies coming, and I'd not want to be there to hear them crying at all hours. It's best that I take myself off, like I'm doing. One more tune or two, and then we'll be going to bed to get some sleep against the morning, when I'll pack up my fine blanket and take my leave. Listen to this, will you? It's a bit sad, but a fine tune for a night like this."

They didn't hear the two people coming down the gully path, Dad and the pretty girl with the hard, bright face like a china doll's. But they heard her laugh, right by the porch, and the tune stopped on a wrong, high, startled note. Dad didn't say anything, but the girl came forward and spoke to Granddad prettily: "I'll not be seeing you leave in the morning, so I came over to say good-by."

"It's kind of you," said Granddad, with his eyes cast down; and then, seeing the blanket at his feet, he stopped to pick it up. "And will you look at this," he said in embarassment, "the fine blanket my son has given me to go away with!"

"Yes, she said, "it's a fine blanket." She felt of the wool, and repeated in surprise, "A fine blanket—I'll say it is!" She turned to Dad, and said to him coldly, "It cost something, that."

He cleared his throat, and said defensively, "I wanted him to have the best. . . ."

The girl stood there, still intent on the blanket. "It's double, too," she said reproachfully to Dad.

"Yes," said Granddad, "it's double—a fine blanket for an old fellow to be going away with."

The boy went abruptly into the shanty. He was looking for something. He could hear that girl reproaching Dad, and Dad becoming angry in his slow way. And now she was suddenly going away in a huff.... As Petey came out, she turned and called back, "All the same, he doesn't need a double blanket!" And she ran up the gully path.

Dad was looking after her uncertainly.

"Oh, she's right," said the boy coldly. "Here, Dad"—and he held out a pair of scissors. "Cut the blanket in two."

Both of them stared at the boy, startled. "Cut it in two, I tell you, Dad!" he cried out. "And keep the other half!"

"That's not a bad idea," said Granddad gently. "I don't need so much of a blanket."

"Yes," said the boy harshly, "a single blanket's enough for an old man when he's sent away. We'll save the other half, Dad; it will come in handy later."

"Now, what do you mean by that?" asked Dad.

"I mean," said the boy slowly, "that I'll give it to you, Dad—when you're old and I'm sending you—away."

There was a silence, and then Dad went over to Granddad and stood before him, not speaking. But Granddad understood, for he put out a hand and laid it on Dad's shoulder. Petey was watching them. And he heard Granddad whisper, "It's all right, son—I knew you didn't mean it. . . . " And then Petey cried.

But it didn't matter—because they were all three crying together.

Questions on "The Blanket"

1. What is the predominant symbol in this tale?
   (A) The fiddle
   (B) The blanket
   (C) The china doll
   (D) The moon
   (E) The scissors

2. What does that main symbol represent?
   (A) The problems of the aged in America
   (B) The enormous rise in divorce and remarriage with all its attendant problems
   (C) The father's attempt to assuage his guilt
   (D) The difficulty of life in rural America
   (E) The importance of cutting bonds and knowing when to let go

3. What is the theme of this story?
   (A) Things were rough for this family, and however unpleasant it may be, it was necessary to hold on to good items like blankets.
   (B) The old man got exactly what was his due.
   (C) Unintentionally, we all do cruel and unpleasant things.
   (D) It can be very difficult having old people around, especially if there is a remarriage.
   (E) Things have changed greatly over the past fifty years.

4. What is the author saying about old age and the difference between generations?
   (A) There really is an enormous difference between the three generations.
   (B) Old age is a golden time.
   (C) It is better to be young than old.
   (D) There is no real "generation gap": we will all be old someday.
   (E) The old are very poorly treated as a general rule.

5. What is the overall tone of this story?
   (A) Melancholic
   (B) Cheerful
   (C) Uplifting
   (D) Sardonic
   (E) Sarcastic

6. The girl is described as a "china doll"
   (A) to show how callow she was
   (B) to show how pretty she was
   (C) to indicate her concern for Granddad, however muted it may appear on the surface
   (D) to indicate what a good wife she would be
   (E) to indicate what a suitable wife she would be

7. The term "china doll" was selected to describe the girl because
   (A) she is very, very pretty and uses cosmetics to the best advantage
   (B) her "hard, bright face" reveals her true nature
   (C) it explains why Petey and Granddad admire her
   (D) she has very fine manners, revealed when she says goodbye to Granddad
   (E) she is like a doll

8. What is the tone of paragraphs 7 to 9?
   (A) Revulsion
   (B) Quiet happiness
   (C) Peaceful contentment
   (D) Bitter resentment
   (E) Sadness and pain

9. How is Granddad's tone in paragraph 10 different from Petey's tone in paragraphs 19–24?
   (A) Brave resignation to bitter sarcasm

(B) Clever subterfuge to childlike solemnity
(C) Disguised sarcasm to cold fear
(D) Melancholy gaiety to bewildered confusion
(E) Open bitterness to bitter sarcasm

10. The "blanket" connotes
    (A) death
    (B) suffocation
    (C) warmth
    (D) marriage
    (E) old age

11. The word "shanty" suggests
    (A) a broad, expansive country estate
    (B) a well-to-do-family
    (C) an historic old home
    (D) a family living a lower-middle-class existence
    (E) abject poverty

12. The "scissors" best represent
    (A) severing the bonds of love, duty, respect
    (B) severing the bonds of unpleasant duty
    (C) cutting loose from that which is holding you back

(D) cutting dead weight
(E) assuming new freedoms and human possibility

13. The point of view in this story is most closely
    (A) first-person observer
    (B) first-person participant
    (C) omniscient
    (D) editorial omniscient
    (E) limited omniscient

14. The story is most closely related to the literary movement known as
    (A) Realism
    (B) Surrealism
    (C) Symbolism
    (D) Naturalism
    (E) Graveyard school

15. Granddad's attitude can best be described as
    (A) considerate and understanding
    (B) carefully controlled resentment toward his son's fiancée
    (C) anxious and worried
    (D) bitter but resigned to the treatment he is receiving
    (E) understandably very upset

Answers to Questions on "The Blanket"

1. (B) A blanket is a symbol of warmth, comfort, home. Obviously, the symbol is being used here in an ironic manner, as that is what is being denied to Granddad.
2. (C) The father feels that by giving his father the best blanket he can buy, he will somehow feel better about sending the old man to the government home.
3. (C) The father did not really mean to be cruel, as evidenced by the ending which shows his love for his father.
4. (D) Petey's line about saving the other half of the blanket for *his* father when he sends *him* away tells us this.
5. (A) This is a melancholy, sad story, as we feel the sad music and lonely times bred by misunderstanding and conflict.
6. (A) "Callow" means shallow and superficial.
7. (B) "Hard and bright" are used to show that she is a cold and unfeeling person; she begrudges the double blanket for the old man, feeling a single would have been more than enough.
8. (E) Petey is sad that he will never hear his grandfather play again, and that his father's wife will "slobber" all over him in her insincere attempts to be a mother to him.
9. (A) Granddad is putting on a brave front about the situation; Petey is being cold and sarcastic when he offers to cut the blanket in two to save the cost of another to send *his* father away with.
10. (C) The good wool blanket is intended to comfort Granddad in his old age.
11. (E) A shanty is a poor hovel.

12. (A) By offering to cut the blanket, Petey is saying that if that is the way you, Dad, treat your father, you can expect me to treat you that way too.
13. (C) The narrator is all-knowing.
14. (A) This is a realistic view of the problems many families face with aged parents and remarriage. See definitions of all other literary movements.
15. (A) We must understand that Granddad is not being sarcastic in what he says; he honestly attempts to see his son's point of view.

ESSAY QUESTIONS ON THE SHORT STORY

Directions: Allow yourself 45 minutes to organize, write, and correct an essay on each of the following topics. Follow the directions for generating and organizing your thoughts as described in **Part 2: Essay Writing Guide**. Be sure to leave time to revise and edit your essay at the end. Suggestions for answers follow the questions.

1. Compare the use of language in any two short stories by different authors. Establish the level of diction (elevated, conversational, colloquial, etc.) and sentence structure (simple, compound, complex) as well as punctuation. Then, cite specific examples to prove the difference between the stories.

2. Discuss how James Joyce uses symbols to convey his theme in any two stories from *Dubliners*.

3. Although he lived during the 1850's, Hawthorne often drew from the Puritan past of the 1600's for his themes of guilt and sin. Show how this is evident in any one of his short stories, drawing specific examples from the tale under discussion.

4. Some collections of short stories are so structured that the stories can be read either individually or as a unit. Individually, they have all the elements that we have come to expect from a short story, but when taken as a whole, the collection works as a novel, with each story, functioning as a chapter, adding something incremental to the plot. Discuss how this is true for one of the following: Joyce's *Dubliners*, Anderson's *Winesburg, Ohio*, or the short stories of F. Scott Fitzgerald or Ernest Hemingway.

5. There are many ways an author can convey his meaning to his audience, but the short story writer, because of the limitations of space, often must telescope his message. Thus we find that some short story writers rely a great deal on the use of symbols to compress a lot of meaning into a short space. Select any one of the short story writers from the list below, or any other writer of equal stature, and show how he/she uses symbols to convey theme effectively in a short story.

Hawthorne	Conrad	James, Henry
Joyce	Lawrence	Mann
Porter, K.A.	Anderson	Hemingway

6. Discuss how the personality of a main character from a short story is established through the use of dialogue. Include as many specific examples as possible.

7. Show how the images from any one short story are consistent, drawn from the same source. These sources may include nature, animals, etc. Then, show how the images determine the theme of the tale.

8. Some authors focus on particular symbols in their tales: One of the most striking is the use of color. Show how any of the following short story writers, or any

others of the same stature, use color symbols in any one of their tales.

Joyce Lawrence Porter Anderson

9. Some short story writers focus on the psychological aspect of man's life to create tales that probe the unconscious. Select any one tale and show how the author uncovers the inner workings of a character's mind.

10. The setting of a short story can often be a pivotal factor in the development of theme. Show how this is true in any one tale.

11. Select any short story and describe how the author's specific choice of words establishes the tone.

12. Show how the ending of any short story is foreshadowed by the beginning. Discuss symbol, image, characterization, and so forth to establish your thesis.

13. Select any short story from the "modern school" (Chekhov, Mansfield, James, Joyce, etc.) and contrast it to any story from the "traditional school" (Poe, Dickens, O. Henry, etc.). Using symbol, image, characterization, tone, mood, etc., show how the tales are different and the same.

Suggestions for Answering Essay Questions on the Short Story

1. Differences in the use of language are especially clear between Edgar Allan Poe and Anton Chekhov, or Daniel Defoe and Katherine Mansfield, or Ernest Hemingway and Charles Dickens. Hemingway, for example, uses simple sentences, commas rather than semicolons, and conversational or colloquial diction. Dickens uses complex sentences and, by twentieth-century standards, far more elevated diction.

2. "Clay" uses the symbol of clay to describe Maria's life, while "The Dead" uses the symbol of snow to show what happened to Gabriel's feelings. None of Joyce's stories is discussed here because of space limitations, but the work bears looking into on your own.

3. In "Roger Malvin's Burial," for example, we see how Reuben Borne must bear the guilt for leaving his father-in-law to die alone, even though Roger Malvin had asked him to leave to save his own life. This sin colors the rest of Reuben's life, affecting his marriage and career. The sin and guilt are not erased until the symbolic murder of his son, Cyrus, who stands for all that was best in Reuben.

4. In *Winesburg, Ohio*, for example, the main character, George Willard, appears in most of the stories as a unifying factor. Even when he is not in the story, however, his presence is felt, as in the story concerning his mother. The entire work shows us *why* George would feel compelled to leave Winesburg, by describing the stultifying lives of its inhabitants.

5. In Hawthorne's "Roger Malvin's Burial," the tree stands for the blight that has descended on Reuben Borne's life. In Anderson's "Paper Pills," the small rolls of paper that Dr. Reefy compresses in his pockets represent his thoughts, crammed into small spaces, no longer expressed to anyone, symbolic of the compression of his life.

6. See the main characters in Mansfield's "The Dill Pickle."

7. See Hawthorne, whose images, usually drawn from nature, illustrate the theme of the effect of sin and guilt on the human heart.

8. The color brown is carried through *Dubliners*, from the clay in the story of the same name to the final stories.

9. Henry James, D. H. Lawrence, Conrad Aiken and Edgar Allan Poe would all be

appropriate choices. In Aiken's "Silent Snow, Secret Snow," for example, we see how a boy retreats from the problems of his environment, escaping into his mind, turning inward like a flower becoming a seed again.

10. Lawrence's "Rocking Horse Winner," for example, describes how a young boy obtains funds to enable his parents to continue to live in the style they covet. Had the tale been set in a different environment, it would not have illustrated the same theme, the parents'—especially the mother's—greed for the more they have become accustomed to, captured in the phrase, "We must have more money, we must have more money."

11. In any of Poe's horror tales, we find that each word is selected to establish the tone of horror and terror. Thus, in the first paragraph of "The Black Cat," we find the words "terrified," "horror," and "torture," to select a few. This technique continues throughout the tale. See "The Philosophy of Composition."

12. In Poe, for example, we see that the character's personality, established in the first paragraph of "The Black Cat," predisposes him to the tragedy that is to follow, for his good nature is destroyed by drink.

13. We find a far greater concern for the "well-made tale" in those tales from the "traditional" school. These "traditional" stories have a clear beginning, middle, and end, and the narration is in the first or third person. They are concerned with a clear "single effect" and the clear transmission of plot. In the "modern" school, in contrast, we find more of a "slice of life" approach, a greater concern for the creation of a specific image than the transmission of a traditional plot. These modern tales usually try to capture the inner workings of the mind rather than employing a third-person or first-person narration; they favor the "stream of consciousness" and compression of detail.

SUGGESTED READING LIST

The following critical analyses and collections of short stories contain introductions and commentaries that are useful for studying the short story:

Bloom, Edward A. and Lillian Bloom, eds. *The Variety of Fiction: A Critical Anthology.* Indianapolis: Odyssey Press, 1969.

Brooks, Cleanth and Robert Penn Warren. *Understanding Fiction.* New York: Appleton-Century-Crofts, 1959.

Lesser, M.X., and J.N. Morris. *Modern Short Stories: The Fiction of Experience.* New York: McGraw-Hill, 1962.

MacKenzie, Barbara. *The Process of Fiction.* 2nd ed. New York: Harcourt Brace Jovanovich, 1974.

West, Ray and Stallman, Robert. *Art of Modern Fiction.* New York: Holt, Rinehart and Winston, 1956.

Achebe, Chinua	"Dead Men's Path"
Aiken, Conrad	"Silent Snow, Secret Snow"
Aleichem, Sholom	"Teyve Wins a Fortune"
Anderson, Sherwood	*Winesburg, Ohio*
	"The Egg"
Babel, Isaac	"The Story of my Dovecot"
Baldwin, James	"Sonny's Blues"
Bambara, Toni Cade	"The Lesson"
Barthelme, Donald	"Report"
Benet, Stephen Vincent	"The Devil and Daniel Webster"
Böll, Heinrich	"Christmas Every Day"
Borges, Jorge Luis	"Deutsches Requiem"
	"The Garden of Forking Paths"
Calvino, Italo	"The Garden of Stubborn Cats"
Camus, Albert	"The Funeral"
Capek, Karel	"Money"
Cather, Willa	"Paul's Case"
Cheever, John	"The Enormous Radio"
	The World of Apples
Chekhov, Anton	"The Bet"
	"Gooseberries"
	"A Father"
	"The Kiss"
Connell, Richard	"The Most Dangerous Game"
Conrad, Joseph	"Heart of Darkness"
	"The Secret Sharer"
Cortazar, Julio	"House Taken Over"
Crane, Stephen	"The Blue Hotel"
	"The Open Boat"
	"The Bride Comes to Yellow Sky"
Defoe, Daniel	"The True Relation of the Apparition of One Mrs. Veal"

de Maupassant, Guy	"The Diamond Necklace"
	"A Piece of String"
	"A Fishing Excursion"
	"The False Gems"
Dickens, Charles	"A Christmas Carol"
Dinesen, Isak	"The Pearls"
Erdrich, Louise	"Marie Lazarre"
Faulkner, William	"A Rose for Emily"
Gogol, Nikolai	"The Overcoat"
Gonzalez, N. V. M.	"On the Ferry"
Head, Bessie	"Snapshots of a Wedding"
Hemingway, Ernest	"The Short Happy Life of Francis Macomber"
Hsun, Lu	"My Old Home"
Hurston, Zora Neale	"Sweat"
Irving, Washington	"Rip Van Winkle"
	"The Legend of Sleepy Hollow"
	"The Devil and Tom Walker"
Jackson, Shirley	"The Lottery"
	"Charles"
Jacobs, W. W.	"The Monkey's Paw"
James, Henry	"The Jolly Corner"
	"The Turn of the Screw"
Joyce, James	*Dubliners*
Kafka, Franz	*The Penal Colony*
	"The Metamorphosis"
	"A Hunger Artist"
Kimenye, Barbara	"The Winner"
Kingston, Maxine Hong	"No Name Woman"
Kipling, Rudyard	"The Gardener"
Lardner, Ring	"Haircut"
Lawrence, D. H.	"The Rocking Horse Winner"
Lessing, Doris	"To Room Nineteen"
	"Our Friend Judith"
	"No Witchcraft for Sale"
	Stories
Levi, Primo	"Weightless"
Mahfouz, Najib	"The Happy Man"
Malamud, Bernard	*The Magic Barrel*
	"Angel Levine"
Mann, Thomas	"Little Herr Friedmann"
Mansfield, Katherine	"Garden Party"
	"The Dill Pickle"
Marquez, Gabriel Garcia	"A Very Old Man With Enormous Wings"
Mason, Bobbie Ann	"Shiloh"
Melville, Herman	"Bartelby the Scrivener"
Munro, Alice	"Royal Beatings"
Narayan, R. K.	"An Astrologer's Day"
O'Connor, Flannery	*The Collected Stories*
O'Flaherty, Liam	"The Sniper"
Ogai, Mori	"Under Reconstruction"
Olsen, Tillie	"I Stand Here Ironing"
	"Questions"

Paley, Grace	"A Conversation with My Father"
Parker, Dorothy	"Standard of Living"
Peng-cheng, Tu	"Lingkuan Gorge"
Pirandello, Luigi	"The Cat, A Goldfinch, and the Stars"
	"A Breath of Air"
Porter, K. A.	"The Jilting of Granny Weatherall"
	"Noon Wine"
Poe, Edgar Allan	*The Complete Stories and Poems of Edgar Allan Poe*
Rojas, Manuel	"The Glass of Milk"
Roth, Philip	"Defender of the Faith"
Saki	"The Open Window"
Salih, Tayeb	"A Handful of Dates"
Salinger, J. D.	*9 Stories*
Sartre, J. P.	"The Wall"
Singer, Isaac Bashevis	"Gimpel the Fool"
Solzhenitsyn, Alexander	"The One Great Heart"
Steinbeck, John	"Chrysanthemums"
Tagore, Rabindranath	"The Artist"
	"The Kabuliwallah"
Thurber, James	"The Secret Life of Walter Mitty"
Tolstoy, Leo	"How Much Land Does a Man Need?"
Twain, Mark	*The Great Short Works of Mark Twain*
	"The Celebrated Jumping Frog of Calaveras County"
	"The Man That Corrupted Hadleyburg"
	"The Mysterious Stranger"
Updike, John	"A & P"
Walker, Alice	"Everyday Use"
Wells, H. G.	"The Time Machine"
Welty, Eudora	*The Complete Stories of Eudora Welty*
Wharton, Edith	"Roman Fever"
Williams, W. C.	"Use of Force"
Wright, Richard	"Bright and Morning Star"
Vonnegut, Kurt	"Report on the Barnhouse Effect"

The Novel

A *novel* is a fictional prose narrative of substantial length. As mentioned in the short story chapter, there is no specific length that distinguishes the two genres, but the terms *short novel* or *novelette* are sometimes applied to narratives of fewer than one hundred pages that seem too short to be considered novels. This is an arbitrary rule at best.

DEVELOPMENT OF THE NOVEL

The novel is related to the epic because it is not limited to historical facts, but allows for the creation of fictional worlds and people. But in the epic, the characters are usually gods and men of supernatural abilities, whereas in the novel, the characters are usually ordinary mortals living in a world closer to the one we inhabit.

A more direct cousin of the novel is the *romance*. As discussed in the short story chapter, such tales described exciting adventures in strange and wonderful lands. The authors felt free to range from the everyday reality and were seldom interested in the details of ordinary, middle-class life. One of the earliest examples, the anonymous *Sir Gawain and the Green Knight*, for instance, includes the story of a green man who neatly survives decapitation. For the romance, then, adventure was far more important than character development.

In Italy, during the Middle Ages and the Renaissance, a prose tale was called a *novella*, meaning a "new short thing," or "news."

The *picaresque novel*, which presents the adventures of *rogue*, (called a *picaro* in Spanish), is usually a detailed satiric picture of middle-class life, describing the shrewd manner in which the rogue triumphs over the less-clever members of the middle and upper classes he encounters on his travels. Because the form originated as a burlesque of the sixteenth-century Spanish tales of chivalric adventures, the picaro wins one encounter after another, and the novel has a very episodic structure. *The Adventures of Huckleberry Finn* by Mark Twain is a more modern version of the picaresque novel.

If a novel includes historical settings or people drawn in such detail that the reader feels that the historical period as well as the characters are the subject, then the whole may be termed an *historical novel*. Dickens' *A Tale of Two Cities*, even though it has no real historical figure developed in the narrative, can be called an historical novel because of its emphasis on the setting—France during the Revolution—but usually there is some historical figure present. In recent years, historical figures have played larger roles in novels, but these have been termed "fictional biographies," because of the depth of character development.

The *roman à clef* (French for "novel with a key") uses as its main characters contemporary figures disguised with false names. For example, D. H. Lawrence appears as Mark Rampion in Aldous Huxley's *Point Counter Point*.

The *bildungsroman* or *erziehungrsroman* (German for "novel of development") deals with growing up, whereby the hero becomes aware of himself as he relates to the world outside his subjective consciousness. Thomas Mann's *The Magic Mountain* is a well-known example of this genre. When the *bildungsroman* is concerned with the development of the artist, as is James Joyce's *A Portrait of the Artist as a Young Man*, it may be termed a *kunstlerroman* (German for "novel of the artist"). This type of work pays great attention to the mental attitudes of its characters, and may also be called a psychological novel. Although this genre dates back at least as far as the Russian novelist Dostoevski, it has been greatly commented upon in the twentieth century. An especially important kind of psychological novel is the *stream-of-consciousness novel.* By means of the *interior monologue,* the stream-of-consciousness novel attempts to look into the minds of its characters, recording their mental activity complete with all apparent irrelevancies. Usually there is little punctuation, few logical transitions, and few author's interventions in these interior monologues, which, while they serve to represent the mind, can be very difficult to read and understand. James Joyce's *Ulysses* is a stream-of-consciousness novel, and its final chapter, the thoughts of Molly Bloom, represent an interior monologue. The entire section, almost fifty pages long, contains only three conventional sentences.

The novel has changed greatly in the twentieth century, largely through the efforts of Henry James (especially in *The Ambassadors*), Marcel Proust (*Remembrance of Things Past*), and James Joyce (*Ulysses* and *Finnegan's Wake*). While these novelists were not personal friends, their works contain similar characteristics and techniques that effected a change in the novel as we have traditionally come to define it.

The traditional novel, something like *Tale of Two Cities* by Charles Dickens, presents a series of events worked out on the stage of external reality that generally is very close to what we have come to expect of everyday life. The *modern novel,* in contrast, presents a series of events enacted on the stage of *internal reality,* and the reader is required to enter into the internal world the writer has created, rather than the external world to which he is accustomed. Further, the artist creates a *special language* to convey this reality. Thus, he does not speak *about* the mind, as in the traditional novel, but rather seeks to *enter* the mind, and make the reader see events through the character's eyes. He may even try to simulate the actual thoughts of a character as they flow through his mind, called "stream of consciousness." At other times, he may try to distill a moment of time and reduce it to exact language, to capture the moment as it has happened. This attempt to find in language the exact equivalent of experience itself allies the modern novelist with the modern poet and makes the modern novel distinctly different from its predecessors.

Another major difference between the traditional novel and the modern version lies in the notion of *plot.* In the traditional novel, such as *David Copperfield,* the reader enters into the action through the plot, the story. But modern novels such as *Ulysses* have no plot as such, and the reader must gather the story for himself, putting together the pieces as he can. Sometimes the events are very discontinuous, as in the final chapter of *Ulysses,* Molly Bloom's interior monologue, and the reader must translate the author's rendition of the complex inner workings of the mind. The result is what Henry James called the "atmosphere of the mind."

LITERARY MOVEMENTS

Existentialism

The writings of this movement stress the loneliness, insecurity, and irrevocability of man's experience and the dangerous situations in which these qualities are most prominent. It also focuses on the serious and anxious attempts of serious people to face these situations and the evasive or desperate and ultimately useless attempts of weak people to escape them. Most followers of this movement think that the future is undetermined and that man is free, but that he has neither fixed potentials nor fixed values to aid him. Our free choice of actions asserts our actions as valid: In Jean-Paul Sartre's own words, "man makes himself." Man must himself form his own character. Existentialist criticism approached literature by asking how well it depicts these complexities of man's situation.

Expressionism

This school presents life as the author (or his character) passionately feels it to be, not as it appears on the surface to the dispassionate eye. Thus the Expressionist's work often consciously distorts the external appearance of an object in order to picture the object as he feels it really is. Scenery in an Expressionist drama, for example, would not be photographically accurate, but would be distorted so that, for instance, the wall of a courtroom may tilt at a weird angle to reveal the accused's state of mind. The movement was especially dominant in German painting during the decade following World War I.

Naturalism

This movement attempted to portray a scientifically accurate, detached picture of life, including everything and selecting nothing for particular emphasis. This is often called the "slice of life" technique when focused on a narrow bit of scientific realism. Many of the Naturalists were very much influenced by evolutionary thought, and regarded man as devoid of free will and soul, a creature whose fate was determined by the twin pulls of environment and heredity. The movement was represented in the works of Emile Zola, Theodore Dreiser, Frank Norris, Stephen Crane, and others to a lesser extent. The emphasis on scientific determinism, heredity, and environment—Social Darwinism— differentiates Naturalism from Realism, and the two should not be confused.

Realism

In contrast to Naturalism, Realism is the detailed presentation of appearances of everyday life. William Dean Howells, a notable Realist, said that the movement "sought to front the every-day world and catch the charm of its work-worn, care-worn, brave, kindly faces." This movement is closely linked to the Local Color school, which concentrated on picturesque details—scenery, customs, language—characteristic of a certain region. Though often sentimental, local color could go beyond externals and delve into character, and thus is an important part of realism. In its humble, everyday subject matter, Realism has its roots in Romanticism, but Realism generally shuns the Romantic interest in the exotic and mysterious. After the Civil War, American Realism showed a note of disillusionment not present in Howells, painting little people who had their share of petty vices. This can be found in the work of Mark Twain, Stephen Crane, and Hamlin Garland. Realism is not the same as Naturalism, which usually paints a picture of life determined by the twin forces of heredity and environment.

Romance

The Romance describes strange lands and wonderful adventures. It allows the writer greater latitude to "mingle the Marvelous . . . as a slight, delicate, and evanescent flavor," in Nathaniel Hawthorne's words (in his preface to *The House of the Seven Gables*). A novel, in contrast to a romance, assumes the writer will aim at a very minute fidelity to facts, but here the writer may, as Hawthorne again remarks, "swerve aside from the truth of the human heart." The romance may include the traditional hero with the white hat on the white horse; the evil villain with the long black mustache; the lovely young woman in need of rescue, and the hairbreadth rescue itself.

Surrealism

The Surrealist aims to go beyond what is usually considered "real" to the "super real," which would include the world of dreams and the unconscious. Surrealists especially shun middle-class ideals and artistic traditions, believing that all these deform the creations of the artist's unconscious. With its emphasis on spontaneity, feeling, and sincerity, Surrealism is linked to Romanticism. The movement was especially strong in France in the 1920s and 1930s.

Symbolist Movement

The Symbolist movement arose in France in the second half of the nineteenth century and included writers Mallarmé and Valéry. W. B. Yeats, the Irish writer, was influenced by the movement. Some Symbolists believed in an invisible world beyond that of concrete events—Yeats, for example, experimented with automatic writing—but other Symbolists found the concrete world functioned to stimulate their writings. Such Symbolists believed that an object was neither a real thing nor the holder of divine essence; it simply called forth emotions, which were communicated by words whose sounds would be able, they thought, to call forth the same emotion in the reader. Extreme followers of the Symbolist movement believed that poetry was sound with associations rather than words with meanings.

Private Symbol. This is a symbol that is not commonly held by a great many people. It is unique to its inventer and user. Thus, for Yeats, a heron came to symbolize subjectivity.

Conventional Symbol. This is a symbol that is widely accepted and used by other writers. It is able to arouse deep feelings and possess properties beyond what the eye alone can see.

ANALYSIS AND INTERPRETATION OF *THE SCARLET LETTER*

Author: Nathaniel Hawthorne
Date of Publication: 1850

Plot Analysis

The Custom-House. This essay was originally published with the book and thus was intended to accompany it. It serves several purposes:

- It tells how the narrator discovered a faded scarlet A and sheets of manuscript that tell the story that follows. (This is not true, for although Hawthorne did indeed work in the Salem Custom House, where he claims the discovery took place, the story is all his invention. The plot actually appeared some nine years previously in one of Hawthorne's short stories.)
- It sets the mood and the feeling for the tale, by gradually placing us back in the seventeenth century.
- It serves as a form of revenge, for Hawthorne had lost his position in the Custom House because of the Whig victory in the 1849 elections. The election of Zachary

Taylor occasioned a shift in personnel and the loss of Hawthorne's political clout. Hawthorne used this essay to sketch biting portraits of his former Whig colleagues, sketches so sharp as to draw immediate fire from the local newspapers.

Chapter 1—The Prison-Door. This chapter serves to establish the *setting,* seventeenth-century Boston, through detailed description: drab, weather-beaten wooden prison; colorless people; unsightly plot of weeds. These descriptions combine to give the reader the impression of a dreary, decayed, miserable piece of land and group of people. A great deal is also accomplished through the use of *symbols:*

rust, decay, ugliness	=	the *mood* of the people, setting, novel
prison	=	*theme* of punishment
cemetery	=	*theme* of death
rose bush	=	love Hester and Dimmesdale share
		invitation to find "sweet moral blossom"
		Hester herself, the one beautiful element

Chapter 2—The Market-Place As the Puritans await Hester Prynne's public punishment, they discuss her sins in a very uncharitable manner. The people who deride her most are the most physically unattractive, and the ugliest woman goes so far as to declare that Hester ought to be killed outright for her sins. Hester's sin, it emerges, is adultery, the proof evident in her little daughter, Pearl. Hester is brought out before the crowd to undergo public punishment, and she is an exceedingly beautiful and impressive young woman. She thinks of her former life.

This chapter serves to introduce us to the main character as well as to establish the smug, self-righteous nature of Puritan society. This is shown in the holier-than-thou attitude of the women who criticize Hester so freely and cruelly.

Chapter 3—The Recognition. Hester, still on the scaffold to be publically humiliated, catches sight of a small, misshapen man on the outskirts of the crowd. He, seeing her, is equally taken aback. We learn that this is her husband, who had sent her ahead to America some two years earlier. She had assumed that he had been lost, and because of these unusual circumstances, she is not being executed for her sin, but instead must wear the Scarlet Letter and withstand public punishment. The stranger, whom no one realizes is her husband, reveals that he has been held by the "heathen-folk." The Reverend Arthur Dimmesdale is called upon to plead with Hester to reveal her lover's name. Despite his pleas, she refuses to name her partner. This is a highly ironic scene as we later realize, for the Reverend himself is Hester's lover, and were this fact known, his career would be ended in humiliation.

This chapter reveals Hester's strength of will, as she undergoes this punishment alone.

Chapter 4—The Interview. After seeing her husband and withstanding the public display, Hester and her child, Pearl, are in a frenzy. Ironically, Hester's husband, who is a physician, is brought in to minister to them. He calms them both with potions. We learn that her husband, who will go under the name of Roger Chillingworth, bears little ill-will against Hester. He had fallen in love with her, and thought that his gentle nature would win her heart. But he is quite old and she never came to love him, nor ever lied and told him that she did. He is determined to discover the man who has violated his marriage and probe his soul. To this end, he makes Hester swear that she will keep his indentity secret.

Chapter 5—Hester at Her Needle. Hester is released from jail and free to go wherever she desires, but her love for Dimmesdale keeps her in Boston, and she rents a small cottage on the outskirts of the town. She supports herself and her infant daughter through her skill at needlework—the same skill evident on the Scarlet A that so inflamed the women of the town in the first chapter—and her work is in great demand for every occasion but weddings. Despite the popularity of her needlework, Hester and her daughter are complete social outcasts. While she shows her penance for her sin by wearing the coarsest clothing and taking the abuse of the Puritans, Hester inwardly rebels at the injustice of the situation, for she did not sin alone.

Chapter 6—Pearl. Pearl, Hester and Dimmesdale's daughter, is an exceptionally beautiful child, which Hester accentuates by dressing her in the most gorgeous clothing, so that Pearl appears as a miniature of the A, so stunning as to cast a circle of light about her. But Pearl will not bend to rules, possessing a character "whose elements are perhaps beautiful and brilliant—but all in disorder." Her fiery passion, love of mischief, and disrespect for authority remind Hester of her own sin of passion. Pearl adds to Hester's sorrow rather than soothing it, for the deep love Hester feels for her daughter is tempered by fear of her wildness. Pearl is also a living reminder of her sin, and in a perverse way, Pearl delights in taunting her mother about the Scarlet A, pelting it with flowers, asking endless questions about it.

This portrayal of Pearl shows us one level of Hawthorne's genius, for it is entirely possible that a child living isolated from society would become wild and disrespectful of rules. It is also logical that she would focus on the A, shining against Hester's somber clothing, as it would appear a wonderful plaything. On the other hand, this functions well as a symbol, a living A juxtaposed against the cloth A Hester wears. Both remind her of her sin; both are inescapable.

Chapter 7—The Governor's Hall. Hester hears that certain influential citizens, feeling it would be better for both mother and child, plan to remove Pearl from her care. Alarmed, she goes to the Governor's mansion to plead to keep her child. Pearl is dressed in scarlet and gold, a perfect representation of the A. When they enter the mansion, the A on Hester's chest is reflected in a suit of armour to such an extent that she seems hidden behind it. Hester's proud and defiant acceptance of her punishment is demonstrated by the way she dressed Pearl as a miniature of the A.

Chapter 8—The Elf-Child and the Minister. The Governor, shocked by Pearl's immodest dress, challenges Hester's fitness to raise her child. To test her, they question Pearl on her knowledge of catechim. Although Hester has taught her much about religion, much more than most three-year-olds would be expected to know, Pearl deliberately pretends ignorance. Horrified, the Governor and the Reverend are ready to take Pearl from Hester at once. Hester protests, and appeals to Dimmesdale for help. Holding his hand over his heart, he speaks so persuasively that they allow Hester to keep Pearl. This is the first hint that we have that there is something in, on, or about Dimmesdale's heart that causes him discomfort.

Chapter 9—The Leech. Chillingworth has been well received in the town, the people believe that he has been helping their beloved minister, Dimmesdale. Dimmesdale entrusts his health to Chillingworth and they spend much time together, even moving into the same house. Gradually some of the townspeople come to suspect that Chillingworth is not what he appears, that he is secretly evil. Finally, the townspeople come to believe that Dimmesdale is in the hands of the devil. All have faith, though, that he will triumph over evil.

Chapter 10—The Leech and His Patient. The title of this chapter is a pun, for a leech refers to the small bloodsucking worm doctors used to remove what they thought to be toxic substances from their patient's bodies. Thus, doctors were also called Leeches. In this instance, though, the pun has greater depth, for Chillingworth is trying to suck the life from his patient in his efforts to plumb Dimmesdale's soul. Chillingworth has become obsessed with his search for Dimmesdale's guilt. One day he finds the minister asleep in his chair, and seizing the opportunity, pulls aside the minister's vestments. What he sees causes him to "turn away with a wild look of wonder, joy, and horror" and do a little dance of joy. The reader is never told what Chillingworth actually sees. Perhaps, indeed, there is nothing there at all, and what Chillingworth perceives is simply that which he wishes to perceive. This motif is picked up again in the very end of the book, as Dimmesdale reveals his chest to the entire community.

Chapter 11—The Interior of a Heart. Now in possession of what he takes to be proof of Dimmesdale's guilt, Chillingworth begins his unrelenting torture of the minister. Ironically, as Dimmesdale's suffering grows greater and his guilt increases, he grows more popular among the congregation. Church members, not knowing of his secret sin, build him up as "a miracle of holiness." Incapable at this point of publically admitting his guilt, Dimmesdale substitutes self-punishment, often beating himself bloody.

This is a very *ironic* situation, for the more Dimmesdale tries to assert his guilt and rid himself of his sin, the more the people believe him to be innocent. In an interesting twist, Chillingworth is "more wretched than his victim," as he tortures the poor minister.

Chapter 12—The Minister's Vigil. Dimmesdale leaves his house one night and walks to the scaffold where Hester stood clutching Pearl seven years ago. He shrieks aloud at the mockery of his position—revered by the townspeople, but really a secret sinner, unable to share in his lover's public humiliation and pain. Laughing at the vision of himself frozen upon the scaffold, he hears Pearl's answering laugh. Hester and Pearl mount the scaffold, and the two adults stand linked by Pearl, the living symbol of their guilt. Dimmesdale promises to speak from the scaffold of his guilt on the great judgment day. At that moment, he looks up, and sees the sky illuminated by a dull red light in the shape of an A. At the same instance he sees that Pearl is pointing toward Chillingworth, who stands nearby, staring at the three on the scaffold. Overcome with terror, Dimmesdale asks Hester who Chillingworth really is. Hester, remembering her promise, remains silent, but Pearl pretends to answer the minister by whispering some nonsense in his ear. Chillingworth leaves. The next day, Dimmesdale ironically preaches one of his finest sermons. Later, the Sexton returns one of Dimmesdale's gloves that was found on the scaffold, and they speak of the red A that appeared in the sky. They suggest that it signified the death of a local dignitary, showing he was an "angel" and is ascending to heaven.

This is the midpoint of the book, structured so that there is a scaffold in the very beginning, in the very middle, and the very end. The scaffold stands for death and public punishment, and the three observers can be said to represent the state, church, and evil. This chapter also plays with variations on the A, with Hester, Pearl, and Dimmesdale forming an A, the A in the sky, etc.

Chapter 13—Another View of Hester. Hester is shocked at Dimmesdale's appearance, for he has greatly withered under Chillingworth's unrelenting torture. But many things have happened in seven years. Hester's quiet duty to the sick and the poor have won her great respect among the townspeople who once hated her. The A is now seen as a positive sign, said to stand for "able," and is greatly welcomed by those in need. Hester, too, has changed physically. The warmth, passion, and charm have been replaced by a coldness and severity. Her once-luxuriant hair is covered by a tight cap, and she resembles a nun. She is determined to speak with Chillingworth and have him cease torturing the minister.

Chapter 14—Hester and the Physician. Hester meets with Chillingworth, and is shocked by the change in his appearance. The visage of the gentle scholar has been replaced by the dark, evil face of the devil, complete with glowing red eyes. She pleads with him to stop plunging into Dimmesdale's soul, but he says that the *situation,* not his character, has created the necessity for his actions. We can see that Chillingworth is evil for violating the sanctity of the human heart, but that he is not a devil. It is the role of fate.

Chapter 15—Hester and Pearl. Pearl asks Hester why she wears the A and why the minister holds his hands over his heart, for by now this has become his way. Hester does not answer, and here we see her loneliness and misery, with only a rather perverse child as her companion. Despite the change in the townspeople's attitude, she has no real friends among them.

Chapter 16—A Forest Walk. Hester arranges to meet with Dimmesdale to discuss Chillingworth's true indentity. They meet in the forest, and the narrow path they trod can be said to symbolize the narrow moral path that Hester has followed for the past seven years. The forest can stand for the moral wildnerness itself, the brook for the current of life.

Chapter 17—The Pastor and His Parishioner. Hester and Dimmesdale meet, and he explains the misery of his position, a minister idolized by his flock but carrying a dark sin in his heart. She reveals to him that Chillingworth is her husband, and they decide that Chillingworth's sin is greater than theirs, for he has "violated the sanctity of the human heart." Dimmesdale's terror of Chillingworth increases, to the point where he sees death as the only possible escape. He appeals to Hester to think for him, and though appalled by his weakness, she advises him to leave Boston with her and Pearl. He makes a reference to a Scarlet Letter, saying his "burns in secret." We do not know, however, if he has an actual letter somehow imprinted on his breast, or guilt eating at his soul.

Chapter 18—A Flood of Sunshine. Hester and Dimmesdale agree to leave Boston. In joy, she throws off the Scarlet Letter, and lets her beautiful hair down. Her youth and beauty return. Symbolically, the sun breaks through the clouds and shines down upon them. In Nature, the two have yielded to their natural impulses (love), and it appears that Nature approves and that all will be well.

Chapter 19—The Child at the Brook-side. Dimmesdale wishes to speak with Pearl but she won't cross the brook. She gazes at her mother's chest without the A and screams. She won't stop screaming until Hester pins the A back on. Dimmesdale kisses Pearl but she washes it off, and stands alone as Hester and Dimmesdale make their final plans for escape.

The living A (Pearl) forces Hester to take up the cloth A once again. This chapter works well on several levels, for it is entirely possible that a small child would be upset by a radical change in her mother's appearance and be unwilling to have a stranger kiss her. It also works well on a symbolic level, for Pearl is unwilling to accept a change in Hester until Dimmesdale has made public penance for his sin; she is equally unwilling to accept him until he has done what is right.

Chapter 20—Minister in a Maze. Dimmesdale goes over the escape plans in his mind. Hester will book passage for them in four days. On the way home he feels wicked impulses, which can be viewed as the subconscious effects of his decision to run away rather than admit his guilt to the townspeople.

Chapter 21—The New England Holiday. Hester and Pearl go to the market-place on Election Day, a very important holiday for the Puritans. We learn that Chillingworth has discovered their plans and has booked passage on the same ship.

Chapter 22—The Procession. Dimmesdale looks strong walking in the Election Day procession. All the strangers in town stare at the A on Hester's chest as though she were a freak. Dimmesdale, in sharp contrast, is treated as though he were a saint by the townspeople. The author comments, "What imagination would have been irreverent enough to surmise that the same scorching stigma was on them both," that they share the same sin, despite the difference in treatment they are accorded. There is some literary foreshadowing, as the Mistress Hibbins (taken as a witch) reveals to Hester that the "saint on earth" (Dimmesdale) carries the Black Man's mark on his chest (an A?) that will soon be revealed.

This chapter shows the wide gulf between Hester (the sinner) and Dimmesdale (the saint), although we know that the definition of "sinner" and "saint" can be applied equally in the reverse. It is all up to Dimmesdale now—he must bridge the gap, reveal his guilt, and show himself for what he really is.

Chapter 23—The Revelation of the Scarlet Letter. This is the most brilliant and triumphant moment of Dimmesdale's life, as the crowd emerges awed by the power of his speech. They shout out a tribute, but it fades as he totters and his face turns ashen. He joins Hester and Pearl on the scaffold, and Chillingworth appears and tries to stop him, for if Dimmesdale reveals the truth, Chillingworth will have been robbed of his full revenge. As Dimmesdale, Hester, and Pearl climb to the top of the scaffold together, Dimmesdale tells Hester that he is dying and must acknowledge his guilt. He cries out to the crowd of his guilt, tears the ministerial band from his chest, and stands flushed with triumph before the crowd. Then he sinks down. Pearl kisses him (compare the kiss he tries to give her at the brook-side), he bids Hester farewell, and dies. This is the climax of the book.

Chapter 24—Conclusion. People are not sure what they saw when Dimmesdale ripped open his clothing. Some swear he had the identical image of Hester's A branded in his chest, while others, equally sure, believe that his breast was as naked as that of a newborn infant. It is possible that his enormous guilt caused an A to appear from within, or that he actually burned or carved one on his chest. Part of the power of the book is that we are not sure what *is* on his chest, what people actually *did* see.

Hawthorne did not want to add this part of the book, but the publisher felt that a moral was necessary. This was very common in nineteenth-century novels. Here, the moral is "Be true! Be true! Show freely to the world, if not your worst, yet some trait whereby the worst may be inferred!" The publisher also felt that some of what he saw as loose ends had to be tied. Thus, Hester returns to her cottage after a trip to Europe, having gained wisdom through suffering, and she wears the A for the rest of her life. She was buried next to Dimmesdale, with the same tombstone, with the motto "On a field, sable, the letter A, gules" (On a black shield, the letter A, in red). It is unknown what happened to Pearl, but some believe that she married and lived happily; some say they saw Hester making baby clothes. Chillingworth dies, his reason for living gone.

One Possible Interpretation of Events in *The Scarlet Letter*

Theme: Hawthorne was showing the moral and psychological results of sin. These include isolation and morbidity as well as a distortion of character. Chillingworth, for example, becomes an evil, twisted, satanic figure, in contrast to the gentle scholar Hester married. Dimmesdale becomes progressively more "dim," as his will is sapped by Chillingworth's endless probing. And Hester sets aside her youth and beauty to serve the poor, becoming nun-like in the severity of her dress and manner. All three are drastically changed as a result of sin. Hawthorne felt that Chillingworth's sin was the worst of all—"violating the sanctity of the human heart"—far worse than Hester and Dimmesdale's initial passion, and even Dimmesdale's inability to share in the sin publicly.

Character: Chillingworth and Dimmesdale can be seen as two aspects of the *will*—the active and the inactive. From its inception, Puritanism generated a strong belief in the power of the will to overcome all obstacles in the path of the New Israelites in America, in the path of the individual who strove toward Election. But at the same time the Puritan doctrine of predestination denied the possibility of any will except God's. This created a bind that many found impossible to overcome.

Chillingworth unites the intellect and the will, and coldly, with sinister motives, analyzes Dimmesdale. This is the unpardonable sin.

Dimmesdale is the intellect without the will (recall the chapter where he begs Hester to think for him, and though appalled by his weakness, she plans their abortive escape to England). He is passive, all eloquence, sensitivity, refinement, and moral scruple. He preyed upon himself as Chillingworth preyed on him, beating himself in secret to punish himself for his weakness.

Pearl is intuition, the lawless poetic view of the world. She is the artistic impulse outlawed by Puritan doctrine.

Chillingworth	probing intellect, almost the stereotypical mad scientist
Dimmesdale	moral sensibility, effete New Englander
Pearl	the artist, the unconscious
Hester	fallible human reality, what we all are

Brief Review of Puritanism for *The Scarlet Letter*

To the Puritans, the Bible was a complete body of laws, bringing all the spiritual life into relation not only with theology and ethics but with all knowledge and conduct.

The Puritans claimed the right of the individual to read and interpret the Bible for himself, yet in the fundamentals of their faith they agreed with the teachings of John Calvin, the French Protestant reformer. The main tenets of Calvinism can be summarized as follows:

1. God—and only God—elects the individual to be saved.
2. God designs complete salvation and redemption only for those elect.
3. Fallen man (All men are fallen because of the orginial sin of Adam and Eve.) is in himself incapable of true faith and repentance. Only God can supply that, if He so desires.
4. God's grace is sufficient for the elect.
5. A soul once regenerated is never completely lost.

Thus, all men are born evil, because of the original sin of Adam and Eve. God elects certain ones for salvation and only those will be saved. You do not know if you are one of the elect—that can only be discovered after you have died—and so life was often spent in a constant state of self-examination.

The Puritan faith made life anything but dull. The world was the setting for a great drama, man in relation to God and Satan, heaven and hell. It was also the drama of Christian society, for having voyaged to America, the Puritans thought of themselves as the chosen people, the new Israelites in the New Israel. In this Holy Commonwealth, the Bible was the Constitution, only church members were citizens, and God's ministers ruled the state. The more this corporate blessedness was undermined by Satan—in the form of Indians, witches, dissenters, and internal church conflicts—the more passionately it was believed in and enforced.

Hawthorne's relative, John Hathorne (Nathaniel added the "w"), was a judge at the Salem witch trials of 1692. He was merciless in his devotion to what he saw as his duty, ridding the state of witches, and was given the name "the hanging judge of Salem." This is thought to have sparked Nathaniel's interest in the past, although his family always had an inward turn. They were not a social family, and the early death of Nathaniel's father, a sea captain, is thought to have contributed to this introspection. In any event, Nathaniel had a deep and abiding interest in the Puritan past, unusual in the 1850s, when his contemporaries were exploring the notion of man as divine and capable of his own salvation.

Some select qualities of the Puritan

God is just, not merciful.	God rewards the just and punishes the wicked.
Pleasure is suspect.	Duty is important.
All men are sinners.	Predestination was real.
There is moral value in all.	Against the Roman Catholic Church

REVIEW OF *PRIDE AND PREJUDICE*

Author: Jane Austen
Date of Publication: 1813

Plot Summary

Chapter 1. As the novel opens, Mrs. Bennet is questioning her husband about a "young man of large fortune from the north of England" who has just rented a mansion not far from the Bennet's home. Mrs. Bennet wishes the eligible bachelor to marry one of her five daughters; she is worried that the Lucases, who also have daughters, will get to him first. Mr. Bennet teases his wife and calls his daughters "silly and ignorant," except for Elizabeth. These opening scenes indicate that one of the main themes of the book is the business of getting one's daughters, or oneself, married. The term "business" is just what the author intends, and she uses a great many business terms, such as "property," to indicate the materialistic and coarse nature of this entire preoccupation.

Chapter 2. Despite his teasing, Mr. Bennet does pay a call on Mr. Bingley, the bachelor, and everyone eagerly looks forward to his return call. In this chapter we see Mr. Bennet's intellectual superiority to his wife and three younger daughters. The daughters, in order from eldest to youngest, are Jane, Elizabeth, Mary, Kitty, and Lydia.

Chapter 3. Mr. Bennet refuses to reveal any details about Mr. Bingley, and so it is that Mrs. Bennet learns that he is handsome as well as rich from her friend Lady Lucas. Mr. Bingley returns Mr. Bennet's visit but meets no one else in the family, and because of an engagement in London, he is unable to accept their dinner invitation. A ball (called an "assembly") in town gives the people a chance to meet Mr. Bingley, and he shows a keen interest in Jane, the eldest of the Bennet daughters. Mr. Darcy, Mr. Bingley's good friend, is also handsome and very wealthy, but he is overly proud at the ball, and many conclude that he is disagreeable. In addition, he insults Elizabeth by saying that he would not care to dance with her because she is not handsome enough. The theme of "pride and prejudice" is introduced in this chapter, as we will see that Darcy's pride stands in the way of his falling in love with Elizabeth. In the same way, his initial insult will prevent Elizabeth from making an objective assessment of his character. The fact that Elizabeth tells the story of his slight to all her friends shows her maturity and sense of humor.

Chapter 4. Jane and Elizabeth discuss Bingley, whom Jane greatly admires. Elizabeth says that his sisters, though, seem very haughty and proud. Although Darcy's reserve and superior attitude are greatly different from Bingley's open and agreeable nature, Bingley greatly admires his friend for his clever mind. In a contrasting scene, Bingley and Darcy discuss the ball, and decide that Jane is an agreeable girl, but Darcy claims to find all the people in the town dull. Among the upper classes in England in the early nineteenth century, business and commerce were looked down on as vulgar pursuits. The Bingley sisters are not the heirs to old, established fortunes, and they act very snobbishly to play down the origin of their wealth, commerce, and try to convey the impression that they are of the established gentry. One of the themes of this book is that snobbery is not an indication of good manners and occupations are not an indication of moral worth.

Chapter 5. The Lucases and the Bennets meet to discuss the ball, and Mrs. Bennet denounces Darcy's pride. Elizabeth says that she could forgive his pride if he had not offended hers. By now, we can see that Darcy and Elizabeth are the two main characters because of their superior intellects, and we also see that Elizabeth was more deeply hurt by Darcy's remark than she has admitted. We may also see a future to their relationship.

Chapter 6. The Bingley sisters and the Bennets exchange visits, and it becomes apparent that Jane is much attracted to Bingley. Elizabeth and her close friend, Charlotte Lucas, discuss marriage. Charlotte says that a woman must catch the man she wants before someone else does. Elizabeth says that one must first be sure of her feelings, but Charlotte believes that the most important thing is to get married, regardless of emotion. This conversation reinforces the theme: Elizabeth sees the necessity for affection as well as good economic status; Charlotte sees simply the importance of being married. Despite his criticism, Darcy is attracted to Elizabeth for her personality and spirit, and admits to one of Bingley's sisters that he finds Elizabeth most pleasing. Miss Bingley discourages his interest, saying no matter how pleasing Elizabeth may be, he would have to contend with the "common" Mrs. Bennet as a mother-in-law. Miss Bingley is single, and her interest in Darcy is not totally without self-serving notions.

Chapter 7. When Mr. Bennet dies, his daughters will receive no inheritance, due to the way in which the property was originally left to him. Mrs. Bennet has a small inheritance of her own as well as two relations who are engaged in trade. Kitty and Lydia are very excited that a military regiment is to pass the winter in the vicinity. Mr. Bennet is annoyed at the shallowness of his daughters, but Mrs. Bennet reminds him that she too was once much taken with soldiers. Jane receives an invitation to visit Bingley's sisters, and through Mrs. Bennet's clever machinations, she is invited to stay the night. Unfortunately, Jane becomes ill, and Elizabeth walks the three miles to see her, arriving splattered with mud. Despite her appearance, Darcy is struck with her beauty and she is invited to stay and help nurse Jane.

Chapter 8. After dinner that evening, Elizabeth returns to Jane's room while the Bingley sisters cynically discuss her appearance and family connections with trade. Darcy concludes that she will not stand a good chance of marrying someone of quality. The discussion turns to Darcy's fine estate, Pemberley, and we see the social differences between Darcy and Elizabeth.

Chapter 9. Elizabeth spends the night with her sister and sends for her mother, who arrives with her two youngest daughters. Mrs. Bennet exaggerates the severity of Jane's illness, insisting that Jane is not well enough to travel home. We see how vulgar and crude Mrs. Bennet can be.

Chapter 10. Darcy is now so taken with Elizabeth's character and appearance that if it were "not for the inferiority of her connections" he would seriously consider marriage. Caroline Bingley, desiring Darcy for herself, again attacks Elizabeth's family connections, and while Darcy does not reply, the barbs do have some sting.

Chapter 11. After dinner, Caroline Bingley tries to attract Darcy's attention by walking back and forth, showing off her figure, but it is only after Elizabeth joins her that Darcy looks up. It is plain that Darcy is taken with Elizabeth, but it is ironic that she is not even trying to attract him.

Chapter 12. Elizabeth writes to her mother that Jane is well, but her mother, contriving to extend their visit with Darcy and Bingley, refuses to send the carriage. Elizabeth borrows Bingley's carriage and returns home anyway.

Chapter 13. The next morning, Mr. Bennet reads a letter to his family that tells them that Mr. Collins, who is to inherit Bennet's estate, had been ordained in the Church of England and receives the patronage of a wealthy Lady, Catherine. He is to visit, the letter says, and he arrives that afternoon.

Chapter 14. Mr. Collins tells of his good fortune in receiving the patronage of Lady Catherine, and Mr. Bennet and Elizabeth are much amused at his pompous airs.

Chapter 15. Collins has decided to visit the Bennets partly to marry one of the daughters, which he feels will somewhat make up for his inheriting the estate. He focuses his attentions on Elizabeth. The next day they go for a walk and meet Mr. Wickham, an officer. They meet with Darcy, and Darcy and Wickham are visibly embarrassed at seeing each other. We see Collins as perhaps the most pompous, snobbish person in the book.

Chapter 16. The next evening, at a party, Wickham tells Elizabeth that Darcy's father had been his godfather and had informally bequeathed a very fine parish to Wickham, who was to enter the church. Darcy ignored his father's wishes, though, and so Wickham has had to enter the military to make a living. Elizabeth finds herself attracted to Wickham and feels that he has indeed been misused by Darcy. Wickham goes on to say that Collin's patron, Lady Catherine, is Darcy's aunt.

Chapter 17. The next day Elizabeth tells Jane what Wickham revealed. Jane, as usual, cannot believe ill of anyone. One of the themes here is appearance vs. reality. Elizabeth knows little of Wickham, yet she believes his tale based on his appearance, as well as Darcy's apparent pride. In the course of the action, Elizabeth learns that appearances can be deceiving. Another aspect of this theme involves the nature of trade, for it would appear that people engaged in commerce would or could be inferior. In reality, Elizabeth's aunt and uncle in London are morally superior to Caroline Bingley and Lady Catherine.

Chapter 18. At the ball, it is announced that Wickham is not attending because he wants to avoid Darcy. Elizabeth feels added resentment against Darcy, but when he asks her to dance, she is too surprised to refuse. He will not talk about Wickham, though, and he finds himself even more attracted to her. Later, Miss Bingley tells Elizabeth that Wickham is responsible for the bad feelings, but Elizabeth refuses to listen. Mrs. Bennet behaves badly, bragging that her daughter Jane will soon marry Bingley. We see Darcy struggle between the attraction of Elizabeth's wit and beauty and her vulgar and tasteless mother and family connections.

Chapter 19. The next day Mr. Collins proposes to Elizabeth and although she quickly declines, he takes this to be mere coyness. This scene is comic, as Collins, a true bore, refuses to believe that anyone could possibly refuse his offer of marriage.

Chapter 20. Mrs. Bennet tries to force Elizabeth to marry Collins, but her father backs her decision completely. Collins finally realizes that Elizabeth is serious and withdraws his offer. This scene, although comic, shows how wide the gulf is between Elizabeth and her mother.

Chapter 21. Elizabeth sees Wickham, and he admits that he missed the ball to avoid Darcy. Jane receives a letter from Caroline Bingley, who tells her that Bingley will marry Darcy's sister. Jane believes that Bingley has lost interest in her; Elizabeth does not agree.

Chapter 22. Collins proposes to Charlotte Lucas, Elizabeth's best friend, and to Elizabeth's astonishment, Charlotte accepts quite happily. This shows us one view of marriage—making a good business transaction. Both are satisfied.

Chapter 23. Lady Lucas arrives at the Bennets to brag of her daughter's engagement, but Mrs. Bennet is furious, since by the terms of the inheritance, Charlotte Lucas will one day be mistress of her home rather than one of her daughters, as she had schemed and planned.

Chapter 24. Jane receives another letter from Miss Bingley, who informs her that they are to stay in London all winter. She also claims that Bingley will marry Darcy's sister. Elizabeth does not believe this. She criticizes Charlotte's marriage, saying that for a marriage to be a success, both affection and material needs must be considered.

Chapter 25. Collins returns to the Bennet's neighborhood, and Mrs. Bennet's brother and his wife come for a Christmas visit. He and his wife are far superior in breeding to his sister, and Mrs. Gardiner, the sister-in-law, convinces Jane to return with them to London for a visit. Mrs. Gardiner had lived in the area and enjoys hearing news of it from Wickham. This will become very important later.

Chapter 26. Mrs. Gardiner discourages Elizabeth's interest in Wickham. Collins arrives for his marriage to Charlotte Lucas. Jane visits with Bingley's sister in London but is coolly received and becomes convinced that Bingley never really cared for her. Wickham has become very interested in a young woman who has inherited a considerable sum of money. It appears his idea of marriage is very much like Charlotte's.

Chapter 27. Elizabeth travels to London, where her aunt teases her about the loss of Wickham's attentions. Although she defends his action, it appears that she is upset by his turn to another for the sake of money.

Chapter 28. The next day Elizabeth and her friends pay a call on Mr. Collins, who speaks at great length about his patron, Lady Catherine. Elizabeth gets a look at the "sickly and cross" girl who is rumored to become the future Mrs. Darcy.

Chapter 29. While everyone is greatly impressed by Lady Catherine, the independent-minded Elizabeth finds her snobbish. Pride and good breeding, two of the themes of this book, are treated ironically in Lady Catherine, who despite her high birth, has neither. The theme is that good breeding does not belong only to the upper classes.

Chapter 30. Elizabeth stays on to visit with Charlotte, and it emerges that Lady Catherine is a general busybody. A week before Easter, Darcy and his cousin, Colonel Fitzwilliam, arrive for a visit.

Chapter 31. The next week, the Collinses and their guests visit Lady Catherine. Darcy is upset at his aunt's ill breeding. Elizabeth engages in banter with Darcy that only increases his attraction to her, but again she is not aware of it.

Chapter 32. Darcy and Elizabeth visit alone; he had expected others to be there and the visit is somewhat uncomfortable. Later, Charlotte suggests that Darcy's visit shows that he is attracted to Elizabeth, but Elizabeth quickly discounts this, despite his repeated visits during the next few days.

Chapter 33. Darcy and Elizabeth continue to meet during her solitary walks, but she is more interested in the attentions of his cousin, Fitzwilliam. He, however, tells her that as the younger son he does not stand to inherit any money and thus must consider money a factor when he marries. He also says that Bingley is much indebted to Darcy for saving him from a poor marriage. Elizabeth had believed that Miss Bingley was the leader in convincing her brother not to marry Jane and is very distressed by this news.

Chapter 34. Darcy calls on Elizabeth to propose marriage, explaining that his pride has stood in the way of his heart. To his astonishment, she refuses his offer, and tells him that she is angry that he prevented Jane and Bingley from marrying. Darcy's pride is so great that he feels compelled, even while he is proposing, to tell her what a great sacrifice he is making.

Chapter 35. The next morning Darcy hands Elizabeth a letter attempting to justify his actions. He also explains his side of the situation concerning Wickham. It emerges that Elizabeth has been mistaken about a number of things: Darcy's pride has not been all snobbishness and Wickham has not been honest and open.

Chapter 36. Elizabeth reads Darcy's letter with great excitement and realizes her great *prejudice* has stood in her way of understanding the situation fully. Now she sees that Wickham's behavior is not consistent and that she has been misled by appearances. She declares, "Till this moment I never knew myself," and begins to shed her prejudice and be honest with herself. Read this chapter very carefully; it shows the correct order of all that has been incorrectly perceived before.

Chapter 37. Elizabeth carefully thinks over what she has learned.

Chapter 38. Elizabeth leaves the Collinses residence and travels to London for a few days. She decides to wait until they return home to tell Jane what she has learned.

Chapter 39. The main function of this chapter is to tell the reader about Lydia's character. She is a great deal like her mother, coarse and vulgar.

Chapter 40. Elizabeth tells Jane what she has learned about Bingley from Darcy, as well as about her prejudice against him.

Chapter 41. Seeing her youngest sisters crying over the departure of the regiment, Elizabeth feels the truth of what Darcy has said about her family. Lydia is invited to join a young wife and follow the officers. Elizabeth tries to get her father to stop what is at best an imprudent and at worst a dangerous trip, but he does not want to upset the family peace. Wickham returns, and Elizabeth hints that she has learned a great deal about him. We see by his fear and refusal to talk with her that Darcy's side is correct. Lydia leaves on her trip.

Chapter 42. Elizabeth realizes that her father married her mother solely for her looks and quickly lost interest in her. This has been a poor example for the family, and he has tended to ignore all his daughters except Elizabeth. Elizabeth goes for a vacation with the Gardiners to the area around Darcy's estate, Mrs. Gardiner's childhood home.

Chapter 43. Elizabeth tours Darcy's home, secure that he is away. The housekeeper describes him in such glowing terms that she cannot believe this is the same man she knows. As they are leaving the house, Darcy appears. Elizabeth is overcome with shame that he will think she is pursuing him. Later, they meet him again, and he treats her and her family with great courtesy. Because she has shed her prejudice and he his pride, they can see each other more clearly and she sees his true interest in her.

Chapter 44. Darcy brings his sister to meet Elizabeth the same day, a great compliment, and because of his behavior, her aunt and uncle conclude that his intentions are sincere and his love true. Elizabeth explores her own feelings about him.

Chapter 45. Bingley's sister receives Elizabeth's visit, which is not warm and cordial, and after Elizabeth leaves, criticizes her. Darcy comes to Elizabeth's defense.

Chapter 46. Jane writes two letters to Elizabeth. The first says that Lydia has run off with Wickham; the second, that he does not intend to marry her. Elizabeth runs to catch her aunt and uncle and meets Darcy, who is very sympathetic toward her plight. She thinks that this disgrace will wipe away any affection he has for her. This is an important chapter, for we see that emotion (feeling) should always be governed by reason. The Gardiners leave to find Lydia.

Chapter 47. Elizabeth and the Gardiners discuss Lydia and Wickham. Elizabeth does not reveal the complete truth about his past, but enough so that the Gardiners realize that he is not honest. Meanwhile, Mrs. Bennet blames everyone but herself for Lydia's misfortune, not seeing that it is the result of a careless upbringing.

Chapter 48. Wickham owes money all over town. Collins writes a letter to the Bennets, in which he says that it would be better if Lydia were dead rather than to dishonor her family so. Again we see how shallow he is. Mr. Bennet tells Elizabeth that he is responsible for what has happened to Lydia, and we see that as with Darcy and Elizabeth, he too has a moment of realization, when he must acknowledge and confess his character faults.

Chapter 49. Gardiner has found Lydia and Wickham and has learned that Wickham has no intention of marrying her. Gardiner arranges a settlement: Wickham will marry Lydia for a sum of money. Elizabeth is worried about a marriage that starts so poorly; her mother, in contrast, is delighted that Lydia will marry. In Jane Austen's time, this was the only sensible solution to the problem, since a decent middle-class man would not marry a woman who had run off with another man. Therefore, Lydia would either have had to marry "beneath" her or remain unmarried.

Chapter 50. Mrs. Bennet looks for a house for Lydia and Wickham, but Mr. Bennet informs her that he will not give her any money and will never receive the couple in his home. Wickham and Lydia will move to another part of the country, and Elizabeth convinces her father to see Lydia off. Elizabeth now sees that she and Darcy would have had a model marriage, but she believes that the alliance between Lydia and Wickham, Darcy's enemy, is the final blow, for Darcy would never marry into such a family.

Chapter 51. Lydia and Wickham arrive and behave poorly. Lydia tells her sisters to go to Brighton, for that is where they will all find husbands. It does not bother her that she has nearly disgraced the family and that Wickham had to be bribed to marry her at all. Lydia reveals that Darcy was at their wedding, which astonishes Elizabeth.

Chapter 52. Mr. Gardiner writes to Elizabeth to tell her what Darcy has done. After Gardiner arrived in London, Darcy contacted him to tell him that he had heard about Wickham and Lydia and gone after them to try to change their minds. Darcy had arranged the financial settlement and had paid the full amount himself—but the Bennets were not to know. Finally, Darcy returned for the wedding and the final financial arrangements. Wickham comes to see Elizabeth, they discuss the truth of his past, and Elizabeth generously asks that they forget the past.

Chapter 53. Wickham and Lydia leave, and Mr. Bennet ironically says that Wickham is a fine fellow. We learn that Bingley is to return to his home in the country, and on the third day after their arrival, Bingley and Darcy come to pay a call on the Bennets.

Chapter 54. Some days later at dinner, Bingley and Jane are excited to be with one another again, but Darcy seems to treat Elizabeth coolly. She believes that this is because she has once refused his offer of marriage.

Chapter 55. Bingley proposes to Jane. Mrs. Bennet's moral and intellectual dullness are made clear by the way she reacts to her daughter's news: She treats it as she did Lydia's, apparently seeing no difference in the way Jane and Bingley regard each other from the way Wickham used Lydia.

Chapter 56. Lady Catherine appears at Elizabeth's door, rudely inquiring if it is true that Darcy is to marry her, since she wants Darcy to marry her daughter. Lady Catherine is insulting and vulgar. Her crude assault is an extreme form of the pride from which Darcy once suffered. All of Lady Catherine's wealth cannot make up for her poor breeding.

Chapter 57. Collins writes a letter revealing Darcy's plan to marry Elizabeth, but warning that it will be what Lady Catherine calls a "disgraceful match." Mr. Bennet is much amused, thinking that Elizabeth greatly dislikes Darcy. She is angry and confused. She would like to be engaged, and others think she is, but she is not.

Chapter 58. Darcy comes to visit and Elizabeth thanks him for what he has done for Lydia. He again proposes, and this time she accepts. They declare their mutual love. They review the details of their relationship, their pride and prejudice.

Chapter 59. Elizabeth tells her father of her match, and he cautions her to not marry unless she feels affection. She tells him that she does indeed love Darcy, despite her earlier condemnations of him. She informs her mother, who is thrilled that Elizabeth is to marry.

Chapter 60. Elizabeth and Darcy discuss how they fell in love. The Collinses come to visit, and Darcy patiently endures the dull Collins and vulgar Mrs. Bennet.

Chapter 61. Jane and Elizabeth each marry. A year later, Jane and Bingley buy an estate about thirty miles from Pemberely, where Darcy and Elizabeth live. Lydia writes to Elizabeth, asking for help. Elizabeth sends money, and Darcy helps Wickham with his army career. All the loose ends are tied up, and we see in Elizabeth and Darcy and Jane and Bingley the portrait of happy marriage, quite different from the business proposition pictured in Chapter 1.

Organization of Plot

The plot of *Pride and Prejudice* is organized *two* ways—by pairs of lovers and by places.

In the first scheme, we can divide the book into five parts:

Part I   The lovers meet, especially Darcy and Elizabeth, Jane and Bingley. The section ends with the marriage of Collins and Charlotte Lucas (Chapter 26).

Part II   Darcy proposes to Elizabeth; she refuses (chapters 27–41).

Part III   Darcy and Elizabeth meet for the third time; Lydia and Wickham have run away (Chapter 42–47)

Part IV   Lydia and Wickham's story (chapter 43–52).

Part V   Double marriage of Elizabeth and Darcy, Jane and Bingley. Resolution of conflicts on all levels.

In the second method of organization, we also see five divisions, based on location:

Part I   Longbourn, Netherfield, Meryton

Part II   Hunsford and Rosings

Theme

The main idea of this book concerns the ways in which we ought to select spouses and conduct ourselves during the selection. Mrs. Bennet, for example, judges success in marriage strictly in economic terms, and we see that despite her conviction that her own marriage was a sound deal, her husband and she have little in common, and the marriage is actually very unsound. In the same way, Lydia's marriage is unsound, as we see in the end, when the author tells us they have little happiness. A "marriage of true affection" must combine emotional as well as practical considerations. Thus, personalities must match, and morality and social breeding must be considered. That is what we see in the models of Jane and Bingley and Elizabeth and Darcy.

Sample Questions to Consider

1. Explore the class structure of the novel: Explain what the hierarchy says about the author's theme.
2. How is the title important?
3. What does a close look at the vocabulary of this novel reveal about its moral underpinnings?

Answers

1. Marriage is the ultimate social act, because through its continuation society conserves and revivifies itself (or disintegrates). All society is hierarchical, there are ranks, orders, or classes. In the time of Elizabeth and Darcy, the late eighteenth century, these were acknowledged with greater formality than now and crossing class lines was a dramatic social event. These marriages afforded us a glimpse of the social facts of life of the eighteenth century: income ("fortune"); aristocratic ideals; snobbery; and breeding ("manners").
2. The novel deals with the effect of pride and prejudice on the characters. By "pride" the author means an unrealistic exaggeration of one's status, and by "prejudice," judging before all the evidence is at hand. While the main part of the story revolves around the relationship of pride and prejudice in Elizabeth and Darcy, it is also manifested in all the minor characters, most notably Lady Catherine, Mr. Collins, and Mrs. Bennet.
3. Certain words are frequently applied to certain people, which helps establish their characters in a subtle and highly effective manner. Thus, we have words dealing with business transactions—charge, worth, debt, business, etc.—applied to those who view marriage as a sort of business transaction, people like Charlotte, Mr. Collins, and Mrs. Bennet. On the other hand, we see abstract words dealing with moral standards—principle, sense, truth, folly, pride, prejudice, conduct, reason—applied to people who see marriage as the uniting of two like souls, people like Elizabeth and, to a lesser extent, Jane and Darcy. Naturally, the vocabulary a character uses ought to conform to the nature of his or her character. This is one of the standards by which we judge a quality work of literature.

EVALUATION OF *PORTRAIT OF THE ARTIST AS A YOUNG MAN*

Author: James Joyce
Date of Publication: 1916

Plot Summary

Chapter 1. The novel opens with some early childhood experiences of the main character, Stephen Dedalus. The scene then shifts to Clongowes, where Stephen is a student. Sensitive and standoffish, Stephen is unwilling to join his classmates in games. His mind wanders to the lavatory at school, the memory of which makes him feel hot and cold. Stephen is taken sick and admitted to the infirmary. He goes home for the Christmas holiday and we meet his family. Christmas dinner is the scene of a violent religious and political argument about Parnell, Ireland's dead hero, but Stephen does not understand what the fighting is all about. After the holidays, we shift back to the playground where Stephen listens to a conversation concerning certain boys leaving school. Again, he refrains from participation. In class Stephen is unjustly punished for neglecting his studies. The prefect of studies, Father Dolan, believes Stephen broke his eyeglasses on purpose to avoid having to do his lessons. Stephen tells the rector about the incident and is welcomed back to the playground as a hero by his classmates.

Chapter 2. His father has undergone a financial setback and Stephen has been withdrawn from school. He spends his free time reading romantic fiction. The family moves to Dublin and Stephen is sent to Belvedere school, where we see he is still proud and sensitive. He takes a trip with his father to Cork and is aware of his lack of communication with his father. In school, his pride and independence lead to trouble with the authorities. The final incident concerns an essay which has been judged to be heretical and which he is asked to recant. Stephen refuses to conform outside the classroom, defending Byron's verse and deriding Tennyson's, even though he is beaten for his opinions. With some prize money he has won, Stephen attempts to heal the rift between himself and his family. He lends them money, takes his family out, etc. but when all the money is gone, he realizes that his plan "to erect a breakwater of order and elegance" is doomed. At the same time, he feels that he is drifting into mortal sin and feelings of lust, feelings which impell him to wander Dublin's streets at night. He soon finds his way to the brothel section.

Chapter 3. Stephen's feelings of lust are sharply altered after Father Arnall's sermons on the horrors of hell and eternal damnation. Feeling that the sermons were directed at him personally, he is overcome with shame and guilt. Stephen is horrified by the graphic descriptions of hell. He is so overcome that back in his room he vomits. Later he prays for forgiveness and promises to reform his life.

Chapter 4. Partly because of his apparent devotion, Stephen is called in to speak with the director about the possibility of becoming a Jesuit priest. He realizes that this is impossible, however, for *non serviam*, I cannot serve, is his credo. He cannot leave the world by assuming a religious life; he must participate in it and accept the guilt and suffering. The symbol of his decision is the bridge over Tolka stream, as his eyes for a moment face the faded shrine of the Virgin and then turn toward his own house. The "disorder, the misrule and confusion of his father's house" is his choice. Later he goes to the shore, and the voice of the waves mingled with the voices of his friends gives shape to his name, Dedalus, the "fabulous artificer," and thus he is fated to become an artist. Seeing a lonely girl wading in the water, he feels he is reborn to the beauty of the world. As Stephen stretches out on the sand for a final vision of this new world, the novel reaches its climax, the point at which Stephen comes to understand not only literal reality but the greater reality that exists beyond.

Chapter 5. Back at the university, Stephen speaks of aesthetics (art) and we see sketches of his friends, Cranly, MacCann, and others. Remaining isolated, he refuses to sign the petition for universal peace, and we see that he is still alone, that his pride is still a motivating factor. A long discussion of aesthetic philosophy takes place between Stephen and his friend, Lynch, in which Stephen concludes that the artist must set his images between himself and "the market place," and that the forms of art must be considered as falling into three related categories: the *lyrical,* as the artist presents the image in relation to himself; the *epical,* as the image is presented in relation to himself and others; and the *dramatic,* as the image is presented in immediate relation to others. The last section of this chapter shows Stephen preparing to leave. An implied comparison is made between Stephen and Icarus, the son of Daedalus. The novel ends with Stephen recording in his diary his feelings about his upcoming escape to Europe, as he declares that his goal is "to forge in the smithy of my soul the uncreated conscience of my race."

Themes

1. Conformity to ritual (suggested by Stephen's dancing to the hornpipe).
2. Stephen's search for identity and, by extension, any artist's search for his own voice (suggested by Stephen's questions about his name).
3. Alienation and loneliness, probably the central theme (suggested by his behavior at school and with his family and friends; he is always alone, even in a crowd): The artist's search for identity and place in the hostile world.
4. Ireland, her history and politics (suggested at the very beginning by the "moocow," a symbol of Ireland, and later by the discussion of Parnell at Christmas dinner. Parnell is one of the most vivid symbols of the country.).
5. The gulf between generations, specifically the rift between father and son (suggested by the parents' behavior when Stephen gives them the prize money—how little difference it makes ultimately in their lives or his).
6. The conflict between the internal and external worlds, between imagination and reality (suggested by the contrast between heat and cold, red and green). The underlying theme in *Portrait* is the role of the artist as he seeks to discover or "forge" his place in an often hostile, or at best indifferent, world. The events take place during the artist's teen years, for this is when the conflict between the ideal (the artist) and the real (the world) is sharpest. Many who have felt themselves destined to create works of art, especially literature, have been very strongly drawn to this book, as *they* try to find a place in the world that often seems to reject them because they seem different from the norm.

Method of Development

Unlike the conventional novel, *Portrait of the Artist as a Young Man* does not depend on the *plot,* the chronological unfolding of events, to develop its themes. Rather, they are woven into the book by means of *expansion,* which takes several different forms. For example, the first, third, and fifth chapters build up ideas that are commented on in the second and fourth chapters. This rise and fall of interwoven ideas is one method of development. Another is the *recurrence of images or incidents,* as the opposites, hot and cold for example, reoccur throughout the novel. A third form of expansion is the movement from *the specific to the universal*—the specific shown, for example, in the scene where Stephen writes his name in the geography text, and moving through a series of wider definitions of himself, arriving finally at "the Universe." In these ways, Joyce was able to work around the straight line plot development of the traditional novel to use: *dialectic* (thesis-antithesis), *cyclic* (circles, returns, recurrences), and *inductive* (specific to general) means of development to suggest whole new meanings.

These expansions fit in with another of Joyce's means of development, the *architectonic,* a medieval concept that explains the integration of clearly defined parts into a unified whole. Therefore, we find a series of parts and motifs that occur again and again. Thus, for example, we see the playground at the beginning and at the end of the first chapter. Joyce's narrative structure has been termed *montage,* a term taken from the movies, a series of scenes that illustrate the daily progression of life. Some readers have felt that they could read *Portrait* in any order and it would still make sense. This would work only if the reader did not realize that one scene builds upon another to create a total effect, although on first reading the scenes may appear randomly selected.

Some Motifs in Detail

Names. Stephen's last name, Dedalus, has meaning on several levels: First, the Daedalus in Greek mythology was the man who tried to escape the ties of time and place by devising a pair of wings. Thus, he can be said to stand for the eternal conflict between man's quest for freedom and the limitations the world imposes. Daedalus also invented the labyrinth, and so, in this book, the name can also be symbolic of the mind's many twisting and turning paths that attempt to prevent the formulation of any absolute solutions.

Artistic consciousness. Very early on, Stephen is aware of his desire to create artistically. The verses that he intends to write, for example, are dedicated to E—— C——, copied from what he had seen in Byron's works. Byron was an exiled poet, as was the Count in *The Count of Monte Cristo,* one of Stephen's favorite works. Stephen will leave Ireland for Europe at the end of the work, becoming an exiled poet himself.

Role of the artist. The artist lives in isolation and solitude, Stephen/Joyce concludes. The role of the artist expressed here is taken from Flaubert's idea that the artist's role is similar to that of a priest (in the real world) and of God (in the ideal world). Yet we recall that Stephen also concludes that life is to be faced and lived, which is one reason he declined to accept the Jesuit's offer to become a priest. This apparent contradiction defines the role of the artist in the modern age: how to be a detached and preoccupied artist, yet go with the crowd at the same time. Stephen's friend MacCann accuses him of being "an antisocial being, wrapped up in [him]self" (Chapter 5), and Cranly suggests that Stephen is unable to communicate. Stephen wants to discover the way in which the artist can express himself freely, and to this end decides to use only "silence, exile, and cunning." It is for each of us to discover for ourselves the role of the artist and to evaluate Stephen's "sins"—pride and egoism. Are they necessary for the artist in the modern world? What *is* the artist's stance?

Sample Questions to Consider

1. What is Joyce's definition of "epiphany"? Give some examples from *Portrait*.
2. What is Stephen's philosophy of art? Is it the same as James Joyce's?
3. How do the sermons in Chapter 3 affect Stephen?

Answers

1. Joyce uses the term epiphany to mean a sudden realization, usually a recognition of the essence of something. Joyce himself said "its soul, its whatness leaps to us from the vestment of its appearance." In the end of *Portrait*, Stephen's epiphany comes when he realizes he must leave Ireland behind to, as he says, "forge in the smithy of my soul the uncreated conscience of my race."

2. Stephen's philosphy is based on the ideas of St. Thomas Aquinas and, and while his philosophy is simplistic it does contain important substance. Go back to lyric, epic, and dramatic (discussed previously) for the theory. Since most critics agree that Joyce is treating the young artist ironically here, most likely parodying himself at Stephen's age, it is likely that when he wrote *Portrait* he did not take these ideas very seriously himself. Much of what Stephen concludes *sounds* better than it is.

3. Impressed by the images in the sermons, Stephen attempts to use Christian faith to avoid reality. But this barrier, like his previous attempt to establish order in his life in Chapter 2, is doomed to fail, for the artist cannot escape the world, even through faith.

ESSAY QUESTIONS ON THE NOVEL

Following are some sample AP essay questions on the novel. Allow yourself 60 minutes to organize, write, and correct each essay. Be certain to cite specific examples from the work under discussion to prove your points. Follow the directions for generating and organizing your thoughts as described in **Part 2: Essay Writing Guide**. Be sure to leave time to revise and edit your essay at the end.

1. First chapters are often important in establishing the personality of a main character through language, symbolism, imagery, and so forth. Select any novel of recognized literary worth that you have read and show how this is true.

2. In the same manner, second and third chapters establish the personality of minor or secondary characters. Select any two novels of recognized literary worth that you have read and show how their second and third chapters establish the personality of secondary characters through the use of language, symbolism, imagery, and so forth.

3. The first chapter of a novel can also establish the *tone* of the entire work through word choice, imagery, symbolism, and language. Select any novel of recognized literary worth that you have read and show how this is true.

4. In some novels, the historical and/or social background is so important to the theme and plot that the work could not have been set in any other time or place. Show how this is true in any novel that you have read.

5. Occasionally the conclusion of a novel seems tacked on, not really an integral part of the narrative. It may seem that the author could not figure a way out of the action and so constructed an artificial ending, or that the beliefs of the time demanded that the book end in a particular way. Sometimes we may find two versions of a book: one with a conventionally expected ending, another with a very different outcome. Select any one novel and show how the ending does not seem to fit with the rest of the book.

6. On the other hand, there are novels whose endings seem perfect; there is no other way the action could have ended. Select any novel that you have read and show how the ending fits the rest of the book and is the best possible resolution of the theme and plot.

7. In some novels, setting is of very little importance. The novel could have taken place anywhere, anytime. Show how any one work you have read could have been set in another time and place with no loss to theme or plot, or perhaps even be improved by another setting.

8. Language is usually an important element in any work of literature. Sometimes it becomes the most significant element in a novel, a metaphor for the theme. Show how this is true in any one novel you have read.

9. Some first chapters set forth all the themes of the novel as well as establish character and setting. Show how this is true in any novel you have read. Trace the themes and show how they are introduced in the first chapter.

10. The final chapter of a novel is sometimes a letdown for the reader for a variety of reasons. Select a novel of recognized literary value and show how the ending does not live up to the promise of the beginning.

11. Oppositely, the ending of a novel may be better than you expected for a variety of reasons. Show how this is true in any novel you have read. Be sure to prove what makes the ending so much better than the text that preceded it.

12. Sometimes you may read and admire several works by the same author, then pick up another of his/her books to find that it is a great disappointment for a variety of reasons. Show how this is true in any one work you have read. First explain what made all the other books better, then show how this book was a disappointment.

13. The inverse may be true: You may not like any of the author's previous works but find one astoundingly good. Use one work you have read as an example. Explain what made the previous works disappointing and then show how this one is better. Refer to language, theme, setting, imagery, characterization, etc.

14. Select any one aspect of the novelist's craft—characterization, imagery, setting, theme, plot, etc.—and show how any one author has used that element to create a masterpiece. Select specific examples to prove your point.

SUGGESTED READING LIST

Austen Jane	*Pride and Prejudice*
	Emma
Baldwin, James	*Go Tell It on the Mountain*
Bellow, Saul	*Seize the Day*
Brontë, Charlotte	*Jane Eyre*
Brontë, Emily	*Wuthering Heights*
Buck, Pearl	*The Good Earth*
Camus, Albert	*The Stranger*
Chopin, Kate	*The Awakening*
Conrad, Joseph	*Heart of Darkness*
Crane, Stephen	*The Red Badge of Courage*
Defoe, Daniel	*Moll Flanders*
Dickens, Charles	*David Copperfield*
	A Tale of Two Cities
Dostoevski, Fyodor	*Crime and Punishment*
	The Brothers Karamazov
Dumas, Alexander	*The Count of Monte Cristo*
Eliot, George	*Silas Marner*
Ellison, Ralph	*Invisible Man*
Faulkner, William	*The Sound and the Fury*
	As I Lay Dying
Fielding, Henry	*Joseph Andrews*
Fitzgerald, F. Scott	*The Great Gatsby*
Flaubert, Gustave	*Madame Bovary*
Forster, E. M.	*Passage to India*
Fowles, John	*The French Lieutenant's Woman*
Golding, William	*The Lord of the Flies*
Greene, Graham	*The Power and The Glory*
Hardy, Thomas	*The Return of the Native*
Hawthorne, Nathaniel	*The Scarlet Letter*
	The House of the Seven Gables
Hemingway, Ernest	*The Sun Also Rises*
	For Whom the Bell Tolls
Howells, William D.	*The Rise of Silas Lapham*
Huxley, Aldous	*Brave New World*
James, Henry	*The Turn of the Screw*
Joyce, James	*A Portrait of the Artist as a Young Man*
Knowles, John	*A Separate Peace*
Lawrence, D. H.	*Sons and Lovers*
London, Jack	*Call of the Wild*
Lee, Harper	*To Kill a Mockingbird*
Mailer, Norman	*The Naked and the Dead*
Malamud, Bernard	*The Fixer*
Maugham, W. Somerset	*Of Human Bondage*
Melville, Herman	*Moby Dick*
	Billy Budd, Foretopman

Morrison, Toni	*Song of Solomon*
Norris, Frank	*The Octopus*
Orwell, George	*1984*
	Animal Farm
Roth, Philip	*Goodbye, Columbus*
Shelley, Mary	*Frankenstein*
Steinbeck, John	*The Grapes of Wrath*
	Of Mice and Men
Stowe, Harriet Beecher	*Uncle Tom's Cabin*
Swift, Jonathan	*Gulliver's Travels*
Tan, Amy	*The Joy Luck Club*
Thackeray, William M.	*Vanity Fair*
Turgenev, Ivan	*Fathers and Sons*
Twain, Mark	*The Adventures of Huckleberry Finn*
Updike, John	*Rabbit, Run*
Walker, Alice	*The Color Purple*
Warren, Robert Penn	*All the King's Men*
West, Nathanael	*Miss Lonelyhearts*
Wharton, Edith	*Ethan Frome*
Woolf, Virginia	*To the Lighthouse*
	Mrs. Dalloway
Wright, Richard	*Native Son*

Satire

The term "satire" is derived from the Latin "satura," which means "full," "a mixture of things." While it seems to have referred originally to food, it has come to be associated with a down-to-earth coarseness. While there are, of course, highly stylized, polite, and refined satires—Pope's *The Rape of the Lock* is a well-known example—these are not typical of satire as a whole. The function of satire was not defined by the Greeks, and so we have nothing comparable to Aristotle's analysis of tragedy. Two main conceptions of the purpose of satire have emerged, however.

TWO KINDS OF SATIRISTS

One type of satirist likes most people, but thinks they are foolish and blind to reality. He tells the truth pleasantly, so that he will not turn people away but rather cure them of that ignorance which is their worst problem. The other type of satirist hates people, and believes that wickedness and evil will triumph in the world. Swift is an example of the second type of satirist. He loves individuals, but hates mankind. He therefore desires not to cure, but to punish and destroy. The famous satirist Juvenal also falls into this category.

The two types have different views of evil. The misanthropic satirist feels that evil is rooted in man's nature and the structure of society. Nothing he can say will cure or eliminate it. Man, or the special group that he is discussing, deserves only hatred, and his laughter carries with it no identification. This type of satirist is close to the tragedian. Many readers find such satire difficult to read, for what is the purpose if man cannot be changed from the folly of his ways? The misanthropic satirist finds life not comic but contemptible.

The satirist who likes people is basically an optimist, believing that evil is not inherent in humanity, or if it is, it is like a disease which can be cured. Some people *are* incurable, and they are offered as examples in order to help the others who *can* mend the folly of their ways. Only those who understand what good really is can follow it and shed evil ways. Satirists such as Horace believed this, and they are kinder, more persuasive than denunciatory. At the worst, such satirists will say that the world's values are twisted, but offer this view as a comment on the ridiculous predicament of mankind. Usually they select a few of the worst offenders to hold up as examples. Even if the satire does cut a little too deeply, it doesn't matter, for they believe that the pain will result in a cure for the evils that they have pointed out.

WHY SATIRISTS WRITE

The different kinds of satirists naturally view their purpose differently. The optimist writes in order to correct man's problems; the pessimist writes in order to punish man for his transgressions. The optimistic satirist sees the world as essentially a healthy place, even though there are those among us who are ill and need to be cured; the pessimistic satirist sees a world full of incurable criminals, a world so mad that some have lost their wits just looking closely at it. So that he will not go insane like the rest of the sick world the pessimitic satirist uses all the hate and derision at his command. All satirists cannot

143

be rigidly classified in this manner, however, for a writer may compose one work that is hopelessly pessimistic and follow it with another that is cheerfully optimistic. Various degrees of optimism/pessimism are even found within the same work, as the satirist's mood changes with his material.

Why does the satirist write? First, he is moved to action by a personal feeling about a specific subject, perhaps hatred or scorn, even though he may claim in his work that he has gotten rid of all personal feelings. He tries to justify his feelings and make his readers share in them. Some satirists have been moved by feelings of personal inferiority, of social injustice, of being excluded from a group to which they wished to belong. Pope and Dryden, for example, were both Roman Catholics in a Protestant country. Pope was unusually small and deformed. Juvenal and Cervantes were men of talent forced into careers they felt useless or beneath their talents.

Some satirists feel a pleasure in the material itself, and many feel the patterns of satire are especially interesting in their complexity. Any writer of satire needs a very large vocabulary, a good sense of humor and imagination, and especially good taste, allowing him to say shocking things without making the reader turn aside in disgust. This aesthetic appeals to some.

Still others like satire because it allows them to set up a model to copy and offer advice. Although some may be too bitter to give voice to positive beliefs and others may be too concerned with humor, we do find a great many satires that establish an ideal for emulation.

CHARACTERISTICS OF SATIRE

What is satire?

- It is topical, referring to its time and place.
- It claims to be realistic, although it is usually distorted or exaggerated.
- It is shocking.
- It is informal in tone and manner.
- It is funny, although it sometimes may be painful or grotesque.

It usually assumes one of three main forms:

1. *Monologue.* The satirist, usually speaking as himself or from behind an assumed mask or persona, addresses us directly. He states his view of the problem, provides examples, criticizes opponents, and tries to make his view ours.
2. *Parody.* The satirist takes an existing work of literature which was created with a serious purpose or a literary form in which some well-regarded books have been written and makes the work or the form look ridiculous, filling it with incongruous ideas or exaggerating its features. He may make the ideas look silly by placing them in an inappropriate setting or form.
3. *Narratives.* The satirist generally does not assume a narrative voice as he does in the monologue. The narratives may be stories, such as Voltaire's *Candide,* or dramatic fictions, such as *Troilus and Cressida.* This seems to be the most difficult type of satire to compose, and hardest for the reader to judge and understand.

If the forms are different, how can we tell what is a satire and what is not? What qualities make an entire work a satire, but another contain only satiric episodes?

HOW TO DETERMINE IF A WORK IS SATIRE

When a satirist writes a parody which follows the originally very closely, when his work is highly ironic, when his humor is subtle or mild, or when he pretends in such a manner as to convince the reader that he is really telling the truth, he may be mistaken for a dispassionate commentator, a skilled comedian, or a genuine admirer of the material he is ridiculing. There have been many readers who have missed the point of a satire entirely and have found themselves in agreement with the most ridiculous satiric suggestions. Fortunately, there are a number of ways to distinguish a satire:

First, the author may clue us in that he is writing a satire. Juvenal, for example, looked at the corruption rampant in Rome and wrote, "It is difficult *not* to write satire," and so we know that he is writing in the satiric mode.

Second, the author may cite previous satires to tell us what he is satirizing. When Erasmus, for example, says that his *Praise of Folly* is justified by such works as *The Battle of Frogs and Mice* and Apuleius' *Metamorphoses* (among others), he is telling us that his work follows the classical line of descent of other satirists.

Third is the choice of traditional satiric subject matter and its treatment. Often, the topic will derive directly from a previously published, well-known satiric work. This can also be accomplished by quoting another well-known satire, even without a direct statement or without mentioning the original author's name, trusting the reader to recognize it. The satirist favors *concrete, topical,* and *personal* subjects. Satires often deal with real cases and many even name real people or describe them unmistakably, and often unflatteringly. Satires often allude to the gossip of the moment in the city in which the writer resides, the here and now. Freshness is one of the most important characteristics of the satire. No one cares fifty or one hundred years later what the talk was about, and few can recall, if they are even concerned, the details of the crisis that had the whole city talking. Dryden's *Mac Flecknoe,* for example, is full of good jokes, but they pale when we have no knowledge of the participants, and we lose interest.

Fourth, while the subject matter varies, the *style* is easy to distinguish in most instances. Most satires contain cruel and even "dirty" words, and all contain comic words and terms. Many use colloquial and nonliterary terms to make their points. The satirist always tries to produce the unexpected, so in plot, tone, vocabulary, sentence structure, and phrasing, the satire will contain the unexpected, unlike the epic or the sonnet forms. We also find many typical satiric weapons—irony, paradox, antithesis, parody, anticlimax, obscenity, violence, vividness, and exaggeration. If these devices are used only in certain sections of work, then those sections can properly be considered satiric, but if they are present throughout the work, then the entire piece is considered a satire.

In almost all satires, two special attitudes, or methods, are usually present:

1. The first is the detailed description of an absurd or painful situation, or a foolish or wicked person or group of people. The satirist believes that most people are dulled by custom and must be made to see the truth as clearly as posible. A tone of scornful amusement may prevail.
2. The satirist may use blunt language to describe unpleasant people and facts in order to shock his readers into awareness. He wants to force them to look at something that they may have overlooked or may wish to overlook. Use of brutally direct language—nauseating images, crude slang, forbidden expressions—will make the people see the truth of what he is saying and be moved to feelings of protest.

There is one final test for satire. The author wishes the reader to feel a mixture of amusement and contempt. In some works the amusement far outweighs the contempt; in others, the amusement nearly vanishes in a grim smile or a sneer of cold contempt.

A MODEST PROPOSAL

For Preventing the Children of Poor People From Being a Burthen to Their Parents or Country, and for Making Them Beneficial to the Public.

by Jonathan Swift

It is a melancholy object to those who walk through this great town, or travel in the country, when they see the streets, the roads, and cabin-doors crowded with beggars of the female sex, followed by three, four, or six children, *all in rags,* and importuning every passenger for an alms. These mothers, instead of being able to work for their honest livelihood, are forced to employ all their time in strolling, to beg sustenance for their helpless infants, who, as they grow up, either turn thieves for want of work, or leave their dear Native Country to fight for the Pretender in Spain, or sell themselves to the Barbadoes.

I think it is agreed by all parties that this prodigious number of children, in the arms, or on the backs, or at the heels of their mothers, and frequently of their fathers, is in the present deplorable state of the kingdom a very great additional grievance; and therefore whoever could find out a fair, cheap, and easy method of making these children sound useful members of the commonwealth would deserve so well of the public as to have his statue set up for a preserver of the nation.

But my intention is very far from being confined to provide only for the children of professed beggars; it is of much a greater extent, and shall take in the whole number of infants at a certain age who are born of parents in effect as little able to support them as those who demand our charity in the streets.

As to my own part, having turned my thoughts, for many years, upon this important subject, and maturely weighed the several schemes of other projectors, I have always found them grossly mistaken in their computation. It is true a child, just dropped from its dam, may be supported by her milk for a solar year with little other nourishment, at most not above the value of two shillings, which the mother may certainly get, or the value in scraps, by her lawful occupation of begging, and it is exactly at one year old that I propose to provide for them, in such a manner as, instead of being a charge upon their parents, or the parish, or wanting food and raiment for the rest of their lives, they shall, on the contrary, contribute to the feeding and partly to the clothing of many thousands.

There is likewise another great advantage in my scheme, that it will prevent those voluntary abortions, and that horrid practice of women murdering their bastard children, alas, too frequent among us, sacrificing the poor innocent babes, I doubt, more to avoid the expense than the shame, which would move tears and pity in the most savage and inhuman breast.

The number of souls in this kingdom being usually reckoned one million and a half, of these I calculate there may be about two hundred thousand couples whose wives are breeders, from which number I subtract thirty thousand couples who are able to maintain their own children, although I apprehend there cannot be so many under the present distresses of the kingdom, but this being granted, there will remain an hundred and seventy thousand breeders. I again subtract fifty thousand for those women who miscarry, or whose children die by accident or disease within the year. There only remain an hundred and twenty thousand children of poor parents annually born: The question therefore is, how this number shall be reared, and provided for, which, as I have already said, under the present situation of affairs, is utterly impossible by all the methods hitherto proposed, for we can neither employ them in handicraft, or agriculture; we neither build houses (I mean in the country), nor cultivate land: they can very seldom pick up a livelihood by stealing till they arrive at six years old, except where they are of towardly parts, although, I confess they learn the rudiments much earlier, during which time they can however be properly looked upon only as *probationers,* as I have been informed by a principal gentleman in the County of Cavan, who protested to me that he never knew above one or two instances under the age of six, even in a part of the kingdom so renowned for the quickest proficiency in that art.

I am assured by our merchants that a boy or a girl, before twelve years old, is no saleable commodity, and even when they come to this age, they will not yield above three pounds, or three pounds and half-a-crown at most on the Exchange, which cannot turn to account either to the parents or the kingdom, the charge of nutriment and rags having been at least four times that value.

I shall now therefore humbly propose my own thoughts, which I hope will not be liable to the least objection.

I have been assured by a very knowing American of my acquaintance in London, that a young healthy child well nursed is at a year old a most delicious, nourishing, and wholesome food, whether stewed, roasted, baked, or broiled, and I make no doubt that it will equally serve in a fricassee, or a ragout.

I do therefore humbly offer it to public consideration that of the hundred and twenty thousand children already computed, twenty thousand may be reserved for breed, whereof only one fourth part to be males, which is more than we allow to sheep, black-cattle, or swine, and my reason is that these children are seldom the fruits of marriage, a circumstance not much regarded by our savages, therefore one male will be sufficient to serve four females. That the remaining hundred thousand may at a year old be offered in sale to the persons of quality, and fortune, through the kingdom, always advising the mother to let them suck plentily in the last month, so as to render them plump, and fat for a good table. A child will make two dishes at an entertainment for friends, and when the family dines alone, the fore or hind quarter will make a reasonable dish, and seasoned with a little pepper or salt will be very good boiled on the fourth day, especially in winter.

I have reckoned upon a medium, that a child just born will weigh 12 pounds, and in a solar year if tolerably nursed increaseth to 28 pounds.

I grant this food will be somewhat dear, and therefore very proper for landlords, who, as they have already devoured most of the parents, seem to have the best title to the children.

Infants' flesh will be in season throughout the year, but more plentiful in March, and a little before and after, for we are told by a grave author, an eminent French physician, that fish being a prolific diet, there are more children born in Roman Catholic countries about nine months after Lent than at any other season; therefore reckoning a year after Lent, the markets will be more glutted than usual, because the number of Popish infants is at least three to one in this kingdom, and therefore it will have other collateral advantage by lessening the number of Papists among us.

I have already computed the charge of nursing a beggar's child (in which list I reckon all cottagers, labourers, and four-fifths of the farmers) to be about two shillings *per annum,* rags included, and I believe no gentleman would repine to give ten shillings for the carcass of a good fat child, which, as I have said, will make four dishes of excellent nutritive meat, when he hath only some particular friend or his own family to dine with him. Thus the Squire will learn to be a good landlord, and grow popular among his tenants, the mother will have eight shillings net profit, and be fit for work till she produces another child.

Those who are more thrifty (as I must confess the times require) may flay the carcass; the skin of which, artificially dressed, will make admirable gloves for ladies, and summer boots for fine gentlemen.

As to our City of Dublin, shambles may be appointed for this purpose, in the most convenient parts of it, and butchers we may be assured will not be wanting, although I rather recommend buying the children alive, and dressing them hot from the knife, as we do roasting pigs.

A very worthy person, a true lover of this country, and whose virtues I highly esteem, was lately pleased, in discoursing on this matter, to offer a refinement upon my scheme. He said that many gentlemen of this kingdom, having of late destroyed their deer, he conceived that the want of venison might be well supplied by the bodies of young lads and maidens, not exceeding fourteen years of age, nor under twelve, so great a number of both sexes in every country being now ready to starve for want of work and service: and these to be disposed of by their parents if alive, or otherwise by their nearest relations. But with due deference to so excellent a friend, and so deserving a patriot, I cannot be altogether in his sentiments; for as to the males, my American acquaintance assured me from frequent experience that their flesh was generally tough and lean, like that of our schoolboys, by continual exercise, and their taste disagreeable, and to fatten them would not answer the charge. Then as to the females, it would, I think with humble submission, be a loss to the public, because they soon would become breeders themselves: And besides, it is not improbable that some scrupulous people might be apt to censure such a practice (although indeed very unjustly) as a little bordering upon cruelty, which, I confess, hath always been with me the strongest objection against any project, however so well intended.

But in order to justify my friend, he confessed that this expedient was put into his head by the famous Psalmanazar, a native of the island Formosa, who came from thence to London, above twenty years ago, and in conversation told my friend that in his country when any young person happened to be put to death, the executioner sold the carcass to persons of quality, as a prime dainty, and that, in his time, the body of a plump girl of fifteen, who was crucified for an attempt to poison the emperor, was sold to his Imperial Majesty's Prime Minister of State, and other great Mandarins of the Court, in joints from the gibbet, at four hundred crowns. Neither indeed can I deny that if the same use were made of several plump young girls in this town, who, without one single groat to their fortunes, cannot stir abroad without a chair, and appear at the playhouse, and assemblies in foreign fineries, which they never will pay for, the kingdom would not be the worse.

Some persons of a desponding spirit are in great concern about that vast number of poor people, who are aged, diseased, or maimed, and I have been desired to employ my thoughts what course may be taken to ease the nation of so grievous an encumbrance. But I am not in the least pain upon that matter, because it is very well known that they are every day dying, and rotting, by cold, and famine, and filth, and vermin, as fast as can be reasonably expected. And as to the younger labourers they are now in almost as hopeful a condition. They cannot get work, and consequently pine away for want of nourishment, to a degree, that if at any time they are accidentally hired to common labour, they have not strength to perform it; and thus the country and themselves are happily delivered from the evils to come.

I have too long digressed, and therefore shall return to my subject. I think the advantages by the proposal which I have made are obvious and many, as well as of the highest importance.

For first, as I have already observed, it would greatly lessen the number of Papists, with whom we are yearly over-run, being the principal breeders of the nation, as well as our most dangerous enemies, and who stay at home on purpose with a design to deliver the kingdom to the Pretender, hoping to take their advantage by the absence of so many good Protestants, who have chosen rather to leave their country than stay at home, and pay tithes against their conscience to an Episcopal curate.

Secondly, The poorer tenants will have something valuable of their own, which by law be made liable to distress, and help to pay their landlord's rent, their corn and cattle being already seized, and *money a thing unknown*.

Thirdly, Whereas the maintenance of an hundred thousand children, from two years old, and upwards, cannot be computed at less than ten shillings a piece *per annum*, the nation's stock will be thereby increased fifty thousand pounds *per annum*, besides the profit of a new dish, introduced to the tables of all gentlemen of fortune in the kingdom, who have any refinement in taste, and the money will circulate among ourselves, the goods being entirely of our own growth and manufacture.

Fourthly, The constant breeders, besides the gain of eight shillings sterling *per annum*, by the sale of their children, will be rid of the charge of maintaining them after the first year.

Fifthly, This food would likewise bring great custom to taverns, where the vintners will certainly be so prudent as to procure the best receipts for dressing it to perfection, and consequently have their houses frequented by all the fine gentlemen, who justly value themselves upon their knowledge in good eating; and a skilful cook, who understands how to oblige his guests, will contrive to make it as expensive as they please.

Sixthly, This would be a great inducement to marriage, which all wise nations have either encouraged by rewards, or enforced by laws and penalties. It would increase the care and tenderness of mothers toward their children, when they were sure of a settlement for life, to the poor babes, provided in some sort by the public to their annual profit instead of expense. We should see an honest emulation among the married women, which of them could bring the fattest child to the market, men would become as fond of their wives, during the time of their pregnancy, as they are now of their mares in foal, their cows in calf, or sows when they are ready to farrow, nor offer to beat or kick them (as it is too frequent a practice) for fear of a miscarriage.

Many other advantages might be enumerated: For instance, the addition of some thousand carcasses in our exportation of barrelled beef; the propagation of swine's flesh, and improvement in the art of making good bacon, so much wanted among us by the great destruction of pigs, too frequent at our tables, which are no way comparable in taste or magnificence to a well-grown, fat yearling child, which roasted whole will make a considerable figure at a Lord Mayor's feast, or any other public entertainment. But this and many others I omit, being studious of brevity.

Supposing that one thousand families in this city would be constant customers for infant's flesh, besides others who might have it at merry-meetings, particularly weddings and christenings, I compute that Dublin would take off annually about twenty thousand carcasses, and the rest of the kingdom (where probably they will be sold somewhat cheaper) the remaining eighty thousand.

I can think of no objection that will possibly be raised against this proposal, unless it should be urged that the number of people will be thereby much lessened in the kingdom. This I freely own, and was indeed one principal design in offering it to the world. I desire the reader will observe, that I calculate my remedy for this one individual *Kingdom of Ireland, and for no other that ever was, is, or, I think, ever can be upon earth.* Therefore let no man talk to me of other expedients: *Of taxing our absentees at five shillings a pound: Of using neither clothes, nor household furniture, except what is of our own growth and manufacture: Of utterly rejecting the materials and instruments that promote foreign luxury: Of curing the expensiveness of pride, vanity, idleness, and gaming in our women: Of introducing a vein of parsimony, prudence, and temperance: Of learning to love our Country, wherein we differ even from* LAPLANDERS, AND THE INHABITANTS OF TOPINAMBOO: *Of quitting our animosities and factions, nor act any longer like the Jews, who were murdering one another at the very moment their city was taken: Of being a little cautious not to sell our country and consciences for nothing: Of teaching landlords to have at least one degree of mercy toward their tenants. Lastly, of putting a spirit of honesty, industry, and skill into our shopkeepers, who, if a resolution could now be taken to buy only our native goods, would immediately unite to cheat and exact upon us in the price, the measure, and the goodness, nor could ever yet be brought to make one fair proposal of just dealing, though often earnestly invited to it.*

Therefore I repeat, let no man talk to me of these and the like expedients, till he hath at least some glimpse of hope that there will ever be some hearty and sincere attempt to put them in practice.

But as to myself, having been wearied out for many years with offering vain, idle, visionary thoughts, and at length utterly despairing of success, I fortunately fell upon this proposal, which as it is wholly new, so it hath something solid and real, of no expense and little trouble, full in our own power, and whereby we can incur no danger in *disobliging* ENGLAND. For this kind of commodity will not bear exportation, the flesh being of too tender a consistence to admit a long continuance in salt, *although perhaps I could name a country which would be glad to eat up our whole nation without it.*

After all I am not so violently bent upon my own opinions as to reject any offer, proposed by wise men, which shall be found equally innocent, cheap, easy, and effectual. But before something of that kind shall be advanced in contradiction to my scheme, and offering a better, I desire the author, or authors, will be pleased maturely to consider two points. First, as things now stand, how they will be able to find food and raiment for an hundred thousand useless mouths and backs. And secondly, there being a round million of creatures in human figure, throughout this kingdom, whose whole subsistence put into a common stock would leave them in debt two millions of pounds sterling; adding those, who are beggers by profession, to the bulk of farmers, cottagers, and labourer with their wives and children, who are beggars in effect. I desire those politicians, who dislike my overture, and may perhaps be so bold to attempt an answer, that they will first ask the parents of these mortals whether they would not at this day think it a great happiness to have been sold for food at a year old, in the manner I prescribe, and thereby have avoided such a perpetual scene of misfortunes as they have since gone through, by the oppression of landlords, the impossibility of paying rent without money or trade, the want of common sustenance, with neither house nor clothes to cover them from the inclemencies of the weather, and the most inevitable prospect of entailing the like, or greater miseries upon their breed for ever.

I profess in the sincerity of my heart that I have not the least personal interest in endeavouring to promote this necessary work, having no other motive than the *public good of my country, by advancing our trade, providing for infants, relieving the poor, and giving some pleasure to the rich.* I have no children by which I can propose to get a single penny; the youngest being nine years old, and my wife past child-bearing.

ANALYSIS OF "A MODEST PROPOSAL"

The best known of Jonathan Swift's shorter pieces, "A Modest Proposal" (1729), composed when he had long been Dean of St. Patrick's, the Protestant cathedral in Dublin, is consistently ironic and relentlessly harsh and satiric. Its aim, in the words of its long title, is to prevent "the children of poor people from being a burthen to their parents or country, and for making them beneficial to the public." Not a single sentence in the essay deviates from this bitter tone. Its persuasive power lies in its irrefutable indictment of Irish and English indifference and sheer folly in the face of unspeakable injustice and misery, but its first attraction is its wildly original and creative idea.

The pamphlet does not claim to be written by Swift himself; as with many monologues, as we mentioned earlier, the author assumes a mask. In this case, Swift claims the document has been penned by an anonymous Irish patriot, whose sole motive was to help the people of Ireland by solving their most pressing social and economic problems. The situation was that under English domination, the people of Ireland were starving to death. One radical solution, Irish independence, could not then be considered and so other measures of complete social, financial, and moral reorganization were obviously correct. Thus, they would never be considered or initiated, Swift felt with the pessimism of the satirist. So, behind the ironic mask of the anonymous philanthropist, he set forth a solution that was framed in blandly persuasive tones, but was so atrocious that no one could possibly take it seriously.

The solution that he proposes is that since so many Irish babies are being born every day, they should be treated as animals, not as humans, and be slaughtered and consumed. The best age at which to eat them, from the consumer's point of view, would be one year, for at that point they would be healthy and tender. Another suggestion is that the children be allowed to grow until the age of 12 or 13 and then served in place of venison, but he is not in favor of this, as the meat would be lean and tough. "And besides," he adds, with not a little touch of sarcasm and irony, "it is not improbable that some scrupulous people might be apt to censure such a practice (although indeed very unjustly) as a little bordering upon cruelty, which, I confess, hath always been with me the strongest objection against any project, however so well intended." In a serious manner, with all apparent concern for the welfare of the Irish people, who are miserably downtrodden and ill treated, the narrator describes the advantages of his modest little proposal. It will, he says, reduce the number of Catholics, increase the country's annual income, and even raise the general standard of living. Even in brief outline the ideas are revolting, but the arguments are so even tempered and well presented that the reader finds himself continuing to follow the argument, despite the horror that underlies the words. Swift, long tortured by the horrors he saw around him, put all his efforts into describing the practical details of actually cooking and serving a child. These details obviously add greatly to the effect he desires.

He claims that a child will provide two dishes at a party, but "the fore or hind quarters will make a reasonable dish" when the family dines alone. He notes that "seasoned with a little pepper or salt [it] will be very good boiled on the fourth day, especially in winter." These specific details—even to the extent of providing cooking directions—add to the satire, as he vents his spleen at the callousness of the authorities that allow people to continue to live in miserable hovels, starving to death.

What is the object of Swift's attack? It may, of course, be argued that his main purpose is to employ satire to reveal the full horror of the Irish economic situation. And we can see that this must be one of the aims, for the speaker implies that cannibalism is a reasonable alternative to the horrible status quo. But when we say that the main purpose of the essay is to underscore the dreadful conditions of the Irish peasants, we run into difficulties. It is true that as an introduction to the essay's proposal Swift gives an appalling view of the hopeless squalor and suffering which afflicted his countrymen. But the "proposal" itself does not serve to reinforce this distressing scene. The conclusion that one is tempted to draw is that the proposal is not itself more shocking than the existing state of affairs Swift had described for us in the beginning of the essay. Yet this implies that the proposal is real, that the ideas he sets forth are taken at face value, seriously—in short, that we are not dealing with satire, but rather with a straightforward proposal of the most brutal economic notion ever to be put to paper.

It is clear that thoughtful readers will not accept his argument at face value, but will look beyond his literal words for some essential object of attack, and thus regard the work as satiric. A number of theories concerning the real object of Swift's venom have been proposed. Some feel that it is the English—specifically the English legislators, landlords, and economic apologists. We can see his argument in this light as an exaggeration and distortion of English indifference to the most basic human needs of the Irish. The problem with this view is that the speaker never identifies himself with the English. Indeed, throughout, he is clearly addressing the Irish and regards the country as his own.

Some have seen "A Modest Proposal" as a parody of previous writings. Certainly in the glib and semi-scientific descriptions of cooking and addressing the children we see mocking echoes of what were, in Swift's time, all-too-familiar discussions of the Irish problem. But the bleakness with which the plight of the Irish peasant is presented, especially in the opening paragraphs, and the savage resentment which the narrator voices, cannot be explained by previous works on the same subject. Nowhere else has the same solution been offered in a published attempt to solve the Irish poverty problem.

We can also see that the Irish people themselves are a target of Swift's venom here, those people who determine the country's policies. Swift is acting the part of the angry preacher, determined to reveal the sloth and stupidity of his congregation. The famous passage which begins, "for this one individual *Kingdom of Ireland, and for no other that ever was, is, or, I think ever can be upon earth,*" shows that he is aiming at least part of his anger at the Irish people themselves. This passage contains a series of solutions that Swift had long advocated himself, and it is clear he bitterly resents that his common-sense ideas have been ignored. In a letter to Alexander Pope the year before "A Modest

Proposal" was written. Swift said that he was feeling ". . . perfect rage and resentment" at seeing daily the "mortifying sight of slavery, folly, and baseness about," which he was forced to endure.

The main satiric thrust, then, can be seen as a devastating assessment of the Irish people's own lethargy and foolishness in the face of horrible social and economic conditions. Their blindness appears all the more awful when we see, after Swift has pointed it out, that they have rejected all reasonable courses of action, and that the incredibly repellent proposal he sets forth is at least better than doing nothing. For a people who should, he thinks, truthfully "think it is a great happiness to have been sold for food at a year old," he offers, in rage and despair, a blueprint for the destruction of a nation which is no more shocking than the current state of affairs in that nation, resulting from their own folly.

Curiously, another plan to solve Ireland's problems, which actually outdid this one in its absurdity, was seriously suggested by an Irish patriot, Colonel Edward Despard. He told a friend that he could solve Ireland's problems through a separation of the sexes. Swift satrically proposed that the Irish institute a system of regulated cannibalism, while Despard very seriously proposed racial suicide, which, had it been instituted, would have eliminated the entire Irish population in a few short generations. In Colonel Despard's suggestion, what had been ironic in Swift became theoretical truth, for it was most seriously proposed.

SATIRE AND GEORGE ORWELL'S *1984*

George Orwell wrote *1984* with two main purposes in mind: To ensure, as far as it lay in his power, that the kind of society that he envisioned would not come about, and to satirize totalitarianism and linguistic abuses. *1984,* then, is a satire whose purpose is not to portray the future, but to warn the present, to alert those whom Orwell considered the decent and reasonable members of his generation to be on their guard against the rise of totalitarian societies.

1984 is a political satire of an activist nature, for Orwell hoped that his work might have some political effect by telling his readers of certain dangers he saw creeping into modern society. It is in the tradition of Utopian literature, which, taking its name from Sir Thomas More's *Utopia* (1515–16), extends back at least as far as Plato's *Republic,* and describes a mythical but ideal society which is intended to shed light on current-day society and change it to conform to the author's view of the ideal. A variation on this model is anti-Utopian society, in which the hypothetical land is presented not as an ideal to emulate, but a distortion of the real, often focusing on the worst and most frightening aspects of the real society. Its object is the same as that of the true Utopia, in that people are supposed to work to improve the society in which they live. Instead of holding up the model of a perfect land, the author of anti-Utopian literature presents a satirical criticism of mankind's pride and folly, combined with a warning that if tendencies shown in the anti-Utopian model are not corrected, man's condition will get worse instead of beter. The most famous anti-Utopian satirical fiction in English is Jonathan Swift's *Gulliver's Travels* (1726). Aldous Huxley's *Brave New World,* written in 1932, is also an example of this genre, but Orwell's *1984* stands as the most famous and influential anti-Utopian work of the twentieth century.

The real structure of the brutal society described in *1984* is explained in the political tract which Winston Smith, the main character, reads as he is about to be apprehended by the Thought Police. It is called "The Theory and Practice of Oligarchical Collectivism," and it was written by Emmanuel Goldstein, the enemy of Big Brother, the leader, and the Party which controls the society of 1984. Oligarchy means that a small group has control over the larger groups, and implies a certain corruption. Without doubt, the oligarchy here is corrupt, for the leaders tyrannize and brutalize the masses into submission.

In *1984* the world has been divided into three superstates: Oceania, Eurasia, and Eastasia. England has become a province of Oceania called Airstrip One. The three powers are constantly at war, although one will occasionally strike an alliance with another to gain an advantage. Partly through the enormous cost of the constant war, and partly through the waste of material and energy which the Party encourages to maintain its power, England has become poor and grim. Oceania has three classes: The Inner Party, the Outer Party, and the Proles. The Inner Party consists of only two percent of the total population and is the ruling class. It maintains its numbers not through hereditary succession, democratic election, or even brute force, but by the selection of people from time to time either from the Inner Party's children or from the most able members of the Outer Party. It is thus a selective aristocracy, including both talent and a fierce devotion to the aims of the Party. Big Brother, whose pictures are everywhere, is the symbol of the Inner Party. It is never clear if he is a real person or not; most likely he is simply the imaginary representative of the Inner Party and has been created by them out of the realization that people need a single all-powerful leader to look up to and even worship. The only member of the Inner Party we ever meet in the book in any detail is O'Brien, Winston Smith's torturer, and we never even learn his first name. As a matter of fact, only three characters in the depersonalized and dehumanized world of this novel are ever given their complete names.

Under the total control of the Inner Party is the Outer Party, made up of fifteen percent of the population and responsible for all the routine administrative duties. The Outer Party may be compared to a small and powerless, but nonetheless indispensable, middle class. Winston Smith, the 39-year-old hero of the book, is a member of the Outer Party. The action of the book revolves around his revolt against the oligarchy and the results of his decisions. His name is symbolic, for Smith is the most common name in the English language, thus suggesting that he is Everyman, representative of all of us. Winston is the first name of the great English war leader and Prime Minister, Winston Churchill, who is generally recognized as one of the greatest heroes of his age. The combination of these two names implies that while Winston Smith is Everyman, he is also unique. For example, in the beginning of the book, Winston Smith, as a minor employee of the Government's Ministry of Truth, sets himself up against Big Brother and the Party, even though he is fully aware that he cannot possibly succeed. All crimes in *1984* are understood to be simply different forms of the same crime—Thoughtcrime— which means having the wrong mental attitude toward the Party and Big Brother, and are punishable by death without a formal legal trial. Winston is a Thoughtcriminal, and this novel, in illustrating his decline and fall, takes us through the most representative parts of the complete society so we may understand the satire fully.

The government of *1984* is centralized in London, the capital city of Airstrip One (England), and is organized into four huge ministries: The Ministry of Truth, which is involved with news, entertainment, education, and the fine arts; the Ministry of Peace, concerned with war; the Ministry of Love, which rules law and order and controls the secret police; and the Ministry of Plenty, which governs economic affairs. In Newspeak, the official language of *1984,* these are referred to as Minitrue, Minipax, Miniluv, and Miniplenty. Winston Smith works for the Ministry of Truth.

His job, when we first meet him, is to rewrite—which means to falsify—history to make it conform to Party doctrine. This is done in accordance with the Party slogan: "Who controls the Past controls the Future." Winston has begun to keep a diary, which is technically not illegal, for since there are no written laws nothing can be considered illegal in the technical sense, but it is nevertheless dangerous, for it shows that one may have private thoughts and by putting them on paper may wish to communicate these private thoughts to others. This is forbidden or at least not at all encouraged, for the maintenance of the oligarchical totalitarianism in 1984 depends not on increasing communication between people by sharing thoughts, but rather on decreasing it to the minimum necessary to carry on a routine life. Therefore Winston's diary would make him suspect, a fact of which he is fully aware.

The three slogans of the Party upon which the government is constructed are:

WAR IS PEACE
FREEDOM IS SLAVERY
IGNORANCE IS STRENGTH

All three superstates are essentially the same: self-contained economies having little or no need for external support. Each has enough raw materials. War would provide them at most, a few million extra people for hard labor and a few more miles of land. Despite the fact that war is not at all an economic necessity, a constant state of war is maintained. War determines the population's condition, and overcrowding, chronic food shortages, and long hours of work for poor pay result. There are even added hours of "voluntary" work for the Outer Party, for which no additional pay is received.

In the past, the objective of war was largely economic, but in the society of *1984*, the purpose of war is not to win, but instead to maintain the status quo. War, therefore, is peace, for the state of war keeps society in balance. The slogan "War is Peace" holds true as long as the war does not build up, for the three states can keep their people too busy with the war effort to allow them any time to plan ways of changing the system. The three states hold each other up, despite their frequent differences, and provide ways of destroying the surpluses which would make life comfortable.

Members of the Party are expected to be hard-working and intelligent (within the narrow limits of Party allegiance, of course). At the same time, they are required to be ignorant fanatics whose prevailing moods are "fear, hatred, adulation (of Big Brother), and orgiastic triumph." The way that Party members can resolve this contradiction is through the practice of Doublethink, a process whereby a person may control his mind so that he will not even allow himself to think of things which are not approved by the Party. Thus the Party members convince themselves that Oceania is fighting a war which will end in victory, and in which Oceania will be the ruler of the world. To think in any other way is to be guilty of a Thoughtcrime.

When we first encounter Winston Smith he is in very dangerous shape, for Doublethink, Party conditioning, is breaking down and he is thinking for himself. He is aware of the mortal difficulty he is in, but he cannot help himself. One day, he hysterically writes in his diary:

DOWN WITH BIG BROTHER
DOWN WITH BIG BROTHER
DOWN WITH BIG BROTHER . . .

and with this forbidden thought and deed, his fate is sealed. Although his downfall will take some time, it is inevitable.

He becomes acquainted with two people from work who will have a great influence on his life: Julia, a 26-year-old woman, who will become his mistress, and O'Brien, a member of the Inner Party who will betray Winston and Julia.

Winston and Julia are expected to behave in a manner approved by the Party. The Party must approve all marriages, and is suspicious of romantic love, for it feels that any attachment of one human being for another will weaken the attachment to or affection for Big Brother. All good Party members are expected to love Big Brother above all else. The only affection tolerated by the Party is called Goodsex in Newspeak—the normal, marital relations between husband and wife only for the purpose of reproduction. Smith had previously been married to a fanatical Party member named Katheríne, but they had separated after discovering they could not do their duty to the Party by having children. They have not been divorced, since the Party rarely allows divorces. The Proles, who are not considered important even though they make up 85 percent of the population, are not restricted in their sexual and marital behavior because Proles exist solely to provide soldiers and workers for the State. They are kept in ignorance, and if a Prole looks like he might cause a problem, he is destroyed by the Thought Police.

Julia works in a division of the Ministry of Truth which provides reading material for Proles to keep them out of trouble. The novels she works on have only six possible plots, shuffled around by machine. This pornographic material, along with cheap gin, is endlessly supplied to the Proles to keep them from any awareness of reality. Party members who indulge in such vices are punished.

Winston and Julia becomes lovers, and in so doing, set themselves up against the Party. They know too that no matter how careful they are, they will eventually be found out. "Thoughtcrime does not entail death; thoughtcrime is death," Winston writes in his diary, realizing that he is as good as dead as a result of his crime.

Big Brother is watching them in the form of O'Brien, an urbane and cultured member of the Inner Party who is several levels above Winston and Julia. He strikes up a relationship with them, and they visit his home. As a member of the Inner Party, he is allowed to turn off the two-way screen which constantly spies on all members of society. They tell O'Brien that they are Thoughtcriminals. Winston says that he has heard of a secret brotherhood, headed by Emmanuel Goldstein, that plots to overthrow Big Brother. But just as no one has ever seen Big Brother, no one has ever seen Goldstein either, and it is likely that both are Party creations.

Winston and Julia join the Brotherhood through O'Brien, whom they suppose is its representative. They are willing to do whatever is necessary to work toward the overthrow of Big Brother. O'Brien gives Winston a copy of Goldstein's book, and promises that they will meet again.

They next meet in the underground rooms of the Ministry of Love, where the Thought Police torture victims. At the same time, Winston and Julia have found a place free of telescreens, a cheap room above an antique shop run by a Mr. Charrington. There, one day while they are in bed, the Thought Police come to arrest them, and it is revealed that even Mr. Charrington is an agent of the Thought Police. Winston is taken to be tortured.

The Party does not wish to kill Winston. Rather, they wish to change his way of thinking, to make him a perfect follower of Big Brother. After this, he may be killed, but the party is far more concerned with the mental destruction than the physical destruction of its enemies.

Next we see Winston's torture, his betrayal of Julia, and his final spiritual destruction, so complete that by the end of the book he does indeed love Big Brother. Winston provides another way the Party can show its power. Since Power is what the Party worships above all, there must be limitless reasons to exercise Power or the Party will cease to exit. The end of Power is Power; and the goal of the Inner Party is to maintain its Power by whatever means are necessary. The last third of the book is a dialogue between Smith and O'Brien on the theme of the Party and Power, in which O'Brien leads Winston through the path that will show him that he must believe anything that the Party decides that he will believe.

The Party has won. No matter what happens to Winston now, the Party has him in its control, for he will think no thought that is not approved by the Party. Just as the Ministry of Peace is concerned with war, so the Ministry of Love is concerned with torture, all in the name of Big Brother. Winston's spirit has been thoroughly crushed by the end of the book, so much so that it matters little whether he lives or dies.

Satire on Totalitarianism

Orwell's satire on totalitarianism in *1984* revolves around the distorted notions of law and justice illustrated. Our ideas of justice have come from the idea that people have what the Declaration of Independence calls "certain inalienable rights," rights which cannot be given or taken away. These rights have no value in society unless they are guaranteed and backed up by law, since otherwise, there would be no way of enforcing them.

One of the rights which we assume to be ours is the right to be ruled by a code of government which does not allow a person to be convicted of a crime unless the person knows that the act (or the omission of an act) is in fact a crime. This means that no one can be punished for breaking the law unless the person knows that there *is* a law. A person does not have to read all the laws, but is expected to know the law; thus, ignorance of the law is not accepted as an excuse. For example, you are expected to know that a red light means stop. If you go through a red light and a police officer stops you and gives you a ticket, you will not be excused if you say that you did not realize that it was illegal to pass red lights.

In *1984* there are no written laws; thus, everything *can* be a crime, but no one knows what really *is*. All crimes are combined into what is called Thoughtcrime, which involves not forbidden acts but thoughts. Our laws take no account of thoughts, only acts. How can someone be held legally responsible for thinking forbidden thoughts? Further, how can this be if he doesn't even know what *is* forbidden? But this is exactly the position of the Party, and it leads to complete tyranny.

Certain rights we have come to expect have been abolished in this book. For example, we take as basic the right of a person held for a crime to be released if there is not enough proof to hold him, or released on bail or certain other ways if the judge rules so. This is called the right of *habeas corpus*. In *1984*, people can be held without trial for months or even years, without even being told what the charges against them are.

In *1984*, people simply vanish, as was the case with Smith's parents, since there are no safeguards imposed on the society to protect the individual. Another right we assume is the integrity of the individual, but this too is violated by the Party. This is what the Party does to Winston and Julia—degrade them to the point where they are no longer what we would consider human.

Common crimes—murder, theft, etc.—still exist in *1984* and while they are punished by the Party, they are not considered as serious as Thoughtcrimes. Ordinary criminals are even treated with some favoritism by the jailers in *1984*.

In short, the absence of a legal code leaves punishment up to the whim of the Party. In the totalitarian states of the 1930s and 1940s, Orwell saw such things as imprisonment without trial, secret murder, and political assassination employed as normal rules of state. He believed that unless people obtained a written guarantee of their rights and freedoms, they would have nothing except that granted by a not always benevolent government.

Linguistic Satire in *1984*

The linguistic satire here is similar to that found in the works of Jonathan Swift, a writer Orwell much admired. Swift's "Tale of a Tub" and Book III of *Gulliver's Travels* contain brilliant satire on the corruption of language for political or religious purposes. Swift's ideal in language involved precision of meaning, which he employs in the works just mentioned. In "Tale of a Tub," for example, a satire on religious controversy and true and false religions, Swift makes the point that if a work is clear and has meaning, the average reader will immediately be aware of it, for it does not take extraordinary intelligence to understand a clear and meaningful work of literature. On the other hand, if a writer decides to conceal his meaning, he will bombard the reader with a collection of ill-selected and imprecise words. Orwell also advocates precision and clarity of meaning.

Orwell felt that much political writing seeks not to reveal the truth but to conceal it. The corruption of language takes two forms: the first involves the limitation of meaning and thought, and the second, the deliberate lack of precision and meaning through the use of words selected to soothe and cover reality.

In the appendix to *1984*, Orwell explains what he means fully. "The purpose of Newspeak was not only to provide a medium of expression for the world-view and mental habits proper to the devotee of Ingsoc, but to make all other modes of thought impossible." This seems to be impossible, but it can be brought about by destroying the *connotations* of words, so that each word will have one and only one possible meaning. Of course, we find exaggeration here for the purposes of satire. Accompanying the destruction of connotative meaning is the decline of the precision of language for political and economic causes, whereby euphemisms (soothing expressions such as "passed on" for "died") are used to obscure the truth. Thus political opponents of a totalitarian regime are not murdered or shot; they are "eliminated" or "liquidated." These words do not carry the same connotations of brutality, and they obscure the truth. These words come to substitute for real thought. Both of these processes—the narrowing of meaning through the elimination of connotation and the use of euphemism—are satirized in *1984*.

Newspeak is used by the Party to help make certain thoughts impossible by removing the very ideas and ways in which these thoughts can be phrased in English. Thus, even a dictionary has political import, as it is used to narrow down the meaning of words. Thus "free" can not be used in any way as to suggest political freedom; it can only be used to suggest that an object is not held by another, as in "the yard was free of small animals." So Newspeak limits the range of thought and expression.

The Party wishes to abolish Oldspeak as soon as possible, but since much of it is still in use, the language in *1984* is a cross between Oldspeak and Newspeak. Newspeak contains three vocabularies, A, B, and C. The A words are used in everyday life; the B words have been invented for political reasons; and the C words are technical and scientific. In practice, then, anti-Party thoughts would be difficult if not impossible.

"Political language," Orwell wrote in his essay "Politics and the English Language," "is designed to make lies sound truthful and murder respectable, and to give the appearance of solidity to pure wind." The process he saw in motion in the totalitarian countries in the 1930s and 1940s were completed in his satiric *1984*. Yet he saw that the process could be reversed if people were aware of the debasement of language and took steps to use it properly, to clarify rather than obscure thought.

We can conclude that *1984* satirizes all absolutist systems of political control of populations, whether we call these systems Communism, Fascism, or Oligarchical Collectivism, which is the form of government in *1984*. What all these forms have in common is that none is democratic. Orwell believed that man was not fully capable of power on his own, and thus government had to be constructed on a system of checks and balances. This book was, therefore, a satiric projection of the trends that Orwell saw surrounding him in the 1930s and 1940s trends about which he hoped to warn people.

ESSAY QUESTIONS ON SATIRE

Allow yourself 45 minutes to organize, write, and correct an essay on any of the following topics. Follow the directions for generating and organizing your thoughts as described in **Part 2: Essay Writing Guide**. Be sure to leave time to revise and edit your essay at the end.

1. Explain the purpose of the satire in any one satiric work that you have read. What exactly is it that the author is attacking? Select specific words or phrases from the text to prove your point; be specific. If possible, explain the background of the subject.

2. Select any one satiric piece that you have read and define the *tone*. To make your point clearly, isolate specific words and phrases that prove your thesis.

3. What are the tools of the satirist? What devices does he/she have at his/her disposal to make a point? How do these literary devices differ from those of the novelist or the short story writer?

4. Define satire in the opening paragraph of your essay. Then, show how any one work of recognized literary value is satiric.

5. Select any one satire and explain its audience. Show the group at which the satire is aimed, and explain how you came to that conclusion. Use specific details from the work to make your point.

6. Select any one satire that you have read and isolate and define the following elements: characters, objects of satire, style, unifying elements. Show how they work together to make the satirist's point.

SUGGESTED READING LIST

Note: For those authors with no specific work listed, any of their works is acceptable for the AP exam.

Ancient Satire

Horace
Juvenal
Martial
Petronius Arbiter

Medieval Satire

Roman de la Rose; thirteenth-century dream allegory
Chaucer, Geoffrey — *The Canterbury Tales* (selected); see especially "The Miller's Tale" and "The Nun's Priest's Tale"

Renaissance Satire

Brant, Sebastian
Rabelais, François — *Pantagruel* and *Gargantua*
Erasmus, Desiderius — *Praise of Folie*
Cervantes, Miguel de — *Don Quixote*
Barclay, Alexander
Butler, Samuel — *Hudibras*
Dryden, John — *Absalom and Achitophel*
Molière

Eighteenth-Century Satire

Gay, John — *Beggar's Opera*
Pope, Alexander — *Dunciad*
Addison, Joseph
Fielding, Henry
Austen, Jane
Smollett, Tobias George — *The Expedition of Humphry Clinker*
Voltaire — *Candide*

Nineteenth-Century Satire

Bierce, Ambrose — *Devil's Dictionary*
Thackeray, William
Twain, Mark
Dickens, Charles
Wilde, Oscar
Shaw, George Bernard

Twentieth-Century Satire

Lewis, Sinclair — *Babbitt*
Thurber, James
Waugh, Evelyn
Huxley, Aldous — *Brave New World*
West, Nathanael — *The Day of the Locust*
Nabokov, Vladimir
Grass, Günter
Hasek, Jaroslav — *The Good Soldier Schweik*
Heller, Joseph — *Catch-22*
Ellison, Ralph
O'Hara, John

The Essay

An essay is a literary composition which does not assume to treat a subject thoroughly. The word "essay," which comes from the French "essai," meaning an "attempt," was first used in the sixteenth century. Although usually written in prose, an essay may be written in verse, such as Pope's "Essay on Criticism." Because the main meaning of the term "essay" is a beginning study, an essay may be only a few pages long, or even less than a page, although there is no fixed length. There have been books of many essays and large books that contain only a single essay, but since the eighteenth century, most essays have appeared in magazines. Famous essayists include Addison, Steele, Lamb, Hazlitt, Macaulay, George Orwell, and Aldous Huxley. Around 1800, the Romantic writers employed a form of the essay called the *informal or familiar essay,* in which the author adopts a personal and chatty tone. He often reveals as much about himself as he does about the subject under discussion, as in Lamb's "Dissertation Upon a Roast Pig." *Formal essays,* in contrast, are impersonal analyses of various subjects, an example being John Locke's "Essay Concerning the Human Understanding." For more on the essay, consult Leslie Fiedler's *The Art of the Essay.*

DETERMINING TONE AND MOOD

An essayist often reveals a specific attitude in the course of developing his thesis. This is important because the speaker's tone or mood can often significantly affect the meaning of a passage; in some instances, the meaning depends on the speaker's attitude. Questions involving this aspect of a writer's craft often appear on Advanced Placement exams, and we find this especially important when considering an essay, which was usually written to convey a specific attitude in a very brief amount of space. A novelist has the room to expand his argument, a short story writer can rely on narration (telling a story) rather than persuasion (proving a point), but the essayist usually has a point to prove and tone/mood are among his most valuable tools.

The following passages illustrate this type of persuasive prose writing. Read them and answer the questions that follow each.

> 1. It takes no calendar to tell root and stem that the calm days of mid-summer are here. Last spring's sprouted seed comes to fruit. None of these things depends on a calendar of the days and months. They are their own calendar, marks on a span of time that reaches far back into the shadows of time. The mark is there for all to see, in every field and meadow and treetop, as it was last year and then years ago and when the centuries were young.
>
> The time is here. This is the point in the great continuity when these things happen, and will continue to happen year after year. Any summer arrives at this point, only to lead on to the next and the next, and so to summer again. These things we can count on; these will happen again and again, so long as the earth turns.

The passage indicates that the author experiences a feeling of
(A) frustration
(B) fear of the forces of nature
(C) pessimism
(D) serene confidence
(E) regret at the rapid passage of time

The answer here is (D), serene confidence, as the phrases "calm days," "great continuity," and "we can count on" reveal. The author has no fear of nature nor any regret at the passage of time; rather, we sense, through the phrases cited above, a calm acceptance of the seasons.

2. Engineers say that the push-button factories may eventually permit a work schedule in which the weekend will be longer than the week. Educators see all this leisure promoting a scholastic renaissance in which cultural attainments will become the yardstick of social recognition for worker and boss alike. Gloomier observers fear the trend toward "inhuman production" will end by making men obsolete.

The passage is developed principally by means of
(A) cause and effect
(B) examples
(C) definition
(D) narration
(E) contrast

The answer is (A), cause and effect, for the causes, such as "push-button factories" result in the effects, such as "the weekend will be longer than the week." Leisure will result in an cultural renaissance; "inhuman production" will result in men becoming obsolete. There are no specific examples here (B), and the author does not define his terms. In the same manner, narration, telling a story, (D), is not an element of this passage, nor is contrast, (E), except between the final sentence and the first two, but the main means of development remains cause and effect.

The writer's *tone* is established through his choice of words and their placement in the passage. This, in turn, reveals his attitude toward the subject matter. The next passage illustrates how tone reveals attitude:

Eventually the whole business of purveying to the hospitals was, in effect, carried out by Miss Nightingale. She, alone, it seemed, whatever the contingency, knew where to lay her hands on what was wanted; she alone possessed the art of circumventing the pernicious influences of official etiquette. On one occasion 27,000 shirts arrived, sent out at her insistence by the Home Government, and were only waiting to be unpacked. But the official "Purveyor" intervened; "He could only unpack them" he said, "with an official order from the Government." Miss Nightingale pleaded in vain; the sick and the wounded lay half-naked, shivering for want of clothing; and three weeks elapsed before the Government released the shirts. A little later, on a similar occasion, Miss Nightingale ordered a Government consignment to be forcibly opened, while the "Purveyor" stood by, wringing his hands in departmental agony.

1. The tone of the author reveals that his attitude toward Miss Nightingale is one of
   (A) amazement and chagrin
   (B) admiration and respect
   (C) prejudice and apathy
   (D) frustration and fright
   (E) dislike bordering on active hatred

2. The use of a phrase like "she alone" gives the reader an idea of Miss Nightingale's
   - (A) loneliness
   - (B) conceit
   - (C) femininity
   - (D) uniqueness
   - (E) inefficiency

3. Describing the influence of official etiquette as "pernicious" reveals the author's awareness of the
   - (A) dangers of red tape
   - (B) efficiency of command procedure
   - (C) lack of blood plasma
   - (D) women's liberation movement
   - (E) horrors of war

4. The description of the sick and wounded as "half-naked" and "shivering" serves as
   - (A) an introduction of physical detail
   - (B) weather information
   - (C) historic documentation
   - (D) contrast to bureaucratic lack of concern
   - (E) a metaphor

5. The Purveyor seems concerned only with
   - (A) humanity
   - (B) the ill men
   - (C) the men's needs
   - (D) departmental procedure
   - (E) Miss Nightingale's requests

6. In this selection, the author's tone is best communicated by his
   - (A) metaphors
   - (B) similes
   - (C) onomatopeia
   - (D) word choice
   - (E) general figurative language

Answers

1. (B) admiration and respect. The final example, where she circumvented official policy to make sure that the suffering were taken care of, reveals his attitude toward her.
2. (D) uniqueness. The first sentence reveals that she alone is responsible for the welfare of the suffering
3. (A) dangers of red tape. The incident concerning the delay in unpacking shirts already in the hospital shows the author's feelings about "red tape," the official tendency to make things more difficult than they need be.
4. (D) contrast to bureaucratic lack of concern. The author underscores the same point with the example of the shirts unreleased.
5. (D) departmental procedure. That he could stand by and watch people suffer shows this. The final incident is the same type of example.
6. (D) word choice. As cited earlier, the use of phrases like "half-naked" reveal the importance of word choice.

SAMPLE AP QUESTIONS ON THE ESSAY

The Advanced Placement Committee suggests the following topics for consideration in the study of the essay: (1) organization and structure of the essay; (2) speaker; (3) tone and mood; (4) style and language; (5) ideas and theme; (6) elements of fiction; (7) audience.

Following are some typical AP questions on the essay. Suggestions for answers follow the last question.

1. As expressed in the essay that follows, what is the cost of man's reliance on and interest in amassing property? Examine the premise of "Reliance on Property" and write an essay in which you show that the author's thesis does or does not hold true today.

RELIANCE ON PROPERTY

And so the reliance on property, including the reliance on governments which protect it, is the want of self-reliance. Men have looked away from themselves and at things so long that they have come to esteem the religious, learned and civil institutions as guards of property, and they deprecate assaults on these, because they feel them to be assaults on property. They measure their esteem of each other by what each has, and not by what each is. But a cultivated man becomes ashamed of his property, out of new respect for his nature. Especially he hates what he has if he sees that it is accidental,—came to him by inheritance, or gift, or crime; then he feels that it is not having; it does not belong to him, has no root in him and merely lies there because no revolution or no robber takes it away. But that which a man is, does always by necessity acquire; and what the man acquires, is living property, which does not wait the beck of rulers, or mobs, or revolutions, or fire, or storm, or bankruptcies, but perpetually renews itself wherever the man breathes. "Thy lot or portion of life," said the Caliph Ali, "is seeking after thee; therefore be at rest from seeking after it." Our dependence on these foreign goods leads us to our slavish respect for numbers. The political parties meet in numerous conventions; the greater the concourse and with each new uproar of announcement, The delegation from Essex! The Democrats from New Hampshire! The Whigs of Maine! the young patriot feels himself stronger than before by a new thousand of eyes and arms. In like manner the reformers summon conventions and vote and resolve in multitude. Not so, O friends! will the God deign to enter and inhabit you, but by a method precisely the reverse. It is only as a man puts off all foreign support and stands alone that I see him to be strong and to prevail. He is weaker by every recruit to his banner. Is not a man better than a town? Ask nothing of men, and, in the endless mutation, thou only firm column must presently appear the upholder of all that surrounds thee. He who knows that power is inborn, that he is weak because he has looked for good out of him and elsewhere, and, so perceiving, throws himself unhesitatingly on his thought, instantly rights himself, stands in the erect position, commands his limbs, works miracles; just as a man who stands on his feet is stronger than a man who stands on his head.

—*Ralph Waldo Emerson*

2. Explain the literary devices the author uses in the essay that follows to show the difference between a "mere thinker" and "Man Thinking."

MAN THINKING

It is one of those fables which out of an unknown antiquity convey an unlooked-for wisdom, that the gods, in the beginning, divided Man into men, that he might be more helpful to himself; just as the hand was divided into fingers, the better to answer its end.

The old fable covers a doctrine ever new and sublime; that there is One Man,—present to all particular men only partially, or through one faculty; and that you must take the whole society to find the whole man. Man is not a farmer, or a professor, or an engineer, but he is all. Man is priest, and scholar, and statesman, and producer, and soldier. In the *divided* or social state these functions are parcelled out to individuals, each of whom aims to do his stint of the joint work, whilst each other performs his. The fable implies that the individual, to possess himself, must sometimes return from his own labor to embrace all the other laborers. But, unfortunately, this original unit, this fountain of power, has been so distributed to multitudes, has been so minutely subdivided and peddled out, that it is spilled into drops, and cannot be gathered. The state of society is one in which the members have suffered amputation from the trunk, and strut about so many walking monsters,—a good finger, a neck, a stomach, an elbow, but never a man.

Man is thus metamorphosed into a thing, into many things. The planter, who is Man sent out into the field to gather food, is seldom cheered by any idea of the true dignity of his ministry. He sees his bushel and his cart, and nothing beyond, and sinks into the farmer, instead of Man on the farm. The tradesman scarcely ever gives an ideal worth to his work, but is ridden by the routine of his craft, and the soul is subject to dollars. The priest becomes a form; the attorney a statute-book; the mechanic a machine; the sailor a rope of the ship.

In this distribution of functions the scholar is the delegated intellect. In the right state he is *Man Thinking*. In the degenerate state, when the victim of society, he tends to become a mere thinker, or still worse, the parrot of other men's thinking.

In this view of him, as Man Thinking, the theory of his office is contained. Him Nature solicits with all her placid, all her monitory pictures; him the past instructs; him the future invites. Is not indeed every man a student, and do not all things exist for the student's behoof? And, finally, is not the true scholar the only true master?

—*Ralph Waldo Emerson*

3. In the essay that follows the author objects to man traveling in hopes of "get[ting] somewhat which he does not carry." Explain what this means by specific references to the essay.

TRAVELING

It is for want of self-culture that the superstition of Traveling, whose idols are Italy, England, Egypt, retains its fascination for all educated Americans. They who made England, Italy, or Greece venerable in the imagination, did so by sticking fast where they were, like an axis of the earth. In manly hours we feel that duty is our place. The soul is no traveler; the wise man stays at home, and when his necessities, his duties, on any occasion call him from his house, or into foreign lands, he is at home still and shall make men sensible by the expression of his countenance that he goes, the missionary of wisdom and virtue, and visits cities and men like a sovereign and not like an interloper or a valet.

I have no churlish objection to the circumnavigation of the globe for the purposes of art, of study, and benevolence, so that the man is first domesticated, or does not go abroad with the hope of finding somewhat greater than he knows. He who travels to be amused, or to get somewhat which he does not carry, travels away from himself, and grows old even in youth among old things. In Thebes, in Palmyra, his will and mind have become old and dilapidated as they. He carries ruins to ruins.

Traveling is a fool's paradise. Our first journeys discover to us the indifference of places. At home I dream that at Naples, at Rome, I can be intoxicated with beauty and lose my sadness. I pack my trunk, embrace my friends, embark on the sea and at last wake up in Naples, and there beside me is the stern fact, the sad self, unrelenting, identical, that I fled from. I seek the Vatican and the palaces. I affect to be intoxicated with sights and suggestions, but I am not intoxicated. My giant goes with me wherever I go.

—*Ralph Waldo Emerson*

4. Read the address that follows and then answer the questions about it.

SECOND INAUGURAL ADDRESS, MARCH 4, 1865

Fellow Countrymen: At this second appearing to take the oath of the presidential office, there is less occasion for an extended address than there was at the first. Then a statement, somewhat in detail, of a course to be pursued, seemed fitting and proper. Now, at the expiration of four years, during which public declarations have been constantly called forth on every point and phase of the great contest which still absorbs the attention and engrosses the energies of the nation, little that is new could be presented. The progress of our arms, upon which all else chiefly depends, is as well known to the public as to myself; and it is, I trust, reasonably satisfactory and encouraging to all. With high hope for the future, no prediction in regard to it is ventured.

On the occasion corresponding to this four years ago, all thoughts were anxiously directed to an impending civil war. All dreaded it—all sought to avert it. While the inaugural address was being delivered from this place, devoted altogether to saving the Union without war, insurgent agents were in the city seeking to destroy it without war—seeking to dissolve the Union, and divide effects, by negotiation. Both parties deprecated war; but one of them would make war rather than let the nation survive; and the other would accept war rather than let it perish. And the war came.

One eighth of the whole population were colored slaves, not distributed generally over the Union, but localized in the southern part of it. These slaves constituted a peculiar and powerful interest. All knew that this interest was, somehow, the cause of the war. To strengthen, perpetuate, and extend this interest was the object for which the insurgents would rend the Union, even by war; while the government claimed no right to do more than to restrict the territorial enlargement of it.

Neither party expected for the war the magnitude or the duration which it has already attained. Neither anticipated that the cause of the conflict might cease with, or even before, the conflict itself should cease. Each looked for an easier triumph and a result less fundamental and astounding. Both read the same Bible, and pray to the same God; and each invokes His aid against the other. It may seem strange that any man should dare to ask a just God's assistance in wringing their bread from the sweat of other men's faces; but let us judge not, that we be not judged. The prayers of both could not be answered—that of neither has been answered fully.

The Almighty has His own purposes. "Woe unto the world because of offenses! for it must needs be that offenses come; but woe to that man by whom the offense cometh." If we shall suppose that American slavery is one of those offenses which in the providence of God, must needs come, but which, having continued through His appointed time, He now wills to remove, and that He gives to both North and South this terrible war, as the woe due to those by whom the offense came, shall we discern therein any departure from those divine attributes which the believers in a living God always ascribe to Him? Fondly do we hope—fervently do we pray—that this mightly scourge of war may speedily pass away. Yet, if God wills that it continue until all the wealth piled by the bondman's two hundred and fifty years of unrequited toil shall be sunk, and until every drop of blood drawn with the lash shall be paid by another drawn with the sword, as was said three thousand years ago, so still must be said, "The judgments of the Lord are true and righteous altogether."

With malice toward none; with charity for all; with firmness in the right, as God gives us to see the right, let us strive on to finish the work we are in; to bind up the nation's wounds; to care for him who shall have borne the battle, and for his widow and his orphan—to do all which may achieve and cherish a just and lasting peace among ourselves, and with all nations.

—*Abraham Lincoln*

Questions on Lincoln's "Second Inaugural Address"

1. According to the passage, what was the North's purpose in entering the war?
2. According to the passage, what was the author's own feeling toward slavery?
3. Did the author believe that the preservation of the Union was important?
4. Why are there quotations from the Bible in this address? What purpose do they serve?
5. Would this address be considered an example of good—even superior—writing? Consider writing elements such as word choice, sentence variety, use of figurative language, tone, etc. in answering this question.

Suggested Answers to Sample Questions on the Essay

1. In "Reliance on Property," Emerson asserts that man's interest in amassing property is achieved at the expense of his self, his independence and self-reliance. "Men have looked away from themselves . . ." would be a line to support this, as would, "They measure their esteem of each other by what each has, and not by what each is." Whether or not this is true today is, of course, a matter of opinion, but most would agree that it is and could cite people's adherence to cults as proof that we seek some sense of self.
2. As stated in "Man Thinking," a "mere thinker" is a person following an intellectual exercise that he is unable to relate to what is happening about him, while a "Man Thinking" is a person who is able, using all his abilities, to experience

feelings of total awareness. The fable is the main literary device employed here; trace its development and parallels to the thesis.

3. In "Traveling," Emerson is referring to knowledge and wisdom, cultural and spiritual growth, and self-awareness, all of which escape those who travel to run away from themselves and their inner lives. The "giant" of the last line is the self that is unable to find beauty at home and cannot be affected by the simple experiences of daily life. No matter where we travel, we can never escape from ourselves.

4. Lincoln's "Second Inaugural Address"

    a) The purpose of the North's involvement was to preserve the Union as well as restrict "territorial enlargement" of slavery.

    b) Lincoln regarded slavery as a moral offense for which God had punished the nation by inflicting war.

    c) The preservation of the Union was Lincoln's main concern. Slavery was regarded as a secondary concern, although he realized it was the underlying cause of the conflict.

    d) The quotation from Matthew 7:1 foreshadows the lack of vindictiveness in the final paragraph: "With malice toward none; with charity for all. . . ." Those quotes from Matthew 18:7 and Psalms 19:9 are used to indicate a share in the responsibility.

    e) The speech is extraordinarily effective in what it seeks to accomplish. It is especially well written for the glimpse that it gives us of the speaker, who reveals himself here to be a wise and compassionate man. It is also almost free from recrimination, the assignment of blame. Slavery is attacked on moral grounds, but the ethics of men "wringing their bread from the sweat of other men's faces" is set forth with little heat, while the "two hundred and fifty years of unrequited toil" and the "blood drawn with the lash"—which are the most emotional lines in the speech—are presented in almost biblical language and thus seem to be missing a lot of their vengeful quality. The diction is simple for the most part, but there are times when the choice of words is amazingly precise and apt. The second sentence of the third paragraph, for example; "These slaves constituted a peculiar and powerful interest." There is nothing that could be substituted for "interest" and "peculiar" without seriously changing the exact meaning that the author desired. It is also a sign of good writing that so much of American history is contained in the words "strengthen, perpetuate, and extend this interest," which follows in the next sentence. Lincoln is also adept at varying his sentences to achieve specific effects. For example, he uses inversion, the switching of the normal, expected order of words within the sentence, to attract attention to specific sentences. Thus, "Fondly do we hope" and the opening sentences of the last paragraph attract our attention by their difference. While his sentences tend to be long and complex in style, he is careful to mix in some short statements for balance. This can be seen in the second and third paragraphs especially. At some points his prose borders on the poetic, as "Fondly do we hope—/ fervently do we pray—/ that this mighty scourge of war/ may speedily pass away." There are also numerous instances of specific poetic techniques such as assonance and alliteration, metaphor, and personification. "Bind up the nation's wounds" in the final paragraph would be an example of personification. But in the final analysis it is not the poetic devices that achieve the success here, but the restrained tone. The holding back of tone, the avoidance of excessive zeal, helps to convey the message of utter sincerity, especially in the final paragraph. The language of this address evokes the ugly realities of the war as well as the hope of people everywhere for a just and lasting peace. It is an especially effective example of clear, persuasive prose.

SUGGESTED READING LIST

Note: For those authors with no specific work listed, any of their essays are acceptable for the AP exam.

Addison, Joseph	
Angelou, Maya	"Graduation"
Bacon, Francis	
Baldwin, James	
Beauvoir, Simone de	
Carson, Rachel	
Chief Seattle	"My People"
de Tocqueville, Alexis	"Influence of Democracy on the Family"
Donne, John	
DuBois, W.E.B.	
Emerson, Ralph Waldo	
Faulkner, William	"Nobel Prize Acceptance Speech"
Fisher, M.K.F.	
Henry, Patrick	
Hughes, Langston	"Let America Be America Again"
Hurston, Zora Neale	"How It Feels to be Colored Me"
Jefferson, Thomas	"The Declaration of Independence"
Keller, Helen	
Kennedy, John F.	
King, Martin Luther, Jr.	"I Have a Dream"
	"Letter from Birmingham Jail"
Kingston, Maxine Hong	from *The Woman Warrior*
Lamb, Charles	
Least Heat Moon, William	
McCarthy, Mary	
Mead, Margaret	
Momaday, N. Scott	
Orwell, George	
Packard, Vance	
Poe, Edgar Allan	
Rodriguez, Richard	"The Achievement of Desire"
Sontag, Susan	
Steffens, Lincoln	
Swift, Jonathan	"A Modest Proposal"
Terkel, Studs	
Thomas, Lewis	
Thoreau, Henry David	*Walden*
Thurber, James	
Turner, Frederick Jackson	"The Significance of the Frontier in American History"
Trilling, Lionel	
Twain, Mark	
White, E.B.	
Wilson, Edmund	
Woolf, Virginia	

Part 4

Understanding Poetry

How to Read and Interpret Poetry

While there are different methods of approaching poetry, the following steps have proved helpful: Read the poem through once and see how much of the author's meaning you can immediately grasp. Then, go back through the poem a second time, line by line, and define all the unfamiliar words, concepts, ideas, and references. Figure out all the images and symbols, referring, if necessary, to outside works or other poems by the same author. Sometimes, it is helpful to "translate" each line into prose, or simply to substitute simpler words for the more difficult ones. When you understand all the basic words and ideas, reread the peom a few more times and pull it all back together.

Poetry will make a great deal more sense to you if you read it in a normal speaking tone, letting the accents fall where they seem natural. Pay attention to the punctuation the author uses, ending a line only when the punctuation indicates it is correct to do so. The punctuation marks in poetry tell us how the author wishes the work to be read. A period or an exclamation mark can be thought of as a complete stop, while a comma, in contrast, would be a half-stop. So there is no need to stop at the end of a line unless there is some punctuation mark to indicate that we must.

> Farewell, too little, and too lately known,
> Whom I begin to think and call my own;
> For sure our souls were near allied, and thine
> Cast in the same poetic mold with mine.

These first four lines of John Dryden's "To the Memory of Mr. Oldham" show several uses of the pause. When a line of verse has a pause at its end, as in "known," "own," and "mine," the line is called *end-stopped*. But when there are pauses indicated within the line, as after "little" and "allied," the term employed is *caesura*. This simply means a "little pause." When there is no pause at the end of the line, as in line 3 of this example, one line flows into the next and the line is called a *run-on line* or an *enjambement*. These effects are common in modern verse especially.

When reading poetry, follow the author's directions. Do not insert punctuation where none is indicated, and do not force a word to be stressed that would not normally be so. Some poets, Gerard Manley Hopkins, for one, frequently indicate to the reader that a certain word is to be stressed by the addition of a stress mark. Readers, of course, should follow such leads. Some lines may be read in more than one way, depending, for example, on the reader's background. A poem read by a Southerner sounds very different from one read by a New Englander, for example. Use your common sense and pronounce each line as you would normally speak, and the poem will make a great deal more sense.

Let's apply the suggestions outlined above to the reading and interpretation of the poems that follow.

SAILING TO BYZANTIUM

1

That is no country for old men. The young
In one another's arms, birds in the trees
—Those dying generations—at their song,
The salmon-falls, the mackerel-crowded seas,
5 Fish, flesh, or fowl, commend all summer long
Whatever is begotten, born, and dies.
Caught in that sensual music all neglect
Monuments of unaging intellect.

2

An aged man is but a paltry thing,
10 A tattered coat upon a stick, unless
Soul clap its hands and sing, and louder sing
For every tatter in its mortal dress,
Nor is there singing school but studying
Monuments of its own magnificence;
15 And therefore I have sailed the seas and come
To the holy city of Byzantium.

169

3

O sages standing in God's holy fire
As in the gold mosaic of a wall,
Come from the holy fire, perne in a gyre.
20 And be the singing-masters of my soul.
Consume my heart away; sick with desire

And fastened to a dying animal
It knows not what it is; and gather me
Into the artifice of eternity.

4

25 Once out of nature I shall never take
My bodily form from any natural thing.
But such a form as Grecian goldsmiths make
Of hammered gold and gold enameling
To keep a drowsy Emperor awake;
30 Or set upon a golden bough to sing
To lords and ladies of Byzantium
Of what is past, or passing, or to come.

—*Willam Butler Yeats*

INTERPRETATION OF "SAILING TO BYZANTIUM"

The first thing to discover here is the meaning of the title. According to the dictionary, Byzantium was an ancient Greek city on the Bosporus and the Sea of Marmara. Its buildings were characterized by highly formal structure and the use of rich color. This, however, doesn't tell us why Yeats selected this particular empire; there were, after all, many other ancient cities noted for the same qualities. Looking through other poems by the same author as well as critical studies of his work, we find that Byzantium had become for Yeats the symbol for art or artifice as contrasted with the natural world of biological activity. As he matured, he turned away from the sensual world of growth and constant change to the world of art. Later, though, he returned to the sensual world. As he wrote in his work, *A Vision*, "I think that if I could be given a month of antiquity and leave to spend it anywhere I chose, I would spend it in Byzantium [what we today call Istanbul] a little before Justinian opened St. Sophia and closed the Academy of Plato [around 535 A.D.] . . . I think that in early Byzantium . . . religious, aesthetic, and practical life were one, that architects and artificers . . . spoke to the multitude in gold and silver." In his old age, the poet rejected the world of growth and death—biological change—to turn instead to structures of what he called "unaging intellect."

This discussion fits in with the opening line reference to "old men," which we also could have discovered by looking up Yeats' age when he wrote this poem and the date of the poem itself. Yeats lived from 1865 to 1939, and this poem was published in 1927 when he was obviously in his later years. Thus, we can also infer that the poem has some autobiographical learnings.

The entire first stanza discusses the natural world of biological activity: the endless process of creatures being "begotten, born," and dying. He is the old man, as he states, turning away from all this.

The second stanza continues with the theme of the aging man, here made into the brilliant and oft-quoted symbol of the "tattered coat upon a stick." And so, seeking the unchanging world of art, the speaker comes, symbolically, to all that Byzantium has come to represent.

The "gold mosaic" in the third stanza refers to the mosaic figures on the walls of the Church of the Hagia Sophia ("Holy Wisdom") in Byzantium. There are two words that must be explained in the third stanza. The first is "perne," which means a bobbin, reel, or spool, and can also be spelled "pirn." The second is "gyre," which means to whirl around in a spiral motion. This became a favorite word of Yeats', and he used it as a verb, meaning "to spin around." He associated this spinning with the spinning of fate. Here he is asking the saints on the wall to descend and enter into this symbolic spinning motion, and thus help *him* enter into their state of being. We see this in the final line of this stanza, ". . . and gather me/Into the artifice of eternity."

Once he is able to leave the natural flux, he says in the final stanza, he shall not again assume a natural shape. Rather, he will assume a form that Grecian workers in gold might fashion. The form is specifically that of a bird. His notes say that he had read somewhere "that in the Emperor's palace in Byzantium was a tree made of gold and silver, and artificial birds that sang."

Therefore, we can conclude that "gyre" and "Byzantium" were key words in the poems of W. B. Yeats, whose special meanings are very important to how he felt about life, art, and approaching old age. Here he is turning away from the natural world to embrace the timeless world of art, represented for him in the symbol of Byzantium.

AMONG SCHOOL CHILDREN

1

I walk through the long schoolroom questioning;
A kind old nun in a white hood replies;
The children learn to cipher and to sing,
To study reading-books and history,
5 To cut and sew, be neat in everything
In the best modern way—the children's eyes
In momentary wonder stare upon
A sixty-year-old smiling public man.

2

I dream of a Ledaean body, bent
10 Above a sinking fire, a tale that she
Told of a harsh reproof, or trivial event
That changed some childish day to tragedy—
Told, and it seemed that our two natures blent
Into a sphere from youthful sympathy,
15 Or else, to alter Plato's parable,
Into the yolk and white of the one shell.

3

And thinking of that fit of grief or rage
I look upon one child or t'other there
And wonder if she stood so at that age—
20 For even daughters of the swan can share
Something of every paddler's heritage—
And had that color upon cheek or hair,
And thereupon my heart is driven wild:
She stands before me as a living child.

4

25 Her present image floats into the mind—
Did Quattrocento finger fashion it
Hollow of cheek as though it drank the wind
And took a mess of shadows for its meat?
And I though never of Ledaean kind
30 Had pretty plumage once—enough of that,
Better to smile on all that smile, and show
There is a comfortable kind of old scarecrow.

5

What youthful mother, a shape upon her lap
Honey of generation had betrayed,
35 And that must sleep, shriek, struggle to escape
As recollection or the drug decide,
Would think her son, did she but see that shape
With sixty or more winters on its head,
A compensation for the pang of his birth,
40 Or the uncertainty of his setting forth?

6

Plato thought nature but a spume that plays
Upon a hostly paradigm of things;
Soldier Aristotle played the taws
Upon the bottom of a king of kings;
45 World-famous golden-thighed Pythagoras
Fingered upon a fiddle-stick or strings
What a star sang and careless Muses heard:
Old clothes upon old sticks to scare a bird.

7

Both nuns and mothers worship images,
50 But those the candles light are not as those
That animate a mother's reveries,
But keep a marble or a bronze repose.
And yet they too break hearts—O Presences
That passion, piety, or affection knows.
55 And that all heavenly glory symbolize—
O self-born mockers of man's enterprise;

8

Labor is blossoming or dancing where
The body is not bruised to pleasure soul,
Nor beauty born out of its own despair,
60 Nor blear-eyed wisdom out of midnight oil.
O chestnut tree, great-rooted blossomer,
Are you the leaf, the blossom, or the bole?
O body swayed to music, O brightening glance,
How can we know the dancer from the dance?

—William Butler Yeats

INTERPRETATION OF "AMONG SCHOOL CHILDREN"

This poem can be read in the same manner as "Sailing to Byzantium." Also by Yeats, it is used here as an example to show how an author's body of work functions as a unified whole. The more examples of a poet's art you read, the more you will understand the symbols and allusions that artist employs.

The first stanza tells us that the speaker, a "sixty-year-old smiling public man," is touring a parochial school (note the reference to a nun), asking what the children are learning. Again, we can infer that the speaker bears some relation to Yeats, as we check the dates and discover that he was indeed in his early sixties when he wrote this poem. A quick look at a biography reveals that he was very well known and well respected at this time.

The second stanza contains many difficult allusions. Zeus visited Leda in the form of a swan. As a result of the union Leda gave birth to Helen of Troy. Yeats saw Zeus' visit as an "annunciation marking the beginning of Greek civilization." In Yeats's private mythology, this is used as a reference to Maud Gonne, a woman he very much admired, who functions in his verse as a kind of Helen, a shining ideal of womanhood—and betrayal. The first two lines of this stanza refer to Aristophanes' explanation of Love in Plato's *Symposium*. He suggested that the primeval man was round with four hands and four feet, back and sides forming a circle, one head having two faces. After the division, the two parts of man, desiring the other half, throw their arms around each other in embrace, not wanting to be alone. As the daughter of Leda and the swan, Helen would have been born from an egg, and this suggests Yeats's image for the coming together. This stanza, then, describes the child telling the speaker some tale that changed their normally happy and carefree childhood day to tragedy (as it would seem to a child). After they shared the sadness of the event, they were in such sympathy and agreement that their very natures bent into the form of a single being. Thus, it suggests how two persons can share the grief and blend into one when their natures are in accord.

Suddenly back in the present again, the speaker wonders if any of the little girls before him look as Maud did all those years ago when they were children. In this third stanza, he suddenly sees a little girl who looks just as Maud did many, many years ago, and his "heart is driven wild."

In the fourth stanza, he thinks of how she looks today, in the present, a mature woman. Quattrocento is a reference to the fifteenth century, and here he is calling to mind the painters of that period, especially Botticelli, noted for his lovely portraits of women. The speaker notes that although he was never as handsome as she was beautiful, he did have "pretty plumage once." He stops his remembrances there, for that is all passed now, and it is better to smile about the past for the sake of all the schoolchildren looking at the famous figure. He now sees himself as a "comfortable kind of old scarecrow," smiling nicely for the children.

In the fifth stanza he thinks of his mother, looking at her infant son now sixty years old. The references here are complex. The phrase "honey of generation" was taken from Porphyry's essay, Yeats tells us, but Porphyry did not consider it a "drug" that destroys the memory of pre-birth freedom. Porphyry was a philosopher who wrote during the third century A.D. "Honey of generation," by erasing the memory of happiness before birth, "betray[s]" an infant into being born into the world. The infant will either "sleep" or "struggle" to escape from the world, depending on whether the drug works or the memory of the bliss of life before birth takes over. Would his mother, looking at her 60-year-old son, think that his present "shape" (ie, condition, status, fame) was compensation for the pain of his birth or her fear of what fate would allot to him?

In the sixth stanza, we see that Plato believed that nature was but an appearance ("spume") covering the final spiritual and mathematical reality ("ghostly paradigm"). Aristotle believed that form was really in the matter of nature and thus nature itself had reality; thus Yeats calls him "soldier." Aristotle was Alexander the Great's tutor and punished him by using "taws," or straps, to beat him. So the first two lines here explain what Plato thought about nature, and the second two tell us that Aristotle disciplined Alexander (the king of kings) with a strap. Pythagoras was a Greek philospher who lived during the early sixth century B.C. and was interested in mathematics and music. His followers, called the Pythagoreans, developed a mythical philosophy of numerical relationships and tied together the fields of mathematics and astronomy in a theory of the music of the spheres. These followers regarded their master as a god with a golden thigh. Thus, these three lines refer to Pythagoras and his followers. The final line of this stanza is a contemptuous description of all three philosophers.

The beginning of the seventh stanza says that both nuns and mothers worship images: Nuns worship images of Christ or the Virgin; mothers worship their own inward images of their children. Mothers do not worship the same images as nuns do, the next line states.

The final stanza expresses Yeats' theme: Life is a cosmic dance, in which every human ability and part joins in smoothly. The individual becomes part of the whole, as the dancer becomes part of the dance. He sees this cosmic dance as a means of bringing together the conflicting parts of everyday life.

A Brief History of Meter

From the very first poems, oral accounts of adventures we date from the eighth century, an individual line of poetry has been the basic unit we recognize as "poetic." Up until the time of Walt Whitman's revolutionary poetic experiments, we were even able to say that a poem "looked like a poem," by which we meant that the lines stood apart in a certain recognizable manner and did not run together like a prose paragraph. The act of breaking down poetic lines into their basic units to discover their rhythm and rhyme is called *scansion*. *Scanning* a poem is not an attempt to discover its meaning; it is breaking down the verse into its textual parts. When we scan, we will discover that there are four basic types of verse: *accentual, syllabic, accentual-syllabic,* and *free verse.*

ACCENTUAL VERSE

The earliest recorded poetry, the eighth-century Anglo-Saxon verse mentioned above, was measured neither by rhyme nor by meter. From its inception in other languages, English has been an *accented* language. This means that certain words receive more spoken emphasis than others, that we stress certain parts or sounds within the word. The Anglo-Saxon poets used this system of accents as the basis of their poetry. The accents determined the length of the line of poetry. We use this system to indicate accents: An ictus (´) over a syllable means that it is to be accented. A breve (˘) over a syllable means that it is *not* accented.

If we look at a few sample lines from the poem <u>Beowulf</u>, from the eighth century, we see how the accentual system works to determine meaning:

Hwǽt! Wē Gár-Dena   in géar-dágum,

þéod-cýninga,   þrym gefrúnon,

hū ðā ǽþelingas   éllen frémedon!

The first line has nine syllables; the second, ten; the third, ten or eleven. But the number of syllables per line doesn't matter in verse that is scanned by accent. What is important is that each line have the same number of accents. Going through the poem, it becomes apparent that *four* accents predominate per line. No matter how you read the lines, though, no one would stress words such as "the" and "to."

Accentual verse comes up again in the works of Gerard Manley Hopkins, mentioned previously. Hopkins, who lived from 1844 to 1889, reintroduced accented verse to the modern ear with a variation called *sprung rhythm,* in which strongly accented syllables are pushed up against unaccented ones to produce a new way of scanning verse. Hopkins hoped to shake up the reader to his meaning by forcing us to look at his words in a new light.

SYLLABIC VERSE

Syllabic verse, has a different basis from *accented verse.* The French language, unlike English, makes little use of strongly accented words. One rarely counts out the number of accents in a line of French verse. Instead, the French developed a way of counting the number of syllables to establish the length of their lines of verse. When William the Conqueror invaded England in 1066, he introduced French poets experienced in syllabic rhythms and rhyme. The next few centuries, until the 1400's, saw the change from Old English (*Beowulf*, as we saw before, for example) to Middle English. Old English and French melded together; the language of the lower classes and the language of the court meshed to form Middle English, a midpoint between Old English and modern English. For a short period, the English court spoke French and listened to French poets composing verse within the strict confines of a syllabic line. Although this was a brief period and syllabic verse was altered quickly into accentual-syllabic poetry, later poets occasionally utilized lines determined solely by the number of syllables. In these verses, the number of accents could vary as long as the number of syllables remained constant. Modern poets continue to experiment with the syllabic idea, for it enables the author to escape the boundaries of a more regulated and often jingling or monotonous rhythmic cadence. Dylan Thomas, the Welsh poet who lived from 1914 to 1953, constructed such a syllabic verse:

> In my craft or sullen art
> Exercised in the still night
> When only the moon rages
> And the lovers lie abed . . .

Each line has seven syllables, even though the accents change in each line, both in their number and position.

ACCENTUAL-SYLLABIC VERSE

Accentual-syllabic verse is the kind of poetry that most people would identify immediately as "poetry." It often rhymes, has a definite beat—called *meter*—and usually moves with a predictable regularity. From the fourteenth century to the present, accentual-syllabic verse has been the norm, following rules strictly enforced. In some instances, the skill of the poet has been equated with ability to follow these rules and manipulate words within their confines.

Accentual-syllabic verse came into being when the counting of accents and the counting of syllables in a line occurred at the same time. Although many modern poets feel that this type of verse sounds forced and artificial, for centuries few were bothered by this at all. Rather, they felt it lovely and truly "poetic"—the measure of the craftsman's skill in forging words and ideas into a preconceived pattern. Poetry was closely linked to music and understood to be little more than the construction of a series of sounds, a work of skill and art. Conventional verse gains much of its success and beauty from the fact that English is a language in which word order is highly significant. When the poet is able to fashion language into a verse that moves with ease, a tension and power are created. It is like a formal garden, trained under the craftsman's eye for symmetry and order. Nature has been subdued, brought under man's control, and the work that results has a structure that many find enormously pleasing.

The *foot* of English poetry was created by counting out the number of accents and syllables together. Because English has an accented base, dividing a line into stressed and unstressed syllables creates certain recurring patterns. These measures also fit the patterns of classical Greek and Latin. In counting stresses, the two classical languages were also counting duration—the length of time it took to express an idea. In Greek and Latin, syllables were separated according to length, not stress. Long and short syllables were equated to what English terms stressed or unstressed, the *quality* of a syllable. Therefore, counting in accentual-syllabic verse came to be measured in *feet*.

There are four basic types of metrical feet in English verse:

$$\text{IAMB} \;\; \breve{}\, \acute{} \qquad \text{ANAPEST} \;\; \breve{}\, \breve{}\, \acute{}$$
$$\text{TROCHEE} \;\; \acute{}\, \breve{} \qquad \text{DACTYL} \;\; \acute{}\, \breve{}\, \breve{}$$

A foot is composed of either two or three syllables, such that the nature of the foot is determined by the placement of the accent. Every English sentence, no matter whether classified poetry or prose, is made up of these units. Their placement determines the *rhythm* of a line. Even more significantly, they establish the *meter* of a line, the regularity of a verse in an accentual-syllabic piece. One particular foot determines the poem's rhythm.

The following examples illustrate the four basic English feet:

Iamb	Ĭ táste/ ă líq/ uŏr név/ĕr bréwed
Trochee	Eárth, rĕ/ céive ăn/ hoňorĕd/ guést
Anapest	Ťe Ašsyř iaň caˇme doˇwn/ likĕ ťe wólf/ oň ťe fóld
Dactyl	Oút ŏf ťe/ crádlĕ/ eńdlešslў/ roćkiňg

A slash / is used as a divider to separate feet in a line.

Poetic lines are usually not composed of only one type of metrical foot, for this would sound dull. Variations are constructed to give the line more exciting movement. There are two rare feet,

$$\text{SPONDEE} \;\; \acute{}\, \acute{}$$
$$\text{PYRRHIC} \;\; \breve{}\, \breve{}$$

that are occasionally mixed in with the more usual ones. An iambic line, thus, may contain other feet, such as trochees, just as a trochaic line could contain iambs for variety. In lines with mixed feet, whichever foot is most prevalent determines the type and name of the line. Thus, a line with six iambs and four trochees would be called an iambic line.

After we figure out the predominant foot in the line, we mark the accents and count the number of feet in order to determine the total length of the line. For example:

Ĭ taśte/ ă liq́/ uŏr név/ eř bréwed

has a total of four iambic feet. This is called iambic tetrameter. The following chart explains the number of feet and the length of the line:

Number of Feet	Line Length
one	monometer
two	dimeter
three	trimeter
four	tetrameter
five	pentameter
six	hexameter
seven	heptameter

While it is possible to have a line containing more than seven feet, in actual practice, the heptameter line—a line from 14 to 21 syllables long—approaches the outer limits of most poems.

The most common foot in English is the iamb, perhaps because the use of articles—the, a, an—establishes that an unstressed syllable will occur before a stressed one. Children's verse, such as nursery rhymes, often has trochees dominating. This is also because children don't use as many articles as adults do in speech. The most common line in English poetry is the iambic pentameter line, in part because a line greater than ten syllables in length requires an intake of breath, which translates as requiring another line.

Even though the measurement of an accentual-syllabic line can be very precise, as illustrated earlier, there is a way for the poet to shorten or lengthen the line, even within strict metrical lines. This is called *elision*. For example, two vowels placed side by side may become a single syllable. We consider the letters h, w, and v as vowels, as well as the more easily recognized a, e, i, o, and u. These four lines by Raleigh illustrate the process:

> The flowers do fade, and wanton fields
> To wayward winter reckoning yields;
> A honey tongue, a heart of gall,
> In fancy's spring, but sorrow's fall.

This poem, "The Nymph's Reply to the Shepherd," is written in iambic tetrameter, which means that it should have eight syllables per line. The first two lines though, count out to nine syllables apiece, while the second two come out to the expected eight. We deal with the extra syllable in the first line by taking the word "flowers" and treating it differently. The vowels o, w, and e come together to create what we call a *diphthong*, meaning two syllables which may be counted or pronounced as one if the poet should so desire. The same is done with the word "reckoning" in the second line, compressing into two syllables what might have been considered three with more formal pronunciation. The same process can be seen in Milton's sonnet "On the Late Massacre," which has an iambic pentameter line with eleven syllables instead of the usual ten:

> ... and they
> To Heaven. Their martyred blood and ashes sow
> O'er all th'Italian fields where still doth sway
> The triple tryant;

Elision occurs here with the words "To Heaven" where the two-syllable word "Heaven" is treated as though it had only one syllable. In the next line, "Over" is written "O'er," indicating elision by spelling. In the same manner, "the Italian fields" is shortened to "th'Italian fields." It is rare today to find words contracted as Milton did to show the elision, for it is felt to be old-fashioned, but it is nonetheless present in modern accentual-syllabic verse. You will be able to find it when you read the lines for their meter.

Accents may also be used to give the poet greater leeway at the end of a line of verse. A line is said to have a *feminine ending* when it ends on an unaccented syllable, a *masculine ending* when it ends on an accented one: These lines from Milton's epic *Paradise Lost* have a feminine ending:

> Thus they in mutual accusation spent
> The fruitless hours, but neither self condemning

The second line has an extra syllable because of its feminine ending, but as an unaccented additional syllable at the close of a line, the "ing" may be discounted. Thus a line that counts out to 11 syllables may, at the poet's decision, become technically a 10-syllable line thanks to the feminine ending.

FREE VERSE

Free verse has no fixed metrical pattern: It is free from counting, measuring, meter. Free verse replaces the expected pattern of a particular foot with a looser movement called *rhythm*. Free verse shares a common basis with accentual and syllabic verse, but it must be devoid of all predominant measurements to be considered truly "free." The placement of accents must follow no pattern; the syllables must not be able to be measured with any regularity. In the same manner, *rhyme,* if used at all, is irregular. A poem may be considered free verse if you can find no accentual or syllabic pattern. It may, of course, have other regularities. This type of verse can be found in the work of e.e. cummings and Walt Whitman, among others.

There are some modern poets who consider free verse to be anything in which no attempt has been made to make the lines of verse fit a definite pattern, even though they do, in fact, have patterns at intervals. Often a page of poetry will look like free verse, but upon closer examination, will reveal itself to be syllabic or accentual. The poems of T. S. Eliot and Dylan Thomas are of this type. There are many other modern poems that have no metric regularity and are thus considered free verse, although they have a great deal of rhythm, such as the work of Lawrence Ferlinghetti.

Some poets have carried matters to such a length that they have created poems where the shape, not the words, is what matters. These are called *concrete poems.* Sometimes just repeating one letter of the alphabet, they leave it to the reader's eye to create a pleasing or important shape and meaning.

We have looked thus far at rhythm and accents, syllables and lines, but it's obvious that these can be grouped in several ways. Often these lines arrange themselves into blocks of specific numbers—two lines, four lines, six lines, etc. Usually there is a space, followed by an equal grouping of lines. A grouping of lines is called a stanza, roughly the same as a paragraph in a prose work. Stanzas may be classified as follows:

Couplets	2-line stanzas
Quatrains	4-line stanzas
Sextets	6-line stanzas
Octets	8-line stanzas

A Quick Review of Meter

Scansion	The act of breaking down lines into their basic units to discover rhythm and rhyme.
Accent	Emphasis or stress on certain words or parts of words.
Ictus	' mark over the syllable to indicate that it is accented.
Breve	˘ mark over the syllable to indicate that it is not accented.
Sprung Rhythm	A reintroduction of accentual verse in the works of Gerard Manley Hopkins (1844–1889), in which strongly accented syllables are pushed up against unaccented ones to produce greater tension and emphasis within the verse.
Accentual Verse	A system of verse in which accents are used to determine the length of lines of poetry. The number of syllables per

	line is unimportant. This is found mainly in the works of the earliest poets, dating from the eighth century.
Syllabic Verse	A system of verse in which syllables are used to determine the length of a line of poetry. This type of verse flourished mainly in the period between 1066–1400, although modern poets have experimented with it.
Accentual-Syllabic Verse	A type of verse in which the counting of accents and syllables occurs within the same line. It is the type of poetry most people instantly recognize as "poetic," for it has a definite beat and often rhymes.
Meter	The "beat" of a line of verse determined by the kind and number of poetic feet.
Foot/Feet	A group of stressed and unstressed syllables combining to form a unit of verse.
iamb ˘ ´	An unstressed syllable followed by a stressed one
trochee ´ ˘	Stressed, unstressed syllables
anapest ˘ ˘ ´	Two unstressed followed by a stressed
dactyl ´ ˘ ˘	Stressed followed by two unstressed
spondee ´ ´	Two stressed syllables
phyrrhic ˘ ˘	Two unstressed syllables
/	Used as a divider to separate feet in a line

Number of Feet	line length
one	monometer
two	dimeter
three	trimeter
four	tetrameter
five	pentameter
six	hexameter
seven	heptameter

Elision	The elimination of a vowel, consonant, or syllable in pronunciation. It usually occurs in verse at the end of a word when the next word begins with a vowel, and is used to shorten or lengthen a line to make it fit metrical requirements.
Diphthong	Two syllables that are counted and pronounced as one, used in poetry to make the words fit the metrical requirements.
Feminine Ending	A line that ends on an unaccented syllable.
Masculine Ending	A line that ends on an accented syllable.
Free Verse	Poetry without a fixed metrical pattern. The rhythmical lines vary in length and are usually unrhymed. Although the form may appear unrestrained, there is a firm pattern to the words.
Concrete Verse	Poems shaped like a specific object.
Stanza	An arrangement of a certain number of lines forming the divisions of a poem.

Types of Stanzas

couplets	2-line stanzas
quatrains	4-line stanzas
sextets	6-line stanzas
octets	8-line stanzas

Rhyme and Figurative Language

Rhyme is the repetition of the same or similar sounds often occuring at set intervals in a poem. Many find it pleasant in itself, and it also serves to suggest order and pattern. In addition, it often relates to the meaning of the verse, for it brings words together and suggests relationships.

The most obvious type of rhyme is called end rhyme, since it appears at the end of a line. For example, the word "light" rhymes with "fight," "sight," etc. The rhyming constant is the sound "ight," on which the poet forms other rhymes by changing the first letter or letters. To some extent, the use of rhyme is similar to the musical pattern of returning to a recognized theme or note. In ancient poetry, before the advent of writing, rhyme was invaluable, for it was far easier to commit to memory poetry that had a strong pattern of rhyme.

KINDS OF RHYME

True or *perfect rhyme* occurs when the first consonants change, but following consonants or vowels stay the same. This can also be referred to as *exact rhyme*. These involve identity of sound, not spelling. "Fix" and "sticks," like "buffer" and "rougher," though spelled diffeently, are perfect rhymes. Anne Bradstreet's "Before the Birth of One of Her Children" (1678) illustrates true rhyme:

> All things within this fading world hath end,
> Adversity doth still our joys attend;
> No ties so strong, no friends so dear and sweet,
> But with death's parting blow is sure to meet.

In the lines quoted, "end," which we shall call *a*, rhymes with "attend," also called *a*, while "sweet," called *b*, rhymes with "meet." The *rhyme scheme*, then, is *aabb*, etc.

Half-rhyme (also called *slant rhyme, approximate rhyme, near rhyme,* or *off-rhyme*) occurs when there are changes within the vowel sounds of words intended to rhyme and only the final consonant sounds of the words are identical. The stressed vowel sounds as well as the initial consonant sounds (if any) differ. Examples include: soul:oil; firth:forth; trolley:bully. The following lines from William Whitehead's "Je Ne Sais Quoi" exemplify half-rhyme:

> Tis not her face that love creates,
>   For there no grace revel;
> Tis not her shape, for there the Fates
>   Had rather been uncivil.

"Revel" and "uncivil in lines 2 and 4 above illustrate half-rhyme because the vowel sound changes, but the "vl" sound has remained the same.

Assonance occurs when the vowels in the words are the same, but the consonants are not, for example, in the words "seat" and "weak." *Consonance* occurs when the consonants agree but the vowels do not, as in the words "luck" and "lick." "Tide" and "mine" are assonantal. Assonance and consonance are both variations of half-rhyme.

Internal rhyme occurs within the line instead of at the end. Oscar Wilde's "Each narrow cell within which we dwell" would be an example of internal rhyme because the words "cell" and "dwell" rhyme.

Masculine and *feminine rhymes* are the equivalents of masculine and feminine line endings. Rhymes that end on a stress, such as "van" and "span," are masculine, while those ending on an unstressed syllable, such as "falling" and "calling," are called feminine. Thus, "stark/mark" and "support/retort" would be masculine while "revival/arrival" and "flatter/batter" are feminine. Feminine rhyme is also referred to as *double rhyme*. Also a feminine rhyme, *triple rhyme* as defined in *A Handbook to Literature** is a rhyme in which the correspondence of sound lies in three consecutive syllables. "Machinery/scenery" and "tenderly/slenderly" are two examples.

Alliteration is the repetition of an initial sound in two or more words. Although not technically considered a type of rhyme, it will be treated here because its use adds to the musical quality of a poem.

About the lilting house and happy as the grass was green

shows alliteration in the repetition of *h* in "house" and "happy" and the *gr* in "grass" and "green." Alliteration is also called *initial rhyme*. In Macbeth's line, "after life's fitful fever," true alliteration is found in the repeated *f*s of "fitful fever" and *hidden alliteration* is found in the *f*s of "after," "life," and "fitful." Accentual Anglo-Saxon poetry, used alliteration a great deal to create the balance and music of its verses.

Eye-rhyme occurs when words are spelled the same and look alike but have a different sound, see the following lines 3 and 4 of Sir Walter Raleigh's poem "The Nymph's Reply to the Shepherd."

"These pretty pleasures might me move
To live with thee and be thy love"

The words "move" and "love" are an example of eye rhyme. These rhymes are also called *historical rhymes* as, in the above example by Sir Walter Raleigh, the pronunciation has changed over the years. The word "tea," for example, once rhymed with "day," but today these two words are, at best, *half-rhymes*.

Onomatopoeia occurs when the sound of word echoes or suggests the meaning of the word. "Hiss" and "buzz" are examples. There is a tendency for readers to see onomatopoeia in far too many instances, in words such as "thunder" and "horror." Many words that are thought to echo the sound they suggest merely contain some sound which seems to have a resemblance to the thing it suggests. Tennyson's lines from "Come Down, O Maid" are often cited to explain true onomatopoeia:

"The moan of doves in immemorial elms
And murmuring of innumerable bees."

Euphony is the use of a pleasant-sounding or harmonious combination of words, while *cacaphony* is harsh or discordant sound used to produce an unharmonious effect.

FIGURATIVE LANGUAGE

Robert Frost, the twentieth-century American poet, once said, "Poetry provides the one permissible way of saying one thing and meaning another." Of course, this is an exaggera-

*William Flint Thrall and Addison Hibbard, *A Handbook to Literature,* ed. C. Hugh Holman (New York: The Odyssey Press, 1960) p. 495.

tion, but it does underline the importance of *figurative language*—saying one thing in terms of another. Words have a literal meaning that can be looked up in any dictionary, but they can also be employed so that something other than that literal dictionary meaning is intended. What is impossible or difficult to convey to a reader through the literal use of language may be highly possible through the use of *figures of speech,* also called *tropes. Figures of speech* make language significant, moving, and fascinating. "My love is a rose" is, when taken at face value, ridiculous, for few love a plant with a prickly, thorny stem. But "rose" suggests many other possible interpretations—delicate beauty, soft, rare, costly, etc.—and so it can be implied in a figurative sense to mean "love" or "loved one."

If a reader comes across the phrase "Brutus growled," he/she is forced, if the poem has indicated that Brutus is a human, to accept "growled" in a nonliteral manner. We understand that it is likely that the poet is suggesting that Brutus spoke like an animal, perhaps a lion or a bear, and indicates Brutus' irritation or unrest. The author calls forth the suggestion of wild animals to describe Brutus most vividly and accurately. It is far more effective than saying "Brutus spoke like an animal," or "Brutus acted like an animal." By using a figure of speech, the author calls the reader's imagination into play.

THE FIGURES OF SPEECH

Simile. A simile is a comparison between unlike objects introduced by a connective word such as "like," "as," or "than," or a verb such as "seems." The following are some examples:

> My heart is like a singing bird (C. Rossetti)
> I am weaker than a woman's tear (Shakespeare)
> Seems he a dove? His feathers are but borrowed (Shakespeare)

Metaphor. A metaphor is a comparison without the "like" or "as." Once established, this relationship between unlike objects alters our perception of both. In the most basic metaphor, such as "My love is a rose," "rose" and "love" are equated. They are not alike, but they interact with one another, so the abstract word, "love," becomes concrete. Now it is not a vague internal emotion but an object that could be picked and caressed. We can make the comparison even more specific by describing the rose in more detail—color, variety, and so forth. The subject of the comparison—in this case, love—is called the *tenor,* and the figure that completes the metaphor—the rose—the *vehicle.* These terms were coined by critic I.A. Richards. In the following metaphor by John Donne, the poet's doctors become the map-makers of the heavens, while the poet's body becomes the map in which the ultimate destiny of his soul can be divined:

> Whilst my physicians by their love are grown
>   Cosmographers, and I their map, who lie
> Flat on this bed . . .

Implicit or Submerged Metaphor. If we do not have both terms of the metaphor present ("My winged heart" instead of "My heart is a bird"), we have what is called a submerged metaphor.

Mixed Metaphor. A mixed metaphor combines two metaphors, often with absurd results. For example, "Let's iron out the bottlenecks," would be silly, for it is obvious that it is an impossibility.

Dead Metaphor. A metaphor that has lost its figurative value through overuse is called a dead metaphor. "Foot of a hill" or "eye of a needle" are examples.

Extended Metaphor. An extended metaphor results when a metaphor becomes elaborate or complex. It has length and the ideas are more fully illustrated.

Conceit. A metaphor that goes beyond the original tenor and vehicle to other tenors and vehicles is called a conceit. In "A Valediction Forbidding Mourning" by Donne, the souls of two lovers become the same as the two legs of a draftsman's compass:

> If they be two, they are two so
>   As stiff twin compasses are two;
> Thy soul, the fixed foot, makes no show
>   To move, but doth, if th'other do.
>
> And through it in the center sit,
>   Yet when the other far doth roam,
> It leans and harkens after it,
>   And grows erect, as that comes home.

Metonymy. Metonymy is the substitution of one item for another item that it suggests or to which it is closely related. For example, if a letter is said to be in Milton's own *hand*, it means that the letter is in Milton's own handwriting. As another example, Sidney wrote in his sonnet "With How Sad Steps, O Moon," "What, may be that even in heav'nly place/That busy archer his sharp arrows tries?" "That busy archer" is a reference to Cupid, the god of love frequently depicted as a cherubic little boy with a quiver full of arrows. Here he is at his usual occupation—shooting arrows into the hearts of unsuspecting men and women. Thus an archer, by relating to the god of love, describes love without specifically using the word.

Synecdoche. Synecdoche substitutes a part of something for the whole, or the whole is used in place of one of the parts. "Ten sails" would thus stand for ten ships. In the stanza below by American poet Emily Dickinson, "morning" and "noon," parts of the day, are used to refer to the whole day. In the same manner, "Rafter of Satin" refers to a coffin, by describing its inner lining rather than the entire object:

> Safe in their Alabaster Chambers—
> Untouched by Morning—
> And untouched by Noon—
> Lie the meek members of the Resurrection—
> Rafter of Satin—and Roof of Stone!

Transferred Epithet. Transferred epithet is a word or phrase shifted from the noun it would usually describe to one which has no logical connection with it, as in Gray's "drowsy tinklings," where "drowsy" literally describes the sheep who wear the bells, but here is figuratively applied to the bells. In current usage, the distinction between metonymy, synecdoche, and transferred epithet is so slight that the term metonymy is often used to cover them all.

Personification. Personification is the attribution of human characteristics and/or feelings to nonhuman organisms, inanimate objects, or abstract ideas. "Death, Be Not Proud" by John Donne addressed Death as if it were a person capable of hearing as well as possessing human emotions, such as pride. Tennyson's "Now sleeps the crimson petal, now the white" and Shakespeare's reference to "Time's cruel hand" are both examples of this process at work.

Pathetic fallacy. This is a specific kind of personification in which inanimate objects are given human emotions. John Ruskin originated the term in *Modern Painters* (1856). Ruskin uses the example of "the cruel crawling foam" of the ocean to discuss the pathetic fallacy: The ocean is not cruel, happy to inflict pain on others, as a person may be, although it may well seem cruel to those who have suffered because of it. Ruskin obviously disapproved of such misstatement, and allowed it only in verse where the poet was so moved by passion that he could not be expected to speak with greater accuracy. But in all truly great poetry, Ruskin held, the speaker is able to contain his excess emotion to express himself accurately. The term is used today, however, without this negative implication.

Apostrophe. Apostrophe is also closely related to personification. Here, a thing is addressed directly, as though it were a person listening to the conversation. For example we have Wordsworth's "Milton! thou should'st be living at this hour," although Milton has obviously passed on. Apostrophe and personification go hand-in-hand in Donne's "Busy old fool, unruly Sun," and Wyatt's "My lute, awake." Milton's apostrophe has only a hint of the laurels as listening things in "Yet once more, O ye laurels."

Invocation. Invocation is an address to a god or muse whose aid is sought. This is commonly found at the beginning of an epic. For example, Milton's "Sing, Heavenly Muse" at the opening of his *Paradise Lost.*

Hyperbole or Overstatement. This is exaggeration for a specific literary effect. Shakespeare's Sonnet 97 contains this example:

> How like a winter hath my absence been
> From thee, the pleasure of the fleeting year!
> What freezings have I felt, what dark days seen!
> What old December's bareness everywhere!

We realize obviously that Shakespeare did not literally freeze with real cold when he was apart from his loved one. We also realize that the days did not turn dark, or June turn to December, but he is saying this to illustrate the depth of his despair at their separation. The same process is at work in Lovelace's "When I lie tangled in her hair/And fetter'd to her eye . . .". Obviously, he is not captured in her hair nor chained to her eye; what he is suggesting, however, is that he is a prisoner to her beauty and finds himself unable to escape its spell.

Understatement. Understatement is the opposite of exaggeration, a statement that states less than it indirectly suggests, as in Jonathan Swift's "Last week I saw a woman flayed, and you will hardly believe how much it altered her person for the worst." In the same way, Auden's ironic poem "The Unknown Citizen" has a great many examples of understatement that combine to show how numbers cannot evaluate the ultimate happiness of a person's life.

Litote. Litote is a special form of understatement. It affirms something by negating its opposite. For example, "He's no fool" means that he is very shrewd.

Synesthesia. This takes one of the five senses and creates a picture or image of sensation as perceived by another. For example, "the golden cry of the trumpet" combines "golden", a visual perception of color, with "cry," hearing. In the same manner, Emily Dickinson speaks of a fly's "blue, uncertain stumbling buzz."

Oxymoron. Oxymoron is the combination of contradictory or incongruous terms. "Living death," "mute cry," and Milton's description of hell as "no light, but rather darkness visible" are all examples of this process. The two words that are brought together to form a description of this nature ought to cancel each other out by the nature of their contradictions; instead, they increase the sense of each word. Thus "sweet pain" aptly describes certain experiences of love.

Onomatopoeia. As mentioned earlier, onomatopoeia refers to the repetition of a sound intended to echo what it is describing. The famous last lines of Tennyson's "Come Down, O Maid," contain an example. "The moan of doves in immemorial elms,/And murmuring of inumerable bees" suggests the sounds of birds and bees among old trees.

Symbolism. Symbolism occurs when an image stands for something other than what was expected. The ocean, for example, may be said to symbolize "eternity," and the phrase "river to the sea" could stand for "life flowing into afterlife." In most instances the symbol does not directly reveal what it stands for; the meaning must be discovered through a close reading of the poem and an understanding of conventional literary and cultural symbols. For example, we realize that the "stars and stripes" stands for the American flag. We know this because we are told it is so, for the flag itself in no way looks like the United States. Without cultural agreement, many of the symbols we commonly accept would be meaningless.

Irony. Irony states things in one tone of voice when in fact the opposite meaning is intended. Auden's "Unknown Citizen," for example, ends ironically by making a statement that the reader knows to be false. As a matter of fact, the entire poem is ironic in that it condemns the State by using the State's own terms of praise: "Was he free? Was he happy? The question is absurd;/Had anything been wrong, we should certainly have heard."

Socratic Irony. This form of irony is named for Socrates, who usually pretended to be ignorant when he was in fact cautious or tentative. The person who states "I do not understand; please explain this to me . . ." is a Socratic ironist, and his words are ironic, for he clearly does understand.

Verbal Irony. This form of irony involves a contrast between what is stated and what is more or less wryly suggested. The statement is somehow negated by its suggestions. Thus, Pope attacks the proud man by ironically encouraging his pride:

> Go, wiser thou! and, in thy scale of sense,
> Weigh thy opinion against Providence . . .
> Snatch from His hand the balance of the rod,
> Re-judge his justice, be the God of God.

What is stated ironically need not always be the direct reverse of what is suggested; irony may, for instance, state less than what is suggested, as in the following understatement: "Men have died from time to time."

Sarcasm. Sarcasm is crude and heavy-handed verbal irony.

Dramatic Irony, Sophoclean Irony, Tragic Irony. Here the irony refers to conditions or affairs which are the tragic reverse of what the participants have expected. Thus, it is ironic that when Eve eats the forbidden fruit she is faced with great sorrow, for she had expected great joy and happiness. Macbeth expected great happiness to follow his killing of King Duncan; instead, he finds that he forfeits all that makes life worth living by his deed. Sophocles' King Oedipus accuses the blind prophet of corruption, but by the end of the play he learns, as we had realized all along, that he is himself corrupt, that he has been blind to what is real, and that the prophet's visions were indeed correct. As in verbal irony, dramatic irony is marked by contrast, but here it is not between what the speaker says and means, but between what he says and means and the real state of affairs.

Irony of Fate or Cosmic Irony. This term describes the view that God, Fate, or some supernatural being is amused to manipulate human beings as a puppeteer would manipulate puppets. It is an irony of fate that the prisoner receives his pardon a moment too late.

Romantic Irony. Romantic irony is most commonly found in German literature and shows the creator detaching himself from his creation to treat it playfully or objectively.

Contrast. Contrast shows the difference between two objects. In this sense it is the opposite of comparison, which shows similarities. In the following example by William Shakespeare, we see his mistress contrasted to various accepted symbols of adoration:

> My mistress' eyes are nothing like the sun;
> Coral is far more red than her lips' red;
> If snow be white, why then her breasts are dun;
> If hairs be wires, black wires grow on her head.

Connotation and Denotation. Connotation is the generally accepted meaning(s) of a word, in contrast to the denotation, which is the dictionary meaning. Connotation adds additional richness to a word's, and by extension a poem's, meaning. In the line, "She was the sickle; I, poor I, the rake," the word "rake" has a clear denotation—a gardening tool designed to pick up clippings from a lawn or a garden that a sickle might have cut down. In the context of the entire poem, though, the word "rake" has the connotative meaning of a debauched man. The two meanings work together to give the poem greater depth and further the author's theme.

Ambiguity. Ambiguity allows multiple meanings to coexist in a word or a metaphor. It does not mean that the word or term is unclear; rather, it means that the perceptive reader can see more than one possible interpretation at the same time. Puns, for example, offer ambiguity, as these lines from Wyatt's "They Flee From Me" show: "But since that I so kindely [*sic*] am served/I fain would know what she hath deserved." The word "kindely" means both "served by a group" and "courteously."

Allegory. Allegory occurs when one idea or object is represented in the shape of another. In medieval morality plays and in some poems, abstract ideas such as virtues and vices appear as people. In this way the reader can understand a moral or a lesson more easily. In Emily Dickinson's poem "Because I Could Not Stop For Death," death appears as the allegorical figure of a coachman, kindly stopping to pick her up on the road to eternity.

Types of Poems and Poetic Movements

POETIC FORMS

Ballads. The *traditional* or *popular ballad* is a story told in song form which has been passed by word of mouth from singer to singer, generation to generation. Unlike formal written verse, ballads underwent change. They were common in the fifteenth century, and one, "Judas," is known to have passed down from the thirteenth century. The oral nature is shown in the effective transitions in the narrative, for weak verses tended to get taken out and forgotten, resulting in a highly effective series of pictures in words.

The tradition of the ballad runs through English and American verse. The anonymous ballads of the fifteenth century have their counterpart in the ballads of the twentieth century, in songs of social protest and stories of ordinary people. Traditional ballads were produced throughout the nineteenth century also, in America, commonly by sailors, loggers, and plantation workers—relatively isolated and illiterate people. In rural areas, such ballads are still flourishing today.

When professional poets write stanzas of this type, such as Auden's "I Walked Out One Evening," they are called *literary ballads*. English and Scottish ballads have been imitated by serious poets. Probably the most famous ballads are Coleridge's "Rime of the Ancient Mariner" and Keats's "La Belle Dame sans Merci."

The ballad stanza rhymes *abcb*. ballads often contain *refrains,* musical reptitions of words or phrases. Some critics believe that ballads were originally two-line rhyming songs, thus explaining why there are only two rhymes in a four line stanza. Because early ballads were nonliterary, half-rhymes and slant rhymes are often used. The common stanza is a quatrain of alternating lines of iambic tetrameter and iambic trimeter. Ballads sometimes employ *incremental repetition,* the repetition of some previous line or lines, but with a slight variation to advance the narrative, as in these lines from "The Cruel Brother":

> O what will you leave to your father dear?
> The silver-shode steed that brought me here.
> And what will you leave to your mother dear?
> My velvet pall and my silken gear.

Interestingly, there are frequent nonsense lines in the refrains—"Every rose is merry in time" is a misunderstanding of "Savory, rosemary, and thyme"—perhaps because of oral transmission.

Though the singers of ballads were usually common folk, the subjects were often noble, and the usual theme was tragic love.

A *broadside ballad* was a poem of any sort printed on a large sheet—thus the "broadside"—and sold by street singers in the sixteenth century. Not until the eighteenth century was the word "ballad" limited to traditional narrative song.

Blank Verse. Blank verse is unrhymed iambic pentameter. It was introduced into English poetry in the middle of the sixteenth century. By the end of the century it had become the standard medium of English drama. An example, by William Shakespeare, is: "Time hath, my Lord, a wallet at his back,/Wherein he puts alms for oblivion."

Burlesque. Burlesque is not a type of verse, but any imitation of people or literary type which, by distortion, aims to amuse. Its tone is neither savage nor shrill, and it tends to ridicule faults, not serious vices. Thus it is not to be confused with Satire, for burlesque makes fun of a minor fault with the aim of arousing amusement rather than contempt or indignation. Also, it need not make us devalue the original. For example, T. S. Eliot's "The Hollow Men" is parodied in Myra Buttle's "Sweeniad." The original reads:

> Between the conception
> And the creation
> Between the emotion
> And the response
> Falls the shadow

while the burlesque is:

> Between the mustification
> And the deception
> Between the multiplication
> And the division
> Falls the Tower of London.

Travesty. Also known as *low burlesque,* travesty takes a high theme and treats it in trivial terms, as in the Greek "Battle of the Frogs and Mice," which travesties Homer.

Mock Epic or Mock Heroic. This is also known as *high burlesque,* the reverse of travesty, for it treats a minor theme in a high, lofty, style. Despite its name, it does not mock the epic, but rather mocks low activities by treating them in the elevated style of the epic. The humor results from the difference between the low subject and the lofty treatment it is accorded. In the theatre, a burlesque may be a play that humorously criticizes another play by imitating aspects of it in a grotesque manner, as in John Gay's "Beggar's Opera," which make fun of serious operas. The term is also used, especially in America, for a sort of variety show stressing crude humor and sex.

Didactic Literature. Didactic literature intends to instruct or teach. It is sometimes used in contrast to *pure poetry,* which is said to be free from instruction and moral content and intends merely to delight and entertain. The term need not be pejorative, though many use it in this manner. A good case can be made that almost all of the world's finest poetry is didactic in some way. Satire makes fun of certain modes of behavior; Milton wrote *Paradise Lost* to "justify the ways of God to men." The problem, then, is one of degree, as true didactic literature deals mainly with instruction. This does not make it any less "poetic." These lines by John Gay, explaining how to clean worms, are an illustration of didactic literature:

> Cleanse them from filth, to give a tempting gloss,
> Cherish the sully'd reptile race with moss;
> Amid the verdant bed they twine, they toil,
> And from their bodies wipe the native soil.

Doggerel. Doggerel is verse made comic because irregular metrics are made regular by stressing normally unstressed syllables. In Butler's lines:

> More peevish, cross, and splenetic
> Than dog distract or monkey sick.

If the subject matter is mock heroic (see previous definition) and the lines are iambic tetrameter couplets (as in the example quoted above), the poem is also referred to as *hudibrastic,* after Samuel Butler's "Hudibras."

Dramatic Monologue. The speaker in a dramatic monologue is usually a fictional character or an historical figure caught at a critical moment. His words are established by the situation, and are usually directed at a silent audience. The speaker usually reveals aspects of his personality of which he is unaware. To some extent, every poem is a dramatic monologue, as an individual speaker is saying something to someone, even if only to himself, but in a true dramatic monologue, the above conventions are observed. Fine examples of this mode include Robert Browning's "My Last Duchess," in which a duke who has eliminated his last duchess reveals his cruelty to an emissary, who wants to arrange for the marriage to the latest duchess. T. S. Eliot's "The Love Song of J. Alfred Prufrock," in which the speaker's timid self addresses his agressively amorous self, would serve as another example.

Elegy. An elegy is a poem that deals solemnly with death. In Greek and Latin verse, they are poems that alternate lines of dactylic hexameter and dactylic pentameter. Gray's "Elegy Written in a Country Churchyard" is an example in point. If an elegy is a short funeral lament, it may be called a *dirge,* which in ancient times was a funeral song. *Threnody* and *monody* are terms used for funeral poems also, although the monody is often more complex and recited by an individual mourner. The elegy is frequently a *pastoral,* in which shepherds mourn the death of a fellow shepherd. They use the conventions of this type of verse, including invocation to the muses, processions of mourners, and lists of flowers. Many poets have used this form to advantage, including Walt Whitman's elegy on Abraham Lincoln, "When Lilacs Last in the Dooryard Bloomed" and Milton's "Lycidas."

Eulogy. Frequently confused with elegy, a eulogy is a poem praising the memory of the living or the dead.

Emblematic Poems. Emblematic poems take the shape of the subject of the poem. An emblematic poem on a swan, for example, would be in the shape of a swan. George Herbert's "Easter Wings" is an example of an emblematic poem.

Epic. An epic is a long and serious narrative poem (a poem that tells a story) about a hero and his heroic companions, often set in a past that is pictured as greater than the present. The hero often possesses superhuman and/or divine traits. In Homer's *Iliad,* for example, the hero, Achilles, is the son of a goddess; in Milton's *Paradise Lost,* the characters are God the Father, Christ, angels, and Adam and Eve. The action is usually rather simple, Achilles' anger in the *Iliad* and the fall of man in *Paradise Lost,* but it is increased by figurative language and allusions that often give it cosmic importance. The style is elevated to reflect the greatness of the events, and certain traditional procedures are employed. For example, the poet usually calls to the muses for help, asks them what initiated the action (the *epic question*), and often begins his tale in the middle of the action (*in medias res*). At this point, the hero is at his lowest fortunes, and later recounts the earlier part of the tale. Gods often participate in the tale, helping the heroes. There may be a trip into Hades. The *epic simile,* also called the *Homeric simile,* is an extended comparison, as a subject is compared to something that is presented at such length or detail that the subject is momentarily lost in the description. For example, in *Paradise Lost,* Satan walking in Eden is compared to a vulture:

> Here walk'd the Fiend at large in spacious field,
> As when a Vultur on Imaus bred,
> Whose snowy ridge the roving Tartar bounds,
> Dislodging from a Region scarce of prey
> To gorge the flesh of Lambs or yearling Kids
> On Hills where Flocks are fed, flies toward the Springs
> Of Ganges or Hydaspes, Indian streams;
> But in his way lights on the barren Plains
> Of Sericana, where Chineses drive
> With Sails and Wind their cany Waggons light:
> So on this windy Sea of Land, the Fiend
> Walk'd up and down alone bent on his prey.

There are two types of epics: the *primary epic* (sometimes called the *primitive epic* or a *folk epic*), which is a stately narrative about the noble class recited to the noble class; and the *secondary epic* (also called *literary epic* or *artificial epic*), a stately narrative about great events designed for a literary person to read from a book. Primary epics include Homer's *Iliad* and *Odyssey* and the anonymous Old English *Beowulf,* while secondary epics include Vergil's *Aeneid* and Milton's *Paradise Lost.* The poet of the primary epic speaks as the voice of the community, whereas the poet of the secondary epic may show more individuality. For example, Homer is not introspective; Milton sometimes is. Homer's poems and *Beowulf* share discussion of aspects of an "heroic age" (virtue is identified with strength, celebrated by the poets). Because the poets in these heroic societies sang memorized poems, their chants contain a great many *stock epithets* and repeated lines. When such repetitions occur at particular positions in lines they are called *formulas,* and they served to help the poet compose his material and remember it. An example of *formulaic poetry* is Longfellow's "The Song of Hiawatha." Modern epics include Hart Crane's "The Bridge," William Carlos Williams's "Paterson," and Ezra Pound's "Cantos." The first two are examples of American epics; the last a case for Western civilization. Epics vary in structure. *Beowulf,* for example, uses alliteration and accentual stress, not rhyme or stanza length, to structure the poem.

Epigram. Originally meaning an "inscription," the epigram became for the Greeks a short poem, usually solemn. But the Romans used the term to mean a short witty poem, with the sting at the end. An example by John Wilmot:

> We have a pretty witty King,
> Whose word no man relies on,
> Who never said a foolish thing,
> Nor ever did a wise one.

The term has come to mean any cleverly expressed thought in verse or prose.

Epitaph. An epitaph is a burial inscription, usually serious but sometimes humorous. John Gay's own serves as an example: "Life is a jest and all things show it:/I thought so once, but now I know it."

Epithalamion. (also spelled **epithalamium**). This is a lyric poem in honor of a bride or bridegroom or both. It is usually ceremonial and happy, and is not simply in praise of marriage, but of a particular marriage. Spenser's "Epithalamion" is the greatest in English. It begins, like its models in Greek and Roman literature, with an invocation, and follows Catullus in calling on young people to attend the bride, in praising the bride, and in welcoming the night. Spenser added deep Christian feeling and realistic description of landscape.

Free Verse. (also called **vers libre**). Free verse is composed of rhythmical lines varying in length, following no fixed metrical pattern, usually unrhymed. Often, the pattern is based on repetition and parallel grammatical structure. Although it may appear unrestrained, it does follow the rules outlined above. An example from Walt Whitman's "Song of Myself":

> I celebrate myself, and sing myself,
> And what I assume you shall assume,
> For every atom belonging to me as good belongs to you.

Haiku. Haiku is an Oriental verse form composed of seventeen syllables in three lines. Such forms were greatly admired models for the Imagist school, an early twentieth century movement that attempted to shed excess words to create poems of clear, concise details.

Idyll. An idyll is a short picturesque piece, usually about shepherds but sometimes a little epic, also called an *epyllion*. It presents an episode from the heroic past, but stresses the pictorial rather than the heroic. The most famous English example is Tennyson's "Idylls of the King," with its detailed descriptions of several aspects of the Arthurian legends.

Light Verse. Light verse is considered playful poetry, since it often combines lightheartedness or whimsy with mild satire as in Suckling's "Why So Pale and Wan, Fond Lover?" which concludes, "If of herself she will not love,/Nothing can make her;/The devil take her." The definition of light verse changed in the late nineteenth century, however, to include less polished pieces such as nursery songs with funny rhymes and distorted pronunciations.

Limerick. A form of light verse, a limerick is a jingling poem composed of three long and two short lines, the long lines (first, second, and fifth) rhyming with each other, and the short lines (third and fourth) rhyming with each other. The rhyming words in the first line can sometimes be misspelled to produce a humorous effect. The following limerick from an early sixteenth century songbook is an example:

> Once a Frenchman who'd promptly said "oui"
> To some ladies who'd asked him if houi
>   Cared to drink, threw a fit
>   Upon finding that it
> Was a tipple no stronger than toui

Lyric. Lyrics have regular rhyme schemes and are of a limited length, as in the fourteen-line sonnet. Burns' famous drinking song "Auld Lang Syne," Robert Frost's short poems, and George Herbert's religious meditations are examples of this form. If the emotion is hate or contempt, and its expression is witty, the poem is usually called a satire, or if very brief, an epigram. A *complaint* is a lyric expressing dissatisfaction, usually to an unresponsive love. Chaucer's humorous "Complaint to His Purse," for example, begins: "To you, my purse, and to noon other wight,/Complayne I, for ye be my lady dere!" For a brief period in the 1800s, nature as well as love became a major subject for lyrics, and poets such as William Wordsworth expressed their thoughts on clouds and daffodils more frequently than those on love.

Macaronic Verse. Macaronic verse is verse containing words resembling a foreign language or a mixture of languages. For example:

> "Mademoiselle got the croix de guerre,
> For washing soldiers' underwear,
> Hinky-dinky, parley-vous."

Narrative Verse. See epic.

Nonsense Verse. See light verse.

Occasional Poems. Poems that commemorate battles, anniversaries, coronations, or any other occasions worthy of poetic treatment.

Ode. This form was usually a song in honor of gods or heroes, but is now usually a very long lyric poem characterized by elevated feelings. The *Pindaric ode,* named for the Greek poet Pindar (c. 522–443 B.C.), has two structurally identical stanzas, the *strophe* and *antistrophe* (Greek for "turn" and "counterturn"). These are followed by a stanza with a different structure, the *epode* (Greek for "stand"). The line length and rhyming patterns are determined by the individual poet. In the original Pindaric ode, the chorus danced a pattern while singing during the strophe, retraced the same pattern while singing during the antistrophe, and sang without dancing during the epode. The odes were characterized by great passion. Notable English Pindaric odes are Gray's "The Progress of Poesy" and Wordsworth's "Ode: Intimations of Immortality." *Horatian odes,* named after the Latin poet Horace (65–8 B.C.), are composed of matched regular stanzas of four lines which usually celebrate love, patriotism, or simple Roman morality. Notable English Horatian odes include Marvell's "Horatian Ode Upon Cromwell's Return to Ireland," and Collins' "Ode to Evening." Keats' "Ode to a Grecian Urn" is probably the best known Horatian Ode. Although the ode is a serious poem expressing the speaker's passion, it may be passion about almost anything. Especially during the 1800s, the ode tended to become less public and more personal and introspective. Shelley's "Ode to the West Wind" or Keats' "Ode to a Nightingale" are examples of this introspection. The *irregular ode,* such as Wordworth's "Intimations on Immortality," has stanzas of various shapes, irregular rhyme schemes, and elaborate rhythms.

Sonnet. For the Elizabethans, sonnet and lyric were often considered one and the same, but to the modern sensibility, sonnet has come to mean a poem of fourteen lines (sometimes twelve or sixteen, but this is rare), written in iambic pentameter. There are two main kinds of sonnet: the *Italian sonnet* (or *Petrarchan*) and the *English sonnet* (*Elizabethan* or *Shakespearean*). The Italian sonnet has two divisions: The first eight lines are called the *octave,* rhyming *abba abba cde cde.* The section sets forth the theme of the poem, traditionally love and romance, and elaborates on it. The second section, the *sestet,* which rhymes *cd cd cd,* or a variant, reflects upon the theme and comes to a conclusion that ties everything together. Sidney's sonnets in English are Petrarchan, while Spencer's are linked rhymes with a variation. Milton, Wordsworth, and Keats have also written notable sonnets in the Italian form. The English sonnet, in contrast, is arranged in three quatrains and a couplet, rhyming *abab cdcd efef gg.* In the Shakespearean sonnet, themes and recapitulations are developed the same way as in the Italian, but seven different rhymes are used instead of four or five. In many sonnets, there is a marked correspondence between the rhyme scheme and the development of thought. Thus the Italian sonnet gives the generalization in the octave and specific examples in the sestet. The English sonnet may give three examples, one in each quatrain, and draw a conclusion in the couplet.

A *sonnet sequence* is a group of sonnets linked by a common theme, such as love betrayed, love renewed, love itself, etc. Some notable sonnet sequences include those of Elizabeth Barrett Browning ("Sonnets from the Portuguese"), George Meredith ("Modern Love"), W. H. Auden ("The Quest"), and Dylan Thomas ("Altarwise by Owl-light").

The *Miltonic sonnet* kept the Italian rhyme scheme, but changed the way the octet and sestet are constructed. Here, the sonnet no longer breaks at the octet but flows over or *enjambs* from line to line into the sestet. This type of sonnet appears to be more unified, beginning at one point and moving toward its inevitable conclusion. Milton also changed the theme of the typical sonnet. He moved into larger intellectual and religious concerns, a development begun by Donne.

Villanelle. A villanelle is a poetic form that not only rhymes but also repeats lines in a predetermined manner, both as a refrain and as an important part of the poem itself. Five stanzas of three lines each are followed by a quatrain. The first and third lines of the first stanza are repeated in a prescribed alternating order as the last lines of the remaining tercets, becoming the last two lines of the final quatrain. Dylan Thomas's "Do Not Go Gentle Into That Good Night" is an example of a modern villanelle.

POETIC MOVEMENTS AND TRENDS

Aesthetic Movement

In the early nineteenth century, a devotion to beauty developed in France. Beauty was thought good and desirable not because it reflected the mind of God, but because in a materialistic and chaotic world, it remained good in and of itself. This movement rejected the notion that the value of literature was related to morality—a sense of right and wrong—or some sort of usefulness. Instead, it put forth the idea that art was independent of any moral or didactic (instructive) end. This was in defiance of much of the traditional thought on the subject of art's place and purpose. The slogan was "art for art's sake" ("*l'art pour l'art*"), and many of the writers involved actively attacked the idea that art should serve any "purpose," in the traditional sense. In the late 1900's in England, the movement was represented by Oscar Wilde and Walter Pater. The term "*fin de siècle*" ("end of the century"), which earlier stood for progress, came to imply decadence—great refinement of style but a marked tendency toward the abnormal or freakish in content. When used as a proper noun, Decadence refers to the aesthetic movement.

Imagists/Imagism

At their peak between 1912 and 1914, these poets sought to use common language, to regard all the world as possible subject matter, and to present in vivid and sharp detail a concentrated visual image. "There should be no ideas but things," said poet William Carlos Williams. Imagists usually wrote in free verse. The most frequently cited example of their aims is summed up in this verse by Ezra Pound, the leader of the Imagist movement:

The apparition of these faces in the crowd;
Petals on a wet, black bough.

The title, "In a Station of the Metro," informs the reader that the poem is about a metro, a European subway, but the poem presents its statement without directly telling the reader what conclusions to draw. The poem means that the colorful faces of people in the subway are like flower petals against dark branches. The poet selects his images and arranges them; the reader must sense the relationships to experience the picture the poem presents.

Imagist poets avoided the old accentual-syllabic rhythms and depended on the poem's image or picture in the reader's mind to create the effect. Poems with obviously spelled-out messages were avoided at all costs. Oriental models, most especially the seventeen-syllable three-line haiku, were much admired. Poems of all kinds contain imagery, carefully described objects of the world, but this movement went further than describing what was seen to create a theory of verse around the idea of the picture.

Metaphysical Poets

The most important Metaphysical poets include John Donne (1572–1631) and his seventeenth-century followers, Andrew Marvell, George Herbert, Abraham Cowley, Richard Crashaw, and Henry Vaughan. These poets reacted against the traditions and rules of Elizabethan love poetry to create a more witty and ironic poetry. Modern critics have also concluded that the verse was more passionately intense and psychologically probing than the Elizabethan poems. Instead of penning smooth lines comparing a woman's beauty to something traditional like a rose, these poets wrote colloquial and often metrically irregular lines, filled with difficult and more searching comparisons. A comparison of this nature is called a *conceit,* which came to refer to a striking parallel of two highly unlike objects, such as the sun partly hidden by a cloud to a lover's head reclining on a pillow. Certain *Petrarchan conceits* were often used in English poetry during this time. They included a lover as a ship tossed by a storm, shaken by his tears, frozen by the coldness of his love. The *Metaphysical conceit* is closely allied, although it may be more original then the Petrarchan conceit. New, rather than traditional, and drawn from areas not usually considered "poetic" (commerce and science, for example), metaphysical conceits usually strike the reader with an effect quite different from the Petrarchan conceit.

Pastoral

Any writing concerning itself with shepherds may be called pastoral. Often set in *Arcadia,* a mountainous area in Greece, known for its simple shepherds who live an uncomplicated and contented life, a pastoral can also be called a *bucolic, idyll,* or an *eclogue.* An idyll sometimes refers to a minature epic, while an eclogue is usually a dialogue between two shepherds.

Rural life is usually shown as superior to tainted city life. Christian poets sometimes added their traditions to the Greek-Roman conventions and painted the shepherd as a holy man, as Christ the Shepherd. The *Georgic* is a poem dealing with rural life, and unlike the pastoral, shows a life of labor rather than a happy existence of singing and dancing through the day.

How Poets Create a Vision

There are three basic parts of any poem: its vision, the speaker who expresses that vision, and the language the poet uses to create voice and vision. This section will examine the ways in which language creates that vision.

When we use the term "vision" in relationship to verse, we are saying that the poet's vision is shared by the audience. By the end of a successful poem, then, we should have something that we recognize, perhaps even a reflection of our inner selves, as we have not before experienced it.

There are two ways in which a poet can create this successful vision. The first is to express his view so clearly that we feel that we are seeing what the poet wishes us to see with a new closeness and clarity. The second way involves using figures of speech or unexpected comparisons or juxtapositions of words that force us to make comparisons we have never before imagined. A look at two poems that use these different methods will show how language operates in each:

THE DALLIANCE OF THE EAGLES

Skirting the river road, (my forenoon walk, my rest,)
Skyward in air a sudden muffled sound, the dalliance of the eagles,
The rushing amorous contact high in space together,
The clinching interlocking claws, a living, fierce, gyrating wheel,
5 Four beating wings, two beaks, a swirling mass tight grappling,
In tumbling turning clustering loops, straight downward falling,
Till o'er the river pois'd, the twain yet one, a moment's lull,
A motionless still balance in the air, then parting, talons loosing,
Upward again on slow-firm pinions slanting, their separate diverse
    flight,
10 She hers, he his, pursuing.
                                    —Walt Whitman

THE EAGLE

He clasps the crag with crooked hands;
Close to the sun in lonely lands,
Ringed with the azure world, he stands

The wrinkled sea beneath him crawls;
5 He watches from his mountain walls,
And like a thunderbolt he falls.
                    —Alfred, Lord Tennyson

It is easy to see that these poems are very different. Tennyson's work, depicting a lone eagle who remains still throughout most of the poem, creates a feeling of space and solitude; Whitman's, dealing with two eagles, seems to have captured a constant rush of movement. This difference in feeling is created in part by the sounds of the words the poets have selected. Tennyson's words, lines, and sentences are all short, and the stop at the end of each line is very sharply marked. Whitman, in contrast, uses longer lines, with less sharp breaks between them, and his sentences are complex and involved. This technique keeps the reader's mind in almost constant motion—like that of the eagles' flight. Yet the basic difference in the presentation of these two poems lies not in the motion or motionlessness of the eagles, but rather in the imagery used to describe them.

A close examination of the poems reveals this difference in imagery. Whitman uses a great many adjectives, especially participles (adjectives formed from verbs), such as, "clinching," "interlocking," "living," "beating," and "grappling" to convey a sense of motion and action, and contribute much of the force of the poet's description. The poet is an observer here. Taking a walk, he has been startled first by the "sudden muffled sound" and then by the sight of the eagles. He describes these two sensations as carefully and fully as he can: "The clinching interlocking claws, a living, fierce, gyrating wheel,/ Four beating wings, two beaks, a swirling mass tight grappling".

Tennyson's verse is also descriptive, but it varies greatly from Whitman's in the types of words chosen to describe the eagle. Where Whitman uses words that could easily be applied to eagles, Tennyson uses words that are not usually associated with birds. His eagle is described in terms which compare it to other things: an old man, grown crooked with age; an explorer in "lonely lands"; a thunderbolt. By calling our attention to the comparison between the eagle and other objects, he draws upon our feelings for these other objects (respect or awe, for example) and uses those emotions to influence our feelings about the eagle itself. Thus, instead of saying, as Whitman does, that the eagle has "clinching . . . claws," Tennyson gives his eagle "crooked hands." He "stands"—a human rather than a birdlike act—and "watches," as both men and birds do. The landscape is also humanized. The lands are described as "lonely," the sea is pictured as "wrinkled," and it "crawls." There are examples of hyperbole (exaggeration) as well. The eagle is said to have a perch "close to the sun," which of course is impossible. In the same way, the sky against which he is pictured is an entire "azure world," and the eagle falls like "a thunderbolt." High and remote, yet in these very qualities very human, Tennyson's eagle presents a stunning image of a being in isolation.

By linking things that we would not ourselves associate, the poet creates new images and calls forth new emotions which make the reader look at things in a different light. Abstract ideas become specific through the use of precise visual images and specific words. The reader derives very different feelings from Whitman's waterfall of precisely denotative adjectives and Tennyson's careful balance of connotations of space, people, and isolation. A closer look at other forms of comparison can show us how imagery works in different settings. Comparative figures of speech include explicit comparisons, similes and metaphors, and implicit comparisons, implied metaphors, and personification.

SIMILES, METAPHORS, AND PERSONIFICATION

Similes are comparisons using the words "like," "as," or a similar word of comparison. Usually the objects under comparison resemble each other in only one or two ways, differing in all other aspects. For example, an eagle and a thunderbolt are really not very much alike, but the fact that they both can travel from the sky to the ground allows Tennyson to use this comparison to say that the eagle falls "like a thunderbolt." The strength of the simile lies in the difference between the eagle and the thunderbolt. The fact that the thunderbolt is much more powerful and dangerous than the eagle gives a sense of speed, power, and danger to the bird's fall. Langston Hughes constructed an entire poem, "Harlem," on the basis of similes. He compares a dream that has been put off to various physical items that have in some manner changed their appearance. He calls forth the image of a raisin, a dried grape, and a cut that has become infected. All the similes he uses in some way appeal to our senses and tell us that deferring our dreams will cause horrible things to happen. No matter how the change occurs in any event, lives will not remain untouched by the disappointment of deferred dreams. While the structure and language used are simple, at least on the surface, the similes lend extraordinary power to the poet's theme.

Like similes, *metaphors* are comparisons of two unlike objects. In this instance, though, the joining of the two objects is more complete, for there is no intervening word such as "like" or "as." Instead, the metaphor simply states that A *is* B; one element of the comparison becomes the other. Some metaphors go one step further and omit the "is." They talk about A as though it were B, and in some cases may not even use the name for B at all, forcing the reader to guess what B is by the language used. In this instance, the metaphor is called an *implied metaphor*.

The following poem by John Keats makes use of metaphors:

ON FIRST LOOKING INTO CHAPMAN'S HOMER

Much have I travelled in the realms of gold,
  And many goodly states and kingdoms seen;
  Round many western islands have I been
Which bards in fealty to Apollo hold.

5 Oft of one wide expanse had I been told
  That deep-browed Homer ruled as his demesne;
  Yet did I never breathe its pure serene
Till I heard Chapman speak out loud and bold:
Then felt I like some watcher into his ken;
10 When a new planet swims of the skies
Or like stout Cortez when with eagle eyes
  He stared at the Pacific—and all his men
Looked at each other with a wild surmise—
  Silent, upon a peak in Darien.

—*John Keats*

The vocabulary in the first eight lines of this poem is drawn mainly from the Middle Ages and its system of feudalism. The word "realms" is used for kingdoms, "bards" for poets, and "fealty" for the system under which a nobleman owed his allegiance to a king or other nobleman with more extensive power. "Demesne" is the word for the nobleman's domain, and "ken" means knowledge. In the same way, we no longer use "serene" for air or "oft" for often. Apollo, in contrast, is drawn from classical mythology, and stands for the god of poets. Homer is an ancient Greek poet and Chapman a sixteenth-century English poet who was noted for his translation of Homer's *Iliad* into English. What we must ask ourselves, then, is why the poet would use the language of the Middle Ages and the metaphor of traveling to talk about his joy in reading poetry and the delight he experienced when his discovery of Chapman's translations made him feel that he was really reading Homer for the first time. (Perhaps he selected the Middle Ages metaphor to show the timelessness of true verse, how it transcends the boundaries of time to speak for all people at all times.)

Here are some further questions to consider:

1. When Keats finds Chapman's translation, two new similes come to him that support the metaphor of the traveler. What is the first, found in lines 9–10? How does the new identity of the poet resemble his earlier pose as a traveler? How is it different? What sorts of feelings go with each identity?
2. The second simile is set forth in lines 11–14. Who does the poet feel like now? How do his new feelings form a climax to the poem?

Answers

1. In lines 9–10, the poet compares his feelings to those of an astronomer discovering a new planet.
2. In lines 11–14, he compares his feelings to those of an explorer (Cortez) discovering a new ocean (the Pacific). It will make no difference in your enjoyment of the poem, but it was Balboa, not Cortez, who was the first European to see the Pacific Ocean. From these two similes we can sense the poet's great excitement and wonder.

Personification. Personification is a type of implied metaphor, in this instance, speaking about something nonliving as though it were living. Or, as in the case of Tennyson's eagle, the attribution of human characteristics ("crooked hands") to something nonhuman (the bird).

One way to read a poem is to scan it once, and then go back and note all the figures of speech. Identify each one and decide what elements make up the comparison—what is being compared to what? Make some notes about why the poet would want his readers to think about these specific comparisons. Then, read the poem through once again. Look again at the figures of speech that you have noted and see how each relates to the meaning of the poem. Decide what the speaker's feelings are toward the subject and how many subjects of comparison there are. Is each subject compared to one thing, or is one subject compared to several? Is the comparison developed at length? If it is, to what purpose? What is the point that the poet is making through an extended metaphor? If the subject is compared to several things, how do the different images fit together? Are they unrelated so that the job of fixing them into a pattern is left to the reader? Or does the poet suggest some sort of relationship or contrast between/among them? How does the pattern thus created form your sense of the poet's vision, meaning, progression? Finally, read the poem through once again to see if the conclusions you have reached hold up. This may sound like a very complex and time-consuming practice, but it is only one way of looking at verse. It is handy for exams when you are expected to be fully aware of the poet's techniques and must be able to discuss how and why he did what he did. Of course, verse may be read in many other ways for many different reasons, but here we are dealing with gaining a clear understanding of poetic conventions and meanings.

Take a look at the two poems that follow. Using the method outlined, see what poetic techniques and meanings you can extract.

From A PINDARIC ODE

It is not growing like a tree
In bulk, doth make man better be;
Or, standing long an oak, three hundred year,
To fall a log at last, dry, bald, and sear:
5   A lily of a day
    Is fairer far, in May,
Although it fall and die that night;
It was the plant and flower of light.
In small proportions we just beauties see,
10 And in short measures life may perfect be.
              —*Ben Jonson*

COMPOSED UPON WESTMINSTER BRIDGE, SEPTEMBER 3, 1802

Earth has not anything to show more fair:
Dull would he be of soul who could pass by
A sight so touching in its majesty;
This City now doth, like a garment, wear
5 The beauty of the morning; silent, bare,
Ships, towers, domes, theaters, and temples lie
Open unto the fields, and to the sky;
All bright and glittering in the smokeless air.
Never did sun more beautifully steep
10 In his first splendor, valley, rock, or hill;
Ne'er saw I, never felt, a calm so deep!
The river glideth at his own sweet will:
Dear God! the very houses seem asleep;
And all that mighty heart is lying still!

—William Wordsworth

Most metaphors have a certain timelessness to them, a quality that endures through the ages. Thus, Wordsworth's picture of London asleep is a vision of something real that holds for all time. We can feel it today, more than a century later, as he must have felt it then. There are poems, usually very modern, that contain metaphors that are transitory and illusory. This is true of the work of Richard Wilbur, particularly the poem entitled "Love Calls Us to the Things of This World." In all poems, metaphors serve to illuminate the poet's view of the world.

SYMBOL AND ALLEGORY

Similes and metaphors tend to make points quickly, for they usually occupy little more than a line or two. They can be linked to others of their kind to make further points, or they may stand alone, secure in their power. Symbol and allegory, though, tend to dominate the poems in which they are used. Further, they tend to stand alone, they are not piled one upon the other as metaphors and similes may be. One symbol or allegorical device is usually all a poem can maintain.

Similes and metaphors are used to make us take a closer look at a subject, or to look at a subject in a new light. Symbols and allegory, in contrast, force us to look beyond the literal meaning of the poem's statement or action. The following poem provides an example:

THE TYGER

Tyger! Tyger! burning bright
In the forests of the night,
What immortal hand or eye
Could frame thy fearful symmetry?

5 In what distant deeps or skies
Burnt the fire of thine eyes?
On what wings dare he aspire?
What the hand, dare seize the fire?

And what shoulder, & what art,
10 Could twist the sinews of thy heart?
And when thy heart began to beat,
What dread hand? & what dread feet?

What the hammer? what the chain?
In what furnace was thy brain?
15 What the anvil? what dread grasp
Dare its deadly terrors clasp?

When the stars threw down their spears,
And water'd heaven with their tears,
Did he smile his work to see?
15 Did he who made the Lamb make thee?

Tyger! Tyger! burning bright
In the forests of the night,
What immortal hand or eye
Dare frame thy fearful symmetry?

—William Blake

In this poem, Blake wishes to focus our attention not on the topic of tigers but on the awesome qualities suggested by the tiger's beauty and the godlike powers involved in its creation. This poem may lead the reader to the question of the existence of evil as symbolized by the tiger's murderous nature. How far the symbol or allegory is carried is frequently left in the reader's hands.

Allegory always tells of an action. The events of that action should make literal sense, but they carry much more meaning in a second interpretation. Usually that second interpretation will have a spiritual or psychological level of meaning, for allegories tend to use physical actions to describe the workings of the mind. Thus, allegory presents a correspondence between some physical action (usually some sort of encounter) and a second action (usually psychological or physical), with each step of the literal tale matching the allegorical one. Symbolism, too, may involve the use of a tale, but it may also set forth a description of some unchanging being or object. And it's far more likely to suggest several different interpretations than to insist on a single one. The following poem, for instance, presents a symbolic tale of a king's fall from power:

OZYMANDIAS

I met a traveler from an antique land
Who said: Two vast and trunkless legs of stone
Stand in the desert . . . Near them, on the sand,
Half sunk, a shattered visage lies, whose frown,
5 And wrinkled lip, and sneer of cold command,
Tell that its sculptor well those passions read
Which yet survive, stamped on these lifeless things,
The hand that mocked them, and the heart that fed:
And on the pedestal these words appear:
10 "My name is Ozymandias, king of kings:
Look on my works, ye Mighty, and despair!"
Nothing beside remains. Round the decay
Of that colossal wreck, boundless and bare
The lone and level sands stretch far away.

—*Percy Bysshe Shelley*

The whole tale of the king's loss of power is symbolic, but within the tale, the most striking symbol is the broken statue with its boastful inscription. For many readers, the vision of the statue comes to mind when anyone says "Ozymandias." The full story of the king tends to come as an afterthought.

And what kind of the symbolism here? Does the king's loss of power symbolize the fall of the proud, which would lend a moral interpretation to the poem? Or is it rather the fall of tyranny, which would throw a political cast on the poem's theme. Or is it simply the inescapable destruction of human lives and civilization by the unceasing motion of times? All three levels of meaning can be read into the poem's symbol, and this contributes to the lasting power of the work. Without doubt, the tyrant with his "sneer of cold command" seems unsavory enough for the reader to welcome his overthrow. But the sculptor, with "the hand that mocked," is dead too, and even the work that was to endure is half destroyed. The picture this sonnet paints is simple enough on the surface; the interpretation of the symbol gives it additional strength.

The following poem is an example of conventional symbolism in verse:

THE LAMB

Little Lamb, who made thee?
  Dost thou know who made thee?
Gave thee life & bid thee feed,
By the stream & o'er the mead;
5 Gave thee clothing of delight,
Softest clothing wooly bright;

Gave thee such a tender voice,
Making all the vales rejoice!
  Little Lamb who made thee?
10 Dost thou know who made thee?

Little Lamb I'll tell thee,
Little Lamb I'll tell thee!
He is callèd by thy name,
For he calls himself a Lamb:
15 He is meek & he is mild,
He became a little child:
I a child & thou a lamb,
We are callèd by his name.
  Little Lamb God bless thee.
20 Little Lamb God bless thee.
                    —*William Blake*

Here Blake is relying on the traditional association of Christ with the lamb, and thus the meaning is less difficult to discern than in other poems where the author may invent a private symbol and an interpretation as well.

CONCEITS AND ALLUSIONS

Metaphors and similes, because they are so easy to recognize and usually easy to understand, are the first kind of figurative language we notice when reading verse. Symbols and allegories need a much closer reading, but are rewarding because they offer richness and deeper significance. Conceits and allusions may be brief or run the entire length of the poem, but in any case, they tend to be the most difficult to discern, often requiring some outside knowledge to make their meaning clear.

A *conceit* is a comparison between two very unlike objects; some have even called it an "outrageous metaphor." Conceits are usually developed at length, comparing and contrasting many different aspects of two objects to make their meaning clear. In love verse, conceits often derive from the Renaissance tradition that paints the woman as the walled village and the man as the conquering warrior; he attacks and she defends or surrenders. Or she might be the warrior, harming him with sharp looks and sharp words. She could be depicted as a goddess of love, and the list goes on and on. Some poets take these poetic conventions very seriously; others use them in fun, making use of the shock that comes from turning an expected comparison upside down.

The unexpected was a crucial part of the poetic conceit for the Metaphysical poets of the seventeenth century. They used conceits in religious verse as well as love verse, and succeeded in forging poetry of unequalled complexity. Any of the sciences—physics, astronomy, navigation—could yield a conceit which charted the soul's progress in relation to the physical universe. Such metaphysical conceits can be very difficult to understand, but they can be very rewarding for the depth of vision they offer.

The following poem provides examples of the use of metaphysical conceits. Note that there are two main groups of imagery in the poem. The first concerns maps and voyages; the second the image of Christ as the second Adam. Also note that the two images are interwoven by the idea of the soul's journey to salvation as an annihilation of time and space and by the physical image of the sick man, flat on his back in bed and suffering with fever. .

HYMN TO GOD MY GOD, IN MY SICKNESS

Since I am coming to that holy room,
    Where, with thy choir of Saints for evermore,
I shall be made thy music; as I come
    I tune the instrument here at the door,
5   And what I must do then, think now before.

Whilst my physicians by their love are grown
    Cosmographers, and I their map, who lie
Flat on this bed, that by them may be shown
    That this is my Southwest discovery
10   *Per fretum febris*, by these straights to die,

I joy, that in these straits, I see my west;
    For, though their currents yield return to none,
What shall my west hurt me? As west and east
    In all flat maps (and I am one) are one,
15   So death doth touch the Resurrection.

Is the Pacific Sea my home? Or are
    The eastern riches? Is Jerusalem?
Anyan, and Magellan, and Gibraltàr,
    All straits, and none but straits, are ways to them,
20   Whether where Japhet dwelt, or Cham, or Shem.

We think that Paradise and Calvary,
    Christ's Cross, and Adam's tree, stood in one place;
Look Lord, and find both Adams met in me;
    As the first Adam's sweat surrounds my face,
25   May the last Adam's blood my soul embrace.

So, in his purple wrapped receive me, Lord,
    By these thorns give me his other crown;
And as to others' souls I preached thy word,
    Be this my text, my sermon to mine own,
30   Therefore that he may raise, the Lord throws down.
                      —*John Donne*

Conceits demand that we bring some outside knowledge to our understanding of the poem under study. For example, we must be able to grasp the distortions of space involved in making a flat map represent a round world if we are to fully grasp Donne's hymn. In the same way, an *allusion* demands that we bring knowledge to our reading. An allusion is a reference to a previous work of literature, or to some well-known person or event. If we do not understand the reference, we may misunderstand the poem. Notice how the speakers in the three poems that follow use conceits or allusions to praise the women they love and expound on the benefits of love. Begin by looking carefully at each poem's imagery, but note also the use of apostrophe, or direct address, and the different tones used in each example.

FROM AMORETTI—SONNET 15

Ye tradefull Merchants, that with weary toyle,
Do seeke most pretious things to make your gain,
And both the Indias of their treasure spoile,
What needeth you to seeke so farre in vaine?
For loe, my love doth in her selfe containe,
All this worlds riches that may farre be found:
If saphyres, loe her eies be saphyres plaine;
If rubies, loe hir lips be rubies sound;
If pearles hir teeth be pearles both pure and round;
If yvorie, her forehead yvory weene;
If gold, her locks are finest gold on ground;
If silver, her faire hands are silver sheene:
    But that which fairest is but few behold:—
    Her mind, adornd with vertues manifold.
                    —*Edmund Spenser*

Some Questions for Your Consideration

1. Toward whom is the poet addressing his remarks? Focus on the first four lines.
2. Why should he select this particular audience?
3. What do the words "weary toyle" and "in vaine" suggest about this audience or their activities?
4. How are the metaphors in lines 7–12 connected?
5. How does the conclusion continue the theme of treasure? How does it change the theme?
6. What new questions does the conclusion raise about the merchants' quest for precious things?

Answers

1. The poet is addressing merchants.
2. He might have selected the merchants because they traveled far and wide to seek riches, in contrast to the poet's feeling that all the riches of the world are right at home, in the person of his loved one.
3. The words suggest that all the travels are useless, for real riches rest in love, not commodities.
4. The poet describes the beauty of his love in terms of the most precious substances on earth: gems, gold, silver, and ivory.
5. The conclusion fits in with the theme of treasure in that the mind of the poet's loved one is also "adornd" with riches. It changes the theme since the mind cannot really be seen, and her virtues, the most valuable of her treasures, cannot be gathered like so many jewels.
6. According to the poet, the merchants' quest is absurd, for all we should seek are the virtues hidden in a fine mind, not the outward show of precious metals and stones.

SONNET 18

Shall I compare thee to a summer's day?
Thou are more lovely and more temperate:
Rough winds do shake the darling buds of May,
And summer's lease hath all too short a date:
5 Sometime too hot the eye of heaven shines,
And often in his gold complexion dimmed;
And every fair from fair sometime declines,
By chance or nature's changing course untrimmed:
But thy eternal summer shall not fade
10 Nor lose possession of that fair thou ow'st,
Nor shall Death brag thou wand'rest in his shade,
When in eternal lines to time thou grow'st.
   So long as men can breathe or eyes can see,
   So long lives this, and this gives life to thee.
                 —William Shakespeare

This sonnet also starts with questions relating to physical qualities and concludes with intangible ones.

Questions

1. By means of what comparisons does Shakespeare achieve this movement from tangible to intangible?
2. Trace his logic to show how he arrived at the movement in question 1.
3. Compare and contrast this poem to Sonnet 15 by Spenser. How are they the same? How are they different?

Answers

1. Shakespeare compares a woman's beauty to the beauty of a summer's day to conclude that art—in the form of this sonnet—insures her immortality. The final line, "So long lives this [the sonnet], and this gives life to thee" sums up the movement from tangible to intangible.
2. See lines 1–12 for the development of the theme. The final couplet presents the conclusion and makes the poet's point. Note especially the phrase "summer's day" (line 1), "the eye of heaven" (line 5), and "eternal summer" (line 9). These phrases signal the beginning of the three stages of the author's argument, with the final two lines marking the conclusion. Also, be aware that "fair" has three meanings: a noun meaning "a lovely thing," an adjective meaning "lovely," and a noun meaning "beauty."
3. Both poems are the same in that they praise a loved one for her appearance. They are different in that Shakespeare's sonnet makes the specific point that this particular poem will immortalize the person spoken of in the poem.

Here's another poem to analyze in the same manner:

THE SUN RISING

Busy old fool, unruly sun,
    Why dost thou thus
Through windows and through curtains call on us?
Must to thy motions lovers' seasons run?
5   Saucy, pedantic wretch, go chide
    Late schoolboys and sour 'prentices,
    Go tell court huntsmen that the king will ride,
    Call country ants to harvest offices.
Love, all alike, no season knows nor clime,
10 Nor hours, days, months, which are the rags of time.

    Thy beams, so reverend and strong
    Why shouldst thou think?
I could eclipse and cloud them with a wink,
But that I would not lose her sight so long.
15   If her eyes have not blinded thine,
    Look, and tomorrow late tell me
    Whether both th' Indias of spice and mine
    Be where thou left'st them, or lie here with me;
Ask for those kings whom thou saw'st yesterday,
20 And thou shalt hear: All here in one bed lay.

> She's all states, and all princess I;
> > Nothing else is.
> Princes do but play us; compared to this,
> All honor's mimic, all wealth alchemy.
> 25   Thou, sun, art half as happy as we,
> > In that the world's contracted thus;
> Thine age asks ease, and since thy duties be
> To warm the world, that's done in warming us.
> Shine here to us, and thou art everywhere;
> 30 This bed thy center is, these walls thy sphere.
> > > > > —*John Donne*

Question

Here again earthly riches are equated with the beauty of a woman and then are devalued by it, as time gives way to timelessness. How does Donne's treatment of these conceits differ from those of Shakespeare and Spenser? How is it the same?

Answer

Donne's treatment is different from Shakespeare's since he is *not* saying that this poem will afford the woman immortality. Also, Shakespeare does not place the woman in the center of the universe ("This bed thy center is, these walls thy sphere.") as Donne argues. Of the three, you could make a case for Spenser's poem being the least sophisticated, because he simply praises the woman for her beauty and virtues, while the other two poets make further arguments. Donne's poem is far more earthly than either Shakespeare's or Spenser's, making specific reference to their love.

IMAGERY

We have isolated the various figures of speech to discuss each one individually with examples, but in actual practice, the various poetic devices are almost always found in combination with one another. Just as form and meaning serve to reinforce each other, so the poem's figures of speech work together to echo the poem's pattern of meaning and imagery. When you first begin to read a poem, you may focus on one striking aspect, but once you have studied it well, the entire pattern should come together and the various figures of speech will enter into your understanding of the poem's meaning.

An *image* is a word or a phrase that appeals to the sense—sight, smell, taste, touch, or sound—in such a way as to suggest objects or their characteristics. Images serve to create pictures in the reader's mind and aid in conveying the poem's theme.

Renaissance poems tended to begin with a position and then build on it, showing little movement within the verse. Metaphysical poems showed more movement, as they often followed a speaker's mind through the ramifications of an idea or situation. Modern poets may create scenes, moods, and speakers with even greater movement and further use of sound and imagery. The nineteenth-century American poet Walt Whitman, for example, relied on a pattern of imagery to give structure to his verse rather than on the more conventional rhymes and meters. "There Was A Child Went Forth' is one example. Read the poem and answer the questions that follow.

THERE WAS A CHILD WENT FORTH

There was a child went forth every day,
And the first object he look'd upon, that object he became,
And that object became part of him for the day or a certain part of the day,
Or for many years or stretching cycles of years.

5 The early lilacs became part of this child,
And grass and white and red morning-glories, and white and red clover, and the song of the phoebe-bird,
And the Third-month lambs and the sow's pink-faint litter, and the mare's foal and the cow's calf,
And the noisy brood of the barnyard or by the mire of the pond-side,
And the fish suspending themselves so curiously below there, and the beautiful curious liquid,
10 And the water-plants with their graceful flat heads, all became part of him.

The field-sprouts of Fourth-month and Fifth-month became part of him,
Winter-grain sprouts and those of the light-yellow corn, and the esculent roots of the garden,
And the apple-trees cover'd with blossoms and the fruit afterward, and woodberries, and the commonest
    weeds by the road,
And the old drunkard staggering home from the outhouse of the tavern whence he had lately risen,
15 And the schoolmistress that pass'd on her way to the school,
And the friendly boys that pass'd, and the quarrelsome boys,
And the tidy and fresh-cheek'd girls, and the barefoot Negro boy and girl,
And all the changes of city and country wherever he went.

His own parents, he that had father'd him and she that had conceiv'd him in her womb and birth'd him,
20 They gave this child more of themselves than that,
They gave him afterward every day, they became part of him.

The mother at home quietly placing the dishes on the supper-table,
The mother with mild words, clean her cap and gown, a wholesome odor falling off her person and clothes
    as she walks by,
The father, strong, self-sufficient, manly, mean, anger'd, unjust,
25 The blow, the quick loud word, the tight bargain, the crafty lure,
The family usages, the language, the company, the furniture, the yearning and swelling heart,
Affection that will not be gainsay'd, the sense of what is real, the thought if after all it should prove unreal,
The doubts of day-time and the doubts of night-time, the curious whether and how,
Whether that which appears so is so, or is it all flashes and specks
30 Men and women crowding fast in the streets, if they are not flashes and specks what are they?
The streets themselves and the facades of houses, and goods in the windows,
Vehicles, teams, the heavy-plank'd wharves, the huge crossing at the ferries,
The village on the highland seen from afar at sunset, the river between,
Shadows, aureola and mist, the light falling on roofs and gables of white or brown two miles off,
35 The schooner near by sleepily dropping down the tide, the little boat slack-tow'd astern,
The hurrying tumbling waves, quick-broken crests, slapping,
The strata of color'd clouds, the long bar of maroon-tint away solitary by itself, the spread of purity it lies
    motionless in,
The horizon's edge, the flying sea-crow, the fragrance of salt marsh and shore mud.
These became part of that child who went forth every day, and who now goes, and will always go forth
    every day.

                    —*Walt Whitman*

Questions on "There Was a Child Went Forth"

1. Describe the image in each of the following group of lines: 1–13; 14–17; 19–26;
   30–34; 35–38.
2. Do these images form a pattern? If so, what is it?

3. How does the imagery serve to unify and connect the poem?
4. Discuss the meaning of lines 19–21. How did the child's parents become "part of him"?
5. What is the poet describing through the use of the images in line 37?
6. How long is the time span in the poem?

Answers

1. 1–13: Spring morning in the country, the beginning of both plant and animal life; 14–17: Fall and re-entry into the town and the world of people; 19–26: Home and the child's parents; 30–34: The movement of the city; 35–38: The shore and nightfall
2. There are several patterns evident here: There is a movement from childhood to adulthood, from home to shore, from morning to evening, from country to city, from self outward to others, through the progression of the seasons (spring-summer-fall), from acceptance to doubt, and finally back to a reaffirmation of life and the goodness of the universe.
3. All the images are connected by the child. He embraces the country and the city, land and water, spring and fall, etc. He is the link that connects all the various pictures the poet creates.
4. The child is more than the result of love between his parents. He is a creation whose development depends on the continued care of his parents. They present him with lessons on how to live, lessons that the child blends into his own self-image.
5. Sunset over the water is the image described here.
6. The poem takes place in one day, from sunrise to sunset.

MEETING AT NIGHT

The gray sea and the long black land;
And the yellow half-moon large and low;
And the startled little waves that leap
In fiery ringlets from their sleep,
5 As I gain the cove with pushing prow,
And quench its speed i' the slushy sand.

Then a mile of warm sea-scented beach;
Three fields to cross till a farm appears;
A tap at the pane, the quick sharp scratch
10 And blue spurt of a lighted match,
And a voice less loud, through its joys and fears,
Than the two hearts beating each to each!
—*Robert Browning*

This is a poem about love, but despite the number of things that we can infer about love—it is a sweet and exciting time when everything seems beautiful and the most minor things become significant—nothing is told to us directly. As a matter of fact, the author does not even use the word "love" in the poem. He is conveying a feeling and an experience, to the readers. This is accomplished by presenting a situation—a man going to meet his love—and describing that situation so clearly in terms of sensory impressions that the reader is able to share in the poet's experience.

Every line in the poem centers about an image: the gray sea, the long black land, the yellow half-moon, the blue spurt of the lighted match. These images allow the reader to experience with the poet, to enter into his world and become part of it. The warm sea smell of the beach appeals to both our sense of smell and touch while the quiet speech of the lovers engages our sense of hearing. By engaging the reader's senses, the poet is able to attract the reader's attention and convey his feelings on the subject under discussion. Read the two Edgar Allan Poe poems that follow. Then, answer the questions about each selection.

ANNABEL LEE

It was many and many a year ago,
  In a kingdom by the sea,
That a maiden there lived whom you may know
  By the name of Annabel Lee;
5 And this maiden she lived with no other thought
  Than to love and be loved by me.

I was a child and *she* was a child,
  In this kingdom by the sea,
But we loved with a love that was more than
    love—
10   I and my Annabel Lee;
With a love that the wingèd seraphs of heaven
  Coveted her and me.

And this was the reason that, long ago,
  In this kingdom by the sea,
15 A wind blew out of a cloud, chilling
  My beautiful Annabel Lee;
So that her highborn kinsmen came
  And bore her away from me,
To shut her up in a sepulcher
20   In this kingdom by the sea.

The angels, not half so happy in heaven,
  Went envying her and me—
Yes! that was the reason (as all men know,
  In this kingdom by the sea)
25 That the wind came out of the cloud by night,
  Chilling and killing my Annabel Lee.

But our love it was stronger by far than the love
  Of those who were older than we,
  Of many far wiser than we;
30 And neither the angels in heaven above,
  Nor the demons down under the sea,
Can ever dissever my soul from the soul
  Of the beautiful Annabel Lee;

For the moon never beams, without bringing me
  dreams
35   Of the beautiful Annabel Lee;
And the stars never rise, but I feel the bright eyes
  Of the beautiful Annabel Lee;
And so, all the night-tide, I lie down by the side
  Of my darling—my darling—my life and my bride,
40   In the sepulcher there by the sea.
  In her tomb by the sounding sea.

TO HELEN

Helen, thy beauty is to me
Like those Nicean barks of yore,
That gently, o'er a perfumed sea,
The weary, wayworn wanderer bore
5 To his own native shore.

On desperate seas long wont to roam,
Thy hyacinth hair, thy classic face,
Thy Naiad airs, have brought me home
  To the Glory that was Greece
10 And the grandeur that was Rome.

Lo! in yon brilliant window niche
How statuelike I see thee stand,
The agate lamp within thy hand!
Ah, Psyche, from the regions which
15 Are Holy Land!

Questions on Poe's Poems

1. Characterize the descriptions of women in these poems. What are they like?
2. The meaning of "To Helen" depends on the classical imagery in which it is expressed. What parallel does Poe draw between Helen and the "Nicean barks" in the first stanza?
3. How does the simile of the above question serve to describe the poet?
4. Find the metaphors in the second and third stanzas of "To Helen." Then, show how they reinforce Poe's theme. What *is* the theme of this poem?
5. Find examples of the following types of figurative language:
   Alliteration
   Assonance
   Repetition
6. Find examples of rhyme, especially end rhyme.

Answers

1. While it appears that women are at the center of both poems, these women seem less than real. What we have here are idealized portraits, removed and abstract. Those women are both untouchable—Annabel Lee because she is firmly in the grave, Helen because she is set so high on a pedestal of classical perfection that it seems impossible to see in her any human quality, "To Helen" has a line that sums this up: "How statuelike I see thee stand."
2. Poe compares Helen's beauty to a ship for it can carry him to the heights of happiness experienced by a weary traveler brought home at last. The meaning of this poem has been much discussed and disagreed upon. It may be that the author was drawing from the people of what is now Nice, France, who were a great seapower in the later part of the Middle Ages. The phrase "perfumed sea" calls forth Nicea (now called Iznik), located just southeast of the Bosporos. This city was important because it was located on the early trade routes to the Orient, but it was not on the sea. The Phaeacians—"lovers of the sea"—are another reference to classical imagery. They were the ones to whom Odysseus recounted his adventures and who sent him home in their enchanted bark (ship).
3. This simile shows the poet, exhausted by his travels on the sea of life, finding succor in thoughts of Helen's ideal beauty, which he seems to link to the happy days of his youth.
4. "Hyacinth hair" serves to call forth the image of beauty and makes a classical reference to Hyacinthus. "Naiad airs" may refer to the Ulysses story, and also reinforces the impression of beauty. "Psyche" in the third stanza is also a classical reference. Psyche was separated from her lover, Cupid, when she ignored his instructions and took a lamp to look at him. She searched for Cupid for years, and finally she was reunited with him. The theme of this poem revolves around the contemplation of Helen's beauty. By thinking of Helen, the ideally remembered figure from his childhood, the poet is able to recapture the classic beauty of the state of mind he enjoyed during his youth. He implies that this state of mind must have been common when the world itself was "young"—in the classical age.
5. Alliteration, the repetition of the initial sound of two or more closely related words, is found, for example, in the last stanza of "Annabel Lee." Line 40 has "sepulcher" and "sea"; "sounding" and "sea" appear in line 41.

   Assonance, the sound of the vowel repeated in two or more accented syllables, can also be found in the last stanza of "Annabel Lee." The long *e* sounds of the internally rhymed words "beams" and "dreams" (line 34) also appears in the "me" of the same line and in "feel" (line 36) and "sea" (lines 40 and 41). Also, the long *i* sound of "rise" and "eyes" (line 36), "night-tide" and "side" (line 38), and "bride" (line 39), is repeated in "bright" (line 36), "lie" (line 38), "my" and "life" (line 39), and "by" (lines 38, 40, and 41). The *o* in "moon" (line 34) is repeated in "tomb" (line 41), and is closely related to the sound in "beautiful" (lines 35 and 37).

Repetition may be seen in "Annabel Lee" in the phrase "kingdom by the sea" (lines 2, 8, 14, 20, and 24). The word "love" is repeated in lines 6, 9, 11, and 27.

6. End rhyme is obvious in both works, but Poe also uses the far more elaborate internal rhyme. This can be seen in the last stanza of "Annabel Lee": "beams" in line 34 rhymes with "dreams"; "rise" in line 36 rhymes with "eyes". "Night-tide" and "slide" in line 38 rhyme with each other and with "bride" at the end of line 39.

TONE

Tone is the writer's or speaker's attitude toward his subject, audience, or himself. It brings emotional power to the poem and is a vital part of its meaning. In spoken language, tone is conveyed through the speaker's inflections, and it may vary from ecstatic to incredulous to despairing to bleak and resigned. A correct interpretation of tone is vital to a correct interpretation of meaning. It is more difficult to discern tone in writing than in speech since inflection cannot be determined in text. To understand tone, we must analyze all the poetic elements that we have previously discussed: imagery, simile, metaphor, irony, understatement, rhythm, sentence structure, denotation, connotation, and so forth. Tone is a combination of all these elements. Let's try to determine the tone of the two poems that follow.

CROSSING THE BAR

Sunset and evening star,
   And one clear call for me!
And may there be no moaning of the bar
   When I put out to sea,

5 But such a tide as moving seems asleep,
   Too full for sound and foam,
When that which drew from out the boundless deep
   Turns again home.

Twilight and evening bell,
10   And after that the dark!
And may there be no sadness of farewell
   When I embark;

For though from out our bourne of Time and Place
   The flood may bear me far,
15 I hope to see my Pilot face to face
   When I have crossed the bar.

          —*Alfred, Lord Tennyson*

Questions

1. What are the two different figures that the poet uses to stand for death?
2. What is the exact moment of death in each instance?
3. What kind of death is the poet wishing for here? Why does he say he wants "no sadness of farewell"?
4. What is the "boundless deep"?
5. What is the tone of this poem?

Answers

1. Each figure begins a section of the poem. The first occurs in line 1, "Sunset and the evening star," while the second is found in line 9, "Twilight and evening bell."
2. In the first instance, death occurs "When that which drew from out the boundless deep/Turns again home" (lines 7–8). In the second, death occurs when the speaker has "crossed the bar" (line 16).
3. The poet is wishing for a death that causes "no sadness of farewell," a death that is neither painful nor protracted. He does not want extended leave-takings, nor people gathering around the bedside of a dying man.
4. The "boundless deep" is that which awaits us after death.
5. The tone is one of calm resignation since the speaker is peaceful and relaxed as he faces death.

ONE DIGNITY DELAYS FOR ALL

> One dignity delays for all,
> One mitred afternoon.
> None can avoid this purple,
> None avoid this crown.
>
> 5 Coach it insures, and footmen,
> Chamber and state and throng;
> Bells, also, in the village,
> As we ride grand along.
>
> What dignified attendants,
> 10 What service when we pause!
> How loyally at parting
> Their hundred hats they raise!
>
> How pomp surpassing ermine
> When simple you and I
> 15 Present our meek escutcheon
> And claim the rank to die!
> —*Emily Dickinson*

Questions

1. What is the "dignity" that "delays for all"?
2. What is being discussed in the second and third stanzas?
3. Look up the following words if you're not sure of their meaning: mitred, escutcheon.
4. What is the tone of this poem and how does it differ from that of Tennyson's "Crossing The Bar?"

Answers

1. This "dignity" is death.
2. The second and third stanzas discuss the actual process of dying.
3. "Mitred" means "raised to a high rank." The poet is using it to describe a very special afternoon, the afternoon of her death. "Escutcheon" is a shield with a coat of arms.
4. The tone of this poem is decidedly more playful than that of "Crossing The Bar."

METER

Sound in verse is created by two elements: the rhythm of a poem's lines and the sound of its words. We have already discussed *meter,* the rhythm of a poem determined by the number of stressed and unstressed syllables, and the common varieties of meter, such as *iambic pentameter. Scanning* a poem is determining its rhythm or meter. As a brief review:

Dimeter	2 stresses per line	Díe soón
Trimeter	3 stresses per line	Dóst thou knów who máde thee?
Tetrameter	4 stresses per line	Tell áll the truth but tell it slánt
Pentameter	5 stresses per line	Leáve me, O Lóve, which reáches bút to dust
Hexameter	6 stresses per line	Which, like a wóunded snaké, drags its slow length alóng.

As we have said before, seldom does the pattern of a poem remain perfectly regular, for to hold too closely to one meter can cause monotony. Poets seek to avoid such monotony by shifting stresses, so that a poem written in iambic meter may have some feet that are spondaic and others that are trochaic. More important, the poet varies meter by making the poem's meaning and the speaker's voice move with the rhythm. These few lines from Matthew Arnold's "Dover Beach" (printed in its entirety on page 64), show this process at work:

> The sea is calm tonight.
> The tide is full, the moon lies fair
> Upon the straits;—on the French coast the light
> Gleams and is gone; the cliffs of England stand,
> Glimmering and vast, out in the tranquil bay.

The first statement meshes beautifully with the meaning of the first line. But the next overlaps the second line, so that you cannot stop reading on "fair," but must continue with "Upon the straits" to make sense of the line. After a pause, the thought continues through that line and half of the next, then pauses more briefly, finishes the line with a slight pause, and comes to an end at the fifth line. The first and fifth lines are called *end-stopped,* because a longer pause is called for at the end of these lines. In the same manner, the second, third, and fourth lines which force your voice to continue are called *run-on* lines. Both end-stopped and run-on lines may contain internal pauses. there is one such pause after the word "full" in the second line. These pauses are called *caesuras,* and their placement gives to poetry the sound of the speaking voice.

Blake's "The Lamb" and "The Tyger" (see pages 187 and 185) offer a marked contrast to Arnold's "Dover Beach." Because of the many end-stopped lines and the regularity of their rhythm, the two Blake poems sound almost like incantations, very different from the musing, gentle tone of Arnold's poem. But even in these two poems Blake varies the length of the lines and includes some caesuras and run-on lines.

> What the hammer? what the chain?
> In what furnace was thy brain?
> What the anvil? what dread grasp
> Dare its deadly terrors clasp?

Blake holds himself to seven-syllables lines in "The Tyger" and a patterned alternation between trimeter and tetrameter lines in "The Lamb," while Arnold varies the length of the lines in "Dover Beach," the lines getting longer as the speaker's argument continues. It is also clear that all the lines quoted from both Blake and Arnold end with stressed syllables. The rising voice at the end of a line creates what is called *rising rhythm*. In contrast, lines that end in unstressed syllables create a *falling rhythm*. "O wild West Wind, thou breath of Autumn's being" is an example of falling rhythm.

Let's look at the following poem to determine both its meaning and its rhythm:

PIED BEAUTY

> Glory be to God for dappled things—
> For skies of couple-colour as a brindled cow;
> For rose-moles all in stipple upon trout that swim;
> Fresh-firecoal chestnut-falls; finches wings;
> 5 Landscape plotted and pieced—fold, fallow, and plough;
> And áll trádes, their gear and tackle and trim.
>
> All things, counter, original, spare, strange;
> Whatever is fickle, freckled (who knows how?)
> With swift, slow; sweet, sour; adazzle, dim;
> 10 He fathers-forth whose beauty is past change:
> Praise him.
> —*Gerard Manley Hopkins*

Questions

1. How do the examples of "dappled things" given in lines 2–4 differ from those in lines 5–6? How do the examples in the first stanza (lines 2–6) differ from those in the second stanza (lines 7–9)?
2. What has Hopkins done to his first definition of "dappled things"?
3. In what way are all these images and examples unified?
4. How important is the speaker's vision of "pied beauty"?
5. What is the rhythm here?

Answers

1. Lines 2–4 present *specific* items (line 2, skies; line 3, trout; line 4, chestnuts, birds' wings), while lines 5–6 present *general* descriptions (line 5, landscape; line 6, trades).
2. Hopkins has gone from the specific to the general to include all of creation as he sees it.
3. The images and examples are connected by theme and language. In the first in-

stance, the theme is that all of the universe is God's glory and reflection. In the second, we see an echo of language techniques:

line 5 fold, fallow, plough

line 9 swift, slow, sweet, etc.

Both these lists show a common technique and serve to unify the poem.

4. The speaker's vision is, of course, the most important thing in the world to him, for he was a priest and saw God's hand in all.

5. This is an example of Hopkins' sprung rhythm, explained earlier.

Rhymed and Unrhymed Verse

Unrhymed verse is rather easy to classify, and can be divided into three main types. First is *accentual verse,* which originated in the eighth century, the earliest known kind of verse. *Beowulf* is an example of early accentual verse and Gerard Manley Hopkins' "Pied Beauty" is an example of nineteenth century accentual verse. Second is blank verse, unrhymed iambic pentameter, a sixteenth-century invention made famous by Shakespeare. Third is modern *free verse,* found in the work of such poets as Walt Whitman, e. e. cummings, Ezra Pound, and Denise Levertov.

Rhymed verse cannot be divided into three simple categories. There are those forms with a fixed length: the limerick with five lines, the sonnet with fourteen lines, and the villanelle with nineteen lines. There are other forms that do not have a fixed number of lines, although almost all are composed of stanzas. While each stanza usually has a fixed length, the number of stanzas may vary, so that a poem can be any length at all. There are a series of patterns, though, that we can isolate and discuss in depth.

The *couplet* is a stanza that has two lines that rhyme. A couplet is found at the end of an English sonnet to make the point and conclude the discussion. An example from Shakespeare:

> So long as men can breathe or eyes can see,
> So long lives this, and this gives life to thee.

The *triplet* or *tercet* is composed of three rhyming lines, as we see here:

> He clasps the crag with crooked hands,
> Close to the sun in lonely lands,
> Ringed with the azure world, he stands.

Another three-line stanza in which only the first and last lines rhyme is called *terza rima*. When several stanzas of *terza rima* are grouped together, the middle line of one stanza will rhyme with the first and third lines of the following stanza. For example:

> O wild West Wind, thou breath of Autumn's being,
> Thou, from whose unseen presence the leaves dead
> Are driven, like ghosts from an enchanter fleeing,
>
> Yellow, and black, and pale, and hectic red,
> Pestilence-stricken multitudes: O thou
> Who chariotest to their dark wintry bed

The *quatrain* is a stanza composed of four lines which may have several different rhyme schemes: the second and fourth lines (*abcb*); the first and third, and the second and fourth (*abab*); the first and fourth and the second and third (*abba*); and the first and second, and third and fourth (*aabb*). Any one of these patterns may be used, or they may be combined in any variation. Thus, you cannot assume that if the first few stanzas follow a certain pattern, the rest of the poem will continue that pattern. It is always best to check the rhyme in each and every line to make sure the pattern follows what you assume. Here are some examples to study:

(*abcb*)   When I was one-and-twenty
                 I heard a wise man say,
                 "Give crowns and pounds and guineas
                 But not your heart away;"

(*abab*)   She even thinks that up in heaven
Her class lies late and snores,
While poor black cherubs rise at seven
To do celestial chores.

(*abba*)   Earth hath not anything to show more fair!
Dull would he be of soul who could pass by
A sight so touching in its majesty
The city doth now, like a garment, wear.

(*aabb*)   "O, Melia, my dear, this does everything crown!
Who could have supposed I should meet you in Town?
And whence such fair garments, such prosperi-ty?"—
"O didn't you know I'd been ruined?" said she.

THE NARRATIVE POEM

A narrative poem tells a story, recounting actions and events. The sequence of events in a narrative poem is called the *plot,* and it must be controlled and directed by the *narrator,* the person telling us the tale. The *point of view,* the position from which the narrative is recounted, must also be controlled, which is accomplished in part by the grammatic *person* in which the author chooses to write. Narrative verse is less popular today, as more stories are told in prose forms.

The following is an example of a *narrative poem:*

MY LAST DUCHESS

1 That's my last Duchess painted on the wall,
Looking as if she were alive. I call
That piece a wonder, now: Frà Pandolf's hands
Worked busily a day, and there she stands.
5 Will't please you sit and look at her? I said
"Frà Pandolf" by design, for never read
Strangers like you that pictured countenance,
The depth and passion of its earnest glance,
But to myself they turned (since none puts by
10 The curtain I have drawn for you, but I)
And seemed they would ask me, if they durst,
How such a glance came there; so, not the first
Are you to turn and ask thus. Sir, 'twas not
Her husband's presence only, called that spot
15 Of joy into the Duchess' cheek: perhaps
Frà Pandolf chanced to say, "Her mantle laps
Over my lady's wrist too much," or "Paint
Must never hope to reproduce the faint
Half-flush that dies along her throat:" such stuff
20 Was courtesy, she thought, and cause enough

For calling up that spot of joy. She had
A heart—how shall I say?—too soon made glad,
Too easily impressed; she liked whate'er
She looked on, and her looks went everywhere.
25 Sir, 'twas all one! My favour at her breast,
The dropping of the daylight in the West,
The bough of cherries some officious fool
Broke in the orchard for her, the white mule
She rode with round the terrace—all and each
30 Would draw her alike the approving speech,
Or blush, at least. She thanked men,—good! But thanked
Somehow—I know not how—as if she ranked
My gift of a nine-hundred-years-old name
With anybody's gift. Who'd stoop to blame
35 This sort of trifling? Even had you skill
In speech—(which I have not)—to make your will
Quite clear to such a one, and say, "Just this
Or that in you disgusts me; here you miss,
Or there exceed the mark"—and if she let
40 Herself be lessoned so, nor plainly set

Her wits to yours, forsooth, and made excuse,
—E'en then would be some stooping; and I choose
Never to stoop. Oh sir, she smiled, no doubt,
Whene'er I passed her; but who passed without
45 Much the same smile? This grew; I gave commands;
Then all smiles stopped together. There she stands
As if alive. Will't please you rise? We'll meet
The company below, then. I repeat,

The Count your master's known munificence
50 Is ample warrant that no just pretence
Of mine for dowry will be disallowed;
Though his fair daughter's self, as I avowed
At starting, is my object. Nay, we'll go
Together down, sir. Notice Neptune, though,
55 Taming a sea-horse, thought a rarity,
Which Claus of Innsbruck cast in bronze for me!

—*Robert Browning*

Discussion

This is a narrative poem, in which we listen to the Duke speak of his dead wife. He tells the story of their marriage and her death. Browning uses a technique called the *dramatic monologue,* and the reader feels almost as though he is overhearing the Duke as he speaks. From his conversation, we are able to piece together the situation, both past and present, and we are able to see what sort of person the Duke is as well as what sort of person his wife was. By the end of the poem, we are even able to see what the poet thought of them both.

Line-by-line Analysis of "My Last Duchess"

Lines 1–2. Addressing an unidentified audience, the Duke discusses a portrait of his "last Duchess." The word "last" hints that the Duke may have had more than one previous wife, and also suggests that he is once again "shopping" for another. The word also intimates that a wife is a commodity, something to acquire as one would any other possession. We know immediately she is dead from the phrase "Looking as if she were alive" (line 2).

Lines 3–4. The Duke is very impressed with the painting, and makes sure to mention the painter. This tells us that he admires works of art and that he is very conscious of status. Already we can tell that he treasures *objects* above *people*.

Lines 5–10. The Duke is eager to talk about the look on his former wife's face. It is also important that he tells us that he is the only one to uncover her face. Even in death, he is in control, the one to allow her to be seen.

Lines 11–24. In line 14, the Duke says that it was not only his presence that called "that spot/ Of joy" to her cheek. She had what he calls "A heart . . . too soon made glad" (line 22), and she liked "whate'er/She looked on" (lines 23–24). This causes him great distress, for he is used to being the one in control, the one—and only one—able to call forth her joy.

Lines 25–30. These lines reinforce the Duke's distress, as he tells us that his admiration was, to the Duchess, the same as the sunset or a gift of a bough of cherries. He feels that he should be the only one able to please her and resents all other things that cause her happiness. We also see that the Duchess was gracious and kind, easy to please, and happy with the simple pleasures of life.

Lines 31–43. Lines 31–32 tell us that the Duke bitterly resented the way his Duchess seemed to rank all gifts the same. What right had she to rank the gift of his name (in marriage) with anyone else's gift, he asserts. He was unwilling to speak with her about her graciousness to all, for he felt that even if he had the skill with language, he would not stoop to correct her (lines 42–43).

Lines 44–46. The Duchess, happy with her life, smiles at each and all. The Duke, furious with what he perceives as a slight, gives commands, "Then all smiles stopped together" (line 46). This line is brilliantly juxtaposed with the next, "There she stands/As if alive," so we know that his command destroyed her, directly or indirectly. Perhaps he deprived her of the daily pleasures that give life its savor—the beauty of nature, human company— or perhaps he did something even more heinous.

Lines 47–53. Here we learn that the Duke has been addressing someone sent by a Count to arrange a marriage between the Count's daughter and the Duke. The Duke smoothly asserts that his main goal is the Count's "fair daughter," but that he fully intends to obtain a fitting dowry in the deal.

Lines 53–56. As they walk down, the Duke points out another of his possessions, a bronze statute of Neptune "Taming a sea-horse." Neptune has tamed the sea-horse much as the Duke tamed his "last Duchess," destroying her spirit—through his unbending pride.

   The Duke emerges as arrogant and ruthless, determined to have his will prevail regardless of the cost. That his child-like wife would find innocent pleasure in commonplace events is insufferable to such an egotist, and so he "gives commands" that reassert his will—and destroys his wife's.

LYRIC VERSE

   As stated earlier, lyric verse was originally a term used to describe short poems meant to be sung to the music of a lyre, but the term has evolved to mean any short poem, regardless of meter or rhyme scheme, that expresses an emotion or records a thought rather than tells a tale. Probably the most common emotion in lyrics is love, or the despair brought on by unreturned love, though grief and pain are also frequent subjects. The following is a lyric from a sixteenth-century songbook:

Western wind, when wilt thou blow,
    The small rain down can rain?
Christ, if my love were in my arms,
    And I in my bed again!

There are many different kinds of lyrics:

epigram	a brief witty expression, usually of contempt
satire	a longer expression of hate or contempt
complaint	an expression of dissatisfaction, usually to a loved one
elegy	a melancholy or mournful contemplative poem
ode	a long poem characterized by heroic or elevated emotions
dirge	a short funeral lament
pastoral	a poem of mourning set in a country setting, usually a shepherd mourning the death of a fellow shepherd
threnody	a funeral poem
monody	a longer and more complex funeral poem
sonnet	a fourteen-line poem expressing emotion
ballad	a simply structured poem, usually dealing with an emotional event

The following is an excerpt from a lyric poem, Walt Whitman's "Crossing Brooklyn Ferry." Here Whitman begins with a seemingly simple topic, the daily trip by ferry from Manhattan to Brooklyn, and uses it to create a lyrical meditation on the diversity, unity, and continuity of all objects, people, places, and time. This poem demonstrates that a lyric is more personal and subjective than other poetic forms, falling back on the imaginative to express personal emotions, thoughts, and attitudes.

CROSSING BROOKLYN FERRY

1

Flood-tide below me! I see you face to face!
Clouds of the west—sun there half an hour high—I see you also face to face.

Crowds of men and women attired in the usual costumes, how curious you are to me!
On the ferry-boats the hundreds and hundreds that cross, returning home, are more curious to me than you suppose,
And you that shall cross from shore to shore years hence are more to me, and more in my meditations, than you might suppose.

2

The impalpable sustenance of me from all things at all hours of the day,
The simple, compact, well-join'd scheme, myself disintegrated, every one disintegrated yet part of the scheme,
The similitudes of the past and those of the future,
The glories strung like beads on my smallest sights and hearings, on the wall in the street and the passage over the river,
10 The current rushing so swiftly and swimming with me far away,
  The others that are to follow me, the ties between me and them,
The certainty of others, the life, love, sight, hearing of others.

Others will enter the gates of the ferry and cross from shore to shore,
Others will watch the run of the flood-tide,
Others will see the shipping of Manhattan north and west, and the heights of Brooklyn to the south and east,

Others will see the islands large and small;
Fifty years hence, others will see them as they cross, the sun half an hour high,
A hundred years hence, or ever so many hundred years hence, others will see them,
Will enjoy the sunset, the pouring-in of the flood-tide, the falling-back to the sea of the ebb-tide.

3

20 It avails not, time nor place—distance avails not,
I am with you, you men and women of a generation, or ever so many generations hence,
Just as you feel when you look on the river and sky, so I felt,
Just as any of you is one of a living crowd, I was one of a crowd,
Just as you are refresh'd by the gladness of the river and the bright flow, I was refresh'd,
Just as you stand and lean on the rail, yet hurry with the swift current, I stood yet was hurried.
Just as you look on the numberless masts of ships and the thick-stemm'd pipes of steamboats, I look'd.

I too many and many a time cross'd the river of old,
Watched the Twelfth-month sea-gulls, saw them high in the air floating with motionless wings, oscillating their bodies,
Saw how the glistening yellow lit up parts of their bodies and left the rest in strong shadow,
30 Saw the slow-wheeling circles and the gradual edging toward the south,
Saw the reflection of the summer sky in the water,
Had my eyes dazzled by the shimmering track of beams.
Look'd at the fine centrifugal spokes of light round the shape of my head in the sunlit water,
Look'd on the haze on the hills southward and south—westward.

Look'd on the vapor as it flew in fleeces tinged with violet,
Look'd toward the lower bay to notice the vessels arriving,
Saw their approach, saw aboard those that were near me,
Saw the white sails of schooners and sloops, saw the ships at anchor,
The sailors at work in the rigging or out astride the spars,
40 The round masts, the swinging motion of the hulls, the slender serpentine pennants.

THE ODE

The *ode* has a regular rhythmic pattern, although meter and verse lengths may vary from time to time. Originally a song in honor of the gods characterized by elevated feelings, there are now three main types of ode:

1. Pindaric or regular ode has three parts: a strophe (where the chorus danced while singing), an antistrophe (where the chorus sang without dancing), and the epode (where the chorus sang without dancing). Within these fixed divisions there are lines of uneven length. More modern models include Gray's "The Progress of Poesy" and Wordsworth's "Ode: Intimations of Immortality."
2. Horation or homostrophic ode has one repeated stanza type, but may vary within its form. Examples include Marvell's 'Horatian Ode upon Cromwell's Return from Ireland," Collins' "Ode to Evening," and Keats' "Ode to Autumn."
3. Irregular odes disregard the strophe and stanza rules of their model, the Pindaric ode. They tend to show great flexibility with regard to length, meter and rhyme, and are thus the most popular form.

The ode that follows, by William Wordsworth, one of the leaders of the Romantic movement in England, uses both rhyme and rhythm to great advantage, but also manages to keep a freshness of style and tone that combine to make it pleasant reading long after its composition. It is an irregular ode, for the stanzas vary among themselves, following the poet's argument. The meter is iambic throughout, although the length of the lines and the rhymes shift. The poem discusses relationships among the human soul, nature, and immortality. It suggests that we know what immortality is after death, but even more interesting, it says that we could also know immortality before birth: "trailing clouds of glory do we come/From God, who is our home" (lines 64–65). It revels in the joy that a child sees in the world of nature as well as laments the fact that the child turns his attention to earthly things, quickly dulling that initial joy. But even so, the conclusion is not sorrowful, as the poet passes beyond mourning this loss to celebrating joys that the mature human soul is capable of appreciating. Trace the way the poet develops his arguments, and notice how the poem has been shaped to echo this train of thought. See how the different stanzas reflect the speaker's change in emotion.

INTIMATIONS OF IMMORTALITY FROM RECOLLECTIONS OF EARLY CHILDHOOD

The Child is father of the Man;
And I could wish my days to be
Bound each to each by natural piety.

1

There was a time when meadow, grove, and stream,
The earth, and every common sight,
    To me did seem
    Apparelled in celestial light,
5 The glory and the freshness of a dream.
It is not now as it hath been of yore;—
    Turn wheresoe'er I may,
    By night or day,
The things which I have seen I now can see no more.

2

10   The Rainbow comes and goes,
    And lovely is the Rose,
    The Moon doth with delight
Look round her when the heavens are bare;
    Waters on a starry night
15   Are beautiful and fair;
    The sunshine is a glorious birth;
    But yet I know, where'er I go,
That there hath past away a glory from the earth.

3

Now, while the birds thus sing a joyous song,
20   And while the young lambs bound
    As to the tabor's sound,
To me alone there came a thought of grief:
A timely utterance gave that thought relief,
    And I again am strong:
25 The cataracts blow their trumpets from the steep;
No more shall grief of mine the season wrong;

I hear the Echoes through the mountains throng,
The Winds come to me from the fields of sleep,
    And all the earth is gay;
30   Land and sea
    Give themselves up to jollity,
    And with the heart of May
    Doth every Beast keep holiday;—
    Thou Child of Joy,
35 Shout round me, let me hear thy shouts,
thou happy Shepherd-boy!

4

Ye blessèd Creatures, I have heard the call
    Ye to each other make; I see
The heavens laugh with you in your jubilee;
    My heart is at your festival,
40   My head hath its coronal,
The fulness of your bliss, I feel—I feel it all.
    Oh evil day! if I were sullen
    While Earth herself is adorning,
    This sweet May-morning,
45   And the Children are culling
    On every side,
    In a thousand valleys far and wide,
Fresh flowers; while the sun shines warm,
And the Babe leaps up on his Mother's arm:—
50   I hear, I hear, with joy I hear!
    —But there's a Tree, of many, one,
A single Field which I have looked upon,
Both of them speak of something that is gone:
    The Pansy at my feet
55   Doth the same tale repeat:
Whither is fled the visionary gleam?
Where is it now, the glory and the dream?

5

Our birth is but a sleep and a forgetting:
The Soul that rises with us, our life's Star,
60   Hath had elsewhere its setting,
      And cometh from afar:
Not in entire forgetfulness,
And not in utter nakedness,
But trailing clouds of glory do we come
65   From God, who is our home:
Heaven lies about us in our infancy!
Shades of the prison-house begin to close
    Upon the growing Boy,
      But He
70 Beholds the light, and whence it flows,
    He sees it in his joy;
The Youth, who daily farther from the east
    Must travel, still in Nature's Priest,
    And by the vision splendid
75   Is on his way attended;
At length the Man perceives it die away,
And fade into the light of common day.

6

Earth fills her lap with pleasures of her own;
Yearnings she hath in her own natural kind,
80 And, even with something of a Mother's mind,
    And no unworthy aim,
    The homely Nurse doth all she can
To make her Foster-child, her Inmate Man,
    Forget the glories he hath known,
85 And that imperial palace whence he came.

7

Behold the Child among his new-born blisses,
A six year's Darling of a pigmy size!
See, where 'mid work of his own hand he lies,
Fretted by sallies of his mother's kisses,
90 With light upon him from his father's eyes!
See, at his feet, some little plan or chart,
Some fragment from his dream of human life,
Shaped by himself with newly-learnèd art;
    A wedding or a festival,
95   A mourning or a funeral;
    And this hath now his heart,
    And unto this he frames his song:
    Then will he fit his tongue
To dialogues of business, love, or strife;
100   But it will not be long
    Ere this be thrown aside,
    And with new joy and pride
The little Actor cons another part;
Filling from time to time his "humorous stage"
105 With all the Persons, down to palsied Age,
    That Life brings with her in her equipage;
    As if his whole vocation
    Were endless imitation.

8

Thou, whose exterior semblance doth belie
110   Thy Soul's immensity;
Thou best Philosopher, who yet dost keep
Thy heritage, thou Eye among the blind,
That, deaf and silent, read'st the eternal deep,
Haunted for ever by the eternal mind,—
115   Mighty Prophet! Seer blest!
    On whom those truths do rest,
Which we are toiling all our lives to find,
In darkness lost, the darkness of the grave;
Thou, over whom thy Immortality
120 Broods like the Day, a Master o'er a Slave,
A Presence which is not to be put by;
Thou little Child, yet glorious in the might
Of heaven-born freedom on thy being's height,
Why with such earnest pains dost thou provoke
125 The years to bring the inevitable yoke,

Thus blindly with thy blessedness at strife?
Full soon thy Soul shall have her earthly freight,
And custom lie upon thee with a weight,
Heavy as frost, and deep almost as life!

9

130   O joy! that in our embers
    Is something that doth live,
    That nature yet remembers
    What was so fugitive!
The thought of our past years in me doth breed
135 Perpetual benediction: not indeed
For that which is most worthy to be blest;
Delight and liberty, the simple creed
Of Childhood, whether busy or at rest,
With new-fledged hope still fluttering in his breast:—
140   Not for these I raise
    The song of thanks and praise;
    But for those obstinate questionings
    Of sense and outward things,
    Falling from us, vanishings;
145   Blank misgivings of a Creature
Moving about in worlds not realised,
High instincts before which our mortal Nature
Did tremble like a guilty Thing surprised:
    But for those first affections,
150   Those shadowy recollections,
    Which, be they what they may,
Are yet the fountain-light of all our day,
Are yet a master-light of all our seeing;
    Uphold us, cherish, and have power to make
155 Our noisy years seem moments in the being
Of the eternal Silence: truths that wake,
    To perish never:
Which neither listlessness, nor mad endeavor,
    Nor Man nor Boy,
160 Nor all that is at enmity with joy,

Can utterly abolish or destroy!
  Hence in a season of calm weather
    Though inland far we be,
Our Souls have sight of that immortal sea
165   Which brought us hither,
    Can in a moment travel thither,
And see the Children sport upon the shore,
And hear the mighty waters rolling evermore.

10

Then sing, ye Birds, sing, sing, a joyous song!
170   And let the young Lambs bound
    As to the tabor's sound!
We in thought will join your throng,
    Ye that pipe and ye that play,
    Ye that through your hearts to-day
175   Feel the gladness of the May!
What though the radiance which was once so bright
Be now for ever taken from my sight,
    Though nothing can bring back the hour
Of splendor in the grass, of glory in the flower;
180   We will grieve not, rather find
    Strength in what remains behind;
    In the primal sympathy

    Which having been must ever be;
    In the soothing thoughts that spring
185   Out of human suffering;
    In the faith that looks through death,
In years that bring the philosophic mind.

11

And O, ye Fountains, Meadows, Hills, and Groves,
Forebode not any severing of our loves!
190 Yet in my heart of hearts I feel your might;
I only have relinquished one delight
To live beneath your more habitual sway.
I love the Brooks which down their channels fret,
Even more than when I tripped lightly as they;
195 The innocent brightness of a new-born Day
    Is lovely yet;
The Clouds that gather round the setting sun
Do take a sober coloring from an eye
That hath kept watch o'er man's mortality;
200 Another race hath been, and other palms are won.
Thanks to the human heart by which we live,
Thanks to its tenderness, its joys, and fears,
To me the meanest flower that blows can give
Thoughts that do often lie too deep for tears.
                  —*William Wordsworth*

THE SONNET

The most popular of the defined poetic forms is the sonnet. It is a lyric poem of fourteen lines, written in iambic pentameter (five accents per line). There are two main sonnet forms. The first was originated by the Italian poets in the thirteenth century and reached its final form a century later in the work of Petrarch, thus, it came to be called the *Petrarchan or Italian* sonnet. The first eight lines, called the *octave*, rhyme *abbaabba* and present the subject of the poem; the final six lines, called the *sestet*, rhyme *cdecde* and resolve the problem or situation set forth in the first eight lines. The English poets of the sixteenth century altered the rhyme scheme of the Italian sonnet, creating an *abab/cdcd/efef/gg* pattern, which has come to be called the *Shakespearean or English* sonnet. Some claim the Shakespearean sonnet is easier to write, for no sound needs to be written more than twice. It is also said that the Italian sonnet has a smother flow and is more graceful. Originally both forms came into the language as love verse, but sonnets have been used for many different themes and subjects. A close look at the models that follow will show this variety. Examine each sonnet and decide (1) Is it an Italian or an English sonnet? (2) What is the rhyme scheme? (3) What is the poet's theme or main idea? (4) How does figurative language and other poetic devices enhance the theme?

From Shakespeare:

SONNET 116

Let me not to the marriage of true minds
Admit impediments. Love is not love
Which alters when it alteration finds,
Or bends with the remover to remove.

5 O no! it is an ever-fixèd mark
That looks on tempests and is never shaken;
It is the star to every wand'ring bark,
Whose worth's unknown, although his height be taken.
Love's not Time's fool, though rosy lips and cheeks
Within his bending sickle's compass come.
Love alters not with his brief hours and weeks,
But bears it out even to the edge of doom.
   If this be error, and upon me proved,
   I never writ, nor no man ever loved.

SONNET 73

That time of year thou mayst in me behold
When yellow leaves, or none, or few, do hang
Upon those boughs which shake against the cold,
Bare ruined choirs where late the sweet birds sang.

5 In me thou see'st the twilight of such day
As after sunset fadeth in the west,
Which by and by black night doth take away,
Death's second self that seals up all in rest.
In me thou see'st the glowing of such fire
10 That on the ashes of his young doth lie,
As the deathbed whereon it must expire,
Consumed with that which it was nourished by.
   This thou perceiv'st, which makes thy love more strong
   To love that well which thou must leave ere long.

Henry Wadsworth Longfellow wrote a series of sonnets with especially deep feeling. In July of 1861, his wife was tragically burned to death, despite Longfellow's frantic efforts to save her. Overcome with grief, he sought relief in his work, and set forth an especially difficult task for himself—translating into English Dante's *Divine Comedy*. The poem has three parts, which describe Dante's fictional journey into Hell, Purgatory, and Paradise. In his version, Longfellow opened each section with two sonnets. While Longfellow's writings said that his purpose here was to describe Dante's verse as a cathedral, he is seemingly using Dante's poem to comfort himself in his grief. The two sonnets which follow preface the first part of Longfellow's translation.

Oft have I seen at some cathedral door
   A laborer, pausing in the dust and heat,
   Lay down his burden, and with reverent feet
   Enter, and cross himself, and on the floor
5 Kneel to repeat his paternoster o er;
   Far off the noises of the world retreat;
   The loud vociferations of the street
   Become an undistinguishable roar.
So, as I enter here from day to day,
10   And leave my burden at this minster gate,
   Kneeling in prayer, and not ashamed to pray,
The tumult of the time disconsolate
   To inarticulate murmurs dies away,
   While the eternal ages watch and wait.

How strange the sculptures that adorn these towers!
  This crowd of statues, in whose folded sleeves
  Birds build their nests; while canopied with leaves
  Parvis[1] and portal bloom like trellised bowers,
5 And the vast minister seems a cross of flowers.
  But fiends and dragons on the gargoyled eaves
  Watch the dead Christ between the living thieves,
  And, underneath, the traitor Judas lowers!
Ah! from what agonies of heart and brain,
10   What exultations trampling on despair,
  What tenderness, what tears, what hate of wrong,
What passionate outcry of a soul in pain,
  Uprose this poem of the earth and air,
  This medieval miracle of song!

SAMPLE AP QUESTIONS ON POETRY

1. Considering the sonnet printed below, explain what the author wishes to be loved for and why she feels this way. Time—20 minutes.

SONNET 14

If thou must love me, let it be for nought
Except for love's sake only. Do not say,
"I love her for her smile—her look—her way
Of speaking gently,—for a trick of thought
5 That falls in well with mine, and certes brought
A sense of pleasant ease on such a day"—
For these things in themselves, Belovèd, may
Be changed, or change for thee,—and love, so wrought,
May be unwrought so. Neither love me for
10 Thine own dear pity's wiping my cheeks dry,—
A creature might forget to weep, who bore
Thy comfort long, and lose thy love thereby!
But love me for love's sake, that evermore
Thou may'st love on, through love's eternity.
              —*Elizabeth Barrett Browning*

Answer

The first two lines state what the author wishes to be loved for "nought [nothing]/ Except for love's sake only." This is picked up again in the final two lines, "But love me for love's sake . . . ." She wishes to be loved for "love's sake" because if love is not based on mere physical attractions ("her smile," "her look," "her way/Of speaking gently"), it will be able to endure for eternity (see last line).

2. Contrast the sonnet below, number 43, with the one above and show how the similarities and differences in the description of love. What is the difference in speaker? Theme? Use specific references to make your point. Time—30 minutes.

SONNET 43

How do I love thee? Let me count the ways.
I love thee to the depth and breadth and height
My soul can reach, when feeling out of sight
For the ends of Being and ideal Grace.
5 I love thee to the level of everyday's
Most quiet need, by sun and candle-light.
I love thee freely, as men strive for Right;
I love thee purely, as they turn from Praise.
I love thee with the passion put to use
10 In my old griefs, and with my childhood's faith.
I love thee with a love I seemed to lose
With my lost saints,—I love thee with the breath,
Smiles, tears, of all my life!—and, if God choose,
I shall but love thee better after death.
—*Elizabeth Barrett Browning*

Answer

While each sonnet discusses love, there are differences in speaker and theme. In Sonnet 14, the author is explaining the love someone else feels for her; in Sonnet 43, she is discussing the love *she feels* for someone else. The first sonnet stresses the mutability and impermanence of the outward show of love, rejecting love based on physical attraction for a love that will endure for eternity. The second sonnet stresses the love she feels here and now for the man, but adds that if God chooses, she will love him even better after death.

3. Show how the two parts of "How Soon Hath Time" are united by the theme. You will have to:
   • find and explain the two parts of the poem
   • describe the theme
   • show how the theme unites the poem. Time—30 minutes.

HOW SOON HATH TIME

How soon hath Time, the subtle thief of youth,
Stolen on his wing my three-and-twentieth year!
My hasting days fly on with full career,
But my late spring no bud or blossom shew'th.
5 Perhaps my semblance might deceive the truth
That I to manhood am arrived so near;

And inward ripeness doth much less appear,
That some more timely-happy spirits endu'th.[1]
Yet be it less or more, or soon or slow,
10 It shall be still in strictest measure even
To that same lot, however mean or high,
Toward which Time leads me, and the will of Heaven;
All is, if I have grace to use it so,
As ever in my great Taskmaster's eye.
—*John Milton*

Answer

The first part of the poem, lines 1–6, discusses the outward changes the speaker has undergone. Such changes are reflected in the statement "Perhaps my semblance might deceive the truth/That I to manhood am arrived so near" (line 5–6), which shows, in the word "semblance", the *outward* changes time has wrought.

The second part of the poem concerns *inward* changes, as found in the phrase "inward ripeness" (line 7).

The theme, stated in the final four lines, is that the changes the speaker has experienced are the will of heaven.

4. Using "How Soon Hath Time," show how the author's theme is reflected in the poem's form. Explain why the particular form selected is best suited to this theme. Discuss the sonnet. Why was this form of the sonnet used here? Time—30 minutes.

Answer

The sonnet takes two forms, the Italian (Petrarchan) and English (Elizabethan). This is an Italian sonnet, which has eight lines (the octave), rhyming *abbaabba,* which present the poet's subject, followed by six lines (the sestet), rhyming *cdecde,* which indicate the importance of the facts set forth in the octave and resolve the problem established there. Milton used the Italian sonnet form rather than the Elizabethan (*abab/cdcd/efef/gg* rhyme) because the Elizabethan form resolves the conflict in the final couplet (*gg*) and usually has a witty turn of phrase. The Italian form allows him six lines to make his point—the changes God wills in man—without any wit or humor at the end.

Milton selected the sonnet form because it allows for a brief and clear presentation of theme. He did not need a narrative—a long story—nor an ode—in elevated language— to make his point about the changes he has undergone and their reason.

5. What appalls Captain Ahab so is the "whiteness" of Moby-Dick, the great whale. Robert Frost is working with that symbolism in the poem below. Discuss the *symbolism* of "Design" and explain how the "whiteness" represents the *theme.* Time—30 minutes.

DESIGN

I found a dimpled spider, fat and white,
On a white heal-all, holding up a moth
Like a white piece of rigid satin cloth—
Assorted characters of death and blight
Mixed ready to begin with morning right,
Like the ingredients of a witches' broth—
A snow-drop spider, a flower like a froth,
And dead wings carried like a paper kite.

What had that flower to do with being white,
The wayside blue and innocent heal-all?
What brought the kindred spider to that height,
Then steered the white moth thither in the night?
What but design of darkness to appall?—
If design govern in a thing so small.

—*Robert Frost*

Answer

Follow the white items listed in the first four lines: spider, fat and white; white heal-all; moth, looking like a white piece of cloth. All are linked by the remark in line 4: "Assorted characters of death and blight." These pictures of death and decay continue: witches' broth, dead wings.

The items listed above are pulled together in the final two lines as the speaker expresses surprise that there is some power governing even the formation and design of items as small and seemingly insignificant as the ones he lists. If there is a hand behind even these petty items, what then rules our lives which we hold so very significant?

6. Show how the form of "Design" is suited to the theme. Time—30 minutes.

Answer

This poem is a sonnet, having fourteen lines with the rhyme scheme:

white	a
moth	b
cloth	b
blight	a
right	a
broth	b
froth	b
kite	a
white	a
heal-all	c
height	a
night	a
appall	c
small	c

This is a variation on the Italian sonnet, whose form is *abbaabba cdecde*. This pattern is followed through the octave (*abbaabba*), but breaks form in the sestet, to *acaacc*, with a final rhyming couplet, the *cc*.

An excellent case could be made that the form is followed in the first eight lines because Frost is talking about *design* and so follows a rigid form. In the conclusion, though, he breaks out of the design to create a new pattern. This is reflected in the theme of design ruling even the smallest item in nature, but not in *his* creation, the poem.

7. Read the poem below and answer the following questions: What is "fire" and what is "ice"? Why does the poet conclude that ice will also suffice for destruction? Time—20 minutes.

FIRE AND ICE

Some say the world will end in fire,
Some say in ice.
From what I've tasted of desire
I hold with those who favor fire.
But if it had to perish twice,
I think I know enough of hate
To say that for destruction ice
Is also great
And would suffice.

—*Robert Frost*

Answer

Fire is passion and desire, that which heats up our lives. Ice is cold, hard hate, devoid of the heat of passion. The poet feels that hatred is strong enough to cause the destruction of the world, even though most might feel that desire, fire, is most apt to set things aflame.

SUGGESTED READING LIST

The following books are helpful for understanding poetry and poetic theory:

Brooks, Cleanth and Robert Penn Warren. *Understanding Poetry*. New York: Holt, Rinehart and Winston, 1960.

Ciardi, John. *How Does a Poem Mean?* Boston: Houghton, Mifflin Company, 1960.

Perrine, Lawrence, *Sound and Sense: An Introduction to Poetry*. New York: Harcourt Brace Jovanovich, 1977.

And for brief essays on poets' lives as well as extended discussions of poetic movements and social settings, consult the appropriate volume of *The Norton Anthology of Literature* (New York: W.W. Norton, 1989). There are two volumes on English Literature (I, II) and two on American Literature (I, II).

NOTE: In some instances specific works will be listed; in others, author's names. When an author is listed with no specific work following his name, any of his poems are suitable for analysis on the Advanced Placement exam. Where all of a poet's work is suitable but specific works are recommended for study these works are listed followed by the word "poems."

Eighth Century

anonymous	*Beowulf*

Thirteenth/Fourteenth Century

anonymous	ballads
Chaucer	

Sixteenth Century

Marlowe, Christopher	*Doctor Faustus*
Shakespeare, William	sonnets
	songs from plays
Sidney, Sir Philip	sonnets
Spenser, Edmund	sonnets
Wyatt the Elder, Sir Thomas	poems

Seventeenth Century

Bradstreet, Anne	poems
Donne, John	sonnets
Dryden, John	poems
Gay, John	poems
Herrick, Robert	poems
Herbert, George	poems
Johnson, Samuel	poems
Jonson, Ben	poems
Marvell, Andrew	poems
Milton, John	"On His Blindness"
	Paradise Lost
Pope, Alexander	"Ode on Solitude"
	"An Essay on Man"

	Eighteenth Century
Burns, Robert	poems
Gray, Thomas	"Elegy Written on a Country Churchyard"

	Eighteenth/Nineteenth Century
Blake, William	*Songs of Innocence*
	Songs of Experience
Bryant, William Cullen	"Thanatopsis"
Lord Byron	"She Walks in Beauty"
Coleridge, Samuel Taylor	"Kubla Khan"
Keats, John	"Ode to a Grecian Urn"
	"Ode to a Nightingale"
Shelley, Percy Bysshe	"Ozymandias"
	"Ode to the West Wind"
Wordsworth, William	poems

	Nineteenth Century
Arnold, Matthew	"Dover Beach"
Browning, Elizabeth Barrett	*Sonnets from the Portuguese*
Browning, Robert	poems
Carroll, Lewis	"Jabberwocky"
Dickinson, Emily	poems
Emerson, Ralph Waldo	poems
Fitzgerald, Edward	"The Rubáiyát of Omar Khayyám of Naishápúr"
Hardy, Thomas	poems
Hopkins, Gerard Manley	"Pied Beauty"
	"Spring and Fall"
Longfellow, Henry Wadsworth	poems
Melville, Herman	"Clarissa"
Poe, Edgar Allan	"To Helen"
	"Annabel Lee"
Tennyson, Alfred Lord	"Ulysses"
	"Crossing the Bar"
Thoreau, Henry David	poems
Whitman, Walt	"Out of the Cradle Endlessly Rocking"
	"A Noiseless Patient Spider"
	poems

	Twentieth Century
Brooke, Rupert	poems
Brooks, Gwendolyn	poems, especially "We Real Cool"
Eliot, T.S.	"The Love Song of Alfred J. Prufrock"
	"The Hollow Men"
	"Journey of the Magi"
	Four Quartets
Frost, Robert	"Stopping by Woods on a Snowy Evening"
	"The Road Not Taken"
	"Design"
	poems
Housman, A.E.	*A Shropshire Lad*
Jarrell, Randall	poems
Larkin, Philip	poems
Lawrence, D.H.	poems

Lowell, Robert	poems
MacLeish, Archibald	"Ars Poetica"
	"You, Andrew Marvell"
Merwin, W.S.	poems
Moore, Marianne	poems
Ortiz, Simon	*Sand Creek*
Plath, Sylvia	poems
Pound, Ezra	"In a Station of the Metro"
	poems
Ransom, John Crowe	poems
Robinson, E.A.	"Miniver Cheevy"
Rois, Alberto	"Advice to a First Cousin"
Sandburg, Carl	"Fog"
Sexton, Anne	poems
Stevens, Wallace	"The Snow Man"
	all poems
Williams, William Carlos	"The Dance"
	"The Red Wheelbarrow"
	"The Yachts"
Yeats, William Butler	"Leda and the Swan"
	"When You are Old"
	"Sailing to Byzantium"
	"The Second Coming"
	poems

Part 5

Analyzing Drama

A Brief Overview of Drama

Drama is a presentation in which actors and actresses imitate for an audience an event (the term "drama" comes from the Greek *dran,* which means "to do") through words and/or gestures. The *mis en scène* is the term used for the actual staging of the performance, including any scenery and *properties* (movable furniture) as well as the actors and actresses themselves. If no words are used and the events are told entirely through the use of gestures, the performance is called a *pantomime* or *dumb show.* The last term is often applied to a silent performance within a performance, as in the second scene of the third act of *Hamlet,* where the players, under Hamlet's direction, wordlessly enact the murder of a king.

Chronological List of Periods and Types of Drama

I. Ancient Drama

A. *Classical tragedy:* A dramatic representation of "an action of high importance," according to Aristotle. In the twentieth century, we generally define tragedy as any play of serious intention ending with the hero either dead or spiritually crushed.

B. *Classical comedy:* A kind of drama that amuses the audience, showing a movement from unhappiness to happiness that entertains rather than distresses the audience and ridicules rather than upsets.

II. Middle Ages

A. *Mystery play:* Dramatization of a biblical story concerning a saint's life that included much secular material, especially in the late Middle Ages. *The Second Shepherds' Play,* for example, takes 6/7 of its space to tell the humorous story of a sheep-stealer, leaving only 1/7 to the events of Christ's birth.

B. *Miracle play:* Also dramatization of a biblical story, such as the story of Cain and Abel. Popular from the twelfth through the fifteenth centuries.

C. *Morality play:* Allegorical dramatization of the conflict between good and evil, including stock characters such as Everyman, Good Deeds, and Avarice. A late medieval development which remained popular far into the sixteenth century.

III. The Renaissance

A. *Masque* (also spelled *Mask*): An entertainment given in the Renaissance court, as noblemen and women performed a dignified little play, usually allegorical and mythological in nature. It was frequently lavish in production but the structure was simple, as the so-called masquers, costumed and masked noblemen, entered, supposedly having traveled from afar. They invited the ladies of the court to dance, they dance, and the masquers leave. Shakespeare's *Henry VIII,* I, iv reenacts the masque at which the king first encountered his second wife, Anne Boleyn. Renaissance England's greatest writer of masques was Ben Jonson, who created them with the famous architect Inigo Jones.

B. *Antimasque* (popularized by Ben Jonson): A grotesque dance of monsters or clowns. The performance was enacted by professionals representing chaos, who are broken up by the courtly performers. "Anti" is derived from the term "antic," meaning a "grotesque caper" or "fool" and does not mean "against" as we might assume today.

C. *Pastoral:* Any writing having to do with shepherds. These plays described rural life as unspoiled and superior to urban existence. They are frequently set in Arcadia, a mountainous district in Greece, well known for its peaceful shepherds.

D. *Chronicle play:* A dramatization of historical material (or material assumed to be historical) for a public ready to view its past. These plays are registers of facts, a history in chronological order. There is some confusion between a tragedy with historical figures, such as Shakespeare's *Richard II,* and a chronicle play with tragic events.

E. *Tragedies and Comedies:* To be discussed later in detail.

IV. Restoration (1660–1700) and the Eighteenth Century

A. *Comedy of manners* (also called comedy of wit): A form of comedy, often cynical in tone, that involved much witty *repartee* (quick and unexpected come-back answers). The best-known authors of such comedies were Etherege, Wycherly, and Congreve. The most common theme was that love, marriage, and commonly held notions of romance are silly. People emerge as selfish, pleasure-loving, and skeptical of traditions that cannot stand up to close study. About 1700, Restoration comedy ended when the satire came to be directed against heartless cleverness rather than deviations in manners. At the same time *sentimental comedy* developed.

B. *Commedia dell'arte:* A dramatic comedy that used so-called stock characters including such figures as the Merchant, the Doctor, Young Lovers, Clever Servants, etc. It was performed especially by Italian troops of actors who improvised as they went along.

C. *Sentimental comedy and drama:* Developed at the end of this period, portray man as basically good. The few who are evil quickly repent, often in a sea of soggy sentiment. There is little wit; the characters are usually drawn from the middle class; and they indicate their virtue by weeping at the sight of any kind of distress.

V. Nineteenth Century

A. *Melodrama:* Originally drama with music expressing the character's thoughts (as is done in the movies today), but by the nineteenth century, it had come to stand for a drama wherein characters who are clearly good or evil are posed against each other in sensational situations filled with suspense. In the nineteenth century, there was an element of exotic horror represented by castles and dungeons, but it was later replaced by local evil, including the wicked landlord. The plot is unbelievable or unlikely, and virtue triumphs over adversity.

B. *Social plays:* Depict social setting and people in their environment.

VI. Twentieth Century

A. *Problem plays:* Ask the audience to address itself to a sociological problem of some sort. Ibsen's *A Doll's House* invites debate on the relationship between a husband and a wife, and Shaw's *Major Barbara* (discussed in the following chapter in depth) involves the audience in a discussion of the merits of the Salvation Army, the ethics of businesses and the people that run them, and the responsibility for war. It may not be either tragic or comedic, but the emphasis is on the social aspects of the problem rather than the fate of individual characters.

B. *Theatre of the absurd:* To be discussed in the following chapter in detail.

The Elements of Drama

TIME

Drama, theater, and the play are all closely related, but for our purposes here, the term *drama* shall be restricted to the written form, the creation of the *dramatist*. Going back 2300 years to Aristotle's *Poetics,* drama is defined as consisting of a *story* (or *fable*) with a beginning, a middle, and an end, which must be told within a specific *time* period. Following the conventions of the ancient Greeks, the modern dramatist, too, must complete his story within the few hours allowed to him, for the audience cannot put his story down and come back tomorrow, nor sit for more than a few hours at a time. Within the strict limits of the time he has, the dramatist must tell his tale in such a way as to get his meaning across and hold the audience's attention. Some of this has changed—rather drastically, too—in contemporary drama, as you will see later, but the theater experience is basically still limited to a few short hours at a time.

Even within the strict limits of the time allowed to him, the dramatist has some freedom. This can be seen even in plays by such traditional playwrights as Shakespeare. There are two distinct "times" in *Othello,* for example. The first, from the beginning of Act II until the end of the play, takes only 33 hours of "play" time (just a few hours—or less, depending on interpretation—of "theater" time). But this is not enough time to account for the repeated adultery with which Iago accuses Desdemona. There would not have been time for the alleged affair between Cassio and Desdemona either in Cyprus or in the brief time in Venice. This is accounted for by a period of time in Cyprus lasting over a week: Bianca scolds Cassio for having been away from her for so long; Lodovocio has time to sail from Venice and reach Cyprus after the news of the Turkish defeat has reached Venice.

SPEAKERS/CHARACTERS

Having decided upon the story, the dramatist must next consider who will tell his tale and perform the action. There must not be too many people on the stage at any one time, for if the stage becomes too crowded, the audience may not be able to follow the action. In Greek drama, for example, each playwright was limited to three speaking actors: one involved in the actor's contest (for best actor) and two others, who divided the remaining roles between them. In tragedy, the number of actors never exceeded three, although in comedy there were sometimes extras who were assigned a few lines. In both tragedy and comedy, there were an unlimited number of nonspeaking walk-on parts. The audience must be able to identify with the characters to establish the dramatist's desired relationship. Because the characters are visible and live, the dramatist must constantly be aware of physical appearance and capabilities of his characters. Will they require costumes? Will they have to appear older? Younger?

The *major characters* are those at the center of the drama. They are either the cause of the crisis or caught up in it through no fault of their own. We see this in Aeschylus' *The Choephori* and Euripides' *Electra*. Orestes and Electra are major characters in both works, and their crisis is the decision to kill Clytemnestra. In a tragedy, the audience must feel sympathy for the major characters, for we must be emotionally affected by the fate of these characters if the play is to be successful. This is not necessarily true for comedy. There we do not forge a bond with the main characters, who are not usually drawn as fully as are the characters in a tragedy.

Minor characters may or may not help to advance the plot, and the audience is not usually as caught up in their fate. They may serve to advance the plot through their roles as messengers or servants. In Greek drama, violence was not allowed to be performed on stage, so the minor characters often gave long speeches describing violent acts that took place out of sight of the audience.

Stock characters are characters whom we instantly recognize as "types." Pylades in *The Choephori* and *Electra* is "the faithful friend." Cadmus appears to be "the foolish old man" in the beginning of *The Bacchae,* but by the play's end, he has discarded his stereotype and grown in stature. Other stereotypical roles include "the sweet young maiden," "the brave soldier," "the dirty old man," etc.

Motivation is essential to a successful play. The audience must be made to feel that the characters have reasons for doing what they do. In Greek tragedy, one of the key motivations is revenge (getting back at a person for what he has done to the main character). Family ties are sacred, and one of the chief responsibilities of family is to revenge wrongs done to relatives. Romantic love as we define it today was not a key motivation in early plays. Since most marriages of the time were arranged for personal or political reasons, little attention was paid to romantic love as a motivating force. This, of course, is very different today, and so we find romantic love as an important motivation in modern drama.

Character development is another major element of drama. How does the character change as the play progresses? Does the character mature in stature or is this not a necessary function of that character in that play? Hippolytus in Euripides' play is an unbearable egotist through most of the drama. When he is close to death, though, he realizes his error of pride and becomes more likable, allowing the audience to feel for him. Comedy, in contrast, usually does not feature character change. Strepsiades is as silly and unthinking at the conclusion of *The Clouds* as he was in the beginning.

There are several ways in which an author can indicate characterization. The first is through *dialogue.* The way in which a character speaks, the words he selects, his specific accent, and his use of grammar and syntax tell us something about him.

A character's *actions* also reveal his personality. How he acts and reacts to events tell us a great deal about him.

The most difficult aspect of characterization for the dramatist is the indication of a *character's thoughts.* Playwrights have adopted several means for stepping inside a character's mind to show what he is thinking. One of these methods is the *soliloquy,* in which a character stands alone on the stage and addresses the audience. Another is the *prologue,* a feature of Greek tragedy in which a character appears before the start of the action to share his thoughts with the audience. Another method used to reveal thoughts in Greek drama involves using the *chorus* as a kind of sounding board. Frequently the chorus is sworn to silence by a character who feels that he has revealed too much.

Other characters also help to define a major character, for what others say about a person can be very revealing. Sometimes, one character has a personal grudge against another character, and so we must carefully sift what is said, recognizing the possibility of bias.

Often the characters in drama function to give *unity* to the plot. The events of a play can be held together because they happen to the same character or are enacted by the same character. Euripides, for example, has been criticized because often the only thing that holds the two halves of his plays together is the fact that they concern the same character. *Hecuba* is a good example of this type of relationship. When plots are held together through time or character, they are said to be *loose* or *episodic.* This is not to say that any one type of structure is superior to another, but naturally some critics and viewers favor one over the other.

DIALOGUE

Dialogue is of vital importance to successful drama. Aristotle wrote that what is said (*thought*) and how it is said (*diction*) are next in importance to character, and if the dialogue is not accurate, the audience will be unable to follow the dramatist's ideas. Even the finest writers of fiction are often unable to pen good dramatic dialogue. Such was the case with Henry James, whose stories have held readers spellbound, but whose plays were all failures. Ironically, many of his stories, when adapted for the stage by good dramatists, were successes. Thus, dialogue is crucial, for it is the only way we can learn what is going through a character's mind. Dialogue is a curious thing, though. Because it keeps going without a pause in traditional plays, it becomes essentially unreal. Yet it must *appear* real. The characters must seem to speak in that manner, whether or not anyone really does. The quality of the dialogue, then, makes the difference between merely *literate* drama and real *dramatic literature*. While all drama is literate, it is the exceptional drama that is passed down through the ages as great, enduring literature. Whether it is written in poetry or prose, enduring dialogue must have a sense of the patterns of speech that are fitting to each speaker and the special situation in which he is placed. The speakers must hold the audience by their words and, simultaneously, reveal the theme.

Shakespeare had four basic tools for dialogue:

1. blank verse
2. prose of different kinds, such as comic prose of clowns, familiar speech of gallants
3. variations on ten-syllable lines, such as couplets, quatrains, stanzas, etc.
4. shorter rhymed lines, usually six or eight syllables each, in couplets or quatrains

The following examples show that we can clearly distinguish the difference between various forms:

> Now, fair Hippolyta, our nuptial hour
> Draws on apace: four happy days bring in
> Another moon: but, O, methinks how slow
> This old moon wanes! She lingers my desires,

and

> Over hill, over dale,
>   Through bush, through briar,
> Over park, over pale,
>   Through flood, through fire,
> I do wander everywhere.

It cannot be overstressed that Elizabethan audiences would be much more readily attuned to differences in sound; indeed, we know from the following example that their ears were acute enough to be able to recognize blank verse from a single line. In *As You Like It*, Orlando says, "Good day, and happiness, dear Rosalind." One of the other characters responds, "Nay then, God buy you, as you talk in blank verse." The point of the joke rests in Shakespeare's assurance that the audience will pick up the blank verse as quickly as Jacques did. The difference in dialogue also alerted the audience to characterization.

In the opening of *Macbeth,* for example, the witches utter the following lines:

> When shall we three meet again,
> In thunder, lightning or in rain?

Immediately, the octosyllabic lines, in place of the expected blank verse, suggest the supernatural, while the falling (trochaic) movement suggests that things are turned upside down, inverted from the normal order. "Fair is foul and foul is fair" illustrates this also.

Similarly, the language used in the opening of *Hamlet* alerts the audience to what is happening. In the first seven short utterances of the play there are three regular blank verse lines.

> Nay, answer me: stand and unfold youself . . .
> You come most carefully upon your hour . . .
> 'Tis now struck twelve; get thee to bed, Francisco.

This is what the play-goers would have expected. However, the rest of the lines in this section are broken, lines such as "Who's there?" and "He." This suggests to the audience that the atmosphere is broken with tension and anxiety, as the blank verse is disrupted with short, disturbing messages.

These passages from *Macbeth* and *Hamlet* show the link between verse form and scene content. Different verse forms are also used for contrast. The balcony scene in *Romeo and Juliet,* for example, is rich in lyrical blank verse, as the following excerpt shows:

> But, soft! what light through yonder window breaks?
> It is the east, and Juliet is the sun.
> Arise, fair sun, and kill the envious moon,
> Who is already sick and pale with grief,
> That thou her maid art far more fair than she: . . .
> O Romeo, Romeo! wherefore art thou Romeo?
> Deny thy father and refuse thy name;
> Or, if thou wilt not, be but sworn my love,
> And I'll no longer be a Capulet. (II, ii, 1–37)

But the following scene, with Friar Lawrence, uses rhymed couplets and heavy spondaic measures to achieve a poetic, serious, and dignified atmosphere:

> Benedicite!
> What early tongue so sweet saluteth me?
> Young son, it argues a distemper'd head
> So soon to bid good morrow to thy bed:
> Care keep his watch in every man's old eye,
> And where care lodges, sleep will never lie;
> But where unbruised youth with unstuff'd brain
> Doth couch his limbs, there golden sleep doth reign (II, iii, 31–38)

LANGUAGE

The *language* of a work of literature refers to the diction, sentence structure, syntax, and so forth. Since some of the words used during the Renaissance, for example, will obviously be unfamiliar to modern readers, we will initially have to put more effort into grasping their meaning and then turn our attention to an appreciation of style. The problem is even more obvious in older works, such as those from the Greek, or in foreign works, such as Molière's plays. Since you will be reading all such plays in translation, you will have to select a well-known edition, preferably one recommended or clearly the work of a well-known, accomplished translator. A poor translation, or one that was done before the discovery of additional material, will hamper your understanding of the play as well as your appreciation of the style.

Aristotle spoke of diction as crucial to an effective style. Diction, as explained in the Writing section, is word choice. *Diction in tragedy,* according to Aristotle, must be elevated in keeping with the lofty themes and concerns. If this rule is not followed strictly, the work is usually classed as a *tragi-comedy.* In the same way, the characters and images must be elevated, focusing on kings or nobles and such significant events as battles or great storms.

Diction in comedy is usually much less elevated and lofty, and here we find scatological words and images. The wit is also coarser, and generally the entire play relies less on descriptions of the upper strata of society. This is not to say that there are not passages of great beauty, but this is not the main goal of comedy.

Song is an important part of Greek comedy and tragedy. There are choral odes that divide the scenes in tragedy, commenting on the action or the theme. They follow a rigid verse form and refer to mythology and history. These odes are not as important to comedy and are usually used to comment on current events or people.

At the heart of all discussions of style is *language,* for the words a playwright selects are obviously crucial to the meaning of his work. Nowhere is this more evident than in Shakespeare's works. In *Othello,* for example, several language motifs are used to make very specific thematic points:

1. **Military Words.** The major characters are army officers, and four of the five acts take place in a town of war. Thus Othello is called "General" (also referred to as "Captain," an Elizabethan word meaning the same). He is a mercenary, as it was the practice of some Italian city-states to employ a foreigner as the head of the army. Cassio is called "Lieutenant"; Iago is called "Ancient," which is the same as "Ensign." Othello as captain selects his two officers, lieutenant, and ensign, and fires one of them.

2. **"Honest."** When applied to Desdemona, it has a double meaning: "chaste" as well as "upright." When applied to Cassio, it usually means "honorable." When used with Iago, the term is an ironic reference to Iago as a virtuous and trustworthy man. Thus, Iago would be able to distinguish vice in others and enjoy the freedom of cynical and truthful speech. Obviously, this is ironic.

3. **"Think."** This word has not changed meaning over the years, and applies mostly to Iago, whereas Othello has been used to *knowing* and then acting. Iago uses it when he is trying to rouse Othello's suspicions, and we see its climax in Othello's description of his torment:

> By the world,
> I *think* my wife be honest, and *think* she is not;
> I *think* that thou are just, and *think* thou are not.
> I'll have some proof. (III, iii, 383–386)

Imagery, another aspect of style, is extremely effective in a play. In *Othello,* continuing with the previous example, the images, pictures suggested by words and phrases, fall into three groups:

1. **Light and Dark.** This is the most obvious in the marriage of black and white, Othello and Desdemona, which would have startled an Elizabethan audience to whom a Moor would have been a rare sight. The following are a sampling of quotes that show this kind of imagery. You will be able to find many more.

(I, i, 76-77)   "As when, by night and negligence, the fire/Is spied in populous cities."
Fire in the night, a recurrent light/dark image in the play, reaches its climax when Desdemona sees Othello holding a burning candle standing by her bed.

(I, iii, 409-10)   "Hell and night/must bring this monstrous birth to the world's light."
This image is used to describe Iago's hellish plan, as darkness and hell bring forth evil into the light of consciousness.

(III, iii, 386-88) "Her name, that was as fresh/As Dian's visage, is now begrim'd and black/As mine own face."
Through Iago's suggestions, Othello sees Desdemona so marred by blackening evil that she seems to be as black as he is physical-

2. **Animal Images.** Several critics have noticed that the more Othello listens to Iago's evil suggestions, the more "lower"animals are used to describe him. The most well-known of these are the "goats and monkeys" (IV, i, 274) Othello mentions when speaking to Lodovico, echoing the suggestion Iago had made to these lecherous creatures in III,iii,403. These images are frequently lewd and obscene. For example:

(I, i, 88-89)   "An old black ram/Is tupping your white ewe." Iago sees Othello as an "old black ram," Desdemona is the innocent lamb, and suggests Othello is defiling the innocent woman.

3. **Ocean Storms.** The renaissance used images of the larger world called the "macrocosm" to reflect the actions of man in the little world, called the "microcosm." The storms of the ocean represent what is happening to the characters, emotionally and spiritually. In I, i, 30, Iago describes himself as "belee'd and calm'd," and describes the success of his plan in terms of a ship being helped on its way by winds and currents: "If consequence do but approve my dream,?My boat sails freely, both wind and stream" (II, iii, 64-64). There is nothing romantic about his view if the seam and it has no storms, no danger, and ultimately, no beauty. Each character tells us about him. In V, ii, 267-68, for example, Othello compares the end of an ocean journey to the approach of death. Both the tempest and the icy currents, the swell of life, with their beauty and their motion, are now gone: "Here is my journey's end, here is my butt,/ and every seamark of my utmost sail."
     For further study of imagery, see Robert B. Heilman's discussion of various images in Othello including birth, burning, pain, clothing, etc. Wolfgang Clemen has also studied this aspect of the play, especially the contrasting imagery of Iago and Othello.

THEATER STYLE AND PRODUCTION

The manner in which a play is presented has only become important in the last hundred years. The styles of drama has varied through the years, designed as it was for specific theaters, the space determining the manner and method of production. Until about a hundred years ago, the style of drama and the style of the physical space within it was presented had not changed for a period of a hundred years or more. Regardless of the subject, theme, or character, for instance, Shakespearean style remained the same with regard to costuming, staging, theater structure, and so forth from about 1576(the opening of the first commercial theater) until the theaters were closed by the Puritans in 1642. In the same way, the style of theater remained the same from the time the theaters were reopened by Charles II after the Restoration in 1660 for quite a long time. Today this has changed, as theater style has adapted to many different forms. There are several different style to be considered.

The classic style is structured in the manner of Greek drama, with the subject matter devoted to a single plot line, dealing with mainly heroic legends of historical myth and tales. There is little physical violence- what the is takes place off stage- although the physical and mental agonies of many characters, such as those of Odeipus, are in full view. It then takes place during a single time span and in a single space. Dialogue is elevated prose, almost poetic, carefully planned and arranged in long sets pieces that alternate with quick exchanges between main characters. Staging is simple, suggesting the cleanliness of classical buildings. These plays are concerned with the relationship of the larger-than-life characters to the gods, or God, Nature, or the Universe as well as to each other and frequently raise deep questions about the forces that control human behavior. Usually the classic and tragic views are found together.

The romantic style is quite different from the classic. Because the romantic writer sees man as essentially good, unaffected by the gods and untainted by original sin, he is uncomfortable with the rigid uniformity of subject matter, theme, and set design of the classic theater. He favors originality, freedom to move about in time and space, and weave multiple plot line. This, in turn, results in a great deal of colorful spectacle and exciting adventure. Romantic plays tend to appeal to the emotions. Central to these plays is the notion that man's various difficulties are the result of the façade forced upon him by "civilization," hiding and stifling his true nature. When this artificial cover is stripped away man will shine forth in all his goodness. "Natural man" is pure and uncontaminated, and thus the romanticist looks to nature, to the woods and streams, sunshine and rain, for an understanding of mankind. Also, since the past in invariably seen as better than the present, the romanticist is historically oriented. These plays emphasize nostalgia, undying devotion, and love; they are eternally optimistic. Oppositely, the romanticist is also obsessed with evil and the mysteries of death, and is far more drawn to the hellish than the heavenly. What is on the other side of the grave? Can we ever know it" The romanticist probes the supernatural, the magical, the fantastic, and the exotic, setting his tales in mysterious valleys and deeply hidden mountains. He is also not above changing history to suit his own needs, preferring as he does the ideal to the real. This trait can be found in the works of Frederich Schiller, the German romanticist.

The realistic and naturalistic style are very different from the classic and romantic styles. A realistic play accepts man pretty much as he is, and presents him as a product of his society. The subject matter mirrors realty, as the characters on stage move through actions that would be found in real life. The characters are closely identified with the audience, for the are presented as products of their society, unromanticized and unsentimentalized. The characters are neither totally good nor totally evil, but rather totally human, appearing strong or weak, heroic or fearful, as the situation demands. The dialogue also fits in with this characterization, and the characters speak as real people, in the rhythms of normal speech.

The naturalistic style makes use of the same subject matter as the realistic style, but the characters are regarded more objectively, even scientifically. To the naturalistic writer, the characters are used as subjects for close analysis, as the naturalist is interested in what makes man function as a creature in the natural world. According to his theory, society has placed upon the individual a certain pattern of behavior made up of the customs of civilized behavior. If that covering is ripped away, man stands revealed in all his animalistic primitiveness. Because naturalists tend to dwell on these things and are not especially selective in the details they highlight, they have been accused of being sensationalists. Naturalists defend themselves on the grounds that it is necessary to strip away society's veneer in order to be able to probe the forces of nature that have combined to make man what he really is. As a result, the naturalist sees life as a jungle. He avoids concerning himself with the past, seeing little to be gained there. He looks at the future darkly, as contrasted to the realist, who is neither a pessimist nor an optimist. The naturalist sees little possibility of things changing for the better. He offers no particular solution to the effect the forces of nature have worked on man, uncertain as to whether or not there are any solutions for the problem. The realist often takes a sharp stand on the social issues of his day, backing a cause, and even offering a solution. Henrik Ibsen, considered the first great dramatic realist, once explained what he saw as the difference between himself and Émile Zola, one of the greatest naturalists of the nineteenth century. Ibsen is supposed to have said, "When I go down to the sewer, I go to clean it out. When Zola goes down, he takes a bath."

Realism has come to be equated with "modern" drama, which is generally dated from about 1880 to the present. Any departure from this style is called *stylization,* which can be the staging of a modern play in a different manner or the revival of an older play in a different fashion. *Expressionism,* first commented upon in 1902 by the Swedish realist August Strindberg, presented a very subjective view of life. In his play *The Dream Play,* Strindberg blended a nightmare in which time, place, and characters chaotically mingled in the manner of a dream. The expressionist fashions reality as he sees it, not as daily life, but as it appears to him. If a person seems to be the same as the machines he operates, that person will act like a machine, speaking in the manner of a mechanical object. If a person's actions seem to make no sense, then that person will speak in gibberish or singsong. Thus, the expressionist expresses his views and displays them with the greatest possible dramatic and theatrical distortion. His work is socially oriented and concerned with the present that man has forged for himself. The expressionist, like the naturalist, has little faith in the lessons of the past, and the present doesn't seem to offer much hope for the future. This style was popular for only two or three decades in the early twentieth century, but it has had a lasting effect on the theater. The expressionist opened up the use of the stage, including even the audience as an acting area, and imposed no limits on what could or could not be done within the theatrical experience.

Impressionism seeks not to create a distorted "expression" but a highly personal "impression" of what the author sees. Thus we find life viewed from a very particular vantage point, through the clouds of personal or physical distance, making use of a variety of sights and sounds neither totally real, nor totally unreal.

The *absurdist* sees life as a ridiculous joke, a pointless experience, a confusing contest with unknown, uninterested forces. He often sends his characters through a totally stylized world to make his point.

The outward, literal, objective presentation of what the dramatist sees is called realism; the inward, imaginative subjective presentation is expressionism. The push and pull of these two styles combined to bring to the modern theater a great many exciting and innovative changes.

ACTION

Aristotle believed the *fable,* or the story, is the soul of drama and the *agon,* or argument, is the heart. He defined tragedy as "the imitation of an action," and the drama must have action in it. Narration, or the mere telling of a story, he left for the epic poem. The elements of drama we shall consider here are action, plot, and conflict.

Action means the things that happen in a play. It consists of several elements that have a unity unto themselves, yet are so interrelated that they become fully understood only when considered as a whole. These elements can be divided up into two distinct types:

1. Outward action, which includes the events we can see each as Orestes' murder of his mother in Aeschyulus' *The Choephori* and Euripides' *Electra.*
2. Inward action, which includes the events that take place in the minds of the characters, such as major decisions, acceptances, plottings not spoken of to the audience, dislikes, etc. An example of inward action would be how Medea decided to kill her children in Euripides' play, as the audience was not privy to her thoughts.

Plot is the arrangement of the action to produce a unified and coherent whole. According to Aristotle, all the events in a drama must be so closely connected that the removal of any one of them would "disjoint and dislocate the whole."

The *conflict* surrounding the argument centers on the opposition of two forces:

1. The protagonistic force, which may be one person or many.
2. The antagonistic force, which may be a person, group, thing, or force that is supernatural, natural, or divine.

The way in which the argument unfolds is the *form* of the play, involving the beginning, middle, and end. First, there must be a starting point, known as the *point of attact,* from which the dramatist leads his audience into the action. If he starts at the beginning and reveals events as they occur, he is using an *accretive plot.* If he starts in the middle of the action and lets the story reveal what has already transpired, he is using a *climactic plot.* Shakespeare's *Hamlet* is an example of an accretive plot; Sophocles' *Oedipus* is climactic.

In *Hamlet,* we have the following order of events:

I.i.	The ghost of Old Hamlet appears to the guards on the platform of Elsinore Castle.
I.ii.	King Claudius speaks about his brother's death and his assumption of power; Voltemand and Cornelius are dispatched with letters to rulers of Norway; Hamlet agrees to remain in Denmark; Horatio tells Hamlet of the ghost.
I.iii.	Laertes and Polonius advise Ophelia to shun Hamlet's advances.
I.iv.	The ghost appears to Hamlet and the guards.
I.v.	The ghost tells Hamlet about his murder at his brother's hand and commands Hamlet to avenge his death.

II.i	Polonius sends his servant Reynaldo to France to spy on Laertes; Ophelia tells her father of her upsetting meeting with Hamlet; Polonius decides to report Hamlet's mad behavior to Claudius.
II.ii	Claudius asks Rosencrantz and Guildenstern to spy on Hamlet. Hamlet greets the players.
III.i.	After contemplating suicide ("To be or not to be . . ."), Hamlet berates Ophelia for her falseness; Claudius plans to send Hamlet to England.
III.ii.	Claudius' shocked reaction to the play-within-a-play reveals his guilt.
III.iii.	Hamlet spares Claudius as the king tries to pray.
III.iv.	While berating his mother. Hamlet kills Polonius. The ghost appears.
IV.i.	Gertrude tells Claudius that Hamlet is mad.
IV.ii.	Hamlet refuses to reveal where he has hidden Polonius' body.
IV.iii.	Claudius sends Hamlet to England to be killed.
IV.iv.	The sight of Fortinbras' army moves Hamlet to soliloquize on his delayed revenge.
IV.v.	Ophelia goes mad and Laertes returns, bent on avenging Polonius' death.
IV.vi.	Hamlet announces his return to Denmark in a letter to Horatio.
IV.vii.	Claudius and Laertes plot Hamlet's death; Gertrude reports Ophelia has drowned.
V.i.	While walking through the churchyard with Horatio, Hamlet ponders human mortality; encounters gravediggers. Ophelia's funeral.
V.ii.	Treachery in the fencing match leads to the deaths of Gertrude, Laertes, Claudius, and Hamlet. Fortinbras assumes the throne.

As you can see, the plot unfolds in an orderly fashion, from the beginning to the end. With the exception of King Hamlet's murder, which occurred before the beginning of the play, the events unfold as we watch in this type of plot.

No matter which way the dramatist decides to structure the action, he must first establish for the audience what is going on and who is involved, which he does with a technique called *exposition,* showing and telling the facts. This can be accomplished by having two characters tell each other—and thus the audience—what is going on, or simply by plunging us into the action, as Shakespeare does in the opening scenes of *Hamlet.* In *Macbeth,* too, the first scene is structured to attract our attention, as the witches speak:

First witch:	When shall we three meet again In thunder, lightning, or in rain?
Second witch:	When the hurlyburly's done, When the battle's lost and won.
Third witch:	That will be ere the set of sun.
First witch:	Where the place?
Second witch:	Upon the heath.
Third witch:	There to meet with Macbeth.

From this brief exchange, we know immediately that there is to be a battle, and it will end before sunset. Somehow Macbeth will be involved with the battle, but what could he have to do with three witches? This first scene has only twelve lines, and the last two, very well known, express one of the themes of the play:

| *All:* | Fair is foul and foul is fair. Hover through the fog and filthy air. |

The play will be concerned with the differences between appearances and reality. Things will be reversed and we shall not know who to trust, as the loyal and wise Duncan is overthrown by Macbeth, his host for the evening. It is a double treachery, as Macbeth was a trusted soldier, well rewarded by Duncan for his brave deeds and loyalty. Act I, scene ii tells us a great deal more, as we learn details of the battle and Macbeth's bravery and rich rewards:

> *Sergeant:* . . . The merciless Macdonwald
> (Worthy to be a rebel, for to that
> The multiplying villainies of nature
> Do swarm upon him) from the Western Isles
> Of kerns and gallowglasses is supplied;
> And Fortune, on his damnèd quarrel smiling,
> Showed like a rebel's whore. But all's too weak:
> For brave Macbeth—(well he deserves that name)—
> Disdaining Fortune, with his brandish'd steel
>
> . . . .
>
> Like valour's minion carved out his passage
> Till he faced the slave;
>
> . . . .
>
> Till he unseam'd him from the nave to the chops

Macbeth has performed valiantly during battle, disdaining personal safety to kill the traitor Macdonwald. For this he is rewarded with the traitor's land and his title, Thane of Cawdor. This opening scene also foreshadows Macbeth's treachery, for he becomes a far greater enemy than Macdonwald in that he does succeed in killing his king. So these opening passages tell us the themes—loyalty and disloyalty, appearance and reality—and explain what is going on, as King Duncan and his troops are completing a battle and prizes are awarded. Once the events are established, the dramatist can continue to the climax and eventual resolution of events. To return to further exposition after this point would most likely confuse the audience.

In Greek drama, *exposition* is usually accomplished in the prologue. A character comes out on the stage and tells the audience what it must know of past events and character relationships before the play can begin. Modern drama has built upon the Greek tradition: We see in Thornton Wilder's *Our Town,* for example, the role of the Stage Manager, built directly on the prologue tradition.

Having established the situation, the dramatist sets forth *complications* that add depth to the action. These complications form the *rising action:* the building of suspense, emotional response, and audience involvement. All these events carry the plot to its *climax,* where all that has happened is pulled together. The protagonistic and antagonistic forces have established their sides of the agon, and have met, face to face, in one way or another. The climactic showdown, or *obligatory scene,* the one that everyone has come to expect, is the turning point after which nothing new is added. Any other high point that follows is called the *anticlimax,* and may lose dramatic emphasis for being placed after the climax. The climax may be one single event, as when Oedipus finally learns who and what he is, or it may be a series of events, as in *Hamlet,* proceeding from the middle of the play on.

The climax is followed by the *falling action,* a winding down of the action. Things fall into place, and the play heads for its conclusion, its *denouement,* or as the Greeks called it in referring to tragedy, its *catastrophe.* The denouement is the resolution of the plot. It is vital that the conclusion be believable, as the audience must feel that the action has been resolved in an acceptable manner.

The denouement may not always leave the audience satisfied. In Euripides' plays particularly, the plots are so confused with subplots that there is often no clear way out. In such cases, Euripides resorted to the *deus ex machina*. Literally a god lowered by a machine from the roof of the playhouse, the term more commonly refers to the employment of an outside agency to resolve the crisis. Artemis appears in Euripides' *Hippolytus* for this purpose. The modern reader tends to judge this type of conflict resolution as unsatisfactory. However, the device has proved successful in comedies, as when Aristophanes had Socrates appear in a basket lowered from the roof in *The Clouds* and Trygaeus ascends to heaven on the back of a giant beetle in *Peace*.

Plays that follow the pattern just outlined are called *well-made,* because the structure rather than the theme or plot becomes the crucial element. Because these plays tend to emphasize popular entertainment, the term "well-made" has long been held in critical disfavor. But many of the most stunning examples of lasting dramatic art are essentially well-made, such as *Hamlet* and *Oedipus*. It is what the dramatist does with the development of character, the conflict of the fable, the clash between the protagonist and antagonist, that makes the real difference in quality.

MEANING

The central question concerning any work of art, no matter what its form, is what does it all mean? Sometimes the meaning is very clear, as in Aristophanes' *Peace*—war is useless and must be stopped. Sometimes in Greek drama the meaning concerns the origin of a religious rite, such as Euripides' *Iphigenia in Aulis,* which explains the substitution of animal for human sacrifice. There are, however, instances where the modern reader will be unable to fathom the meaning of Greek drama because the historical allusions have been lost or because part of the play itself has been lost.

There are several ways to discern meaning.

Plot. Sometimes a brief summary of the plot will help make the meaning clear, hence all the plot summaries given in this guide. When all the events are set down on paper, often the meaning becomes clear. You can, of course, chart the events of the play for yourself.

Conventions. Sometimes the playwright uses a well-known device to make his meaning clear. In Greek drama, this device is usually the chorus, which explains the main ideas of the play as no character is able to do, standing both within and outside of the action. *Deus ex machina* is another device that may be used to make sure the audience and the characters understand what has happened.

Symbols. In some instances, especially in modern drama, symbols can illuminate meaning. Ibsen's *A Doll's House* is a case in point.

Images. Like symbols, images are often used to reinforce meaning. See the section on *Othello* for a discussion of various images and their meaning.

No matter what the meaning or how you have discerned it, when you are writing your essay, you must back up your assertions with clear, specific examples drawn directly from the text. This means that you will use specific passages and incidents to describe symbols, images, and so forth.

SPECTACLE AND AUDIENCE

The dramatist must ultimately be aware that his play will be performed before a live audience, and he must be versed in theatrical considerations, or *spectacle* in Aristotle's terms. Actually, Aristotle placed *spectacle* very far down his list of important dramatic considerations, for he believed that the dramatist who was concerned mainly with the showy parts of theater would write inferior drama. Furthermore, this entire aspect of theater—costumes, scenery, lighting, etc.—is intended to serve the drama, not to dominate it. The *director* alone has the final say on what will appear on the stage. He approves the setting, lighting, costumes, sound and special effects, and so forth. More important, he is the one who selects the actors, with or without the advice of the dramatist, and in his hands rests the final responsibility for the production.

The *audience* also figures in the final production, for the dramatist and director must be concerned with the living group of people who will willingly suspend their disbelief (to paraphrase Samuel Taylor Coleridge) and accept as truth what is being presented on the stage. Both the actors and the audience participate in this suspended belief: the actors in pretending that they are who they are playing, and the audience in believing that, for the moment, Mary Smith is indeed Shakespeare's Ophelia. For this process to work, there must be a balance between the actor and the spectator. On one side there is *empathy,* an emotional identification with the character and his difficulties. The audience must be interested in and identify with the character. On the other side is *aesthetic distance,* which means that even as it is moving toward emotional identification with the characters, the audience must constantly pull back with the knowledge that what it is seeing is art, not life.

Tragedy

ARISTOTLE'S DEFINITION OF TRAGEDY

All discussion of serious drama begins with an examination of Aristotle's *Poetics*. Tragedy is "an imitation of an action that is serious, complete, and of a certain magnitude; in language embellished with each kind of artful ornament, the several kinds being found in separate parts of the play, in the form of action, not of narration; through pity and fear effecting the proper purgation of these and similar emotions." To fully understand Aristotle's definition, you must comprehend the meaning of his terms:

Imitation means getting at the heart of the situation; finding the universal in the particular.

Action means more than just the moving about of characters; it refers to the great decisions that the central character makes, and the ramifications that these decisions cause.

Magnitude means that the action and characters must rise above the ordinary. Arthur Miller challenged this assumption in *Death of a Salesman* with the creation of Willy Loman, the "low man" common to all of us. For Aristotle, the plays had to revolve around kings, gods, or great military leaders.

Ornament includes *diction* and *song*. The diction must be elevated; people must talk in a refined manner. The songs, choral odes, are sung in ritualistic and often complicated manners. Different ornaments are suited for different parts of the play. Arthur Miller challenged this notion too, with the diction he used in *Salesman*, the everyday talk of a common man.

Purgation, or in Aristotelian terms, *catharsis,* refers to the cleansing that the audience experiences at the end of the play. We feel fear for the fate of the main character, and we pity this character, basically noble and good, who has been put through such travail.

The term tragedy does not refer to a sad play with an unhappy ending. The root of the word has nothing to do with sadness and death. Rather, it comes from the Greek *tragos,* or goat, plus *aedein,* to sing, which means the "singing of the goat." The goat was a sacred animal to Dionysus, god of wine and fertility, in whose honor the early festivals of song and dance were held out of which drama evolved. The entire notion of tragedy as we now accept it is a product of Greek civilization, founded on the special view Greeks held with regard to man and his relationship to the gods. The Greeks created their gods in their own image, endowing them with beauty, power, and immortality, yet subjecting them to the same passions endured by mortal men and women. Thus, Zeus, the king of the gods, could fall in love with an earthly being, and his queen, Hera, could be jealous. The gods did not always possess common sense, no more than did their human models. When they did act, it was following human lines which could be understood by mortals if not always entirely appreciated. The Greek gods were not independent, for they were under the rule of the Fates, the three sisters who controlled the thread of life. From this we can see how tragedy developed. As an assertion of the basic greatness of man, it demonstrates the individual's ability to ascend to the heights of human possibility in the face of an antagonistic force he knows will eventually destroy him. The protagonist of a tragedy, do what he will, may suffer from the curses of the gods for generations, for the gods, like their mortal counterparts, are capable of carrying grudges and taking offense. The point of all tragedy is that the protagonist, even when faced with the knowledge that the forces laid out against him are to cause his literal or symbolic death, can rise and assert his splendor, defy the forces, and even bring the forces down with him on occasion. There is no possibility of escape, and we watch as the hero proceeds in full recognition of his fate. Since the forces move with an absolute finality, it is what the protagonist does in the struggle that counts. The hero rises in the ultimate human courage and defiance to display the godlike qualities that lie within each of us.

Thus, tragedy is not a sad or depressing genre. It is positive and optimistic in its view of the possibilities of human beings. The tragic protagonist is not a martyr, for the martyr suffers for a certain cause and his death implies that something will follow, making the suffering and sacrifice worth the effort. The martyr, having a cause, may actually seek his own end. The tragic protagonist, in sharp contrast, has every reason to survive, and makes a heroic struggle to that end. At the moment of his death, he has shown the very best qualities of mankind, and his death is a very real loss. In displaying his greatness, the protagonist actually becomes godlike, and the giving of his life is a kind of reverse act, a sacrifice for mankind, not for the gods.

At the end of a tragedy there is usually a deep emotional involvement on the part of the audience. Aristotle discussed this when he spoke of *catharsis,* the arousal in the audience of pity, terror, and fear. When we view a tragedy, we are moved by a compassionate pity for the protagonist. In the same manner, we feel terror when we realize the size and the power of the forces that have caused the protagonist's downfall. At the tragedy's end, a calmness descends, and the audience undergoes a spiritual cleansing when it realizes how great the human being can be when called to the proper occasion.

Aristotle described the "ideal" tragic hero as human, not a god, and of noble stature. By this he intended royalty, for those were the deaths that could make empires crumble. Today we have redefined the term to mean that the individual must contain within himself a greatness and a stature beyond the ordinary. Thus, in modern tragedies, the protagonist may be a "little man," but not in any sense a "little person." The tragic hero cannot be predominantly evil, for then the audience would welcome his demise. Neither can he be all good, for then his death would be truly shocking, and displeasing to the audience.

Aristotle attributes *hamartia* to the tragic hero, which we translate as a "tragic flaw" or "shortcoming." In many plays, it is a character flaw or a vice, such as *hubris,* a Greek word meaning overwhelming arrogance or pride, that leads to his demise. But in other plays, a hero's flaw may be merely a poor choice, or a choice that turns out badly. There have been instances in which the tragic hero is undone because of his virtue, as he may be courageous when others are not. Therefore, the tragic hero need not always have a flaw. For instance, in the case of Romeo and Juliet, neither rashness nor lust fits their case, and they are undone more by circumstance than by anything they themselves lack or have caused. Regardless of the reason, the hero suffers and then comes to some sort of an awareness, either of his vice—if he has one—or his virtue—which he now sees cannot exist in the world of ordinary people.

In the end, the hero must be fully aware of what has happened to him and must face that realization. He proclaims his defiance, as Macbeth did in the end of the play, and welcomes his adversary.

Tragedy is ironic, as the audience, aware of what is going to happen, waits for the protagonist to reach awareness. Tragedy may involve the twists of fate: the harder the protagonist may seek to avoid his fate, the faster it approaches. This is true in *Hamlet,* for example.

There are two more terms to consider when discussing Aristotle's definition of tragedy.

Peripeteia (also spelled peripety) occurs when an action produces the opposite of what was intended or expected. It is a *reversal.* Thus, Macbeth kills his king, Duncan, to gain happiness through power, but reaps misery instead.

Anagnorisis means disclosure, discovery, or recognition. For Aristotle, the disclosure was usually a simple recognition of who was who through a clear external sign such as a birthmark or even clothing, but the term has been extended to include the tragic hero's recognition of himself or his place in the universe. So we see that Othello, who killed his faithful wife, learned that he was tricked into thinking her dishonest, and finally sees himself as "one not easily jealous, but being wrought/Perplexed in the extreme" and enacts justice by killing himself.

Melodrama, like tragedy, has come to mean something quite different from what its word roots would seem to portray. *Melo* (music) and *drama* (play) originally meant "a play with music." The term was coined during the eighteenth century, when the popular theaters of the day, offering diversion outside the "classical" theatres, made extensive use of background music. These plays were full of broad action, blood, and excitement. By the end of the eighteenth century, the innocent maiden persecuted by villains and saved by dashing heroes had been added to the format. The difference between tragedy and melodrama lies in the degree of emphasis, for while action is an integral part of a tragedy, melodrama creates action for its own sake, to divert the audience and keep it amused. Characters in tragedy are well-rounded and fully developed; those in melodrama tend to be "types" easily recognized so the plot can move quickly without the dramatist's having to establish motives. The tragic end is unrelated to justice; melodrama punishes the bad and rewards the good. Melodrama sets up the action so that things will work out well for all but the villain in the end.

The nontragic, nonmelodramatic, noncomedic play known as the *middle genre,* the *"straight" drama* or the *drame* comes from the traditions of literary realism. It achieves its success in describing people in terms of their humanity, in everyday situations, not in terms of the contrived plots and settings of the melodrama nor the outrageous fortunes of someone like Hamlet. In this genre, people face the challenges of everyday life in a recognizable setting. These very human figures may sway an audience far more easily than do those of tragedy and melodrama.

Summary of Tragedy

1. The term "tragedy" is applied to literary and especially dramatic representations of serious actions which turn out disastrously for the chief character.
2. "Comedy" is applied to dramatic works in which the characters undergo embarrassments which, on the whole, are so managed that they interest and amuse us without engaging our profoundest sympathy. In comedy, the action turns out well for the chief characters.
3. Discussion of tragedy begins with Aristotle's *Poetics,* where he defined tragedy as "the imitation of an action that is serious and also, as having magnitude, complete in itself." Tragedy must be presented dramatically in poetic language rather than as narrative, with "incidents arousing pity and fear, wherewith to accomplish its catharsis of emotion."
4. "Catharsis" is the feeling of relief on the part of the audience that leads to a cleansing of the mind.
5. Since tragedy must elicit pity and fear from the audience, the tragic hero will do this most effectively if he is neither thoroughly good nor thoroughly evil, but human with flaws like the rest of us. The tragic hero suffers a change in fortune from happiness to misery because of a mistaken act due to his "tragic flaw" or to a tragic error in judgment. One tragic flaw is "hubris," pride that leads man to overlook a divine warning or to break a moral law.
6. The tragic hero whose character is marked by some tragic flaw, which is ultimately responsible for his downfall, moves us to pity, because his misfortune is greater than he deserves, and to fear, because we recognize similar possibilities and consequences in our own fallible selves.

GREEK TRAGEDY

Greek theater grew out of the worship of the god Dionysus, known to the Romans as Bacchus, who was especially significant to the Greeks as a fertility figure. Once every spring he died, was buried, and rose again, standing for the rebirth of the crops which sustained life.

Most likely the first literary form developed to help in the religious ritual was the *dithyramb,* a poem chanted and danced by a chorus of priests. Critics have theorized that as the service became more complex the dithyramb became a *dialogue,* with verses sung or chanted alternately by the religious leader and the chorus, much as is practiced today in religious services. From this it is thought that the leader would assume the role of another, usually a god. From this point on, the Dionysian religious service can be considered drama.

In Athens in the fifth century B.C., drama was organized and run by the state as the main feature of an important religious event, the worship of the god Dionysus, as outlined above. In addition, it was part of a contest. The plays were judged and prizes awarded to the best comedy and best tragedy. There were two main festivals, the more important of the two being the Greater Dionysia, which took place at the end of March or the beginning of April and lasted three days. During the last quarter of the fifth century B.C., three playwrights competed in the tragedy division, three in comedy. Each tragedian entered three plays in the morning contest, and each comedic writer contributed one play to the afternoon festivities.

The second festival was called the Lenaea, and took place at the end of January or the beginning of February. It emphasized comedy and three comedic writers entered, each with one play. Three tragedians also took part, but with two plays each instead of the three allowed in the Greater Dionysia.

The actual production of the plays in both festivals lay entirely in the state's hands. Athens annually elected two officials called "archons," who were in charge of the festivals. Any interested playwright could submit a script to these officials, and the archons decided which ones were to be produced. All entries were in verse, for no prose was allowed, and most scenes were written in iambic hexameter lines, which the actors delivered in ordinary speech. There were also more complex rhymes and lyric passages, which were sung with the accompaniment of a flute or lyre.

The state took care of all expenses, the most significant of these being the chorus. There were 24 people in the chorus of a comedy who had to be paid, costumed, and trained by a dancing coach and a flute player. Since the cost of all this was too great for the state to assume directly, the archon assigned a "choregus," or "chorus handler" to each playwright. These more wealthy Athenians paid all expenses.

The next most significant expense was the actors. In the very early days of the Greek drama, the playwright himself played the leading role, but soon professional actors came to be used. The archon selected the leading men and assigned them to each playwright. The leading men competed against each other for the prize awarded to the best comic actor and the best tragic actor. The state also paid for all the other actors required, and for reasons not clear to us today—perhaps cost—each playwright was limited to only three speaking actors. No female actors were allowed on the stage. The playing of multiple roles was made easier by the use of masks. Made of linen and stiffened with clay, these masks covered the whole head and rested on the shoulders. Actors in comedies also wore silly padded costumes. Because the audience sat far away from the stage in most instances, the masks stood for different facial expressions. We are most familiar with the masks representing tragedy and comedy, but there were masks which stood for a wide variety of emotions. In tragedy, regardless of the emotion represented, the masks often served to maintain nobility and a high tone, while in comedy they were often ugly and ridiculous. Some critics and historians feel that the masks also served to amplify the sound, as the mouthpiece could function as an amplifier. The masks also distanced the audience and the actors, removing the actor from everyday life and rendering him unrecognizable. This would tend to give his actions a significance they would not otherwise carry. The tragic actor also wore high-heeled boots, called *cothurnus,* which added to his distance and impressiveness.

On the morning of the contest, people arrived early, bringing food and cushions, for the seats were hard and the day long. Although the state charged admission to cover the cost of maintaining the theater, there were funds set aside to pay for admission for all those who could not afford it. The first row was set aside for dignitaries.

When the last play was concluded, the panel of ten judges announced the ratings, and the first-place winners were crowned with ivy leaves. The names of the winners, and the order of placement of the losers, was inscribed in stone.

All plays during the fifth century B.C. were performed in the Theatre of Dionysus on the south side of the Acropolis. It looked very different then than it does today, for there was no stage and the construction was, for the most part, of wood. There were enough seats for 14,000 people set into the steep hillside. The first row was a great circle, about 85 feet in diameter. Within it was a smaller circle, about 65 feet around, where the chorus performed. In back of this circle was a building called the *skene*—the "scene building"—that served as a backdrop and the actors' dressing rooms. It was a long, two-story building flanked by two wings opening toward the circle, the whole in the shape of a U with a wider opening. The backdrop had three doors that could be used for entrances and exits and spaces that separated the scene building from the seating area. The entire theater was called the *theatron* or *koilon* and was most like the half-circle end of a football stadium. The *orchestra* is the end zone; the *skene* is on the goal line. The entrance ramps were called *parodos* and were used by the actors and the audience. There was a machine on the roof, called a *logeion,* that was used to raise or lower a symbolic god onto the stage.

This setting limited possible action in Greek plays. Most of the scenes had to take place outside, in front of the same place or setting, if possible. If an indoor scene was necessary, the skene could be opened or set on wheels, called an *eccyclema,* which would be rolled out from inside the skene. Every now and again, painted flats showing mountains or forests were placed against the skene walls. The Greek audience did not expect a great deal of scenery, relying upon imagination to create the atmosphere. There was, of course, no curtain, nor were there any acts or scene divisions. The plays were very short, running about an hour, and when breaks in the action were necessary, the chorus took over for a brief song and dance.

MEDEA BY EURIPIDES

Background

Jason was the heir to the throne of the Greek city Iolcos, but his place was usurped by his uncle, Pelias. Trying to kill his nephew, Pelias sent him to obtain the magic Golden Fleece, which the barbarian Aeetes, King of Colchis, had in his possession. Medea, Aeetes's daughter and a magician in her own right, fell in love with Jason. By deceiving her father and killing her brother, she helped Jason get the Fleece. Back in Iolcos, Medea brought about the death of Pelias, but Jason still could not ascend to the throne. Jason,

Medea, and their two sons fled to Corinth, where Jason, still trying to advance his position, deserted Medea and married Glauce, daughter of the Corinthian King Creon.

Summary of the Play

Standing in front of Medea's house in Corinth, the old Nurse describes Medea's grief over Jason's desertion. An attendant says that he has heard that Creon is to banish Medea and her sons from Corinth. The chorus, hearing Medea's lamentation, tries to soothe her by discussing the unfairness of women's position. Creon enters and tells Medea that she is indeed to be banished, but he allows her 24 hours to find refuge. After Creon leaves, Medea tells the chorus that she plans to murder Jason, Glauce, and Creon, although she does not have a plan yet. Jason, showing little sympathy or tact, arrives to tell Medea that he has married Glauce to provide a better life for Medea and her children. She tells him all the things that she has done to help him, including the murders, but he responds that she should be glad that he has brought her to a place as civilized as Greece. He offers her money, but she refuses. The chorus sings. The King of Athens, Aegeus, enters, and Medea promises that she will help him overcome his childlessness if he will grant her and her children refuge. He agrees, but only if she can get to Athens on her own, for he is worried about angering the Corinthians. She tells the chorus of her plan for the murders: She will send her children to Jason with a present for his bride—a headdress and robe that will burn to death anyone touching them—then murder her children and flee to Athens. Jason returns, and Medea sends the gift and her sons with him. The children return, and she takes them inside, determined to kill them so that Jason will be left with nothing. A messenger arrives to tell Medea that Glauce was engulfed in flames; Creon, coming to her aid, was also burned to death. She rushes inside to kill her children. Jason rushes in search of his children, and the chorus tells him they are dead. Suddenly Medea appears above the house in a chariot drawn by dragons; she tells Jason that she is now beyond his reach. He calls her a monster; she tells him he is not able to love fully. She refuses to allow him even the consolation of burying his children's bodies.

Like Othello, Medea has "loved not wisely, but too well." The extent to which she goes to punish Jason indicates this. She has committed murder to further Jason's career and to be cast aside for another is more than she can bear. Her violent nature erupts, destroying everything that Jason values. Jason, in contrast, is a reversal of the traditional portrayal of a hero. He is usually regarded as a sympathetic person, an adventurer searching for the Golden Fleece. Here, however, he is an opportunist who uses women to obtain what he desires. This play advocates that the dramatic contrasts between cultures—the Greek and the barbarian, for example—would make marriage outside one's caste unwise. Jason makes this point at the end of the play.

Discussion and Essay Questions on Medea

1. *Medea* is set in the city of Corinth, but for the resolution of its problem, the cleansing of guilt, the play looks to Athens. Why?
2. In *Electra,* Orestes' guilt was incurred wittingly, by command of a god; in *Heracles,* the crime was committed innocently. By sharp contrast, Medea's only excuse was her natural passion for revenge and her barbarian heritage. Why, then, is she granted sanctuary?
3. Was Jason a man of entirely respectable ambitions? Can we say that Medea brought her fate upon herself by standing in the way of Jason's ambitions? After

all, she had involved him in a murder before he ever came to Corinth, and as a non-Greek, she could never be recognized by Greeks as his legal wife.

4. Does Jason stand for a civilized life: a life without excess, a life of control and order? If this is the case, can we say that he is opposed to barbarism and all of its ways?

5. Can we conclude that Jason's concern for civilized values is joined with a calculating coldness and an unscrupulous want of feeling?

6. Is the theme of this play that civilized people ignore—at their dire peril—the world of instinct, emotion, and irrational experience; that their carefully worked out notions of right and wrong are mortally dangerous unless these ideas are flexible and allow for constant adjustment?

7. Is it true, that in his revenge plays Euripides first enlists the spectators' sympathy for the avenger and then extends that sympathy to the avenger's victim?

8. Is Medea selecting the most effective way of punishing Jason when she decides to enact her revenge on their children? Support your answer with specific references from the play and your own experiences.

9. Which gods, if any, determine Medea's passion? How does this fit in with other works by Greek playwrights that you have read from this period?

10. Which of her adversaries, if any, have sufficient stature to modify the plot?

11. Is Medea simply the victim of circumstance? Is what happens to Medea more the result of her own nature than anything else?

12. It has been said that Medea is not really different in the end of the play than in the beginning, and it is a mistake to see her as a good but a passionate woman who descends into the ultimate horror only when forced to by circumstances. Agree or disagree with this statement.

13. Some critics claim that Medea is not tragic. Rather, they say, she is a purely passive figure, a helpless victim of her own passions, doomed by her nature to suffer and cause disaster.

14. Others regard Medea as a real tragic heroine, engaged in a real agon and a real choice. Decide whether you see Medea as a helpless victim or a tragic heroine, and support your argument with specific references from the drama.

RENAISSANCE TRAGEDY

During the first half of the sixteenth century, teachers in England began to produce Roman plays in the schools. The effect of this became clear when Nicholas Udall wrote *Ralph Roister Doister* (1538–1553), the first "true" English comedy, based on these Latin models. Strolling bands of players obtained these new plays as soon as they were available, and dozens of new plays, of dubious literary value, flooded the stages.

In 1572, laws were passed that categorized strolling players as vagabonds, and forbade their presence on the streets of London. The effect of these laws was to bring the players under the patronage of the nobility and eventually under the crown itself. Best known of all such troops was the King's Servants, so named after James I ascended to the throne.

Because of local opposition, when the first public theater was built in 1576 by James Burbage, it was located outside the city proper. James Burbage's sons rebuilt their theater in 1599 and named it the Globe. It was known as London's finest theater until it burned down in 1613, during a performance of Shakespeare's *Henry VIII*. It was rebuilt shortly thereafter.

Although there were individual differences, the theaters were basically very much alike. The playhouse itself was round or octagonal, with an open space or courtyard in the center. Spectators' seating surrounded the yard on three levels: At the front and projecting into the yard was the stage itself. Behind the stage were dressing rooms, script rooms, and a space for properties and costumes.

Most scholars believe that the stage had two parts: the inner stage, which was under the roof and fitted with a curtain, and the outer stage, which extended into the yard. In the later theaters, performances could take place on three levels of the inner stage. There was a trapdoor near the center of the apron (outer) stage.

Performances took place during the day. Evening was represented by characters carrying candles or torches, or saying appropriate lines of dialogue. There was copious use of music and elaborate, costly costumes.

OTHELLO BY WILLIAM SHAKESPEARE

Plot Summary

Act I. Iago and Roderigo are discussing Othello's marriage to Desdemona. Roderigo had been one of Desdemona's suitors, and he is furious that he did not know about the affair. Iago declares that since he was passed over for Othello's lieutenant, he too has reason to hate the Moor. They arrive at Brabantio's home to tell him that his daughter has eloped with Othello. Cassio tells Othello that he has been called before a military council. Brabantio and Roderigo enter and the scene becomes violent, as Brabantio, accusing Othello of having bewitched his daughter, demands that he be thrown into jail. Othello convinces him to take his complaint before the Duke. Later that night, Brabantio presents his case before the Duke. Othello tells how he courted his wife. Desdemona arrives, and while making it clear that she still loves her father, she asserts that she now belongs to Othello. Brabantio rejects his daughter. The Duke returns his attention to the war effort, directing Othello to defend Cyprus and become its new governor. Desdemona will rejoin him later. All the others leave, and Iago convinces Roderigo that he still may have a chance to win Desdemona. When Roderigo leaves, Iago asserts that money and fun are his real reasons for befriending Roderigo. Then he begins to plan his deception of Othello.

Act II. A storm at sea has crippled the Turkish fleet and delayed Othello's arrival at Cyprus. Iago's ship, with Desdemona on board, arrives before Othello's does, and Iago jokes to reassure her that her husband will arrive safely. Iago privately notes that Cassio is also distracting her with polite conversation, and makes plans to use this against him later. Finally Othello arrives and he and Desdemona joyously reunite. After they leave the stage, Iago convinces the foolish Roderigo that Desdemona actually loves Cassio and urges him to pick a fight with the lieutenant that night. Alone, Iago tells his wife, Emilia, about his suspicions concerning Othello's and Cassio's affairs. That night they feast in celebration of safe arrival and Othello's wedding, and Iago succeeds in making Cassio drunk and quarrelsome. Urged on by Iago, Cassio and Roderigo fight. Montano breaks in, accusing Cassio of being drunk. Enraged, Cassio wounds him, and Roderigo sounds the alarm. Othello hurries in, and based on what Iago implies, Othello finds Cassio at fault and fires him. Cassio realizes what has happened, and Iago convinces him to try to regain Othello's favor through Desdemona. Iago gloats over the trouble he has caused.

Act III. Some musicians serenade Othello and Desdemona as Iago helps Cassio arrange a private meeting with Desdemona. After Iago leaves, his wife takes Cassio to Desdemona.

Othello requests that Iago meet him to inspect the castle fortifications. Desdemona promises Cassio that she will do all that she can to help his cause. Othello and Iago enter, and Cassio, feeling ill at ease, leaves quickly. Othello notices this, and Iago points out how "guilty" Cassio seemed. Desdemona immediately presents Cassio's case, and Othello bends to her wishes. Iago begins to undermine Othello's faith in Desdemona, going so far as to suggest that she and Cassio are having an affair. Iago leaves, and Desdemona enters. She tries to soothe Othello's headache with a handkerchief, and they depart, the handkerchief left behind. Emilia picks it up and gives it to Iago, not realizing its importance: It was the first gift Othello gave to Desdemona. Othello re-enters, and demands that Iago give him proof of Desdemona's unfaithfulness. Iago responds that he heard Cassio talking in a dream of making love to Desdemona and says that he has seen Cassio wipe his beard with Desdemona's handkerchief. Enraged, Othello plots revenge and promotes Iago. Later, Desdemona again brings up Cassio's case, but Othello is only concerned about the handkerchief. Desdemona lies and says that she has not lost it, for Othello had told her that the token had magical powers and its loss would be a misfortune. Othello leaves. Iago and Cassio enter and discuss Othello's bad temper. Later, Cassio meets Bianca and asks her to copy the embroidery of the handkerchief, which he had found in his room.

Act IV. Othello rages when Iago tells him that Cassio admits that he is having an affair with Desdemona. Cassio enters, but Iago tells him to leave, for Othello has suffered an epileptic fit. Othello, recovered, agrees to hide while Iago questions Cassio about his behavior. Iago speaks to Cassio about his girlfriend, Bianca, but Othello, who cannot hear well where he is hiding, misinterprets the discussion, and assumes they are speaking about Desdemona. Bianca enters and refuses to copy the embroidery on the handkerchief; she and Cassio leave. Again Othello is enraged at what he sees as proof of his wife's infidelity. At Iago's suggestion, he agrees to strangle Desdemona in her bed while Iago murders Cassio. Lodovico arrives with a letter that orders his return to Venice and appoints Cassio Governor of Cyprus. Desdemona tells Lodovico of the breach between Othello and Cassio. Her sympathy for Cassio angers Othello and he strikes and torments her. Othello, who has lost all control, leaves. Othello questions Emilia, who swears that Desdemona is true to him. He sends for Desdemona and she too swears that she has been chaste, but he will not believe her. She sends for Iago and asks how she can make Othello believe her. He tells her to remain calm. Later, Iago convinces Roderigo that they must murder Cassio. Emilia helps Desdemona prepare for bed and Desdemona swears that she loves her husband and would never deceive him.

Act V. Iago and Roderigo wait to murder Cassio. Cassio wounds Roderigo, and Iago wounds Cassio without being seen. Othello, passing by, hears Cassio calling out and believes that Iago's plan has succeeded and Cassio is dying. Lodovico and Gratiano enter, and we see that Cassio is still alive. Iago stabs Roderigo fatally while no one is watching. Bianca enters and Iago tries to fix the blame on her. Emilia enters and Iago sends her to Othello to tell him what has happened. Othello enters Desdemona's bedroom and smothers her, despite her pleas for mercy. Emilia pounds at the door with the news of Roderigo's murder, but Othello does not let her in until Desdemona seems to be dead. With her dying breath, Desdemona tries to hide Othello's guilt. Othello confesses the truth, explaining that Iago convinced him Desdemona was unfaithful. Emilia, horrified, tells him that Iago was lying and rushes out to publicize the crime. Othello explains what has happened to the others as they rush in. Emilia, realizing his error, explains that she took the handkerchief herself for Iago. Furious, Iago kills his wife. Othello wounds Iago for his lies, as the full truth is exposed. In complete despair over Desdemona's death, Othello stabs himself and dies kissing his wife.

Theme of Othello

The theme of this play is *jealousy*, affecting all the characters, but most evident in Othello when interwoven with his *pride*. For example, in III, iii, Othello says concerning his wife:

> I had rather be a toad
> And live upon the vapour of a dungeon
> Than keep a corner in the thing I love
> for others' uses. (III, iii, 270–73)

At first Othello thinks that the solution to jealousy is easy: he need only convert his love to hate. But he finds that this is impossible, for the love and hate are interwoven, and in his conflict, he convinces himself that killing Desdemona will bring about justice (V, ii, 1–17). But after he is convinced of his horrible error, he berates himself before rising to the proud resolution of his final speech. Although jealousy is shown most heartrendingly in Othello, the motivating spirit of envy is Iago.

If we believe what Othello himself says, he is not easily made jealous (V, ii, 345), while Iago, in contrast, is the very embodiment of the emotion. We see in him pride and hate, love transformed into self-admiration. Iago has been considered by several critics, Samuel Taylor Coleridge the most well known, to be an incarnation of "motiveless malignity"; others have seen him as a morality Vice figure. If we consider him a true portrait of a human being, his jealousy—as well as any motivation for it—is difficult to account for. He may, as critic Marvin Rosenberg has suggested, be a proud man resentful of the necessity of bowing before his superiors. It may also be that his hatred is abnormal and irrational, especially as directed toward women. What we can be sure of is the strength of his anguish; it gnaws at his innards (II, i, 306).

Other characters who exhibit signs of jealousy are Roderigo, Bianca, and as some have suggested Brabantio. The most obviously jealous of these characters is Roderigo, whose unrequited love for Desdemona leads him, with Iago's backing, to attempt murder.

Setting of Othello

The setting here of *Othello* is not as crucial as it is in *Macbeth* or *King Lear,* and there is no symbolic enlargement of the scene from the realm of the physical to that of the supernatural. There are two clear settings: The play begins in Venice, and at the beginning of Act II, moves to Cyprus for the rest of the action. Venice is the base of the action, and all the major characters except Othello and Cassio are Venetians. They bring with them to Cyprus what they had been in Venice. Venice represents a peaceful, sophisticated, law-abiding city, as the scene with the Duke (I, iii) shows. We see that despite Brabantio's hysteria over his daughter's elopement, Venice metes out fair judgment and all of its citizens, except Iago, are fair people. We see the sophistication in Brabantio's description of the kind of possible husbands his daughter had rejected (I, ii). Cyprus, in sharp contrast to Venice, is "a town at war,/Yet wild, the people's hearts brimful of fear" (II, iii, 213–14). When she elects, to follow her husband to Cyprus, Desdemona leaves behind all friends and family, creating an island of fatal isolation. As with other islands in Shakespeare, Cyprus is the site of strange happenings. But unlike many of his other plays, the events taking place on the island are not supernatural, for without Iago, Cyprus would be peaceful and pleasant.

Discussion/Writing Questions on *Othello*

1. Evaluate the "completeness" of Othello's love for Desdemona. Othello is convinced of her faithlessness by Iago, and some critics have said that he is too ready to believe her treacherous. Is this a flaw in Othello's character or is it evidence of a less than total love? Consider, for example, the following quote from I, iii, 167–68: "She lov'd me for the dangers I had passed,/And I lov'd her that she did pity them."

2. Some critics have said that Othello's tragic flaw is excessive pride; others have claimed that he is but the pawn of circumstances with a nature too open and easily convinced. Consider the following quote in your evaluation: "Come, Desdemona, I have but an hour/Of love, or worldly matters and direction,/To spend with thee. We must obey the time." (I, iii, 299–301)

3. Is Othello able to feel the sorrow of his ideal being corrupted, even in the midst of his passion? If so, how does this affect our opinion of him, and indeed, his stature as a tragic hero? Consider the following quotation: "So delicate with her needle! . . . Of so high and plenteous wit and invention! . . . But yet the pity of it, Iago! O Iago, the pity of it, Iago!" (IV, i, 198–207)

4. The idealism which colors Othello's love and creates his jealous rage is the cause of some of his self-deception, and turns the murder from passion into a ritual purge. Does Othello at last realize that it is not simple to cast off love? Does he ever fully understand his own motivation for the murder? Consider: "It is the cause, it is the cause, my soul. . . . Yet I'll not shed her blood, . . . Yet she must die, else she'll betray more men. . . . and I will kill thee,/And love thee after. . . . This sorrow's heavenly;/It strikes where it doth love." (V, ii, 1–22)

5. Describe Othello's character in the beginning of the play, especially as shown through the actions and descriptions of others. Consider I, iii, 284–286 and I, iii, 405–06. How do these early descriptions affect his later downfall?

6. Some critics have seen Othello's confidence in himself as a kind of naive complacency. Consider I, iii, 81–87: "Rude am I in my speech,/And little blessed with the soft phrase of peace; . . . And little of this great world can I speak/More than pertains to feats of broil and battle."

7. Samuel Johnson believed that the first act of the play could be omitted without harming the play in any way. What would change in not initially presenting the character of Brabantio, the setting, and the scene where the two lovers defend their marriage?

8. Do most of the vital scenes of the play take place in the evening or the daytime? What effect does this have on the atmosphere and theme of the play?

9. Iago calls the pair "an erring barbarian and a supersubtle Venetian," and some critics have seen this to refer to Othello and Desdemona as opposites. Explain what he means. Is this the reason for what follows in the play or is the tragedy caused by other factors? Explain.

10. Samuel Taylor Coleridge and Harley Granville Barker call Iago "motiveless," believing that he has no reasons for his actions. What reasons does Iago himself give? Other critics, such as Marvin Rosenberg credit him with definite reasons for his actions. Explain who is correct by citing specific reasons for your belief.

11. Of the main characters, Desdemona has the fewest lines, yet her character—courage, devotion, chastity among the most evident qualities—is very clear. How is this accomplished? Trace specific examples.

12. Can nontraditional interpretations of the play be justified? For example, Sir Laurence Olivier portrayed Iago as a homosexual. Use specific examples to support your point of view.

13. Roderigo is the only character to whom Iago reveals his evil nature. What does this tell you about Roderigo's character?
14. Does the "universal appeal" of Othello suffer because Othello is less intellectually gifted than Hamlet or less socially important than Lear? Support your answer.
15. What "moral" can we draw from this play? What lessons does it have to teach us?
16. Iago believes that he is exacting revenge. If so, for what slights(s)?
17. Reconcile Emilia's lie to Desdemona about the stolen handkerchief with her impassioned defense of Desdemona in the final scene.
18. How does Othello's view of love change throughout the play? Is it ever a view held by another character?
19. Write an essay in which you describe one character as he/she appears through the eyes of another, such as Iago as seen by Othello.

MODERN TRAGEDY

Departing from conventional notions of realism, Arthur Miller redefined tragedy in his best-received play, *Death of a Salesman* (1949). His essay written the same year, "Tragedy and the Common Man," explains his aims in this play.

Miller begins by noting that there have been very few tragedies written in the modern age, most likely because man is "often held to be below tragedy—or tragedy above us." But he believes that "the common man is as apt a subject for tragedy in its highest sense as kings were." When tragedy is not the issue, he says, we never hesitate to attribute the same emotional and mental processes to the lowly as to the well-born, and if the tragic ability were truly only for the kingly, it would not happen that the mass of people would cherish tragedy above all other forms, let alone understand it.

He feels that "the tragic feeling is evoked in us when we are in the presence of a character who is ready to lay down his life . . . to secure personal dignity." Tragedy, then, is the result of a person's desire to evaluate himself justly.

A tragedy reveals in the hero what has been called the "tragic flaw," a characteristic not unique to the high-born. Miller feels that this flaw is not necessarily a weakness, but rather "an inherent unwillingness to remain passive in the face of what he [the hero] perceives to be a challenge to his dignity, his image of his rightful status." Those who accept their fate without active struggle are the flawless, he says, and most people fall into that category.

The terror and fear that are associated with tragedy result when this person acts against the scheme of things and, in the process, everything that has previously been blindly accepted is taken out and examined. In this attack on the seemingly stable universe, the individual and the audience feel the tragic emotions of terror and fear.

Most important, he concludes, we learn from this process, and we fear being displaced from our niche in the world, of losing our images of ourselves. It is the common man who experiences this fear most profoundly.

If we accept that tragedy is the result of man's desire to evaluate himself fairly, his destruction in the attempt points to an evil in the environment, not in himself, Miller asserts. This is the discovery of moral law.

Tragedy celebrates, then, the desire for freedom, and the struggle to assert this freedom demonstrates the "indestructible will of man to achieve his humanity." As opposed to the Greek definition, Miller feels that in tragedy the possibility of victory must be present; otherwise it descends to the level of pathos.

It is time, he concludes, that the modern civilization, bereft of kings, takes up the mantle of tragedy and locates it in its logical place—"the heart and spirit of the average man."

DEATH OF A SALESMAN BY ARTHUR MILLER

Plot Summary

As the play opens, Willy Loman, a traveling salesman for 34 years, has returned from a trip to New England. Exhausted, he tells his wife, Linda, that he is having difficulty keeping his mind on driving. He asks about his 34-year-old son, Biff, who has come home after being away a long time. Willy thinks back on the climactic football game of Biff's high school career, some 14 years ago, when universities around the country offered Biff football scholarships. But something thus far unexplained happened that year, and Biff flunked math, never graduated from high school, and never fulfilled his early promise. Later in the play, we find out that Biff had gone to Boston to tell his father that he had flunked math, confident that Willy, whom he greatly admired, would be able to reason with the math teacher. Biff discovered his father having an affair, and crushed that his idol could dishonor his family, lost all faith in Willy and to this day has held a grudge against his father.

Now Biff has returned home. He and his brother, Happy, discuss various jobs for which Biff might be suited. They decide that Biff should ask a former employer, Bill Oliver, for a $10,000 loan to start a business. They tell Willy of their plans, and Willy responds that together the "Loman Brothers" could conquer the world. Willy explains that the important thing is to be "well-liked" and personally attractive. They make plans to meet in a fancy restaurant the next day to celebrate.

Willy is so pleased with his boys' plans that he decides to ask his present boss, Howard Wagner, for a transfer from the New England territory to New York. Howard refuses his request and fires Willy, explaining that Willy's erratic behavior has been harming the firm. Willy, crushed and disoriented, goes to an old friend, his next-door neighbor Charley, to borrow enough money to pay his insurance premium. We find out that Willy has been borrowing $50 a week from Charley for quite some time, and pretending to Linda that he is still being paid salary and commission, when in fact he has received no salary for months. Even though Charley offers Willy a good job in New York, Willy refuses, saying he could never work for Charley. He goes to the restaurant.

Biff and Happy meet, and Biff tells Happy that his whole life has been an illusion. He explains to Happy that he has stolen himself out of every job that he has had, and wants to make everyone, especially Willy, understand that he no longer is bringing home any prizes. But when Willy arrives, he tells his sons that he has been fired, and he refuses to listen to Biff's realizations. Willy pretends that Biff has another appointment with Bill Oliver the next day, despite Biff's confession that he was fired from Oliver's employ for stealing a carton of basketballs. Willy is furious and about to make a scene. When Willy gets up to go to the bathroom, Biff leaves the restaurant. Happy, who has picked up two women—his usual behavior—follows suit, leaving Willy all alone when he returns to the table.

Later that night, Biff returns home to find Willy planting seeds in the backyard and talking to his long-dead brother, Ben. Biff explains to Willy that he thinks it would be better for the whole family if they break off and never see each other again. He again explains that he is a "lo-man," a "dime a dozen," and not a leader of men. But Willy once again refuses to see the truth in what Biff is saying, and Biff breaks down and cries to Willy to see what they really are. Willy thinks Biff is still a child who once again needs him and resolves to commit suicide to leave Biff the $20,000 insurance money and enable him to once again be magnificent. Willy goes through with his plan, but at his funeral we see that he has died a forgotten man, mourned by a handful of family and friends.

Structure

The structure of the play is unusual, told partly through the mind and memory of Willy Loman. Thus, the time fluctuates between 1942 and 1928, and the audience must be aware of the differences in time. To accomplish this, the *setting* must be employed in a suggestive way. When the action is in the present (1942), the characters observe all the doors and walls, but when the time shifts, they ignore the physical barriers and walk right through them. Another tool to show the shift in time is music. When the time shifts into the past, we have the flute, evocative of Willy's father and his lost youth; the blaring music of Willy's affair; the joyous music of the boys' past accomplishments. The characters' posture also changes to show the change in time. In the present, Willy is stooped with the weariness of an old man, but in the flashbacks, he carries himself forcefully. In the same way, Biff and Happy change, appearing in the past dressed as youngsters. The structure of the set underscores one of the main themes of the play, *illusion versus reality,* and shows how Willy has carried the illusions of the past into the present, especially when he calls on his dead brother Ben to guide him.

Recurrent Motifs

Debts. Willy and Linda, unable to afford all they wish, have bought many items on installment and discover that the items break before the payments are finished. They are constantly in debt, as they fall victim to the advertisements for the "best" of everything. The motif rises to the tragic as Willy makes the last payment on his house and then commits suicide so that as the house is all paid up, he is all used up. This is summarized in the "Requiem."

Personal attractiveness/Being well-liked. Willy believes that a person must not just be liked, but must be *well*-liked in order to be a success. Willy decided this after an encounter with a salesman named Dave Singleman (Single-man vs. Lo-man), who was so loved and respected that he could enter any town, pick up a phone, and get an order. When he died, people came from all over to his funeral. Willy decided that this is what he wants for himself, and for his favorite son, Biff. He cannot understand why a boy with such personal attractiveness could be so lost. We discover that Willy has rationalized many of the boy's mistakes and outright crimes with the notion of personal attractiveness: Willy tells Biff early on that the coach won't mind that Biff has stolen a ball because Biff is "well-liked." We see at the funeral that despite his belief, being well-liked does not guarantee success or happiness and that Willy's life has been based on false dreams.

Stealing. We see that Biff has stolen himself out of every job that he has ever had, and that Willy excuses the thefts if performed by someone who is well-liked. This motif brings the drama to its climax, for when Biff steals the pen from Bill Oliver's office during the interview, he is forced to face the fact that he is a thief. This, in turn, makes him see himself and try to explain his character to his father.

Vital to New England. Willy refuses to ask for a transfer to New York initially because he says that "he is vital to New England." We see clearly that he is a hindrance to the company, but for his own self-respect, Willy must continue to believe that he is the cornerstone of New England sales. In a flashback, we see Willy promising to take his sons to New England, but the plan never materializes, for it would force Willy to see that he is not important there or anywhere else. He cannot face the fact that he is not popular or well-liked, and has no friends. He falls easily for the affair, as it serves to build his ego. Here he feels the importance that is denied him as he waits outside closed doors hoping for orders. When Howard fires him, he must construct new illusions, but the world that he has created is so strong that he retreats further and further into his illusions. As he is preparing for suicide, he visualizes all the hundreds of salesmen and buyers who will come to his funeral—but none did come. This motif comments on Willy's life of illusion and how he has transformed illusion to reality to enable him to continue his drudgery of daily life. When maintaining the illusion becomes impossible, there is no reason for him to continue living.

Boxed in. The physical image that best describes Willy's inner state is one of enclosure. The more Willy feels boxed in, the more he feels the need to do something with his hands, to leave something physical for his family. This is introduced in the first scene, as Willy comments that their house has become so boxed in by the larger apartments around them that they no longer have any sunlight and cannot grow anything in the garden. Later we see that Biff feels the same way that Willy does, but when Biff suggests that the Lomans should be "mixing cement on some open plain," Willy refuses to acknowledge even this truth, and responds that even "your grandfather was better than a carpenter." We see throughout the play that Willy is boxed in by the city and that the only way out is through his death. After his death, with his sons unworthy of the sacrifice, Willy is permanently boxed in his little plot of ground.

Time: "The woods are burning". When Willy says that "the woods are burning," he means that life is closing in on him, and he no longer has the time to accomplish what he once thought he could. This is contrasted to Willy's image of his brother, Ben, who escaped to conquer the jungle of life. Ben walked into the jungle at 17 and walked out four years later a rich man. This is what Willy so desired for himself—to conquer life, not to be conquered by it. Therefore, to Willy, life is a jungle that he is unable to penetrate, and it becomes a burning woods constantly closing in on him. By the end, when time has completely closed in on him, the jungle becomes the darkness of death which Willy thought he could conquer by suicide.

Ben. Willy's brother, Ben, stands for all that Willy wants to be. Ben is a financial success, the opposite of Willy. Ben is also shown as cruel and cold, ruthlessly manipulative. He represents another side of Willy's illusions, as Willy refuses to see Ben for what he really is and admires him unquestioningly for his financial success.

Flute. Flute music opens and closes the play. We discover halfway through the play that Willy's father made and sold flutes. His father was also a salesman, but with one important difference: Willy sells things that others have made; his father sold items he made himself. Unlike Willy, his father was a great adventurer. Thus, the flute at the end mocks Willy, capturing his inability to be bold and brave, and suggesting the failure of the illusions that have controlled his world.

Stockings. Linda mends stockings and seems to be continually doing laundry, suggesting she is the eternal wife and mother figure, unable to help Willy strike out on his own.

There has been much written on Linda: Some say she is as guilty as Willy for tying him down to his meaningless illusions; others say she was the mainstay that gave him the strength to continue as long as he did. The mended stockings also evoke the image of the stockings that Willy gave to his mistress, showing, to Biff at least, that Willy denied things to Linda to support his wanderings with at least one other. Therefore, the stockings symbolize both Linda's personality and Willy's guilt.

Losing Weight. Happy is the neglected son, all the attention having been focused for so long on Biff. Thus it comes as no surprise when Happy deserts Willy at the restaurant, for he is acting toward Willy as he perceives Willy acted toward him. He speaks of losing weight in an attempt to gain attention, as he lies down and backpedals to illustrate the sincerity of his efforts, but no one pays him any attention. In the same way, he announces that he is going to get married when the scene gets too tense or he wishes attention. It should come as no surprise that he is shallow and a dedicated chaser of women.

Miller's style

Miller tries to recast tragedy into an American mold, using a "lo-man" as the hero rather than the traditional high-born, heroic model. Additionally, he captures the essential patterns of American speech and recasts them into phrases that remain in our minds, like the refrains of ballads. "Isn't it remarkable" and "He is not just liked but well-liked" are examples. The scenes of the present have a heavy and serious quality to the speech while the past carries a lighter, happier note.

Sample Questions to Consider

1. In what ways is this play a reworking of the traditional notions of tragedy?
2. Does Willy qualify as a tragic hero? Support your answer with specific examples and compare Willy's situation and behavior with the traditional mold.
3. Who is the central character of this play and why?
4. Is Linda Loman the helping, caring wife she appears to be on the surface or is she another force that drags Willy down, tying him to his pathetic illusions?
5. How much of Willy's tragedy is caused by his own personality and how much is caused by the reality of American life? What comments on American society is Miller making in this play?
6. How do illusion and reality function in this play?

Modern Drama

PSYCHOLOGICAL DRAMA—EUGENE O'NEILL

Eugene O'Neill (1888–1953) is considered by many modern critics to be the only American dramatist who can be ranked among the great figures of the European theatre. His brooding presence looms over the landscape of modern drama to affect all subsequent dramatists. His seriousness and devotion to artistic integrity remain landmarks in the American theater tradition. Most see August Strindberg as the main literary influence upon O'Neill, as both mercilessly exposed the corrosive and destructive cruelty family members can practice against one another when bound together in an ultimately fatal love-hate relationship. What some see as the best of his long plays appeared between 1928 and 1933: *Strange Interlude, Mourning Becomes Electra,* and *Ah, Wilderness* (his only successful comedy).

O'Neill's Philosophy

The Atmosphere of the Times. Many had begun to question the traditional values of Western civilization, feeling that God was dead and that it was up to man to create an ideal world using science in place of religion. This new world would benefit the common man, so long repressed by the wealthy. We can see this change acted out in the schools of Naturalism and Realism, which flourished in the modern period. As mentioned previously, the Naturalists felt that man was prey to the twin influences of environment and heredity. Stephen Crane, Frank Norris, and Theodore Dreiser, the chief Naturalists, often exposed conditions in the lower classes of society. This intellectual change was paralleled in social swings, as the rise of mass media (movies, chiefly), affordable automobiles for the masses, and a shift to the cities from the country, brought about the decline of the close-knit family.

Schopenhauer and Nietzsche. Arthur Schopenhauer (1788–1860) and Friedrich Nietzsche (1844–1900) were two German philosophers who had a great influence upon O'Neill. From Schopenhauer, O'Neill concluded that man is at the mercy of his emotions and that individuality and originality are thus illusions. From Nietzsche, he found encouragement to rebel against Christianity and the middle-class values of the day and to embrace the credo of an atheistic freethinker who had rejected middle-class mores. This, of course, fit right in with the change in temper of the beginning of the twentieth century.

Freud. Sigmund Freud (1856–1939), an Austrian physician and psychiatrist, had a profound influence on the literature of the early twentieth century with his writings on the unconscious, the underside of man's personality. He felt that the unconscious, which holds the keys to man's sexuality, was the determining factor in all of man's actions. This was corrupted into the notion that it is not good to repress basic desires, particularly sexual desires. Freud felt that religion would fade away as science came to dominate all of life. These notions were also shown in the temper of the time.

In the works of these three men, O'Neill found backing for his belief that man is controlled by forces he can neither understand nor control. Man's goal is to be able to express himself freely and to set himself against these forces. Despite the ensuing battle, which may be wonderful in its power, life is, in the end, meaningless and sad, especially when man is no longer in his prime.

O'Neill's Changes in the Theater

O'Neill is considered an important playwright because his plays almost singlehandedly created a *serious* American theater; before O'Neill, little had been performed but romantic melodrama. With the coming of O'Neill, the theater became a place where audiences could question man's place in the scheme of things and probe the darker sides of their own natures.

In O'Neill's plays, man is pitted against human and physical nature, as man is indifferent to his fellow man, competing for sexual and individual fulfillment. Above all, man is in conflict with a force that drives him to his doom. He is compelled to fight against this power, even though his efforts are always doomed to fail.

The main structural change O'Neill effected in the theater is the *long monologue*. This is paralleled in the experimental novel, as practitioners of both forms were seeking means to express internal workings to their audience. In *Strange Interlude,* the characters wear masks in an attempt to externalize the internal; in *The Hairy Ape* O'Neill uses backdrops to express the play's meaning symbolically.

MOURNING BECOMES ELECTRA

Source

O'Neill's play is taken from the Greek trilogy, the *Oresteia,* by Aeschylus (525–456 B.C.). The source describes the Trojan War and the events that follow. The Atreus family has been cursed by a terrible deed: When Thyestes seduced his wife, Atreus chopped up Thyestes' children and served them to him to eat. Only Aegisthus escaped. Many years later when Atreus' two sons, Menelaus and Agamemnon, had grown up, Paris, a visitor from Troy, kidnapped Menelaus's wife, Helen, setting off the Trojan War. Agamemnon, commanding the Greek army, met with ill fortune and sacrificed his daughter, Iphigenia, to ensure calm winds and a good voyage. His wife, Clytemnestra, pledged revenge. She gave her son, Orestes, to the King of Phocis (for him to raise) and waited for the day she could get her revenge. Aegisthus and Clytemnestra became lovers, and plotting together, were able to bring about Agamemnon's death. Orestes returned and vowed to avenge his father's murder, urged on by the promptings of his sister, Electra. Orestes killed both his mother and her lover, Aegisthus. He was punished by the Furies, spirits of vengeance, who drove him from place to place. After a trial held by the gods, Orestes was freed from the Furies.

O'Neill's Changes in the Source

Classical Greek drama has at its root the belief that man is controlled by the gods. O'Neill used the twin forces of heredity and environment instead of the Furies, thereby making Fate an internal force. Thus a person's behavior is determined by his past and his psychological background.

Instead of basing the play around the male figure, Orestes, O'Neill decided to use the female, Electra, as his protagonist.

Also there is no matricide. Instead, the mother, here called Christine Mannon, kills herself after murdering her husband.

There is no idea of justice—only the haunting of the living by the sins of the dead. Here we follow the aftermath of a crime of passion, not its expiation.

Comparison chart

Clytemnestra = Christine Mannon
Electra   = Lavinia Mannon
Agamemnon   = Ezra Mannon
Orestes   = Orin Mannon
Aegisthus   = Adam Brant

Setting

There are three plays here, which take place either in the spring or summer of 1865–66, as he tells us in the beginning. The plays are set "on the outskirts of one of the small New England seaport towns." Some critics have said that O'Neill often selected New England settings because the tradition of that part of the United States is characterized by introspection, religious and philosophic questioning, and deep relationships between people. (This is found in the writings of Ralph Waldo Emerson, Henry David Thoreau, and Emily Dickinson, to name a few of the New England writers of the middle to late nineteenth century). Most of the action takes place in the Mannon house itself, built as a Greek temple, with six tall columns. In *Homecoming,* the first play of the trilogy, the first act begins at sunset outside the home. The second takes place in Ezra's study, at the same time of day. The third act is outside the house during the night. The fourth act is in Ezra's bedroom at night. The background music is "Shenandoah," which O'Neill felt "more than any other [song] holds in it the brooding rhythm of the sea." In *The Hunted,* the second play, the first act takes place outside the house during the night. The second act is in the sitting room; the third act in the study. The fourth act is set in the clipper ship; the fifth act again in front of the house. The music is the same. In *The Haunted,* the final play, we begin in Act I outside the house, but this time the house is all boarded up. In Act I scene 2, we move inside and remain there for the next two acts; we go back outside for Act 4.

Theme

The characters in the play destroy themselves because they cannot get along with one another—or with anyone else, for that matter. They will not reach out to form relationships, and so they cannot love. We see here the *isolated self,* in an *amoral universe,* as the characters act out what seems right to them without regard for those around them. What they see as vital is self and self-gratification. Only in the sexual act do we see the possibility of the desire to live a full life, as we see in the relationship of Christine and Adam, and in the world of Adam's mother. They are warm and unrestrained, and represent life, as the Mannons—especially Ezra and Lavinia—represent death.

Structure

Mourning Becomes Electra is divided into three parts, as mentioned earlier. The first and third plays have four acts each; the middle play has five. Obviously, O'Neill was balancing the plays this way.

The play is also organized in a *circular* manner. We see this in the character of Lavinia. In *Homecoming,* she is an unattractive and sexless woman, but by the beginning of the final play, she is a mature and attractive woman. At the conclusion of the trilogy, she is once again wooden and lifeless, cloistered within the Mannon house. Her character development, to trace just one of the players, demonstrates O'Neill's use of a circular organization.

The play is also organized *thematically*. In *Homecoming*, for example, the themes of return, retribution, and curse form a thematic unity. The play marks a return to center as the Mannons move back into their house to work out the old hatreds. Here, though, we have an inversion of the usual meaning of "center" from a place of love and comfort to a place of hatred and evil. The characters must work through the hatred until death can expiate all sins.

Sample Questions to Consider

1. Why is Eugene O'Neill considered the most important dramatist of the twentieth-century American stage?
2. What is O'Neill's philosophy and how did it evolve from the contemporary intellectual movements of his day?
3. How did O'Neill change the theater and its conventions?
4. What was the source of *Mourning Becomes Electra* and how did O'Neill change it to suit his thematic needs?
5. How is the setting of this play important to its theme?
6. Does O'Neill's notion of structure differ from or concur with the classic Aristotelian theory?
7. Does O'Neill follow the traditions of tragedy with regard to theme here?
8. What symbols are present here and how do they function?

A VARIATION ON FORM—THORNTON WILDER

Thornton Wilder (1897–1975), unlike such contemporary dramatists as Samuel Beckett, Harold Pinter, and Eugène Ionesco, felt that man is welcome in the universe and that his attitude must be one of affirmation, not despair. This is shown in his theory of drama. In "Some Thoughts on Playwriting" (1941), Wilder sets forth his guidelines:

- Drama depends on collaborators, and a dramatist should write so as to take advantage of the skills of an actor.
- Drama must appeal to the majority of people. To hold the audience, the main techniques must be action and movement.
- Drama depends on pretense, so little spectacle is necessary.
- Time is always in the present (He violates this in "The Skin of Our Teeth").

These precepts are evident in his best-known play, *Our Town.* It has universal appeal, as shown first in the *setting,* a typical and fictional small town in America called Grover's Corners. The stage set is also in keeping with his precepts, for there is a very minimal set here—a table and a few chairs, two ladders, and two stools. The ladders are used at one point to stand for the second-floor rooms of the Gibbs and Webb homes; at another, they represent the drug store counter. The *time* is the present, as the stage manager tells us. The *characters* also evince this universality, for Wilder provides all we would expect in Small Town, U.S.A.: a paperboy, a milkman, a soda jerk, a high school sports hero, a church organist, a country doctor, the next-door neighbors who fall in love, etc. We also see this in the names, common to any American town. The action takes place from 1901 to 1913, covering the cycles of love, marriage, and death. The events of this small town achieve mythic proportion as the Stage Manager links them to the same cycle of an ancient Babylonian George and Emily, and we realize that love, marriage, and death are events common to all people at all times.

ANALYSIS OF *OUR TOWN*

Structure and Time

As the play opens, we see that there is no curtain and little scenery. The most unusual aspect of this play is the Stage Manager, a figure who can most probably be traced back to Greek drama and the chorus. The chorus commented on the play, interspersing its observations with the characters' dialogue. As the number of characters in the Greek plays increased, the chorus's role diminished. This same technique is also used in some of the plays by Eugene O'Neill, T. S. Eliot, and Tennessee Williams. In *Our Town,* the Stage Manager assumes the roles of a woman in the street, the druggist, and the minister. The play is divided into the usual three acts, and the Stage Manager opens each. He is also the last character to speak in each, and so functions as a framing device. His final remarks in acts I and II are brief, but at the end of act III he talks at greater length, in order to recapture the informal mood of the beginning of the play.

Act I, called "Daily Life," takes place on May 7, 1901, and is a typical day in the life of a small New England town. Act II is called "Love and Marriage," and the majority of the action takes place on July 7, 1904, the day George and Emily are married. There is a flashback in this act which takes us back to the day George and Emily first realized their love for each other. Act III takes place on a summer day in 1913. The act is not directly named, but the reader can surmise that it concerns death since most of the action concerns Emily's funeral and conversations among the dead in the graveyard. There is a flashback in this act also, to February 11, 1899, the date of Emily's twelfth birthday. The development of the action in acts I and II is parallel, as the dialogue switches from the Gibbs to the Webb home. The two scenes played in this way are the breakfast scene and the wedding morning scene.

Scenery

As mentioned earlier, there is no curtain and little scenery. The stage is half lit, and as the audience enters, the Stage Manager is placing a table and three chairs on the left of the stage and another table and three chairs on the right. He also sets out a bench which represents the corner of the Webb home and two flower-covered trellises which show the backyards of the adjacent Gibbs and Webb homes.

Through his gestures and descriptions, the Stage Manager creates an impression of the town, bordered by mountains and hills, and containing the railroad station, the churches, and the various ethnic neighborhoods. The town hall, post office, and jail are contained in the same building. He then describes the cemetery and the train whistle announces the arrival of the 5:45 train for Boston.

Many of the conventional props in the kitchen are imaginary, and the actors pretend they are using them. Thus Mrs. Gibbs raises an imaginary kitchen shade; Dr. Gibbs sets down an imaginary black doctor's bag; Mrs. Webb goes through the motions of putting wood on the stove, lighting it, and then preparing breakfast; Dr. Gibbs reads an imaginary newspaper. The actual props are few: an apron for Mrs. Webb, and hat and handkerchief for Dr. Gibbs, and books encircled by a strap for the children hurrying off to school. We hear the sound of milk bottles rattling, but Howie Newsome carries imaginary bottles, and strokes Bessie, the imaginary horse. This continues through the play, as Mr. Webb mows an imaginary lawn, and the children mount ladders to the imaginary second floor. In the flashback in the final act, on the day of Emily's twelfth birthday, the audience is given a summary of all the imaginary props and scenes of the beginning of the play, including the newspaper, milk bottles, and breakfast scene.

Some of this technique is taken from the Japanese Noh drama, where a player walks around the stage to indicate a long journey or rides a stick to simulate a horse.

Music

Music is used symbolically to underscore the theme of the typical small town and the universality of its appeal. The works are well known to the audience. At Emily's wedding, for example, Simon plays the traditional entrance hymn from Lohengrin and the familiar exit hymn from Mendelssohn's "Wedding March." As weddings are the most staid and traditional of the archetypal ceremonies common to most people, the music is exactly what we would expect to hear. In the same manner, the choir sings "Blessed Be The Tie That Binds" and "Love Divine, All Loves Excelling" at the wedding. Another traditional hymn is practiced by the choir in act I: "Art Thou Weary, Art Thou Languid." These selections fit perfectly with Wilder's description of Grover's Corners as a symbolic farm town.

Sound Effects

Sound effects function here in the same manner as the music, to underscore the nature of Grover's Corners and the appeal the small town holds for all of us. Only those sounds common to a small town in the early 1900s are used, and these are kept to a minimum. Since the story begins at dawn, we hear the cock crow and the whistle from the train headed toward Boston. This is followed by the sounds of Howie Newsome's imaginary horses and the clinking of imaginary milk bottles. Later in the morning, we hear the factory whistle from the Cartwright factory, the sounds of children headed for school, and the sounds of Mrs. Gibbs feeding the chickens.

Theme

Juxtaposed against the backdrop of the small town, Wilder is telling us that we do not appreciate life and all the wonderful little moments it has to offer until it is too late. Wilder celebrates all these little moments: rising, eating breakfast, going off to school, homework, etc., and he succeeds in raising these little pieces of time, the common events of daily life, to the level of ritual, a sequential celebration of the rites of life. This is important in the mainstream of twentieth-century literature, for most of Wilder's contemporaries were satirizing small-town America at the very time Wilder was celebrating it. Sinclair Lewis' *Main Street,* Sherwood Anderson's *Winesburg, Ohio,* Hamlin Garland's *Main Travelled Roads,* and Edgar Lee Master's *Spoon River Anthology* all decry the stultifying effects of the small town on the inhabitants, particularly on the sensitive artistic soul, who must escape to survive. Many of the writers of this period came from such small towns themselves—F. Scott Fitzgerald, Ernest Hemingway, Ezra Pound, T. S. Eliot, Sherwood Anderson, Sinclair Lewis—and initially did not look upon their hometowns with pleasure. Even people like Edith Wharton, who came from a very wealthy

New York area, created a mean and nasty vision of small town life in her "Starkfield" (the very name is symbolic) in *Ethan Frome*. The bitter cold of the town is reflected in the cold of the inhabitants' hearts, and the town, as much as the character's personality and circumstances, traps the individual and destroys him. Wilder, in sharp contrast to his contemporaries, points out these little details of small town life as vital and strengthening. Emily regrets that she never lived her life more fully, appreciating every tiny detail of everything about Grover's Corners. While some critics have said that the real theme and tragedy of *Our Town* is that the characters are not interested in anything beyond Grover's Corners and their everyday mundane life, the fact remains that the people here do not view life any differently and less intensely than any other person in any other setting, despite what other writers were saying at this time about the soul-destroying effects of small-town life.

Symbols

In order to underscore the universality of his message, Wilder uses the symbol of numbers. For example, the Stage Manager does not say that three years have passed but that the sun has risen over a thousand times. When he tells us how hardworking Mrs. Gibbs and Mrs. Webb are, he mentions the thousands of meals they have cooked in their lives, and adds that all 2,642 of the town's inhabitants have eaten dinner and that all those dishes have been washed. His purpose here is to give the play the necessary size to make its theme meaningful to every person, not just the handful that actually live in small towns in America.

THEATER OF THE ABSURD

"Absurd" originally meant "out of harmony" in a musical sense, and in common language, "ridiculous," but when applied to the Theater of the Absurd, the term takes on a different meaning. According to Eugène Ionesco, "Absurd is that which is devoid of purpose." When man is cut off from his roots, all his actions become senseless, useless, and absurd. This sense of anguish and uselessness in man's contemporary condition is found in the works of Samuel Beckett, Arthur Adamov, Eugène Ionesco, Jean Genet, and even Jean-Paul Sartre and Albert Camus, slightly earlier writers. The main difference between Sartre and Camus and the others in the list is that these two present their themes—the senselessness of life and devaluation of ideals—in a lucid and highly structured manner, while the other dramatists do not. The Theater of the Absurd expresses its themes through the disregard of rational devices and anticipated forms of structure. The Theater of the Absurd strives to blend form and content: If the world lacks form and focus, if all is useless, then the *form* of the play must be equally amorphous. The Theater of the Absurd does not *argue* about the absurdity of man's condition; it simply *presents* it, in terms of concrete stage images of the uselessness of life in the modern world. It is this attempt at integration of matter and form which distinguishes the Theater of the Absurd from the Existentialist theater (Camus and Sartre).

Luigi Pirandello. Pirandello has sometimes been considered the first of the Absurdists. Certainly he was one of the first to question who we are and how we appear to ourselves and others. Much of what he writes is hilariously funny, but it is also terrifying in what it says about man and the contemporary world. In *Six Characters in Search of an Author,* we are set in the middle of a play-within-a-play, and we must set aside our ability to rationalize, for in this play "real" people play at being what they are not. Suppose, questions the author, that there is a further "reality" that transcends "real" actors and "real" theater. Suppose there is an absolute reality that is art, the reality experienced by the characters the artist has created, who have undergone such an immediate reality that they must be set aside. And further suppose that they turn up in the world of make-believe that people create in the theater, and feel that their own version of "reality" is not able to be imitated and interpreted, existing as it does in an absolute that is known only to themselves and is not accesible to "real" people. Thus Pirandello is questioning what makes up reality and illusion. The audience realizes that the characters exist in a loop of time that circles back onto itself, as the characters are doomed to be what they are, nothing more and nothing less, for all eternity of written expression. They are, in the final analysis, far more "real" than the audience, who lives, after all, in a world of its own illusions. What we are left with is the question of what is real and who is really alive? What is imagination and who is trapped within it?

Harold Pinter. Harold Pinter generally rejects all labels, but his work is usually classified with the Theater of the Absurd, because of the elements of his plays. Thus the settings are often claustrophobic rooms and the atmosphere or mood is so frightening as to lead one critic to call his plays the "Comedy of Menace." Like Kafka and Beckett, Pinter finds menace in the ambiguity of the contemporary world. The characters express themselves in language that is often inarticulate and sometimes incoherent. As with the language of many other Absurdist plays, the rhythm of the idiom delves more deeply into reality than does the commonplace speech it seems to echo. The language expresses one of Pinter's themes: There can be no verbal certainty in this modern universe. We also find enormous violence in his plays, a reflection of the violence in twentieth-century life. In his later works, sex becomes a metaphor for the destruction of the individual. *The Dumb Waiter* is a case in point.

Edward Albee. Edward Albee's *themes* are similar to Pinter's: the substitution of false for real values in contemporary society, a criticism of smugness, and an exploration of violence and its effects. *The Zoo Story,* for example, looks into the animalistic violence that is barely covered by a thin veneer of civilization; this violence is revealed by the end of the play. It also details the loneliness and frustration of contemporary man, isolated from human contact by society and self. Albee's *symbols* and *allusions* underscore the emptiness of man's life today. Classical mythology, recalling the greatness of myths no longer applicable to modern life, is summoned up in Jerry's reference to his landlady and her dog as "the gatekeepers of my dwelling" and to the dog as "a descendant of the puppy that guarded the gates of hell or some such resort." Biblical parallels, suggesting how empty man's life is without faith, are present in such lines as Jerry's "So be it!" and "I came unto you . . . and you have comforted me. Dear Peter." Peter's response, "Oh my God!" is ironic in this context. Several critics have noticed parallels between Peter and the rock on which institutions are erected and Jerry as a Christ-figure or a Christ-parody. In any event, Albee's plays echo the themes and techniques of the Theater of the Absurd.

COMEDY

Comedy is a type of drama wherein the audience is amused. Generally it shows a movement from unhappiness to happiness, entertaining rather than distressing the audience.

Comedy is generally divided into two categories: *high* and *low*. High comedy is also called *social comedy, comedy of manners,* or *drawing room comedy*. It is intellectual and sophisticated. There may not be much action as it is given more to words than to frantic rushing around. The character development tends to be rather extensive, and the humor arises through a reversal of normal values. At the other end of the scale is *farce,* which shares many of the qualities of melodrama, but is intended to amuse and provoke laughter. Farce is defined as *low comedy,* but that does not imply it is of lesser quality than high comedy. High comedy tends to have a rather narrow intellectual appeal, while low comedy, such as farce, has a much broader, anti-intellectual appeal. There are a great many jokes and sight gags in low comedy, operating on the premise that this is a wacky world, populated by a lot of wild people, where logic and reason have flown out the window. The more a character attempts to find sanity in this insane world, the more likely things are to go awry.

Etherege, Wycherley, Congreve, and other playwrights immediately following the Restoration of Charles I to the throne of England in 1660 wrote what is called *Restoration comedy* of a special sort often referred to as *comedy of manners* or *comedy of wit,* full of cynical and quick repartee.

Comedy of humors is a term applied to plays whose characters represent types of moods, such as the jealous husband, the silly wife, and so forth. A "humor" was the term applied to body fluids that were thought to control man's behavior. There were four "humors"—blood, phlegm, yellow bile, and black bile—and a proper mixture of these elements was thought to produce a well-adjusted person while too much of any one element would distort personality. The word "humor" survives in such phrases as "He's in a bad humor today." Words like "phlegmatic" and "choleric" are still applied to personality. Ben Jonson's plays exemplify this type of comedy.

"Humor" characters are common in *situational comedy,* where the characters are placed by a clever plot into a situation that displays their absurdity; for example, a man who wishes for nothing but silence is forced into the company of a woman who talks constantly.

Farce is a variety of comedy that is based not on clever language or character subtleties, but on broadly humorous situations, such as a man entering the ladies' room by mistake. There is usually a great deal of meaningless movement and very broad facial expressions.

Slapstick is farce that relies on physical assault for humor. There is a lot of falling down and hitting in these works.

There is an in-between area of comedy, neither low nor high, which we call *straight comedy,* or *comedy of sensibility*. Like their counterparts in the drama, the characters here tend to be unsophisticated people who can experience suffering as well as fun. The plot is developed mainly through characterization, shunning what it sees as the vulgarities of farce as well as the narrow intellectualization of high comedy. This genre shows the charm of the ordinary man, not allowing the audience to become sentimental, even if the pain and suffering strike a little too close to home.

Comedy can also be classified according to specific subject matter:

Romantic comedies   show the stage-universe as a delightful pretend land where the main figures are lovers and all works out for the best. This is seen in Shakespeare's comedies.

Critical comedies	have main characters who are often ridiculed, seen especially in Molière's works.
Rogue comedies	such as Jonson's *Alchemist,* have as main characters pleasant scoundrels whose adventures entertain us, perhaps because they represent what we would like to experience in our more rebellious moments.

WHAT IS COMIC?

What is comic has been the topic of studies too numerous to count. Most begin with the distinction between *wit* and *humor*. *Wit,* from the Old English "witan," to know, has various meanings, but most agree with John Locke's definition: "The assemblage of ideas, and putting those ideas together with quickness and variety." In the court of Charles II, a wit was an intellectual, as defined by the above. But "wit" has had various definitions, even within the work of a single author. In the eighteenth century, Alexander Pope, in his "Essay on Criticism," speaks of works that are "one glaring chaos and wild heap of wit," where "wit" is defined as something like fanciful imagination instead of judgment. But Pope also says that "True wit is nature to advantage dressed,/What oft was thought, but ne'er so well express'd." Here "wit" means something like a well-phrased and true common expression, or good sense. Later in the eighteenth century, Dr. Johnson commented on Pope's second definition, and called "wit": "That which is not obvious is, upon its first production, acknowledged to be just." In our day, wit has come to be associated with a particular kind of cleverness that is compressed and mocking, a striking observation so phrased as to evoke laughter and amusement. *Humor,* in contrast, is genial and pokes fun at eccentricities, including the speaker's. As George Meredith says in *On the Comic Spirit,* "If you laugh all round him [a ridiculous character], tumble him, roll him about, deal him a smack, and drop a tear on him, own his likeness to you, and yours to your neighbor, spare him as little as you shun, pity him as much as you expose, it is a spirit of Humor that is moving you." Sometimes wit is said to be a recognition of resemblances while humor is the recognition of incongruities.

Theories about what is funny generally fall into two categories: (1) laughter is evoked by "a kind of sudden glory" (in Hobbes' famous phrase), as the spectator suddenly realizes his superiority to others, for example, when he sees how ridiculous someone looks who has slipped on a banana peel; (2) laughter is called forth by a "transformation of a strained expectation into nothing" (in Kant's famous phrase), as when we find funny a comedian who says, "I have enough money to last me the rest of my life—provided I die a week from Friday." In this instance the humor arises when we suddenly release the tension we have held in because we think we are with a very wealthy person. A great deal has been written on the division between wit and humor, as well as what actually constitutes "funny."

Aristotle did not write about comedy as extensively as he did tragedy (or his writings have been lost), but he did say that tragedy shows men greater than they are, while comedy shows them lesser. Comedy reminds us how unlike the gods we are, no matter how we may wish to emulate them. A comedy is usually thought of as "funny," and as having a happy ending. While this may be true, there may also be a great deal of suffering and even death along the way.

The main difference between comedy and tragedy is that comedy has a *detached point of view.* Comedy forces us to keep our distance, as we see the pain is not permanent nor the disaster real. We do not become emotionally involved with the characters, for if we do, the comedy has ended. Comedy emphasizes the foolishness of many of our poses, tripping us by a sudden reversal, a silly comparison, a gross exaggeration. Even as we fall flat on the ground, those watching us do not take the pain seriously, and so do not become involved with our pratfalls. While things that make people laugh have not changed drastically through the ages, artistic taste has altered. Physical defects, race, or mental problems are no longer acceptable comic devices, but still with us are the sexual jokes, the pratfall, the pie-in-the-face routine, the wit, and wisecrack.

GREEK COMEDY

Comic drama appears to have been drawn from ancient fertility rites, as it usually celebrates renewal, variety, and man's triumph over life's harshness. Even enraged parents and horrible natural events—earthquakes and shipwrecks—cannot prevent happy endings. *Greek comedy,* the earliest form of comedy, is usually divided into three categories: (1) old comedy; (2) middle comedy; and (3) new comedy.

Old comedy is best represented by Aristophanes (445?–380? B.C.) and combines fantastic elements, such as a utopia founded by birds, with wild political satire. Aristophanes was only one of a number of talented writers of comedy during this time, but after his death, his reputation far exceeded all others. The only examples of old comedy that survive are his, about 11 of the 40 plays he wrote.

Since Greek comedy was part of a religious festival, its purpose was to educate as well as entertain. This is true of Aristophanes' comedies. He used humor and satire to urge his audience to become good citizens, to drive away hypocrisy from the Athenian culture. Nevertheless, he had his own set of preconceived ideas, coming as he did from a wealthy family, whose aristocratic and conservative upbringing brought him into conflict with the popular political parties of the day. He tended to see hypocrisy there more easily than in the party he supported.

All of his plays concern three main themes: politics and the war with Sparta; literature, especially the writings of Euripides; and education, especially the teachings of the Sophists, whose beliefs he did not support. This can make much of what he wrote very difficult for the modern audience to understand. Since almost all of his humor was topical, it is necessary for us to refer to notes by critics and scholars.

When Aristophanes presented his first play in 427 B.C. (the earliest surviving comedy in Western literature), Athens was locked in a life-and-death struggle with the other leading power of Greece, Sparta. Athens was no longer the greatest nation on earth; Pericles was dead and his power dissipated.

In 404 B.C., after 27 years of fighting, the war finally ended in complete victory for Sparta. Athens was stripped, her treasure gone. We see this in Aristophanes' final plays.

Although Athens regained her former glory, old comedy never returned. In 338 B.C., Athens fell under the rule of the kings of Macedonia, and freedom of speech became a thing of the past. Life was dictated from above and was terribly unsure. The purpose of new comedy was to entertain, its subject was people, and its main source of humor derived from the gentle mockery of all. It soon became even more popular than tragedy.

Middle comedy does not survive. Many critics have seen it as a bridge to new comedy.

New Comedy is best represented by Menander (342?–291?B.C.) and has the plot we've come to expect in a comedy: Boy meets girl, boy and girl encounter problems, boy and girl overcome problems. There are adventures interwoven with tales of ordinary life. Even though he was not very popular during his lifetime (his rivals' humor had far greater appeal), Menander's reputation caught fire after his death. Some of his work was discovered in 1905 in an Egyptian tomb, greatly adding to his fame. His "formula" was continued in Rome by Plautus (254?–184? B.C.) and Terence (190–159? B.C.).

A century after Aristophanes, Greek comedy had spread to the world. It played in theaters from Italy to Asia Minor, although a performance in Athens remained the goal of every playwright.

Greek comedy generally followed a set formula, having three elements:

Idea: A character thinks of a "happy idea," and calls together a group to discuss it.

Application: After the discussion, the idea is put into practice, usually with very silly results.

Conclusion: There is some sort of union of the sexes at the end of a comedy. Some critics have again seen this as allied to the fertility rites of the ancient Greeks.

Some further qualities of Greek Comedy:

Characters: All are treated in a light manner, no matter what their status.

Purpose: To reform man through laughter. Ideas that people foolishly hold to be true are shown to be ridiculous, so that people will reform their ways.

Diction: Spans all levels, from crude and coarse jokes to lovely poetical passages. Often these shifts are used to illuminate character or theme, showing someone's personality through language.

Plot: Often came from political situations and philosophical questions. Wars, subsequent peace treaties, abuses in power, and prevailing philosophical ideas were often bantered around. While playwrights invented characters, it was not uncommon for well-known citizens to figure in the action.

ANALYSIS OF *THE FROGS* BY ARISTOPHANES

The Frogs was presented at the Lenaea in 405 B.C. and won first prize. The Athenians had been at war almost continually since 431 B.C., and their position was desperate; one defeat would lose the war. Six months after *The Frogs* was performed, Athens did indeed lose to Sparta. But when Aristophanes was writing this play, one great victory could still enable the Athenians to be victorious, provided that they used such a victory wisely, as a bargaining point for a lasting peace.

This was Aristophanes' view, and he felt that if all people banded together their talents and resources, a lasting peace could be achieved. The last lines of the play can be read in this manner.

The first part of *The Frogs* takes the form of a comic journey beyond the limits of the world, similar to *The Birds*. During the course of the journey, the Dead are encountered, who are used to voice the poet's own views and speak on behalf of peace. At the end of the journey, a conversation between two slaves, Xanthias and Aiakos, introduces the final *agon* between Euripides and Aeschylus.

The agon, after introductory preparation, is argued on five issues or rounds, as follows:

1. General style, subject matter, and effect upon audiences
   Choral interlude
2. Prologues, including skill at exposition and the use of iambic meter
   Choral interlude
3. Lyrics and lyric prose
   Choral interlude

4. The weighing of lines
   Interlude by Dionysos and Pluto
5. Advice to the Athenians

In each round, Euripides attacks first. In the first three rounds he achieves some victories. But Aeschylus, the ultimate winner, has the better position for an agon, since the last word belongs to him.

The arguments are as follows:

Round 1. Euripides says that Aeschylus' work is turgid, undramatic, obscure, and too militaristic. His own plays, in contrast, are lucid, plausible, and meaningful for all. Aeschylus responds that he has always maintained a high heroic standard and urged the citizens to greater virtue, while Euripides, in lowering tragedy by bringing it down to earth, has dragged it in the dust. Especially with his morbid interest in sex, he had succeeded in unmanning the Athenians.

Round 2. Euripides charges Aeschylus with an obscure and repetitious style. Aeschylus retorts with a charge of metrical monotony. In prologue after prologue of Euripides, the main verb is delayed and a subordinate clause completed in such a way as to conclude both the metrical line and the sentence.

Round 3. Aeschylus, having raised the question of metrical dullness, spurs Euripides to respond in kind. Aeschylus' lyrics are monotonous, he charges, for however he may begin, he always ends with a dactyl phrase. This can be seen in a line such as "O ho what a stroke come you not to the rescue?" These metrical criticisms repeat the general criticism of style: When Euripides makes sense, he is dull; when Aeschylus sounds wonderful, he means little. Aeschylus responds by saying that Euripides writes free verse and the lyric meters lose their form and lines cease to make any sense. This results in a shoddy, sentimental flow of words, especially marked by one special flaw which Aristophanes always finds in Euripides: the combination of magnificence and homeliness.

Round 4. The weighing of lines has often been regarded as the least important section of the play, but nevertheless it advances the opinion that the verse of Aeschylus has more mass and substance than that of Euripides.

Round 5. What shall Athens do? The speakers may be taken to represent the poet's own struggle. Euripides expresses Aristophanes' doubts about the good purpose of the heirs of Pericles, those who follow the support of naval warfare, while Aeschylus speaks for Aristophanes' unwilling conclusion, that these people alone have a chance to save what remains of the city.

We can conclude from all this that Euripides' Aeschylus, even in parody, is not as simple a figure as we might conclude from his plays. *Seven Against Thebes* is more than a simple-minded glorification of patriotism. *Agamemnon* condemns war-makers and sackers of cities. Aristophanes picked out and exaggerated certain aspects of Aeschylus, not from ignorance, but because he was concerned with the success of his agon rather than the validity of his presentation of historical people. The attack is on the moderns, and Euripides is their spokesman. Whatever Euripides is, Aeschylus must, for argument's sake, be the opposite. So, if Euripides is against war, Aeschylus must be pro-war. If Euripides takes the women's side in discussions, Aeschylus must be against women. And since Euripides was popular with the audience (although he did not win with the judges), Aeschylus must be unpopular, haughty, and aristocratic.

FRENCH COMEDY

During the seventeenth century, tragedy dominated the French theater. It was generally felt that all art must follow the Greek and Roman models and adhere to Aristotle's theories. Although Greek and Roman comedies were known, there were no established rules for comic drama. Molière (Jean-Baptiste Poquelin) stepped in to fill the void in the theater and create an original form.

While Molière is not considered solely a writer of comedies, many of his plays are very witty and humorous. He excelled at using humor to make a serious point. One of the main influences on Molière's work was the tradition of *farce*: a short skit, broadly humorous and satirical of society and its followers. Molière first won acclaim for his farces and returned to this form frequently. His last play, *The Imaginary Invalid*, is largely farcical.

TARTUFFE BY MOLIÈRE

Tartuffe, originally written in verse rather than prose, is Molière's most controversial play. It is based on a particular incident as well as a general problem of his day: There was a real priest who, while serving as the spiritual guide for a family, stole their money and committed adultery with the wife. Molière was also attacking a secret society of religious fanatics who tried to gain entrance to homes and control the personal lives of the families. It is not surprising that these people, seeing themselves so accurately portrayed on the stage, sought to destroy Molière. Many moderate churchmen as well as laypeople attacked the play because they viewed it as the work of an atheist and a freethinker. To them, *Tartuffe* denounced the church, religion, and religious practices.

The present version of *Tartuffe* is not the original script, which was banned by the king in 1664. That play is thought to have concluded in Tartuffe's victory over his enemies, Orgon's declaration of trust in his spiritual advisor, and his assent to Tartuffe's watch over his wife, Elmire. Louis XIV lifted the ban with the revised edition, submitted five years later. We can conclude that one of the reasons for the very weak conclusion, the use of the *deus ex machina* (an incredible and unbelievable device to solve the plot), was to flatter the king. How could Louis XIV not permit a play which praised him as the defender of the mistreated, the wise judge of all wrongs? When the revised edition was performed, it was hailed as a great success. Today it is one of Molière's best-known and most highly admired plays.

The theme is religious hypocrisy, obviously, but the play is also concerned with character and manners. The play focuses on the three points of view of Tartuffe, Orgon, and Cleante. It is difficult to support the thesis that Tartuffe is the main character, for he does not appear directly in the action until act III. The manners of the day, both religious and social, are noted in great detail here, along with the role of religion in family and household, the relations between family members, and the role and nature of friendship.

Summary of Tartuffe

Act I. The play opens in the midst of a family quarrel. Mme. Pernelle is very unhappy with the way her son's household is being managed. She complains about the children's manners and especially criticizes her daughter-in-law Elmire's extravagance. Mme. Pernelle rebukes the entire family for their disregard of Tartuffe, whose presence everyone except Mme. Pernelle resents. Damis, Orgon's son and Elmire's stepson, is the most outspoken, calling Tartuffe a pious fraud. They all describe him as a hypocrite enriching himself at the family's expense. They equally mistrust his servant, Laurent. Mme. Pernelle replies that Tartuffe hates sin and is trying to rescue their souls from eternal damnation. Dorine cannot accept his dictate that the family not be allowed visitors and claims that Tartuffe is emotionally interested in Elmire. Mme. Pernelle claims that visitors cause scandal, and Cleante, Elmire's brother, supports the majority of the family by asserting that they live innocently and have nothing to fear from visitors. Once gossipers start, he says, there is no stopping them. They cite the example of Orante, a neighbor whose current virtuous life-style conceals a wild past. Mme. Pernelle, realizing that she cannot sway the family, delivers one long final speech before her departure, saying that her son's actions in admitting Tartuffe to the house were correct, for he will rid it of evil. She warns them that unless they give up parties and evil ways, she will not visit them again. Cleante and Dorine discuss the reason for Tartuffe's overwhelming influence over Orgon. Prior to Tartuffe's arrival, he was a man of good sense and reason. The others return, and Damis asks Cleante to intercede with Orgon about Mariane's marriage to Valere, which Tartuffe opposes. Orgon enters and shows no interest in his wife's illness of the previous night; rather, he is concerned about Tartuffe's welfare. Cleante tries to make Orgon see how foolishly he is behaving, but Orgon says that Tartuffe has caused all worldly cares to vanish. He even goes so far as to say that he would not be upset if any of his family died. Orgon then explains how he met Tartuffe: his pious behavior in church, his entrance into the family, the upward turn in family fortunes. Cleante thinks that Orgon has lost all reason, and states with vigor that true religion does not concern itself with the blind acceptance of appearances. Why will man not stay within the boundaries of reason and seek the middle path of moderation? Why does man have so much difficulty distinguishing between appearance and reality? The main thrust of his attack is against religious hypocrisy, and he denounces those who use religious practices for their own ends. He praises those who practice what they preach. Insulted, Orgon wants to leave, but Cleante asks him about Valere and Mariane's marriage plans. Orgon says that he will follow the will of heaven—Tartuffe—and Cleante knows that the path will be rocky.

Act II. Orgon and Mariane discuss her wedding. He stresses obedience; she agrees, until he announces that Tartuffe is to be her husband. She refuses, and they quarrel. Dorine enters unnoticed, and Orgon scolds her for being an eavesdropper. She defends herself with an attack on Tartuffe. For example, she does not understand why he could want Tartuffe for a son-in-law, since Tartuffe is penniless. Orgon defends Tartuffe by saying that he has renounced all earthly possessions, including land that would make him rich. Dorine claims that these boasts are not signs of humility. They discuss the wedding, and Dorine says that Mariane will be wretched with Tartuffe as a husband. Orgon objects to Valere because he has heard that Valere does not attend church and plays cards. He believes that piety will bind together Tartuffe and Mariane as love cannot. He finally threatens to strike Dorine unless she keeps quiet, although she continues to make snide comments. Every time he tries to hit her she ceases, but she is at last forced to flee from his rage. Orgon is so angry that he has to leave the room, and Dorine returns to encourage Mariane in her rebellion. Mariane is torn between love and duty. Valere enters and demands to know if the rumor he has heard concerning Tartuffe as his love's intended is true. Mariane seems to be passively accepting her fate and he, too, mocks her. Dorine intervenes and effects a truce between the lovers. She tells Mariane to pretend to accept Tartuffe but to keep postponing the marriage as long as possible.

Act III. Damis and Dorine make plans to trap Tartuffe. Tartuffe enters and begins to assume pompous and false airs, warning against the temptation of the flesh and giving various orders. Elmire begins to discuss the wedding plans with Tartuffe, but he begins to flirt with her, declaring his love and saying he wishes to seduce her. She sets this condition: Tartuffe must give his support to Valere and Mariane's wedding or she will tell Orgon of Taruffe's bold seduction attempt. Damis rushes from the closet where he has been hiding, determined to tell his father what Tartuffe really is like. Orgon enters, and Elmire confirms Damis' tale. Tartuffe refuses to defend himself, kneeling before Damis to hypocritically accept all accusations. Orgon rises to Tartuffe's defense, and Tartuffe has to convince Orgon not to punish his son. Orgon claims the family is jealous of the man—Tartuffe—who is trying to help them. He vows to arrange the marriage sooner as a lesson to the family. Damis objects and Orgon drives him from the house. Tartuffe offers to leave, but Orgon wants him to stay, remain near his wife, be the sole heir to his fortunes, and marry Mariane. Tartuffe pretends to demur, but agrees only to be in accord with the will of heaven.

Act IV. Cleante tells Tartuffe that the townspeople are gossiping about his role in Damis' exile from his own home, and that Tartuffe should mend the fight between father and son for the sake of his, Tartuffe's, reputation. Tartuffe declines to get involved, invoking God's will. In order to escape Cleante's valid criticisms, Tartuffe leaves the room. Elmire, Mariane, and Dorine run in, asking Cleante to protect them against Orgon. When Orgon enters, Mariane begs him not to make her marry Tartuffe; she would rather enter a convent. Elmire is deeply upset by Orgon's acceptance of Tartuffe's version of affairs, and in desperation, asks Orgon if he would believe her if he could see Tartuffe trying to seduce her. He accepts the challenge, and Elmire hides him under the table as the others leave the room. Elmire and Tartuffe flirt, and although initially suspicious about her change in heart toward him, he soon accepts her words completely. She asks Tartuffe how he can justify his sin with his religious beliefs. He hypocritically says that sinning in silence is no sin at all and that he can warp conscience to justify behavior. When she mentions her husband to Tartuffe, he laughs and says that he can lead the foolish Orgon around by the nose. While Tartuffe checks to make sure the coast is clear, Orgon comes out from hiding too soon, and Elmire hides him quickly behind herself. As Tartuffe returns and continues his advances, Orgon comes out from hiding and demands that he leave the house immediately, but Tartuffe brazenly refuses to go, saying that the house is his. Orgon recalls the deed in inheritance he has signed and wants to get to his safe at once.

Act V. Orgon's safe is missing, and in despair, he asks for Cleante's advice. Damis and his father reunite to defeat Tartuffe, and although Mme. Pernelle still refuses to admit any wrongdoing on Tartuffe's part, the rest of the family is solidly against the faker. When Tartuffe sends a notice of eviction to the family, they believe all is lost. Even Mme. Pernelle now accepts Tartuffe for what he is. Valere hurries in to advise Orgon to leave the country; Tartuffe has turned the missing safe over to the king and some papers inside have made it appear that Orgon is a traitor for aiding an outlaw. Before Orgon can escape, Tartuffe comes with a policeman to arrest him. In a surprising ending, the police arrest Tartuffe, not Orgon. The policeman offers a very flattering speech that Louis XIV had immediately recognized Tartuffe for what he is. The king declared the contract between Orgon and Tartuffe null and void, and straightened out the matter of Orgon's friend the outlaw. Cleante does not allow the family to attack Tartuffe physically, but turns him over to the police.

SUGGESTED READING LIST

The following critical studies contain material useful for studying drama.

Boynton, Robert and Maynard Mack. *Introduction to the Play*. Rochelle Park, New Jersey: Hayden, 1969.

Brooks, Cleanth and William Heilman. *Understanding Drama*. New York: Holt, Rinehart and Winston, 1948.

Cubeta, Paul. *Modern Drama for Analysis*. 3rd ed. New York: Holt, Rinehart and Winston, 1962.

Felheim, Marvin, ed. *Comedy: Plays, Theories, and Criticism*. New York: Harcourt Brace Jovanovich, 1969.

Kernan, Alvin. *Character and Conflict: An Introduction to Drama*. New York: Harcourt Brace Jovanovich, 1969.

Levin, Richard, ed. *Tragedy: Plays, Theory, and Criticism*. New York: Harcourt Brace Jovanovich, 1960.

Aeschylus	*Agamemnon*
Albee, Edward	*Who's Afraid of Virginia Woolf?*
	Zoo Story
Anonymous	*Everyman*
	The Second Shepherd's Play
Aristophanes	*The Frogs*
Beckett, Samuel	*Endgame*
	Waiting for Godot
Bolt, Robert	*A Man for all Seasons*
Brecht, Bertold	*The Caucasian Chalk Circle*
Capek, Karel	*R.U.R.*
Chekhov, Anton	*The Cherry Orchard*
	The Sea Gull
Congreve, William	*The Way of the World*
Eliot, T. S.	*Murder in the Cathedral*
Euripides	*Medea*
Gibson, William	*The Miracle Worker*
Gilbert, W. S.	*The Mikado*
Goldsmith, Oliver	*She Stoops to Conquer*
Hansberry, Lorraine	*A Raisin in the Sun*
Hellman, Lillian	*The Little Foxes*
Ibsen, Henrik	*A Doll's House*
	Ghosts
	The Enemy of the People
	The Wild Duck
Ionesco, Eugene	*The Lesson*
Lerner and Loewe	*My Fair Lady*
MacLeish, Archibald	*J. B.*
Marlowe, Christopher	*Dr. Faustus*
Miller, Arthur	*The Crucible*
	Death of a Salesman
Molière	*Tartuffe*
	The Physician in Spite of Himself
O'Casey, Sean	*Juno and the Paycock*
	The Plough and Stars

O'Neill, Eugene	*The Emperor Jones*
	The Hairy Ape
	Mourning Becomes Electra
Pinter, Harold	*The Birthday Party*
Pirandello, Luigi	*Six Characters in Search of an Author*
Rostand, Edmond	*Cyrano de Bergerac*
Sartre, Jean-Paul	*No Exit*
Shakespeare, William	*Hamlet*
	King Lear
	Othello
	Julius Caesar
	As You Like It
	Macbeth
	Romeo and Juliet
	The Tempest
Shaw, George Bernard	*Arms and the Man*
	Man and Superman
	Major Barbara
	St. Joan
	Pygmalion
Sheridan, Richard	*The Rivals*
	The School for Scandal
Sophocles	*Antigone*
	Oedipus Rex
Stoppard, Tom	*Rosencrantz and Guildenstern Are Dead*
Synge, John Millington	*Playboy of the Western World*
Wilde, Oscar	*The Importance of Being Earnest*
Wilder, Thornton	*Our Town*
Williams, Tennessee	*The Glass Menagerie*
	Cat on a Hot Tin Roof
Wilson, August	*Fences*

Part 6

Three Sample Advanced Placement Exams in Composition and Literature

Sample Examination A

SECTION 1

Part A: Time—25 minutes

Directions: Read the poem and answer the questions that follow it.

NATURE

1 As a fond mother, when the day is o'er,
    Leads by the hand her little child to bed,
    Half willing, half reluctant to be led,
    And leave his broken playthings on the floor,
5 Still gazing at them through the open door,
    Nor wholly reassured and comforted
    By promises of others in their stead,
    Which, though more splendid, may not please him more;
    So Nature deals with us, and takes away
10   Our playthings one by one, and by the hand
    Leads us to rest so gently, that we go
    Scarce knowing if we wish to go or stay,
    Being too full of sleep to understand
    How far the unknown transcends the what we know.
    —*Henry Wadsworth Longfellow*

1. What two situations are being compared here?
   (A) A mother reassuring her child that his broken toys will be replaced to Nature's destruction of the world's "toys."
   (B) Life to sleep
   (C) Death to sleep
   (D) Parenthood to childhood
   (E) A "fond mother" and her sleepy child to "Mother Nature" and natural disasters

2. What is such a comparison called?
   (A) Simile
   (B) Hyperbole
   (C) Pun
   (D) Oxymoron
   (E) Synesthesia

3. What is the author's attitude toward his subject matter?
   (A) We have much to fear from death's embrace, he says.
   (B) Death ought to hold little fear.
   (C) We ought to be terrified of the suddenness of death; the author recommends suicide.

   (D) Life usually terminates abruptly, but this is good, for it relieves us of the trials of parenthood.
   (E) Life is a boring affair at best and death is preferable for it is exciting.

4. How does the author's use of comparison illuminate his theme?
   (A) It shows that the mother–child relationship is central to Nature.
   (B) It really doesn't illuminate the theme to any great extent; that is done through poetic devices.
   (C) It portrays life's dilemma accurately, as our "toys" often break and we may not always be solaced by others.
   (D) It pictures the approach of death, and casts it in a light of calm reassurance.
   (E) It describes the enormous difficulty of raising children and reassures us that all share this situation.

5. What are the "playthings" in line 10?
   (A) All the people and things with which we fill our lives
   (B) All the minor annoyances of daily life

(C) Status items
(D) Leisure activities
(E) Wicked and evil habits

(C) Gentle and contemplative
(D) Bewildered
(E) Straightforward

6. What does the use of the word "playthings" tell you about the speaker's view of life?
(A) Life is best appreciated by the young.
(B) Life is an extended childhood.
(C) Man is immature and subject to folly all his life.
(D) Man is unaware of the true value of life until it is terminated.
(E) Life is a bitter affair at best.

7. What is the form of this poem?
(A) An ode
(B) Free verse
(C) A sonnet
(D) A ballad
(E) Light verse

8. What is the prevailing foot of this poem?
(A) Dactyl
(B) Spondee
(C) Trochee
(D) Iamb
(E) Anapest

9. What is the rhyme scheme of this poem?
(A) *abbaabba cdecde*
(B) *ababcdcdefefgg*
(C) *aaaa bbbb cccc dd*
(D) *aaba aaba cde cde*
(E) None of the above; it is unrhymed.

10. What is the tone of this poem?
(A) Euphuistic
(B) Baroque

11. The speaker shifts point of view in which of the following lines?
(A) Line 9
(B) Line 4
(C) Line 5
(D) Line 3
(E) Line 2

12. Which line best states the poem's meaning?
(A) Line 14
(B) Line 9
(C) Line 4
(D) Line 11
(E) Line 12

13. The author states that
(A) life far exceeds death
(B) we have little to fear from death because the afterlife exceeds all our expectations
(C) we have an enormous amount to fear from death
(D) we shall never know what awaits us after death
(E) there is nothing after life

14. The poet's attitude toward life and death shows that he was most likely influenced by
(A) the death of a loved one
(B) the Transcendentalists of the 1830–1860's
(C) the rhythm of nineteenth-century slave verse
(D) the Puritan attitudes of the seventeenth century
(E) the Revolutionary War

Part B: Time—20 minutes

Write a brief essay in which you demonstrate how the author of "Nature" views life, death, and eternity. Be sure to draw specific examples from the poem.

SECTION 2

Part A: Time—45 minutes

Directions: Read the following passage carefully; then write the assignment given after the passage.

CAPTAIN JOHN SMITH AMONG THE INDIANS

The winter [of 1607] approaching, the rivers became so covered with swans, geese, ducks, and cranes, that we daily feasted with good bread, Virginia peas, pumpkins, putchamins, fish, fowl, and diverse sorts of wild beasts as fat as we could eat them, so that none of our tuftaffety humorists desired to go for England.

But our comedies never endured long without a tragedy; some idle exceptions being muttered against Captain Smith for not discovering the head of Chickahamania River, and taxed by the Council to be too slow in so worthy an attempt. The next voyage he proceeded so far that with much labor by cutting of trees asunder he made his passage; but when his barge could pass no farther, he left her in a broad bay out of danger of shot, commanding none should go ashore till his return: himself with two English and two savages went up higher in a canoe, but he was not long absent but his men went ashore, whose want of government gave both occasion and opportunity to the savages to surprise one George Cassen, whom they slew, and much failed not to have cut off the boat and all the rest.

Smith, little dreaming of that accident, being got to the marshes at the river's head, twenty miles in the desert, had his two men slain (as is supposed) sleeping by the canoe, whilst himself by fowling sought them victual; who, finding he was beset with two hundred savages, two of them he slew, still defending himself with the aid of a savage his guide, whom he bound to his arm with his garters and used him as a buckler; yet he was shot in his thigh a little and had many arrows that stuck in his clothes but no great hurt, till at last they took him prisoner.

When this news came to Jamestown, much was their sorrow for his loss, few expecting what ensued.

Six or seven weeks those barbarians kept him prisoner, many strange triumphs and conjurations they made of him, yet he so demeaned himself amongst them, as he not only diverted them from surprising the fort, but procured his own liberty, and got himself and his company such estimation amongst them, that those savages admired him more than their own Quiyouckosucks. The manner how they used and delivered him is as follows.

The savages having drawn from George Cassen whither Captain Smith was gone, prosecuting that opportunity they followed him with three hundred bowmen, conducted by the King of Pamaunkee, who in divisions searching the turnings of the river, found Robinson and Emry by the fireside; those they shot full of arrows and slew. Then finding the Captain, as is said, that used the savage that was his guide as his shield (three of them being slain and divers others so galled) all the rest would not come near him. Thinking thus to have returned to his boat, regarding them as he marched more than his way, slipped up to the middle in an oozy creek and his savage with him; yet durst they not come to him till being near dead with cold, he threw away his arms. Then according to their composition they drew him forth and led him to the fire, where his men were slain. Diligently they chafed his benumbed limbs.

He demanding for their captain, they showed him Opechankanough, King of Pamaunkee, to whom he gave a round ivory double compass dial. Much they marveled at the playing of the fly and needle, which they could see so plainly, and yet not touch it because of the glass that covered them. But when he demonstrated by that globelike jewel the roundness of the earth, the skies, the sphere of the sun, moon, and stars, and how the sun did chase the night round about the world continually; the greatness of the land and sea, the diversity of nations, variety of complexions, and how we were to them antipodes, and many other suchlike matters, they all stood as amazed with admiration.

—*John Smith*

Directions: Write an essay in which you evaluate the author's purpose in writing and publishing this selection. Take into account the time period in which it was written as well as the way in which the action is described.

Part B: Time—30 minutes

Directions: Read the following passage carefully and consider the questions which follow it.

From SINNERS IN THE HANDS OF AN ANGRY GOD

THE wrath of God is like great waters that are dammed for the present; they increase more and more and rise higher and higher, till an outlet is given; and the longer the stream is stopped, the more rapid and mighty is its course when once it is let loose. 'Tis true that judgment against your evil work has not been executed hitherto; the floods of God's vengeance have been withheld; but your guilt in the meantime is constantly increasing, and you are every day treasuring up more wrath; the waters are continually rising and waxing more and more mighty; and there is nothing but the mere pleasure of God that holds the waters back, that are unwilling to be stopped, and press hard to go forward. If God should only withdraw his hand from the floodgate it would immediately fly open, and the fiery floods of the fierceness and wrath of God would rush forth with inconceivable fury, and would come upon you with omnipotent power; and if your strength were ten thousand times greater than it is, yea, ten thousand times greater than the strength of the stoutest, sturdiest devil in hell, it would be nothing to withstand or endure it.

The bow of God's wrath is bent, and the arrow made ready on the string, and justice bends the arrow at your heart and strains the bow, and it is nothing but the mere pleasure of God, and that of an angry God, without any promise or obligation at all, that keeps the arrow one moment from being made drunk with your blood.

Thus are all you that never passed under a great change of heart by the mighty power of the Spirit of God upon your souls; all that were never born again and made new creatures, and raised from being dead in sin to a state of new and before altogether unexperienced light and life (however you may have reformed your life in many things, and may have had religious affections, and may keep up a form of religion in your families and closets and in the house of God, and may be strict in it), you are thus in the hands of an angry God; 'tis nothing but his mere pleasure that keeps you from being this moment swallowed up in everlasting destruction.

However unconvinced you may now be of the truth of what you hear, by and by you will be fully convinced of it. Those that are gone from being in the like circumstances with you, see that it was so with them; for destruction came suddenly upon most of them; when they expected nothing of it, and while they were saying, Peace and Safety. Now they see that those things that they depended on for peace and safety were nothing but thin air and empty shadows.

The God that holds you over the pit of hell much as one holds a spider or some loathsome insect over the fire, abhors you, and is dreadfully provoked; his wrath toward you burns like fire; he looks upon you as worthy of nothing else but to be cast into the fire; he is of purer eyes than to bear to have you in his sight; you are ten thousand times so abominable in his eyes as the most hateful and venomous serpent is in ours. You have offended him infinitely more than ever a stubborn rebel did his prince; and yet it is nothing but his hand that holds you from falling into the fire every moment. 'Tis ascribed to nothing else, that you did not go to hell the last night; that you were suffered to awake again in this world after you closed your eyes to sleep and there is no other reason to be given why you have not dropped into hell since you arose in the morning, but that God's hand has held you up. There is no other reason to be given why you have not gone to hell since you have sat here in the house of God, provoking his pure eyes by your sinful wicked manner of attending his solemn worship. Yea, there is nothing else that is to be given as a reason why you don't this very moment drop down into hell.

O sinner! Consider the fearful danger you are in. 'Tis a great furnace of wrath, a wide and bottomless pit, full of the fire of wrath, that you are held over in the hand of that God whose wrath is provoked and incensed as much against you as against many of the damned in hell. You hang by a slender thread with the flames of divine wrath flashing about it.

—*Jonathan Edwards*

1. What is the *tone* of this passage?
2. What is the *style*?
3. What is the relationship between the *style* and *content*?
4. What is the speaker's attitude toward people? Toward God?
5. How do the *tone* and *style* underscore and support his attitude?

Write an essay in which you show how the author's tone and style are effective in giving his view of God's attitude toward man.

SECTION 3

Time—60 minutes

Choose two literary works in which a character views the past with such feelings as reverence, bitterness, or longing. With clear evidence drawn from the works, show how the characters' views of the past are used to develop a theme in the work. You may wish to select your examples from the list of authors provided, but any two works of comparable literary excellence may be used.

F. Scott Fitzgerald   Toni Morrison

John Updike   Charles Dickens

Bernard Malamud   Henry James

Arthur Miller   Ernest Hemingway

Henrik Ibsen   Theodore Dreiser

ANSWERS AND EXPLANATIONS FOR SAMPLE EXAMINATION A

Section 1, Part A: "Nature"

1. **(C)** Henry Wadsworth Longfellow (1807–1882) is using the Italian (also known as Petrarchan) sonnet form to compare death to sleep, a common theme in sonnets. Lines 1–8 describe a mother leading her child to bed and rest at day's end; lines 9–14 describe Nature leading man to his final sleep.

2. **(A)** Longfellow is using a simile here, a direct comparison of two unlike objects, using "like" or "as." The first line, "*As* a fond mother . . . " tells us this. Hyperbole, (B), is overstatement or great exaggeration for effect. A pun, (C), is the humorous use of words to stress their different meanings, or the use of words that are alike or almost alike in sound but different in meaning; a play on words (*e.g.,* "tail" and "tale"). An oxymoron, (D), consists of contradictory terms brought together to express a paradox in order to establish a strong poetic effect. See poetry section for examples. Synesthesia, (E), occurs when the stimulus applied to one sense triggers another, for example, when hearing a certain sound induces the visualization of color.

3. **(B)** Longfellow's use of the mother-child comparison is intended to reassure the reader and to remove death's sting. Furthermore, words such as "gently" in line 11 suggest the calmness with which we ought to approach death. The final line clarifies his attitude: What lies after our mortal existence far exceeds what meager "playthings" we might have relinquished and the afterlife promises far more splendid treasures (lines 8, 14).

4. **(D)** See explanatory answer for question 3.

5. **(A)** As a child has his treasures, so adults fill their lives with the people and things they value.

6. **(B)** Longfellow does not condemn man for his diversions, as answer (C) implies. Rather, man is unaware of what lies beyond, and man remains in a state of childlike innocence, not realizing what is of value until he has passed through life.

7. **(C)** A sonnet is a lyric poem of 14 lines written in iambic pentameter. Originated by the Italian poets during the thirteenth century, it reached perfection a century later in the work of Petrarch, and later came to be known as the Italian or Petrarchan sonnet. When the English poets of the sixteenth century discovered Petrarch, they were challenged by his format and adopted the

number of lines but changed the rhyme scheme, as will be discussed later. An ode, (A), is an elaborate lyric verse which usually deals with an important and dignified theme. Free verses, (B), has unrhymed lines without regular rhythm. A ballad, (D), is a simple verse which tells a story to be sung or recited. Light verse, (E), falls into a general group of poems written to entertain. Epigrams and limericks show the less serious side of light verse; parody or satire illustrate its more profound aspects.

8. **(D)** Meter is the rhythm of poetry, a pattern of stressed and unstressed syllables measured in units called "feet." This is more fully explained in the Poetry Section. Sonnets are constructed of iambs. An iambic foot consists of an unstressed syllable followed by a stressed one (˘ ´). Other poetic feet include: (A) dactyl: stressed, unstressed, unstressed (´ ˘ ˘); (B) spondee: stressed, stressed (´ ´); (C) trochee: stressed, unstressed (´ ˘); and (E) anapest: unstressed, unstressed, stressed (˘ ˘ ´).

9. **(A)** This is the rhyme scheme of the Italian sonnet. The first group, called the octave, presents the poet's subject; the second group, called the sestet, indicates the importance of the facts set forth in the octave. The sestet lines may resolve the problem presented in the octave. The rhyme scheme of a poem is determined by assigning a letter to each new sound found at the end of a line of verse. (See the Poetry Section for more detail).

10. **(C)** The tone of a poem is derived from the author's attitude toward his audience and subject matter. Here, the tone is gentle and contemplative, as the mother-child situation suggests. (A) Euphuistic describes a very ornate and affected style characterized by euphemism. (B) A baroque tone would be elaborate and extravagantly ornamented. (D) Far from bewildered, the speaker is certain that the unknown afterlife exceeds that which we know. (E) The compassion and tenderness evidenced argue against a straightforward tone.

11. **(A)** Line 9: "So Nature deals with us . . . ."

12. **(A)** The final line (line 14) sums up Longfellow's point, as discussed previously.

13 **(B)** See answer 3.

14. **(B)** The Transcendentalists believed that there was some knowledge of reality or truth that man grasps not through logic or the laws of nature but through his intuition. There is obviously no other way Longfellow could have knowledge of the afterlife. (A) We have no way of knowing from the poem if the poet had suffered a personal loss. (C) This answer would be absurd in reference to Longfellow. (D) The Puritans preached God's wrath and the fearsomeness of the afterlife for all but a very few who were "elect" or saved. There was no way of knowing prior to death if one was saved or not. (E) The Revolutionary War is too general a response to suffice as a correct answer.

Section 1, Part B

The author's view of life and death were explained earlier. The essay should stress this view with specific examples drawn from the poem.

Section 2, Part A

John Smith's famous account is our first advertisement, intended to convince people that, contrary to truth, the New World was a land of plenty (see first paragraph). It was intended to draw single young men hungry for adventure, hence the references to exciting captures and rescues. Also, Smith was not above promoting his own interests and depicting himself as a great leader of men. He hoped to attain greater position and power, but was replaced by other leaders. The essay must stress the references to an abundance of food and adventure. It should also mention that much of what is described is greatly exaggerated, as in the adventure of Smith facing 200 savages or impressing the Indian leader with his compass.

Section 2, Part B

Edwards' "terror" sermon illustrates the Puritan belief in the ultimate depravity of man and the unlimited power and beneficence of God. The tone is angry, strong, biting, and vituperative: It is intended to frighten man into abandoning his wicked ways and following God. The style relies upon figures of speech, such as similes, metaphors, etc. Examples are found in the second paragraph ("bow of God's wrath") and fifth paragraph ("a spider or some loathsome insect" and "offended him infinitely more than ever a stubborn rebel did his prince"). Edwards does not have an overly elaborate style. The figures of speech are used to best advantage because there are only three in the selection. The *style* works very well with the *content*, for the use of figures of speech underscores God's hatred of man. The speaker obviously feels people are all wicked sinners and deserve to be denied God's grace if they do not repent of their evil ways. God, in contrast, is all-powerful, capable of forgiving even the most wicked of men. It is only God's grace that allows man to survive as long as he has. The *tone* and *style* reinforce the content, adding up to what has been called a "fire and brimstone" sermon.

Section 3

F. Scott Fitzgerald's *The Great Gatsby* centers around Jay Gatsby's attempt to recapture the past in the form of his first love, Daisy Buchanan. Gatsby, a gangster and bootlegger, partially succeeds in winning Daisy from her husband, wealthy and amoral Tom Buchanan, but never realizes that she is not what he believes her to be and that one cannot recapture the past. This is shown in a conversation he has with the narrator, Nick Carraway, when Nick tells Gatsby that one cannot regain the past. "Of course you can," Gatsby replies, supremely confident that with enough money and possessions, he can succeed in turning the clock back five years. Gatsby's attitude toward the past is one of "reverence" and "longing," and the theme developed by the novel is that one can never recapture what is gone. Arthur Miller's *The Crucible* shows how John Proctor, the farmer who had had an affair with the serving girl, Abigail Williams, tries to erase the bitterness of the past to clear his family of the charge of witchcraft. Updike's *Rabbit, Run* would also suit here, as would Thornton Wilder's *Our Town*.

Sample Examination B

SECTION 1

Part A: Time—25 minutes

Directions: Read the poem that follows and answer all the questions about it.

UPON THE BURNING OF OUR HOUSE
JULY 10TH, 1666

In silent night when rest I took,
For sorrow near I did not look,
I waken'd was with thund'ring noise
And piteous shrieks of dreadful voice.
5 That fearful sound of fire and fire,
Let no man know is my desire.

I, starting up, the light did spy,
And to my God my heart did cry
To strengthen me in my distress
10 And not to leave me succorless.
Then coming out beheld a space,
The flame consume my dwelling place.

And, when I could no longer look,
I blest his Name that gave and took,
15 That laid my goods now in the dust:
Yea so it was, and so 'twas just.
It was his own: it was not mine;
Far be it that I should repine.

He might of all justly bereft,
20 But yet sufficient for us left.
When by the ruins oft I past,
My sorrowing eyes aside did cast,
And here and there the places spy
Where oft I sat, and long did lie.

25 Here stood that trunk, and there that chest;
There lay that store I counted best:
My pleasant things in ashes lie,

And them behold no more shall I.
Under thy roof no guest shall sit,
30 Nor at thy table eat a bit.

No pleasant tale shall e'er be told,
Nor things recounted done of old.
No candle e'er shall shine in thee,
Nor bridegroom's voice ere heard shall be.
35 In silence ever shalt thou lie;
Adieu, adieu; all's vanity.

Then straight I gin my heart to chide,
And did thy wealth on earth abide?
Didst fix thy hope on mould'ring dust,
40 The arm of flesh didst make thy trust?
Raise up thy thoughts above the sky
That dunghill mists away may fly.

Thou hast an house on high erect,
Fram'd by that mighty Architect,
45 With glory richly furnished,
Stands permanent tho' this be fled.
It's purchased, and paid for too
By him who hath enough to do.

A prize so vast as is unknown,
50 Yet, by his gift, is made thine own.
There's wealth enough, I need no more;
Farewell my pelf, farewell my store.
The world no longer let me love,
My hope and treasure lies above.

—*Anne Bradstreet*

1. Many people try to find logical explanations for unfortunate events. Does the poet, anywhere in the poem, attempt to place blame for the fire?
   (A) She attributes the cause to God, but not the blame.
   (B) Initially she blames the bridegroom, but realizes that it is really God's fault by line 40.
   (C) She blames the initial builder for his use of substandard materials and workmanship.
   (D) She really doesn't care that much about the loss of her possessions, for she already has another house in a better neighborhood.
   (E) She blames God, for He cruelly took back His possessions, as line 17 shows.

2. The "arm of flesh" in line 40 refers to
   (A) hope, promise
   (B) death, decay
   (C) secular, mundane concerns
   (D) the destruction of the fire
   (E) spiritual renewal

3. The poet's attitude toward her home
   (A) remains the same throughout the poem
   (B) changes in the seventh stanza, best summarized in lines 37–42
   (C) changes in the fifth stanza, best summarized in line 26
   (D) is never really made clear, and is especially ambiguous in the eighth stanza
   (E) is not important to the meaning of this poem

4. The poet speaks of two homes in this poem. Who is the nominal owner of each?
   (A) The bridegroom owned the first home; the wealthy architect the second.
   (B) The poet owns the first home; the bridegroom the second.
   (C) The poet owns both homes.
   (D) The plantation overseer owns both homes.
   (E) The poet is the nominal owner of the first home; God, the second.

5. In a philosophical sense—the way the poet really intends it—who is the true owner of both homes?
   (A) The poet feels she owns all homes, but she does have a mortgage on the first.
   (B) God owns both homes, for the poet believes that everything man has is a gift from God.
   (C) The homes are both really unowned, as line 47 and 44 reveal.
   (D) Mankind owns both homes, for all possessions are commonly shared.
   (E) The reader is never sure of ownership here, for it is not critical to the poet's message.

6. "Pelf" in line 52 most nearly means
   (A) a home
   (B) furniture
   (C) money or riches
   (D) a small shop
   (E) furs

7. The connotation of the word "pelf" is
   (A) the poet's earthly nature that must be overcome if she is to find salvation
   (B) the poet's greedy attitude toward her possessions
   (C) The poet's cavalier attitude toward her possessions
   (D) the poet's secret love of death and desire for release from travails
   (E) the poet's deep love of God and His kingdom

8. When the poet finds herself unable to look at the fire any longer, she
   (A) curses God and His unjust actions
   (B) blesses God, but finds His action incomprehensible
   (C) consoles herself with plans for the new house on which a famous architect is already working
   (D) consoles herself with the thought of the new house her husband is building high on the hill
   (E) blesses God, for she believes His actions were just

9. Which adjective best describes the language of the poem?
   (A) Ironic
   (B) Argumentative
   (C) Colloquial
   (D) Pedantic
   (E) Highly figurative

10. Which of the following is the most accurate description of the way material possessions are treated in the poem?
    (A) Their value diminishes when compared to God's treasures.
    (B) Although initially highly valued, the author realizes by the end of the poem that she can easily replace her goods. Thus, their value diminishes.
    (C) Select items—her trunk and chest especially—mean more than anything else to the author.
    (D) They were never highly regarded.
    (E) She is just thankful that her family has been spared.

11. The verse pattern here is
    (A) free verse

(B) rhymed couplets
(C) sprung rhythm
(D) highly alliterative
(E) irregular

12. Judging from the situation and its description, most probably
(A) this is a true story
(B) this never could have occurred
(C) the author is not very religious
(D) this happened to someone the author knew very well
(E) this is a totally false story

13. The attitude of the speaker can best be described as
(A) ironic
(B) sarcastic
(C) moody
(D) religious
(E) irreligious

14. "The world no longer let me love,/My hope and treasure lies above" makes a suitable ending for all of the following reasons EXCEPT:
(A) The ending shows the speaker's growing realization of God's majesty, and proves the theme.
(B) The first thing the speaker did when she saw the fire was pray to God.
(C) The author is really not very devout.
(D) The thought behind the words helps console the author on the loss of her possessions.
(E) The destruction of her worldly goods was followed by prayer to God.

15. In which stanza does the speaker's attitude toward her home change?
(A) sixth

(B) first
(C) third
(D) seventh
(E) ninth

16. Which line best summarizes her change in feeling?
(A) "And to my God my heart did cry" (line 8)
(B) "Then straight I gin my heart to chide" (line 37)
(C) "Thou hast a house on high erect" (line 43)
(D) "I blest his Name that gave and took" (line 14)
(E) "In silent night when rest I took" (line 1)

17. The point of view in this poem is
(A) objective
(B) limited omniscient
(C) omniscient
(D) first-person participant
(E) first-person observer

18. In the eighth stanza, the "house on high erect" stands for
(A) heaven
(B) her newly constructed house on the hill
(C) her store
(D) the richly furnished home provided by her architect friend
(E) none of the above

19. The literary device in the eighth stanza is called
(A) metaphor
(B) understatement
(C) paradox
(D) oxymoron
(E) hyperbole

Part B: Time—35 minutes

One can imagine how sacred home was in the colonial period when Anne Bradstreet wrote this verse: a place of refuge against hostile Indians and bitter weather; a place of order in an alien wilderness. Discuss Bradstreet's attitude toward her loss. Be sure to include specific references from the poem.

SECTION 2

Time—60 minutes

Directions: Read the following passage carefully. Then write an essay in which you describe the author's attitude toward America. What points does he make toward his conclusion?

WHAT IS AN AMERICAN?

What, then, is the American, this new man? He is neither an European nor the descendant of an European; hence that strange mixture of blood, which you will find in no other country. I could point out to you a family whose grandfather was an Englishman, whose wife was Dutch, whose son married a French woman, and whose present four sons have now four wives of different nations. *He* is an American, who, leaving behind him all his ancient prejudices and manners, receives new ones from the new mode of life he has embraced, the new government he obeys, and the new rank he holds. He becomes an American by being received in the broad lap of our great Alma Mater. Here individuals of all nations are melted into a new race of men, whose labours and posterity will one day cause great changes in the world. Americans are the western pilgrims who are carrying along with them that great mass of arts, sciences, vigour, and industry which began long since in the East; they will finish the great circle. The Americans were once scattered all over Europe; here they are incorporated into one of the finest systems of population which has ever appeared, and which will hereafter become distinct by the power of the different climates they inhabit. The American ought therefore to love this country much better than that wherein either he or his forefathers were born. Here the rewards of his industry follow with equal steps the progress of his labour; his labour is founded on the basis of nature, self-interest; can it want a stronger allurement? Wives and children, who before in vain demanded of him a morsel of bread, now, fat and frolicsome, gladly help their father to clear those fields whence exuberant crops are to arise to feed and to clothe them all, without any part being claimed, either by a despotic prince, a rich abbot, or a mighty lord. Here religion demands but little of him: a small voluntary salary to the minister and gratitude to God; can he refuse these? The American is a new man, who acts upon new principles; he must therefore entertain new ideas and form new opinions. From involuntary idleness, servile dependence, penury, and useless labour, he has passed to toils of a very different nature, rewarded by ample subsistence. This is an American.

British America is divided into many provinces, forming a large association scattered along a coast of 1,500 miles extent and about 200 wide. This society I would fain examine, at least such as it appears in the middle provinces; if it does not afford that variety of tinges and gradations which may be observed in Europe, we have colours peculiar to ourselves. For instance, it is natural to conceive that those who live near the sea must be very different from those who live in the woods; the intermediate space will afford a separate and distinct class.

Men are like plants; the goodness and flavour of the fruit proceeds from the peculiar soil and exposition in which they grow. We are nothing but what we derive from the air we breathe, the climate we inhabit, the government we obey, the system of religion we profess, and the nature of our employment. Here you will find but few crimes; these have acquired as yet no root among us. I wish I were able to trace all my ideas; if my ignorance prevents me from describing them properly, I hope I shall be able to delineate a few of the outlines; which is all I propose.

Those who live near the sea feed more on fish than on flesh and often encounter that boisterous element. This renders them more bold and enterprising; this leads them to neglect the confined occupations of the land. They see and converse with a variety of people; their intercourse with mankind becomes extensive. The sea inspires them with a love of traffic, a desire of transporting produce from one place to another, and leads them to a variety of resources which supply the place of labour. Those who inhabit the middle settlements, by far the most numerous, must be very different; the simple cultivation of the earth purifies them, but the indulgences of the government, the soft remonstrances of religion, the rank of independent freeholders, must necessarily inspire them with sentiments, very little known in Europe among a people of the same class. What do I say? Europe has no such class of men; the early knowledge they acquire, the early bargains they make, give them a great degree of sagacity. As freemen, they will be litigious; pride and obstinacy are often the cause of lawsuits; the nature of our laws and governments may be another. As citizens, it is easy to imagine that they will carefully read the newspapers, enter into every political disquisition, freely blame or censure governors and others. As farmers, they will be careful and anxious to get as much as they can, because what they get is their own. As northern men, they will love the cheerful cup. As Christians, religion curbs them not in their opinions; the general indulgence leaves every one to think for themselves in spiritual matters; the law inspects our actions; our thoughts are left to God. Industry, good living, selfishness, litigiousness, country politics, the pride of freemen, religious indifference, are their characteristics. If you recede still farther from the sea, you will come into more modern settlements; they exhibit the same strong lineaments, in a ruder appearance. Religion seems to have still less influence, and their manners are less improved.

Now we arrive near the great woods, near the last inhabited districts; there men seem to be placed still farther beyond the reach of government, which in some measure leaves them to themselves. How can it pervade every corner, as they were driven there by misfortunes, necessity of beginnings, desire of acquiring large tracks of land, idleness, frequent want of economy, ancient debts; the reunion of such people does not afford a very pleasing spectacle. When discord, want of unity and friendship, when either drunkenness or idleness prevail in such remote districts, contention, inactivity, and wretchedness must ensue. There are not the same remedies to these evils as in a long-established community. The few magistrates they have are in general little better than the rest; they are often in a perfect state of war, that of man against man, sometimes decided by blows, sometimes by means of the law; that of man against every wild inhabitant of these venerable woods, of which they are come to dispossess them. There men appear to be no better than carnivorous animals of a superior rank, living on the flesh of wild animals when they can catch them, and when they are not able, they subsist on grain. He who would wish to see America in its proper light and have a true idea of its feeble beginnings and barbarous rudiments must visit our extended line of frontiers, where the last settlers dwell and where he may see the first labours of settlement, the mode of clearing the earth, in all their different appearances, where men are wholly left dependent on their native tempers and on the spur of uncertain industry, which often fails when not sanctified by the efficacy of a few moral rules. There, remote from the power of example and check of shame, many families exhibit the most hideous parts of our society. They are a kind of forlorn hope, preceding by ten or twelve years the most respectable army of veterans which come after them. In that space, prosperity will polish some, vice and the law will drive off the rest, who, uniting again with others like themselves, will recede still farther, making room for more industrious people, who will finish their improvements, convert the loghouse into a convenient habitation, and rejoicing that the first heavy labours are finished, will change in a few years that hitherto barbarous country into a fine, fertile, well-regulated district. Such is our progress; such is the march of the Europeans toward the interior parts of this continent. In all societies there are off-casts; this impure part serves as our precursors or pioneers; my father himself was one of that class, but he came upon honest principles and was therefore one of the few who held fast; by good conduct and temperance, he transmitted to me his fair inheritance, when not above one in fourteen of his contemporaries had the same good fortune.

Forty years ago, this smiling country was thus inhabited; it is now purged, a general decency of manners prevails throughout, and such has been the fate of our best countries.

Exclusive of those general characteristics, each province has its own, founded on the government, climate, mode of husbandry, customs, and peculiarity of circumstances. Europeans submit insensibly to these great powers and become, in the course of a few generations, not only Americans in general, but either Pennsylvanians, Virginians, or provincials under some other name. Whoever traverses the continent must easily observe those strong differences, which will grow more evident in time. The inhabitants of Canada, Massachusetts, the middle provinces, the southern ones, will be as different as their climates; their only points of unity will be those of religion and language.

—*J. Hector St. John de Crèvecoeur*

SECTION 3

Time—60 minutes

Private vs. public conscience—the desire to do what an individual perceives as right vs. the responsibility of carrying out the dictates of society—figures as a central conflict in many important works of literature. Select one literary work in which a character is faced with the choice of doing what he/she believes to be right or what society demands. You may select from the following works or from another of comparable quality.

Madame Bovary   *The Adventures of Huckleberry Finn*

The Crucible   *The Scarlet Letter*

Ethan Frome   *Jude the Obscure*

Sister Carrie   *The Red Badge of Courage*

ANSWERS AND EXPLANATIONS FOR SAMPLE EXAMINATION B

Section 1, Part A

At the age of 18, Anne Bradstreet, the author of "Upon the Burning of Our House," came to America with her husband, settling in the Massachusetts Bay Colony. She had received a better education than most women of her day, and in spite of the demands made upon her as the mother of eight children, she found time to write poetry. Her brother-in-law took some of her verse back with him to England and had it published, establishing her as the first published poet of the New World. This particular poem is based on a true incident, as the date below the title suggests.

1. **(A)** Lines 14–18 tell us that God "gave and took" and that His actions were "just." The other house she mentions is not a physical house at all, as in choice (D), and she assigns no blame to God.

2. **(C)** Rather than an "arm of flesh," anchored to the mundane world, she knows now she ought to have realized that her "hope and treasure [lie] above" (last line).

3. **(B)** As mentioned in question 2 she now realizes that she ought to "Raise up [her] thoughts above the sky" to assuage her the loss of her home. There is another home—heaven—awaiting her on high, much more splendid than her temporal one.

4. **(E)** The word "nominal" is important here, for God actually owns all, as she realizes. The second home is heaven.

5. **(B)** See the third stanza.

6. **(C)** "Pelf" most nearly means accumulated goods. Do not be confused by choice (D), a small shop. The author uses the word "store" in line 52 to indicate a group of objects that she owns, not sells.

7. **(A)** She values her possessions very highly, especially since she would be unable to replace most of them, for there was no insurance and she lacked the means to send back to England for all the items, even if they were all available. Nonetheless, she believes that she must reject her reliance on earthly things if she is to achieve God's grace in heaven. These items are meaningless, of course, when she compares them to what God has to offer in salvation. Obviously, Bradstreet was very religious.

8. **(E)** See stanza 3.

9. **(E)** The language uses many figures of speech (see Poetry Unit). (A) The term ironic means that the words express a meaning that is often the direct opposite of what is intended; Bradstreet makes her meaning quite clear. (B) There is no argumentative tone here; she assumes that her reader will agree with her conclusion. (C) Colloquial language is characteristic of ordinary conversation rather than formal speech or writing. Bradstreet uses a great many inversions ("For sorrow near I did not look" [line 2] rather than "I did not look near for sorrow") and thus her language is not characteristic of the way people usually speak. (D) The term pedantic refers to an excessive or inappropriate show of learning, which is not the case here, although it was typical of much of the writing of the seventeenth century.

10. **(A)** See previous discussions.

11. **(B)** In the first stanza, for example, "took" and "look"; "noise" and "voice"; "fire" and "desire" all rhyme. Thus, the rhymes are in pairs, also called couplets. (A) Free verse has unrhymed lines without regular rhythm. (C) Sprung rhythm is characterized by the use of strongly accented syllables pushed up against unaccented syllables. It was brought into favor by Gerard Manley Hopkins in the late nineteenth and early twentieth centuries. (D) Alliteration is not a verse pattern. It refers to repeated sounds throughout a poem. (E) Rhymed couplets cannot be considered irregular verse.

12. **(A)** From Bradstreet's use of detail and description, as well as the obvious emotion and date on the top of the poem, we can infer that this is a true story.

13. **(D)** As discussed earlier, the poem reveals the speaker's deeply religious attitude. Nowhere is she sarcastic or ironic about her subject.

14. **(C)** As mentioned before, she is highly religious.

15. **(D)** As mentioned previously.

16. **(B)** As mentioned previously.

17. **(D)** The author is a participant in the action, as mentioned above. Far from objective, (A), she is very much involved in what happened. Omniscient (B,C) means having complete or infinite knowledge, and this could be true only in God's case, in her way of thinking. She finds out what is happening as events unfold.

18. **(A)** As mentioned previously.

19. **(A)** A metaphor is a comparison of two unlike objects; here she compares heaven to a house. (B) Paradox is a statement which appears self-contradictory, but underlines a basis of truth, while an oxymoron, (D), consists of contradictory terms brought together to express strong effects. Hyperbole, (E), is exaggeration.

Section 1, Part B

The essay must stress that Bradstreet does not dismiss her worldly possessions lightly—they were of enormous value to her—and she is dismayed by the loss of a gathering place for her family and friends. No more will people visit and eat under her roof (stanza 5); no more will marriages take place (stanza 6); no more pleasant evenings will be spent telling stories (stanza 6). Nonetheless, she is highly devout and solaces herself with the thought of God's grandeur that awaits her in heaven.

Section 2

This selection, from J. Hector St. John de Crèvecoeur's *Letters from an American Farmer,* reveals his affection for and deep faith in the promise of the New World. "Here individuals of all nations are melted into a new race of men, whose labours and posterity will one day cause great changes in the world," he says. This and the next few lines can be cited as examples of his belief in America's promise. In America, man is rewarded for his labor, and all people gladly contribute to the common cause.

Section 3

The Adventures of Huckleberry Finn provides a fine example of the conflict of self vs. society in the character of Huck, who must go against all that he has been taught about slavery to effect the rescue of Jim. He finds Jim a far finer human being than the hypocritical Widow Douglas, who tells Huck not to smoke yet takes snuff, and who tells him to respect all men yet owns Jim and his family. His decision at the fork of the Mississippi River, Cairo,—"All right, then, I'll go to hell"—shows that he will relinquish conventional, public morality to embrace what he feels is right, even if it means that he will suffer everlasting damnation for it.

In *Ethan Frome,* the main character, Ethan, is also faced with a public vs. private conscience decision: Should he leave his wife, the sickly Zeena, for the young and vibrant Mattie Silver, whose very name rings with the promise of bright, shiny things? In Dreiser's *Sister Carrie,* should sister Carrie live with a man without benefit of matrimony? Should she use him to further her career? Should the soldier in *The Red Badge of Courage* stand in battle and risk being killed, as conventional morality demanded, or should he turn and run, as his private conscience advised? Should Reverend Dimmesdale in *The Scarlet Letter* reveal that he is Hester Prynne's lover? Should he acknowledge their child and shoulder his portion of sin and guilt, or should he suffer in silence and self-torment?

Sample Examination C

SECTION 1

Part A: Time—45 minutes

Questions 1–13 refer to the following poem.

TO S. M., A YOUNG AFRICAN PAINTER ON SEEING HIS WORKS

To show the lab'ring bosom's deep intent,
And thought in living characters to paint,
When first thy pencil did those beauties give,
And breathing figures learnt from thee to live,
5 How did those prospects give my soul delight,
A new creation rushing on my sight!
Still, wondrous youth! each noble path pursue;
On deathless glories fix thine ardent view:
Still may the painter's and the poet's fire,
10 To aid thy pencil and thy verse conspire!
And may the charms of each seraphic theme
Conduct thy footsteps to immortal fame!
High to the blissful wonders of the skies
Elate thy soul, and raise thy wishful eyes.
15 Thrice happy, when exalted to survey
That splendid city, crowned with endless day,
Whose twice six gates on radiant hinges ring:

Celestial Salem blooms in endless spring.
Calm and serene thy moments glide along,
20 And may the muse inspire each future song!
Still, with the sweets of contemplation blessed,
May peace with balmy wings your soul invest!
But when these shades of time are chased away,
And darkness ends in everlasting day,
25 On what seraphic pinions shall we move,
And view the landscapes in the realms above!
There shall thy tongue in heavenly murmurs flow,
And there my muse with heavenly transport glow;
No more to tell of Damon's tender sighs,
30 Or rising radiance of Aurora's eyes;
For nobler themes demand a nobler strain,
And purer language on the ethereal plain.
Cease, gentle Muse! the solemn gloom of night
Now seals the fair creation from my sight.

—*Phillis Wheatley*

1. What has S. M. done to win the poet's admiration?
   (A) He can make people come alive on canvas and reveal the human soul in art.
   (B) He is both a poet and a painter, as line 9 reveals.
   (C) He has built a radiant city with 12 gates (lines 16–17).
   (D) He has died after a glorious career as a painter, poet, builder—a man of the world.
   (E) He was a noble Greek warrior as well as a painter.

2. "Seraphic" in line 11 most nearly means
   (A) a long, flowing robe; hence, a long, involved theme
   (B) a singer of melodious songs
   (C) foreign, mysterious
   (D) angelic
   (E) colorful, vivid

3. What hopes does the poet have for S. M.'s future?
   (A) That he will always burn with creative energy
   (B) That his work will attain immortality
   (C) That his soul will ascend to heaven
   (D) None of the above
   (E) All of the above

4. What do "shades of time" symbolize in line 23?
   (A) Temporal, unsubstantial life in heaven
   (B) Temporal, unsubstantial life on earth
   (C) Temporal, unsubstantial life devoid of art
   (D) The specific cares and woes of all painters, permanent and universal
   (E) The dull, dark days common to even the most talented

5. What may "darkness" symbolize in line 24?
   (A) The suffering the Roman slaves experienced each day
   (B) The blindness of the poet Homer
   (C) Death
   (D) The suffering the black slaves experienced daily
   (E) The suffering of a person who never received adequate recognition for his work

6. What does the poet envision for both herself and the painter?
   (A) A life of promise and hope
   (B) A life of creativity and perpetual bloom
   (C) A realm of noble companions
   (D) A better command of the resources of the temporal world
   (E) Nothing better than what they now have

7. The poet's style is marked by
   (A) metaphysical conceits
   (B) ironic commentary
   (C) inverted phrases
   (D) an unusual rhyme scheme
   (E) onomatopoeia

8. How does what the poet envisions differ from the life both poet and painter lead?
   (A) They will be three times happier.
   (B) They will finally be able to move to Salem.
   (C) All people will be able to be artists.
   (D) All people will again be young and vigorous.
   (E) They will no longer be hostages to other men.

9. What does "everlasting day" symbolize in line 24?
   (A) Heaven

   (B) Salem
   (C) Greece during the Golden Age
   (D) Africa
   (E) It has no symbolic meaning.

10. The metaphors in lines 29 and 30 are derived from
    (A) romance
    (B) religion
    (C) art
    (D) mythology
    (E) music

11. Which term best describes the tone of this poem?
    (A) Resigned
    (B) Formal, lofty
    (C) Angry
    (D) Despairing
    (E) Informal, relaxed

12. The theme of this poem can most precisely be stated as follows:
    (A) Artists will finally be appreciated only when they are dead.
    (B) Slaves will be released from bondage and enjoy endless creativity when they enter heaven.
    (C) Heaven is for the talented; there they can flourish and grow.
    (D) Art is the highest human attainment.
    (E) None of the above.

13. The rhyme scheme of this poem is
    (A) *abcd abcd efgh efgh*
    (B) *aaab bbbc ddde*
    (C) *abba cddc effg*
    (D) *aa bb cc dd*
    (E) *abc abc def def*

Questions 14–26 are based on the following poem.

HIS EXCELLENCY GENERAL WASHINGTON

Celestial choir! enthron'd in realms of light,
Columbia's scenes of glorious toils I write.
While freedom's cause her anxious breast alarms,
She flashes dreadful in refulgent arms.
5 See mother earth her offspring's fate bemoan,
And nations gaze at scenes before unknown!
See the bright beams of heaven's revolving light

Involved in sorrows and the veil of night!
The goddess comes, she moves divinely fair,
10 Olive and laurel binds her golden hair:
Wherever shines this native of the skies,
Unnumber'd charms and recent graces rise.
Muse! bow propitious while my pen relates
How pour her armies through a thousand gates;

15 As when Eolus heaven's fair face deforms,
Enwrapped in tempest and a night of storms;
Astonish'd ocean feels the wild uproar,
The refluent surges beat the sounding shore,
Or thick as leaves in Autumn's golden reign,
20 Such, and so many, moves the warrior's train.
In bright array they seek the work of war,
Where high unfurl'd the ensign waves in air.
Shall I to Washington their praise recite?
Enough thou know'st them in the fields of fight.
25 Thee, first in place and honours,—we demand
The grace and glory of thy martial band.
Fam'd, for thy valour, for thy virtues more,
Here every tongue thy guardian aid implore!

One century scarce performed its destin'd round,
30 When Gallic powers Columbia's fury found;
And so may you, whoever dares disgrace
The land of freedom's heaven-defended race!
Fix'd are the eyes of nations on the scales,
For in their hopes Columbia's arm prevails.
35 Anon Britannia droops the pensive head,
While round increase the rising hills of dead.
Ah! cruel blindess to Columbia's state!
Lament thy thirst of boundless power too late.
Proceed, great chief, with virtue on thy side,
40 Thy every action let the goddess guide.
A crown, a mansion, and a throne that shine,
With gold unfading, *Washington,* be thine.

—*Phillis Wheatley*

14. What purpose do the two opening lines serve?
   (A) They introduce the poem and state its subject.
   (B) They establish the tone and theme.
   (C) They explain Washington's role as a leader.
   (D) They explain the suitability of Washington as a subject.
   (E) They establish the poet's unconventional style.

15. What is Columbia?
   (A) A metaphor for the future
   (B) A metaphor for the past
   (C) A metaphor for the Gallic powers
   (D) A metaphor for Washington
   (E) The personification of America

16. What figure of speech is used in line 2?
   (A) Metaphor
   (B) Simile
   (C) Irony
   (D) Symbolism
   (E) Personification

17. Lines 2–22 describe Columbia. What impression do they give?
   (A) She is a shining goddess gracing the land.
   (B) She is a symbol of freedom.
   (C) She is a symbol of military might.
   (D) None of the above.
   (E) All of the above.

18. How does the poet regard Washington?
   (A) He is the unquestioned leader of Columbia's army, strong and virtuous.

   (B) He is a strong leader, but by no means omnipotent.
   (C) He is brave and forceful, but subject to enormous human doubt.
   (D) He is a fine leader, but no match for the Gallic powers.
   (E) He is soon to be replaced by Columbia, a true leader.

19. The poet views England as
   (A) a fair, honest power
   (B) a greedy, imperialist power
   (C) a true friend to Washington
   (D) a fair-weather friend
   (E) The poet makes no comment on England.

20. How do the other countries regard the struggle between England and the colonies?
   (A) They place their hopes in France.
   (B) They place their hopes in America.
   (C) They have made no formal declaration of where their hopes lie.
   (D) They are filled with fear.
   (E) They believe this is a no-win situation.

21. The rhyme scheme of this poem is
   (A) aa bb cc dd
   (B) *abc abc def def*
   (C) *abba cddc effg*
   (D) *aaab bbbc ddde*
   (E) There is no rhyme scheme; this poem is written in free verse.

22. "Celestial choir" (line 1) is an example of
   (A) personification

(B) symbolism
(C) alliteration
(D) metaphor
(E) irony

23. What will be the outcome of the struggle discussed in this poem?
(A) Britain will win.
(B) France will win.
(C) No one will win.
(D) America will win.
(E) The Gallic powers will win.

24. What two subjects are combined in the close of the poem?
(A) France and England
(B) Columbia and Washington
(C) England and Washington
(D) Gallic powers and Washington
(E) Columbia and France

25. What opinions and hopes are voiced at the end of the poem?
(A) Both France and England will enjoy victory and crowning glory.
(B) Both England and the Gallic powers will enjoy victory and crowning glory.
(C) Both America and Washington will enjoy victory and crowning glory.
(D) No one will win.
(E) Only in heaven will the outcome be made evident.

26. The tone of the poem is
(A) enervated
(B) elevated
(C) sarcastic
(D) ironic
(E) peaceful

Part B: Time—60 minutes

Compare the style, tone, and poetic devices employed in the two poems you have just read by Phillis Wheatley. Show both similarities and differences. Do you believe they were written in the same time period?

SECTION 2

Time—45 Minutes

Using any novel from the list below or any other novel of comparable quality, show how the main character is unwilling or unable to accept members of his community or family and is thus isolated and alone. Also explain how the author prepares the reader for this rejection of human companionship. Consider at least two elements of fiction such as theme, symbol, setting, characterization, or any other aspect of the writer's craft in your discussion.

Ethan Frome

The Scarlet Letter

The American

Hamlet

The Adventures of Huckleberry Finn

Gulliver's Travels

The Sound and the Fury

Invisible Man

The Sun Also Rises

McTeague

SECTION 3

Time—30 Minutes

In his Preface to *The House of the Seven Gables* (1851), Hawthorne explained some differences between the romance and the novel:

> When a writer calls his work a Romance, it need hardly be observed that he wishes to claim a certain latitude, both to its fashion and material, which he would not have felt himself entitled to assume, had he professed to be writing a Novel. The latter form of composition is presumed to aim at a very minute fidelity, not merely to the possible, but to the probable and ordinary course of man's experience. The former—while, as a work of art, it must rigidly subject itself to laws, and while it sins unpardonably, so far as it may swerve aside from the truth of the human heart—has fairly a right to present that truth under the circumstances, to a great extent, of the writer's own choosing or creation. If he think fit, also, he may so manage his atmospherical medium as to bring out or mellow the lights and deepen and enrich the shadows of the picture. He will be wise, no doubt, to make a very moderate use of the privileges here stated, and, especially, to mingle the Marvellous rather as a slight, delicate, and evanescent flavor, than as any portion of the actual substance of the dish offered to the public.

Select any novel that you have read that shows elements of romance. Isolate at least three examples of how the work functions as a Romance and show how they are evident in the novel. You may consider works by Hawthorne, or any other author whose works are suitable: Cooper, Melville, Thackeray, Faulkner, (Harriet Beecher) Stowe, or H. Rider, for example.

ANSWERS AND EXPLANATIONS FOR SAMPLE EXAMINATION C

Section 1, Part A

1. **(A)** The first two lines of the poem explain the basis for the poet's admiration of S. M. He can "show the lab'ring bosom's deep intent" (line 1), which is closest in meaning to "reveal the human soul in art." He is also able to paint "living characters" (line 2) or "make people come alive on canvas." (B) is incorrect, for the author is not saying that S. M. is both a painter and a poet, rather, she refers to him as the painter and herself as the poet, as "wondrous youth" pursues different "noble" paths. (C) is also wrong, because S. M. has not built the city 12 gates (heaven). (D) is wrong because S. M. has not yet died. (E) is incorrect, because S. M. is a young African painter, as the title indicates, not a Greek warrior.

2. **(D)** "Seraphic" means angelic, and relates to the discussion of heaven in the rest of the poem. The word "immortal" in line 12 is a context clue.

3. **(E)** The poet wishes that (A), he will always burn with creative energy (see line 20); (B) his work will attain immortality (see line 12); and (C), his soul will ascend to heaven (lines 20–34).

4. **(B)** We know that "shades of time" in line 23 stands for temporal, unsubstantial life on earth, as the following line, "darkness ends in everlasting day," tells us. The rest of the poem refers to heaven and the afterlife, another clue.

5. **(D)** The word "darkness" in line 24 refers to the suffering of black slaves, as shown by the

title, ". . . a Young African Painter." We are given no indication that any other answers are suitable.

6. **(B)** Lines 27, 28, 31, and 32 indicate that the author envisions an eternity of creativity in heaven. (D) is incorrect, for the ending of the poem moves the action to heaven. (C) is incorrect, for the poet does not indicate that heaven will be populated with any but themselves

7. **(C)** is the best answer, as a great many of the poet's sentences are inverted. For example, "May peace with balmy wings your soul invest!" (line 22) may be stated as "May your soul be invested with peace on balmy wings!" (A) is incorrect, since this poem contains no extended comparison of two unlike objects. (B) is incorrect, for the author is not ironic in her discussion. Rather, she is very serious and straightforward in her admiration of S. M.'s talent and future. (D) The rhyme scheme is common, made up as it is of rhymed couplets (pairs). (E) is wrong, for onomatopeia is the use of words whose sound suggests their meaning.

8. **(E)** is the answer, as lines 23 and 24 show.

9. **(A)** "Everlasting day" is a metaphor for heaven.

10. **(D)** Damon and Aurora are figures from Roman mythology. (A) Romance is incorrect, for, as discussed later in this practice exam, it is a genre that allows the writer greater use of the marvelous and the mysterious than the novel. It bears no reference to the two mythical characters cited above. (B) is incorrect, for neither of these are religious figures. (C) and (E) are also wrong, for these figures do not pertain to art or music.

11. **(B)** The elevated, formal tone is evident in the poet's use of language (see first two lines, for example), lofty themes (ascension to heaven and everlasting creativity), and style (word choice, poetic contractions). (A) The poet is not resigned at all. Rather, she sees a brilliant future for them both. (C) The poet is not angry, for the painter's skill inspires her admiration and she foresees a glorious afterlife. (D) and (E) are incorrect for the reasons cited above.

12. **(B)** The title and the last half of the poem tells us that the theme here concerns the author's belief that she and S. M. will be released from their earthly bondage to enjoy everlasting creativity in heaven. (A) is wrong, for the poet appreciates S. M. now, and he is not dead. (C) While heaven may indeed be for the talented, (B) is a more complete answer. (D) The poet does not state this belief in the poem.

13. **(D)** The poem is written in rhymed couplets (pairs): intent/paint (aa); give/live (bb); delight/sight (cc); etc.

14. **(A)** The poet will write of Columbia's "glorious toils," as she states in line 2. (B) The theme and tone are *introduced*, but not established. (C) and (D) Washington has not yet been mentioned. (E) The poet's style is very conventional.

15. **(E)** Columbia stands for America, as the poem tells of America's quest for freedom under General Washington.

16. **(E)** The author assigns human qualities to a non-living object when she makes America, or Columbia, a person. Columbia "toils" and experiences "anxious breast alarms" (lines 2–3). Line 4 assigns gender: "She flashes dreadful in refulgent arms."

17. **(E)** All of the above are correct. The poet admires America enormously.

18. **(A)** The poet believes in Washington without reservation. The praise increases as the poem continues; the final four lines sum up the poet's admiration.

19. **(B)** See lines 35–40, as Britannia (England) is defeated by America's great chief, who has virtue on his side.

20. **(B)** All place their hopes in America.

21. **(A)** This poem, like the previous one, is written in rhymed couplets: light/write (aa); alarms/arms (bb); bemoan/unknown (cc).

22. **(C))** Alliteration is the repetition of two or more initial sounds within a line of poetry or prose. Thus, the two C's or "celestial choir" show alliteration. All the other answers have been previously explained; see the Poetry Unit for further explanation of terms.

23. **(D)** The final four lines make it clear America, under the leadership of Washington will attain victory.

24. **(B)** Line 37 discusses Columbia; line 42, Washington. It is also clear that Washington will be in charge of Columbia/America.

25. **(C)** See answer 23.

26. **(B)** The poem's tone is elevated, as it employs a great many lofty words and phrases to praise Washington. Metaphors like "celestial choir" in line 1 further serve to raise the tone and underscore the theme. **(A)** Enervated means weakened, and is not to be confused with elevated. **(C)** The poet is not at all sarcastic toward her subject; her admiration is genuine.

Section 1, Part B

Both poems were written by the same person, Phillis Wheatley (c. 1753–1784). She was born in Africa and brought to Boston at the age of eight on a slave ship. By the time she was 13, she was translating Latin and writing poetry, for her owner, John Wheatley, encouraged her studies. Considered a member of the family and never treated as a slave, she was granted her freedom at the age of 20. Her later life was marred by great unhappiness: Her marriage was unsuccessful and two of her three children died young. She died alone and in poverty at the age of 31, her death coinciding with that of her third child. They were buried together in an unmarked grave.

The style, tone, and poetic devices employed in the two poems are the same. Wheatley was fond of classical literature and modeled her poetry after such contemporary English poets as Pope and Gray. We find that the style is elevated, employing sophisticated language, poetic contractions, and frequent use of figurative language. She was especially fond of alliteration, metaphor, and personification. Both poems use images of heaven, the first discussing the afterlife of the poet and S. M., the second linking Washington's quest to a heavenly undertaking. This would of course be shown by isolating specific lines from both poems and comparing them. The tone in both poems is the same: elevated and formal with lofty diction. This too would be shown by specific reference to the poems. All the similarities should allow the conclusion that the poems were written in the same period.

Section 2

In *Gulliver's Travels,* the main character, Gulliver, lost during a ship voyage, encounters three different versions of eighteenth-century civilization. He finds each repellent in different ways, and ends up living with a civilization of horses, totally rejecting "Yahoos," or human beings. Theme and setting would be appropriate for discussion here, as you would draw specific examples from the book.

Hamlet would be another good choice for the question, as the main character, Hamlet, attempts to establish contact with members of his family and community but finds that his efforts are rebuffed or misunderstood. Hamlet, who returned from school to attend his father's funeral, has discovered that his mother has married his father's brother a scant two months after his father's death. He finds himself unable to talk to his mother after she has remarried with such unseemly haste, and he distrusts his uncle, which turns out to be very wise indeed. His lover, Ophelia, is of no help either, for her father, Polonius, has told her to rebuff Hamlet's overtures. Thus, she returns his letters and gifts and denies him access to her. His two old friends, Rosencrantz and Guildenstern are turncoats, accepting pay from Hamlet's uncle, King Claudius, to spy on their friend. The famous "to be or not to be" speech shows his isolation. Characterization and theme would be considered here.

Frank Norris' *McTeague* is also suitable, but in a very different way. Unlike Hamlet,

McTeague is not a man who thinks a great deal about his actions. An unlicensed dentist on Polk Street in San Francisco at the turn of the century, McTeague is never very articulate or sure of himself. When his cousin Marcus reveals that McTeague lacks a license (Marcus is jealous that McTeague has successfully wooed the delicate Trina and won the lottery), he quickly reverts to an animal-like state and loses any veneer of civilization. Thus, he stops keeping himself clean, well fed, or neat, and he and Trina move from one hellish apartment to another, until he finally murders her to find the gold she has hidden. Like a wild animal, he runs for the desert, rejecting all human companionship. Setting (wretched apartments and the desert) and theme (overriding greed) would be suitable for discussion.

Ralph Ellison's *Invisible Man* is also fitting, as the main character, a black man alienated from all society, describes how he gradually came to reject all human companionship. He is invisible because people refuse to see him, refuse to recognize a black man in America, as he shows by tracing childhood and college humiliations. Any of these tragic stories would serve to show why he has rejected all human companionship and has gone underground.

Section 3

A romance is characterized by removal from reality and a certain use of the mysterious. Very often there will be a handsome hero on a shining white horse, a dastardly villain, or fair maiden in need of rescue. There may also be daring rescues and hairbreadth escapes, as well as various mysterious happenings. *The Blithedale Romance,* for example, describes the mysterious death of Zenobia, the beautiful and unusual dark heroine, as well as the strange performances of Westervelt and his Veiled Lady. *The House of the Seven Gables,* also by Hawthorne, describes the mysterious curse of the Maules, who were all supposed to die gurgling on blood. Maule's Well, where the curse originated, was said to be haunted. In the *Scarlet Letter,* Reverend Dimmesdale rips apart his vestment before the entire community to reveal mystery. Some say they see the very semblance of an A, identical to that displayed on the chest of his lover, Hester Prynne, all these years. Others swear that his breast is as clean as that of a new born babe's. The entire matter of the A on Dimmesdale's chest weaves through the book, as the evil Chillingworth dances with glee when he believes he has discovered, very early on, that he has seen it on the minister's chest. Even Chillingworth is removed from reality, as his eyes glow an evil red.

Any of Cooper's leatherstocking tales would suffice to answer this question. The *Deerslayer,* for example, describes how Natty Bumppo, a young man reared by the Delaware Indians, attempts to rescue Hist, his best friend Chingachgook's girl, from an unfriendly tribe of Huron Indians and is in turn captured himself. After a great deal of talk and various acts of torture, the Deerslayer (Natty) is rescued by his friend and the entire cavalry. The Deerslayer manages to kill a great many of the Hurons and general carnage results. This is the good guy–bad guy/daring rescue version of romance.

"HOW TO" COMPANION GUIDES